Data Mining Approaches for Big Data and Sentiment Analysis in Social Media

Brij B. Gupta
National Institute of Technology, Kurukshetra, India

Dragan Peraković
University of Zagreb, Croatia

Ahmed A. Abd El-Latif
Menoufia University, Egypt

Deepak Gupta
LoginRadius Inc., Canada

A volume in the Advances in Data
Mining and Database Management
(ADMDM) Book Series

Published in the United States of America by
> IGI Global
> Engineering Science Reference (an imprint of IGI Global)
> 701 E. Chocolate Avenue
> Hershey PA, USA 17033
> Tel: 717-533-8845
> Fax: 717-533-8661
> E-mail: cust@igi-global.com
> Web site: http://www.igi-global.com

Library of Congress Cataloging-in-Publication Data

Names: Gupta, Brij, 1982- editor.
Title: Data mining approaches for big data and sentiment analysis in social
    media / Brij B. Gupta, Dragan Perakovic, Ahmed A. Abd El-Latif and
    Deepak Gupta, editor.
Description: Hershey, PA : Engineering Science Reference, 2021. | Includes
    bibliographical references and index. | Summary: "This book explores the
    key concepts of data mining and utilizing them on online social media
    platforms, offering valuable insight into data mining approaches for big
    data and sentiment analysis in online social media and covering many
    important security and other aspects and current trends"-- Provided by
    publisher.
Identifiers: LCCN 2021019408 (print) | LCCN 2021019409 (ebook) | ISBN
    9781799884132 (h/c) | ISBN 9781799884149 (s/c) | ISBN 9781799884156
    (eISBN)
Subjects: LCSH: Data mining. | Sentiment analysis. | Big data. | Discourse
    analysis. | Webometrics. | Online social networks.
Classification: LCC QA76.9.D343 D382266 2021 (print) | LCC QA76.9.D343
    (ebook) | DDC 006.3/12--dc23
LC record available at https://lccn.loc.gov/2021019408
LC ebook record available at https://lccn.loc.gov/2021019409

This book is published in the IGI Global book series Advances in Data Mining and Database Management (ADMDM) (ISSN: 2327-1981; eISSN: 2327-199X).

British Cataloguing in Publication Data
A Cataloguing in Publication record for this book is available from the British Library.

All work contributed to this book is new, previously-unpublished material.
The views expressed in this book are those of the authors, but not necessarily of the publisher.

For electronic access to this publication, please contact: eresources@igi-global.com.

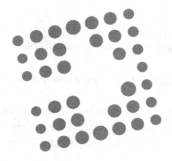

Advances in Data Mining and Database Management (ADMDM) Book Series

ISSN:2327-1981
EISSN:2327-199X

Editor-in-Chief: David Taniar, Monash University, Australia

MISSION

With the large amounts of information available to organizations in today's digital world, there is a need for continual research surrounding emerging methods and tools for collecting, analyzing, and storing data.

The **Advances in Data Mining & Database Management (ADMDM)** series aims to bring together research in information retrieval, data analysis, data warehousing, and related areas in order to become an ideal resource for those working and studying in these fields. IT professionals, software engineers, academicians and upper-level students will find titles within the ADMDM book series particularly useful for staying up-to-date on emerging research, theories, and applications in the fields of data mining and database management.

COVERAGE

- Profiling Practices
- Data Analysis
- Factor Analysis
- Decision Support Systems
- Data Warehousing
- Educational Data Mining
- Customer Analytics
- Neural Networks
- Cluster Analysis
- Enterprise Systems

IGI Global is currently accepting manuscripts for publication within this series. To submit a proposal for a volume in this series, please contact our Acquisition Editors at Acquisitions@igi-global.com or visit: http://www.igi-global.com/publish/.

Titles in this Series

For a list of additional titles in this series, please visit:
http://www.igi-global.com/book-series/advances-data-mining-database-management/37146

Handbook of Research on Essential Information Approaches to Aiding Global Health in the One Healh Context
Jorge Lima de Magalhães (NOVA University of Lisbon, Portugal) Zulmira Hartz (NOVA University of Lisbon, Portugal) George Leal Jamil (Informações em Rede Consultoria e Treinamento, Brazil) Henrique Silveira (NOVA University of Lisbon, Portugal) and Liliane C. Jamil (Independent Researcher, Brazil)
Medical Information Science Reference • © 2022 • 400pp • H/C (ISBN: 9781799880110) • US $395.00

Ranked Set Sampling Models and Methods
Carlos N. Bouza-Herrera (Universidad de La Habana, Cuba)
Engineering Science Reference • © 2022 • 276pp • H/C (ISBN: 9781799875567) • US $195.00

New Opportunities for Sentiment Analysis and Information Processing
Aakanksha Sharaff (National Institute of Technology, Raipur, India) G. R. Sinha (Myanmar Institute of Information Technology, Mandalay, Myanmar) and Surbhi Bhatia (King Faisal University, Saudi Arabia)
Engineering Science Reference • © 2021 • 311pp • H/C (ISBN: 9781799880615) • US $245.00

Transforming Scholarly Publishing With Blockchain Technologies and AI
Darrell Wayne Gunter (Gunter Media Group, USA)
Information Science Reference • © 2021 • 336pp • H/C (ISBN: 9781799855897) • US $205.00

Political and Economic Implications of Blockchain Technology in Business and Healthcare
Dário de Oliveira Rodrigues (Instituto Politécnico de Santarém, Portugal)
Business Science Reference • © 2021 • 389pp • H/C (ISBN: 9781799873631) • US $225.00

For an entire list of titles in this series, please visit:
http://www.igi-global.com/book-series/advances-data-mining-database-management/37146

701 East Chocolate Avenue, Hershey, PA 17033, USA
Tel: 717-533-8845 x100 • Fax: 717-533-8661
E-Mail: cust@igi-global.com • www.igi-global.com

Dedicated to our families and friends for their constant support during the course of this book

-Brij B. Gupta, Dragan Peraković, Ahmed A. Abd El-Latif, Deepak Gupta

Table of Contents

Preface xvi

Acknowledgment xviii

Chapter 1
Approaches and Applications for Sentiment Analysis: A Literature Review 1
    M. Govindarajan, Annamalai University, India

Chapter 2
A Survey on Building Recommendation Systems Using Data Mining
Techniques 24
    Rajab Ssemwogerere, Islamic University in Uganda, Uganda
    Wamwoyo Faruk, Makerere University, Uganda
    Nambobi Mutwalibi, Islamic University in Uganda, Uganda

Chapter 3
A Survey on Sentiment Analysis Techniques for Twitter 57
    Surabhi Verma, National Institute of Technology, Kurukshetra, India
    Ankit Kumar Jain, National Institute of Technology, Kurukshetra, India

Chapter 4
Role of Social Media in the COVID-19 Pandemic: A Literature Review 91
    Kriti Aggarwal, Chandigarh College of Engineering and Technology,
        India
    Sunil K. Singh, Chandigarh College of Engineering and Technology,
        India
    Muskaan Chopra, Chandigarh College of Engineering and Technology,
        India
    Sudhakar Kumar, Chandigarh College of Engineering and Technology,
        India

Chapter 5
Data Mining Approaches for Sentiment Analysis in Online Social Networks
(OSNs) 116
    Praneeth Gunti, National Institute of Technology, Kurukshetra, India
    Brij B. Gupta, National Institute of Technology, Kurukshetra, India
    Elhadj Benkhelifa, Staffordshire University, UK

Chapter 6
Sentiment Analysis and Summarization of Facebook Posts on News Media....142
    Yin-Chun Fung, Hong Kong Metropolitan University, Hong Kong
    Lap-Kei Lee, Hong Kong Metropolitan University, Hong Kong
    Kwok Tai Chui, Hong Kong Metropolitan University, Hong Kong
    Gary Hoi-Kit Cheung, Hong Kong Metropolitan University, Hong Kong
    Chak-Him Tang, Hong Kong Metropolitan University, Hong Kong
    Sze-Man Wong, Hong Kong Metropolitan University, Hong Kong

Chapter 7
An Improved Cross-Domain Sentiment Analysis Based on a Semi-
Supervised Convolutional Neural Network 155
    Lap-Kei Lee, Hong Kong Metropolitan University, Hong Kong
    Kwok Tai Chui, Hong Kong Metropolitan University, Hong Kong
    Jingjing Wang, Hong Kong Metropolitan University, Hong Kong
    Yin-Chun Fung, Hong Kong Metropolitan University, Hong Kong
    Zhanhui Tan, Hong Kong Metropolitan University, Hong Kong

Chapter 8
Detection of Economy-Related Turkish Tweets Based on Machine Learning
Approaches...171
    Jale Bektaş, Mersin University, Turkey

Chapter 9
The Stakes of Social Media: Analyzing User Sentiments 196
    Elodie Attié, Capgemini Engineering T.E.C., France
    Anne Bouvet, Capgemini Engineering T.E.C., France
    Jérôme Guibert, Capgemini Engineering T.E.C., France

Chapter 10
Predicting Catastrophic Events Using Machine Learning Models for Natural
Language Processing..223
    Muskaan Chopra, Chandigarh College of Engineering and Technology,
        India
    Sunil K. Singh, Chandigarh College of Engineering and Technology,

India

    Kriti Aggarwal, Chandigarh College of Engineering and Technology,
      India

    Anshul Gupta, Chandigarh College of Engineering and Technology,
      India

Chapter 11

Clubhouse Experience: Sentiment Analysis of an Alternative Platform From
the Eyes of Classic Social Media Users 244

    Ipek Deveci Kocakoç, Dokuz Eylul University, Turkey

    Pınar Özkan, Dokuz Eylul University, Turkey

Compilation of References 265

About the Contributors 305

Index 311

Detailed Table of Contents

Preface xvi

Acknowledgment xviii

Chapter 1
Approaches and Applications for Sentiment Analysis: A Literature Review 1
    M. Govindarajan, Annamalai University, India

With the increasing penetration of the internet, an ever-growing number of people are voicing their opinions in the numerous blogs, tweets, forums, social networking, and consumer review websites. Each such opinion has a sentiment (positive, negative, or neutral) associated with it. But the problem is that the amount of data is simply overwhelming. Methods like supervised machine learning and lexical-based approaches are available for measuring sentiments that have a huge volume of opinionated data recorded in digital form for analysis. Sentiment analysis has been used in several applications including analysis of the repercussions of events in social networks, analysis of opinions about products and services. This chapter presents sentiment analysis applications and challenges with their approaches and tools. The techniques and applications discussed in this chapter will provide a clear-cut idea to the sentiment analysis researchers to carry out their work in this field.

Chapter 2
A Survey on Building Recommendation Systems Using Data Mining
Techniques 24
    Rajab Ssemwogerere, Islamic University in Uganda, Uganda
    Wamwoyo Faruk, Makerere University, Uganda
    Nambobi Mutwalibi, Islamic University in Uganda, Uganda

Classification is a data mining technique or approach used to estimate the grouped membership of items on a basis of a common feature. This technique is virtuous for future planning and discovering new knowledge about a specific dataset. An in-depth study of previous pieces of literature implementing data mining techniques in the design of recommender systems was performed. This chapter provides a broad study of the way of designing recommender systems using various data mining classification techniques of machine learning and also exploiting their methodological decisions in four aspects, the recommendation approaches, data mining techniques, recommendation types, and performance measures. This study focused on some selected classification methods and can be so supportive for both the researchers and the students in the field of computer science and machine learning in strengthening their knowledge about the machine learning hypothesis and data mining.

Chapter 3

A Survey on Sentiment Analysis Techniques for Twitter 57

Surabhi Verma, National Institute of Technology, Kurukshetra, India
Ankit Kumar Jain, National Institute of Technology, Kurukshetra, India

People regularly use social media to express their opinions about a wide variety of topics, goods, and services which make it rich in text mining and sentiment analysis. Sentiment analysis is a form of text analysis determining polarity (positive, negative, or neutral) in text, document, paragraph, or clause. This chapter offers an overview of the subject by examining the proposed algorithms for sentiment analysis on Twitter and briefly explaining them. In addition, the authors also address fields related to monitoring sentiments over time, regional view of views, neutral tweet analysis, sarcasm detection, and various other tasks in this area that have drawn the researchers ' attention to this subject nearby. Within this chapter, all the services used are briefly summarized. The key contribution of this survey is the taxonomy based on the methods suggested and the debate on the theme's recent research developments and related fields.

Chapter 4

Role of Social Media in the COVID-19 Pandemic: A Literature Review 91

Kriti Aggarwal, Chandigarh College of Engineering and Technology,
    India
Sunil K. Singh, Chandigarh College of Engineering and Technology,
    India
Muskaan Chopra, Chandigarh College of Engineering and Technology,
    India
Sudhakar Kumar, Chandigarh College of Engineering and Technology,
    India

Today, social networks and media have become an integral part of everyone's daily existence. The rising popularity of social media has increased tenfold during the times of COVID-19 when people were forced to isolate following social distancing norms. Between July 2020 and July 2021, active social users grew to 520 million. The COVID-19 crisis has resulted in the usage of digital platforms not only for entertainment purposes but also for educational and corporate reasons. Hence, the spread of information has increased excessively on every social media platform. This has resulted in an equal rise of false information. The term infodemic was widely introduced during COVID-19 to explain the harmful effects of misinformation through social media. The chapter, hence, argues that the advantages of social media surpasses the dangers of misinformation. It discusses the role of COVID-19 in digitalization and how social media has helped in provision of various industries.

Chapter 5
Data Mining Approaches for Sentiment Analysis in Online Social Networks (OSNs) 116
    Praneeth Gunti, National Institute of Technology, Kurukshetra, India
    Brij B. Gupta, National Institute of Technology, Kurukshetra, India
    Elhadj Benkhelifa, Staffordshire University, UK

IoT technology and the widespread usage of public networking platforms and apps also made it possible to use data mining in extracting useful perspectives from unorganised knowledge. In the age of big data, opinion mining may be applied as a valuable way in order to classify views into various sentiment and in general to determine the attitude of the population. Other methods to OSA have been established over the years in various datasets and evaluated in varying conditions. In this respect, this chapter highlights the scope of OMSA strategies and forms of implementing OMSA principles. Besides technological issues of OMSA, this chapter also outlined both technical problems regarding its production and non-technical issues regarding its use. There are obstacles for potential study.

Chapter 6
Sentiment Analysis and Summarization of Facebook Posts on News Media....142
    Yin-Chun Fung, Hong Kong Metropolitan University, Hong Kong
    Lap-Kei Lee, Hong Kong Metropolitan University, Hong Kong
    Kwok Tai Chui, Hong Kong Metropolitan University, Hong Kong
    Gary Hoi-Kit Cheung, Hong Kong Metropolitan University, Hong Kong
    Chak-Him Tang, Hong Kong Metropolitan University, Hong Kong
    Sze-Man Wong, Hong Kong Metropolitan University, Hong Kong

Social media has become part of daily life in the modern world. News media companies (NMC) use social network sites including Facebook pages to let net users keep updated. Public expression is important to NMC for making valuable journals, but it is not cost-effective to collect millions of feedback by human effort, which can instead be automated by sentiment analysis. This chapter presents a mobile application called Facemarize that summarizes the contents of news media Facebook pages using sentiment analysis. The sentiment of user comments can be quickly analyzed and summarized with emotion detection. The sentiment analysis achieves an accuracy of over 80%. In a survey with 30 participants including journalists, journalism students, and journalism graduates, the application gets at least 4.9 marks (in a 7-point Likert scale) on the usefulness, ease of use, ease of learning, and satisfaction with a mean reliability score of 3.9 (out of 5), showing the effectiveness of the application.

Chapter 7

An Improved Cross-Domain Sentiment Analysis Based on a Semi-Supervised Convolutional Neural Network 155

Lap-Kei Lee, Hong Kong Metropolitan University, Hong Kong
Kwok Tai Chui, Hong Kong Metropolitan University, Hong Kong
Jingjing Wang, Hong Kong Metropolitan University, Hong Kong
Yin-Chun Fung, Hong Kong Metropolitan University, Hong Kong
Zhanhui Tan, Hong Kong Metropolitan University, Hong Kong

The dependence on Internet in our daily life is ever-growing, which provides opportunity to discover valuable and subjective information using advanced techniques such as natural language processing and artificial intelligence. In this chapter, the research focus is a convolutional neural network for three-class (positive, neutral, and negative) cross-domain sentiment analysis. The model is enhanced in two-fold. First, a similarity label method facilitates the management between the source and target domains to generate more labelled data. Second, term frequency-inverse document frequency (TF-IDF) and latent semantic indexing (LSI) are employed to compute the similarity between source and target domains. Performance evaluation is conducted using three datasets, beauty reviews, toys reviews, and phone reviews. The proposed method enhances the accuracy by 4.3-7.6% and reduces the training time by 50%. The limitations of the research work have been discussed, which serve as the rationales of future research directions.

Chapter 8

Detection of Economy-Related Turkish Tweets Based on Machine Learning Approaches...171

Jale Bektaş, Mersin University, Turkey

Conducting NLP for Turkish is a lot harder than other Latin-based languages such as English. In this study, by using text mining techniques, a pre-processing frame is conducted in which TF-IDF values are calculated in accordance with a linguistic approach on 7,731 tweets shared by 13 famous economists in Turkey, retrieved from Twitter. Then, the classification results are compared with four common machine learning methods (SVM, Naive Bayes, LR, and integration LR with SVM). The features represented by the TF-IDF are experimented in different N-grams. The findings show the success of a text classification problem is relative with the feature representation methods, and the performance superiority of SVM is better compared to other ML methods with unigram feature representation. The best results are obtained via the integration method of SVM with LR with the Acc of 82.9%. These results show that these methodologies are satisfying for the Turkish language.

Chapter 9
The Stakes of Social Media: Analyzing User Sentiments 196

    Elodie Attié, Capgemini Engineering T.E.C., France
    Anne Bouvet, Capgemini Engineering T.E.C., France
    Jérôme Guibert, Capgemini Engineering T.E.C., France

The COVID-19 context affected the use of social media. Video and voice chat facilitate social interactions during the current social distancing requirements. However, social media creates unrealistic reference points of comparison. The time spent on social media can thus diminish well-being. Researchers and managers aspire to understand how sentiments can control social media. Another research interest regards which techniques create positive sentiments and enhance user experience. This chapter introduces the main stakes of social media, how sentiments change social media, and in turn, social media influences sentiments. The main focus presents a literature review regarding the techniques to analyze sentiments. Finally, solutions and recommendations contemplate the use of social media, for both users and social media platforms.

Chapter 10
Predicting Catastrophic Events Using Machine Learning Models for Natural Language Processing..223

    Muskaan Chopra, Chandigarh College of Engineering and Technology, India
    Sunil K. Singh, Chandigarh College of Engineering and Technology, India
    Kriti Aggarwal, Chandigarh College of Engineering and Technology, India
    Anshul Gupta, Chandigarh College of Engineering and Technology, India

In recent years, there has been widespread improvement in communication technologies. Social media applications like Twitter have made it much easier for people to send and receive information. A direct application of this can be seen in the cases of disaster prediction and crisis. With people being able to share their observations, they can help spread the message of caution. However, the identification of warnings and analyzing the seriousness of text is not an easy task. Natural language processing (NLP) is one way that can be used to analyze various tweets for the same. Over the years, various NLP models have been developed that are capable of providing high accuracy when it comes to data prediction. In the chapter, the authors will analyze various NLP models like logistic regression, naive bayes, XGBoost, LSTM, and word embedding technologies like GloVe and transformer encoder like BERT for the purpose of predicting disaster warnings from the scrapped tweets. The authors focus on finding the best disaster prediction model that can help in warning people and the government.

Chapter 11
Clubhouse Experience: Sentiment Analysis of an Alternative Platform From the Eyes of Classic Social Media Users...244
    Ipek Deveci Kocakoç, Dokuz Eylul University, Turkey
    Pınar Özkan, Dokuz Eylul University, Turkey

Clubhouse is an invitation-only social networking application that differs from the usual social media platforms in that it is "audio only." In this chapter, the sentiments in the social media messages about Clubhouse in the classic SMPs are examined by supervised learning (by using Hugging Face Transformer Library), and the user feelings are analyzed. Because Turkey is in the first ranks among European countries in terms of both the number of social media users and the number of messages, the analysis is conducted using the Turkish users. Mentions of Clubhouse have begun on Twitter and Sourtimes platforms in Turkey in early 2021. In this study, the aim is to demonstrate how Clubhouse, a new and different SMP, is evaluated by Twitter and Sourtimes users and to reveal user thoughts about this SMP along the timeline by using sentiment analysis.

Compilation of References 265

About the Contributors 305

Index..311

Preface

Social media sites are constantly evolving with huge amounts of scattered data or big data, which makes it difficult for researchers to trace the information flow. It is a daunting task to extract a useful piece of information from the vast unstructured big data; the disorganized structure of social media contains data in various forms such as text and videos as well as huge real-time data on which traditional analytical methods like statistical approaches fail miserably. Due to this, there is a need for efficient data mining techniques that can overcome the shortcomings of the traditional approaches.

This book on *Data Mining Approaches for Big Data and Sentiment Analysis in Social Media* encourages researchers to explore the key concepts of data mining, such as how they can be utilized on online social media platforms, and provides advances on data mining for big data and sentiment analysis in online social media, as well as future research directions. Covering a range of concepts from machine learning methods to data mining for big data analytics, this book is ideal for graduate students, academicians, faculty members, scientists, researchers, data analysts, social media analysts, managers, and software developers who are seeking to learn and carry out research in the area of data mining for big data and sentiment.

This book contains chapters dealing with different aspects of Big Data Analytics, Data Mining, Machine Learning, Market Analysis, Multilingual Aspects of Sentiment Analysis, Multimodal Sentiment Analysis, Predictive Models, Recommendation Systems, Security of Social Media, Sentiment Analysis, Sentiment Analysis approaches for Twitter, Social media in Covid-19 Pandemic, Predicting Catastrophic Events, Sentiment Analysis of Facebook Posts, Classic Social Media.

Specifically, this book contains discussion on the following topics:

- Approaches and Applications for Sentiment Analysis: A Literature Review
- A Survey on Building Recommendation Systems Using Data Mining Techniques
- A Survey on Sentiment Analysis Techniques for Twitter
- Role of Social Media in COVID-19 Pandemic: A Literature Review

- Data Mining Approaches for Sentiment Analysis in Online Social Networks (OSNs)
- Sentiment Analysis and Summarization of Facebook Posts on News Media
- An Improved Cross-Domain Sentiment Analysis Based on Semi-Supervised Convolutional Neural Network
- Detection of Economy-Related Turkish Tweets Based on Machine Learning Approaches
- The Stakes of Social Media: Analyzing User Sentiments
- Predicting Catastrophic Events Using Machine Learning Models for Natural Language Processing
- Clubhouse Experience: Sentiment Analysis of an Alternative Platform From the Eyes of Classic Social Media Users

Acknowledgment

Many people have contributed greatly to this book on Data Mining Approaches for Big Data and Sentiment Analysis in Social Media. We, the editors, would like to acknowledge all of them for their valuable help and generous ideas in improving the quality of this book. With our feelings of gratitude, we would like to introduce them in turn. The first mention is the authors and reviewers of each chapter of this book. Without their outstanding expertise, constructive reviews and devoted effort, this comprehensive book would become something without contents. The second mention is the IGI Global staff for their constant encouragement, continuous assistance and untiring support. Without their technical support, this book would not be completed. The third mention is the editor's family for being the source of continuous love, unconditional support and prayers not only for this work, but throughout our life. Last but far from least, we express our heartfelt thanks to the Almighty for bestowing over us the courage to face the complexities of life and complete this work.

Brij B. Gupta

Dragan Peraković

Ahmed A. Abd El-Latif

Deepak Gupta

October 10, 2021

Chapter 1
Approaches and Applications for Sentiment Analysis:
A Literature Review

M. Govindarajan
Annamalai University, India

ABSTRACT

With the increasing penetration of the internet, an ever-growing number of people are voicing their opinions in the numerous blogs, tweets, forums, social networking, and consumer review websites. Each such opinion has a sentiment (positive, negative, or neutral) associated with it. But the problem is that the amount of data is simply overwhelming. Methods like supervised machine learning and lexical-based approaches are available for measuring sentiments that have a huge volume of opinionated data recorded in digital form for analysis. Sentiment analysis has been used in several applications including analysis of the repercussions of events in social networks, analysis of opinions about products and services. This chapter presents sentiment analysis applications and challenges with their approaches and tools. The techniques and applications discussed in this chapter will provide a clear-cut idea to the sentiment analysis researchers to carry out their work in this field.

INTRODUCTION

Sentiment analysis is the automated mining of attitudes, opinions, and emotions from text, speech, and database sources through Natural Language Processing. The sentiment or opinion expressed emotions are classified in different classes as positive, negative and neutral. The basic task of sentiment analysis is to classify the

DOI: 10.4018/978-1-7998-8413-2.ch001

polarity in different levels like Document level, Sentence level and Aspect level or entity level. In document level the whole document is classify either into positive or negative class. Sentence level sentiment classification classifies sentence into positive, negative or neutral class. Aspect or entity level sentiment classification concerns with identifying and extracting product features from the source data. The sentiment classification approaches can be classified in: (i) machine learning (ii) lexicon based and (iii) hybrid approach. The machine learning approach is used for predicting the polarity of sentiments based on trained as well as test data sets. While the lexicon based approach does not need any prior training in order to mine the data. It uses a predefined list of words, where each word is associated with a specific sentiment. Finally in the hybrid approach, the combination of both the machine learning and the lexicon based approaches has the potential to improve the sentiment classification performance. On considering the tools used for sentiments analysis, the most used tools for detecting the feelings polarity are Emoticons, LIWC, SentiStrengh, Senti WordNet, SenticNet, Happiness Index, AFINN, PANAS-t, Sentiment140, NRC, EWGA and FRN. Sentiment analysis is used mainly in different fields such as marketing, political and sociological. This chapter presents sentiment analysis applications and challenges with their approaches and tools. The techniques and applications discussed in this chapter will provide a clear cut idea to the sentiment analysis researchers to carry out their work in this field. The rest of the chapter is organized as follows: the background section describes the related work. A brief description of sentiment analysis, levels, applications and challenges with their approaches and tools of sentiment analysis is presented in section of main focus of the chapter. Finally, the chapter concludes with future research directions.

BACKGROUND

Vishal A Kharde et al., (2016) provide a survey and comparative analyses of existing techniques for opinion mining like machine learning and lexicon-based approaches, together with evaluation metrics. Megha Joshi et al., (2017) describe different applications of sentiment analysis, techniques and challenges of sentiment analysis. Shamsa Umar et al., (2018) have discussed different researcher's work on sentimental analysis approach and classification. This paper also presents the importance of opinion mining and sentiment analysis. Lin Yue et al., (2019) focus on presenting typical methods from three different perspectives (task-oriented, granularity-oriented, methodology-oriented) in the area of sentiment analysis. Specifically, a large quantity of techniques and methods are categorized and compared. On the other hand, different types of data and advanced tools for research are introduced, as well as their limitations. On the basis of these materials, the essential prospects lying ahead for sentiment analysis are identified and discussed. T. Nikil Prakash et al., (2020) emphases on sentiment analysis applications, methods, and challenges in sentiment analysis. Mainly this paper highlighted in sentiment analysis applications and challenges. Moreover, this paper covers different levels of sentiment analysis. Alexander Ligthart et al., (2021) present the results of a tertiary study, which aims to investigate the current state of the research in this field by synthesizing the results of published secondary studies (i.e., systematic literature review and systematic mapping study) on sentiment analysis.

FOCUS OF THE ARTICLE

The purpose of this chapter provides a brief description of sentiment analysis, applications and challenges with their approaches and tools of sentiment analysis.

Figure 1. Sentiment Analysis

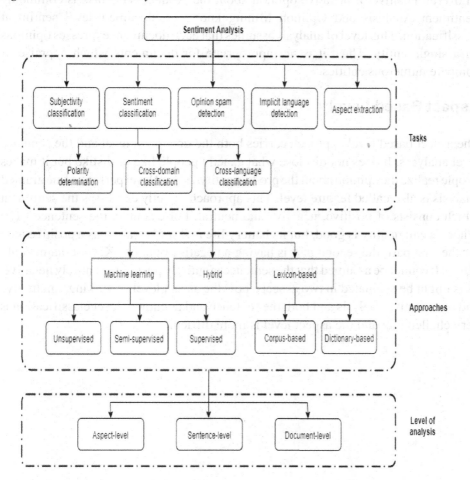

LEVELS OF ANALYSIS

Sentence Level

Sentence level approach goes to the sentences to determine whether the sentence communicated as positive, negative, or neutral opinion. Usually neutral means no opinion. This level of analysis is closely related to subjectivity classification which decides sentences called objective sentences (Xing Fang et al., 2015). The factual information from sentences called subjective sentences that prompt subjective views and opinions. However, the subjectivity is not equivalent to sentiment as many objective sentences can imply opinions.

Document Level

The document level approach is to classify whether the whole document expresses as positive or negative sentiment. The system concludes whether the review states an overall positive or negative opinion about the product. This task is commonly Sentiment Analysis and Opinion Mining known as document-level sentiment classification. This level of analysis assumes that each document expresses opinions on a single entity. Thus, it is not appropriate for documents which appraise or compare numerous entities.

Aspect Based Level

The aspect based level approach carries both the document level and the sentence level analyses. It does not disclose what exactly people like or dislike but it makes people realize the opinion about the product entity. Aspect level performs fine grained analysis is also called feature level. This approach directly expresses the sentiment which consists of positive, negative and neutral. For example, the sentence "The iPhone's call quality is good, but its battery life is short" clearly has a positive tone for the first part, the second part is having a negative opinion (K. Mouthami et al., 2013). It cannot be assumed that the sentence is entirely positive or entirely negative. This might be evaluated in two aspects, how the aspect level is working, qualitative and quantitative analysis and both the sentence and document level classification is very challenging and the aspect level is more difficult.

SENTIMENT ANALYSIS APPROACHES AND TECHNIQUES

Sentiment Analysis "It is the computational study of people's opinions, appraisals and emotions toward entities, events and their attributes. Opinions are important because whenever we need to make a decision –"we listen to other's opinions"." (Bing Liu).

Lexicon Based Approach

The lexical or lexicon approach is a method for teaching dictionary based described by Michael Lewis in the early 1990s (Lei Zhang et al., 2011). The basic concept of this approach respites an idea that the significant part of education involves understanding and produce lexical phrases as chunks. In this pattern of language like grammar as well as consume meaningful set of words at their dumping.

Dictionary-Based Approach

Dictionary-Based approach involves using a dictionary which contains synonyms and antonyms of a word. Thus, a simple technique in this approach is to use a few seed sentiment words to bootstrap based on the synonym and antonym structure of a dictionary. Specifically, this method works as follows: A small set of sentiment words (seeds) with known positive or negative orientations is first collected manually, which is very easy. The algorithm then grows this set by searching in any online available dictionary for their synonyms and antonyms. The seed list will be added with the new found words. The process iteratively keeps on adding the words until no more new words are found. Manual inspection can be used to clean up the list at last.

Corpus Based Approach

The Corpus-based approach helps to solve the problem of finding opinion words with context specific orientations. Its methods depend on syntactic patterns or patterns that occur together along with a seed list of opinion words to find other opinion words in a large corpus. There are two methods in the corpus based approach:

Statistical Approach

If the word appears intermittently amid positive texts, then its polarity is positive. If it appears frequently among negative texts, then its polarity can be considered as negative. If it has equal frequencies, then it can be considered as neutral word. Seed opinion words can be found using statistical techniques. Most state of the art

5

methods are based on the observation that similar opinion words mostly appear together in a corpus. Thus, if two words appear together frequently within the same context, then there is high probability that they have same polarity. Therefore, the polarity of an unknown word can be determined by calculating the relative frequency of co-occurrence with another word. This could be done using Point wise Mutual Information (PMI) as in example suggested by Turney P, 2002, SO of a given phrase is calculated by comparing its similarity to a positive word ("Awesome") And its similarity with negative word ("Awful"). More explicitly, a phrase is given a numerical rating by taking the mutual information between the given phrase and the positive reference word "Awesome" and subtracting the mutual information between the given phrase and the negative reference word "Awful". Using part-of-speech (POS) patterns, this technique then classifies the text by extracting the bigrams. PMI is then calculated by using the polarity score for each bigram.

Semantic Approach

This principle assigns similar sentiment values to semantically close words. These Semantically close words can be obtained by getting the list of sentiment words and iteratively expanding the initial set with synonyms and antonyms and then determining the sentiment polarity for an unknown word by the relative count of positive and negative synonyms of this word (Neviarouskaya Alena et al., 2010).

LEXICON-BASED AND NATURAL LANGUAGE PROCESSING TECHNIQUES

Natural Language Processing (NLP) techniques are sometimes used with the lexicon-based approach to find the syntactical structure and help in finding the semantic relations (Bolshakov Igor, et al., 2004). Moreo and Romero (2012) have used NLP techniques as pre-processing stage before they used their proposed lexicon-based SA algorithm. Their proposed system consists of an automatic focus detection module and a sentiment analysis module capable of assessing user opinions of topics in news items which use a taxonomy-lexicon that is specifically designed for news analysis. Their results were promising in scenarios where colloquial language predominates.

Discourse Information

The importance of discourse in SA has been increasing recently. Discourse information can be found either among sentences or among clauses in the same sentence.

OTHER TECHNIQUES

There are techniques that cannot be roughly categorized as ML approach or lexicon-based Approach. Formal Concept Analysis (FCA) is one of those techniques. FCA was proposed by Wille, 1982 as a mathematical approach used for structuring, analyzing and visualizing data, based on a notion of duality called Galois connection (Priss U, 2006). The data consists of a set of entities and its features are structured into formal abstractions called formal concepts. Together they form a concept lattice ordered by a partial order relation. The concept lattices are constructed by identifying the objects and their corresponding attributes for a specific domain, called conceptual structures, and then the relationships among them are displayed. Fuzzy Formal Concept Analysis (FFCA) was developed in order to deal with uncertainty and unclear information. It has been successfully applied in various information domain applications (Li S, et al., 2011).

Machine Leaning Approach

Machine learning is a subset of computer science that developed from the study of pattern acknowledgement and computational study theory in artificial intelligence (Andrius Mudinas et al., 2012). Machine learning gives study for computer learning ability with explicit program which explores the study and creation of algorithms that can be made a prediction on data. The algorithms function of constructing a model from an example training set of input clarifications in order to make data-driven predictions or decisions stated as outputs. Machine learning is associated to computational statistics. It has a strong mathematical optimization. There are two different types of machine learning is applicable (Zhaoxia Wang et al., 2014).

Supervised Learning

Supervised learning is the machine learning task of deducing a function from labelled training data. The training data contain a set of training examples. Fashionable supervised learning, every examples are pair comprising of input object and a desired output value. This process required wide practices in the machine learning. Different types of techniques are obtainable in supervised learning such as classification and regression. Here the goal of the classification is to learn the mapping input from x to output y, where $y \in \{1,..., C\}$, with C being the number of classes. If C =2, this is called binary classification (in which case we often assume $y \in \{0, 1\}$); if C>2, this is called meticulous classification. Regression has been just like classification excluding the response variable is unremitting.

Naïve Bayes

The Bayesian Classification is a supervised statistical method for classification and contains practical learning algorithms. The posterior probability of a class can be computed using Naive Bayes model. This model works is suitable for a large data set. The use of the Bayes Theorem is to presume the chance of the inclined feature set matches to specified label.

Bayesian Network

A Bayesian network is part of probabilistic graphical models (GMs). An ambiguous domain can be represented using these structures. Every node in the graph points to a arbitrary variable and the edges represents their chance of dependence. These conditional dependencies in the graph are calculated by using known statistical and computational methods (V. Vapnik, 1995).

Support Vector Machine Classifiers

Support vector machines (SVM) are supervised learning models with associated learning algorithms.SVM are effective approaches for non linear separation and regression analysis.

Rule-Based Classifiers

The rule-based classifier is a machine learning methods that learn 'rules' to apply, knowledge and store. The characteristics of the rule-based model are an identification of the set of rules that represents the knowledge. Association rule mining is part of the rule-based approach. The training phase generates the rule based on certain constraints. Support and confidence is the general constraints. Support indicates the frequency of item-set in the database and confidence refers success or truth of the rule.

Decision Tree Classifier

Decision tree classifier is a statistical model uses a decision tree which represents the class labels in the leaves and features of those labels in branches. Algorithm for decision tree works by picking the suitable attribute to split the data and expanding the leaf nodes of the tree until it satisfies the required condition. Decision tree classifier is all about finding attributes that return the highest information gain (Nan Li et al., 2010).

k-Nearest Neighbour

K-Nearest Neighbour is an Instance-based classifier works on unknown instances. It relates the known to unknown instances by distance or similarity. It does not involve prior assumptions about the distribution of data taken from set of positive and negative samples. A new sample is categorized by computing the interval to the nearest training pattern. Positive or negative sign of that point decides the classification of sample. This approach of locating nearest neighbour and marking the unfamiliar item with the located instance as that of the known neighbour is referred as nearest neighbour classifier.

Unsupervised Learning

Unsupervised learning is a type of machine learning algorithm, which is used to draw inferences from data sets containing of input data without labelling reactions. The most common unsupervised learning method is cluster analysis, this is used for examining the data analysis to discover hidden patterns or grouping data.

Hybrid Approach

Hybrid approach is used for combinations of machine learning approaches. This approach has to prove the combination whether it is enhanced results or performance of classification.

Implementation

In this section, how to use WEKA tool to build the machine learning models for the restaurant review dataset will be demonstrated based on accuracy.

INTERPRETING THE RESULTS

The performances of machine learning approaches were compared using restaurant review dataset based on accuracy. Based on the performance of various machine learning approaches, it has been concluded that hybrid approach outperforms the other approaches of machine learning in terms of accuracy. Restaurant reviews could be utilized to create sustainable marketing strategies in the restaurant industry, which contributes to national sustainable economic development. The restaurant industry is highly competitive, and analyzing consumer opinion using social media data can enhance their marketing targets and objectives. The results of this chapter could be used as sustainable marketing strategy for review website developers to design sophisticated, intelligence review systems by enabling customers to sort and filter helpful reviews based on their preferences. The extracted aspects and their assigned sentiment could also help restaurateurs better understand how to meet diverse customers' needs and maintain sustainable competitive advantages.

Table 1. Evaluation of Restaurant Review Dataset

Machine Leaning Approaches	Accuracy
Naïve Bayes	85.00%
Support Vector Machine Classifiers	85.20%
Rule-based classifiers	85.10%
Decision tree classifier	85.30%
k-Nearest Neighbour	83.11%
Hybrid Approach	85.35%

Application Areas of Sentiment Analysis

Sentiment Analysis or Opinion Mining is basically used for determining the subjective nature of the data. The domains where Sentiment Analysis is used are as follows:

- **Aid in decision making:** Decision making is an important part of new life. It ranges from "which car to buy", "which cafe to go" and "which tourist place to visit". The reviews given by old customers of a particular product are processed by Sentiment Analysis and a best case answer is provided to the user (Zhai Zhongwu et al., 2011).
- **Improving the Quality of the Products:** For every product, there is series of manufacturing firms which leads to a tough competition. Firms use Sentiment Analysis for the better analysis of product. The reviews and opinions of customers are used to improve the quality of product. This concept also leads to the development of innovative products (K.R. Chowdhary, 2012).
- **Recommendation Systems:** It is provided to the users for providing their views. This system also provides the development of a great corpus. There are numerous websites with an in-built recommendation system. These types of websites are generally related to the books, music, online media, and film industry. Recommendation system also maintains some important information of user like personal information likes and dislikes previous history and his friend's information to provide more suggestions.

- **Business Strategies:** Developing a strategy for business is not the work of an individual, but a team work. This team includes the higher authorities, experts, developers, junior staff and the most important is the customers. Now, the issue arises, how to communicate with the customers for their assistance. Sentiment analysis used the response of the customers, their needs and demands to generate a future strategy and cover the previous flaws.
- **Business Intelligence:** Sentiment analysis is used to search the web for opinions and reviews of these opinions from different Blogs, Amazon, tweets, etc. It also helps in Brand analysis or competitive intelligence, new product perception, product and service benchmark and market forecasting.
- **Political SA:** It has numerous applications and possibilities viz. analyzing trends, identifying ideological bias, targeting advertising or messages, gauging reactions, etc. It is also useful in evaluation of public opinions and views or discussions of policy.
- **SA and Sociology:** Idea propagation through groups is an important concept in sociology. Opinions and reactions to ideas are relevant to adoption of new ideas and analyzing sentiment reactions on blogs can give insight to this process e.g. modeling trust and influence in the blogosphere using link polarity (Mikhail Bautin et al., 2008).
- **SA and Psychology:** It has potential to augment psychological investigations or experiments with data extracted from natural language text.
- **Drive choices:** Sentiment investigation gives discernment on any adjustment in public-related opinions identified with ones image that will either bolster or nullify business. High or low estimation scores help everyone to recognize the approaches to remake the organization or grow new innovative methodologies.
- **Highlight Competitive Advantage:** There are vital advantages in knowing purchaser sentiments identified with rivals. Sentiment analysis or classification can help to foresee client patterns, so keeping a pulse on general opinions of the public of different organizations and gives a control gathering to analyze against scores.
- **Social Media Monitoring:** Social media observing is otherwise called measurement and listening of social media. It is utilized to gather and mine information, particularly by associations looking for client insight to decide current industry patterns. The procedure has turned out to be simpler - yet increasingly boring because of free and promptly accessible outlets, similar to online journals, wikis, news destinations, person to person communication locales, discussions, video/photograph sharing destinations and message sheets.

- **Employees Assessment:** Sentimental investigation can likewise be utilized to acknowledge assessment from the representatives of the organization and examine feelings, frame of mind towards their activity. It is additionally used to decide whether users are happy with their activity or not.

- **Providing Better Services:** Text mining can give a channel about which administration of the organization is getting increasingly negative criticism. This will assist the organization with knowing, what the issues are emerging with that specific administration. Also, in light of this data the organization can redress these issues. So, analysis can be used to find out faults in products based on actual users' involvement. Customers' reviews can assist to increase the profits and reduce difficulties (P.Haseena Rahmath, 2014).

- **Monitoring Market Research:** It won't just assistance the organization to remain refreshed and associate more with the group of spectators, yet it will likewise encourage the ascent of new thoughts, for growing new items. This will permit the organization figure out what most of the group of spectators' requests and build up an item as indicated by these requests (P.Haseena Rahmath, 2014).

- **Acquiring any Product:** While obtaining a product online and offline, catching correct selection is a challenging job. Analysis of emotions provides evaluated opinion that can be efficiently used for choice making. With the help of this approach, people can figure out other user's judgment about product and also they can compare the competing brands (P.Haseena Rahmath, 2014).

- **Policy Making:** With the help of opinion mining, policy inventor can take people's perspective towards some scheme and they can use this data in creating new scheme. By analyzing reviews into good and bad, scheme say which policy should get confirmed and which should not get confirmed (P.Haseena Rahmath, 2014).

- **Politics:** In Politics, opinion mining can be used to drive the reviews of the people regarding particular entity or situation, for what people are angry or happy for, etc (Suman et al., 2017 and Alessia D'Andrea et al., 2015). Assessment investigation can assist political association with understanding which issues are near the voter's heart. So, opinion gathering can produce relevant judgment and thus support politic parties to develop impressive plans.

- **Students Feedback:** Universities and colleges can also use analysis to analyze the scholar's assessment or feedback about their teaching methods, practical labs, course and other facilities they are providing. Feedback can be collected either from surveys, or from online sources. Then institutes can use the results to find out the areas of student disapproval, as well as they can identify and build on those areas where scholars are showing positive feedback.

- **Government Intellect:** By analyzing comments on social media sites, ministry division can check audience emotions towards their administration and the advantages they transfer. Government can use these reviews to solve social issues, enhance benefits such as parking, relaxation, policing, transport system and the condition of roads (Alessia D'Andrea et al., 2015).

- **Customer Serviceability:** Customer service agents mainly use sentiment classification to fundamentally description of user email into "urgent" or "not urgent". Then agent directs their time toward resolving the users with the most urgent needs first. Now customer service support becomes more and more programmed with the help of machine learning.

- **Online Commerce:** The most general use of sentiment analysis is in ecommerce activities. Websites allows their users to submit their experience about shopping and product qualities. They provide summary for the product and different features of the product by assigning ratings or scores. Customers can easily view opinions and recommendation information on whole product as well as specific product features. Graphical summary of the overall product and its features is presented to users. Popular merchant websites like amazon. com provides review from editors and also from customers with rating information.

- **Voice of the Market (VOM):** Voice of the Market is about determining what customers are feeling about products or services of competitors. Accurate and timely information from the Voice of the Market helps in gaining competitive advantage and new product development. Detection of such information as early as possible helps in direct and target key marketing campaigns. Sentiment Analysis helps corporate to get customer opinion in real-time. This real-time information helps them to design new marketing strategies, improve product features and can predict chances of product failure. Zhang et al, (2012) proposed weakness finder system which can help manufacturer's find their product weakness from Chinese reviews by using aspects based sentiment analysis. There are some commercial and free sentiment analysis services are available, Radiant6, Sysomos, Viralheat, Lexalytics, etc. are commercial services.

- **Voice of the Customer (VOC):** Voice of the Customer is concern about what individual customer is saying about products or services. It means analyzing the reviews and feedback of the customers. VOC is a key element of Customer Experience Management. VOC helps in identifying new opportunities for product inventions. Extracting customer opinions also helps identify functional requirements of the products and some non-functional requirements like performance and cost.

- **Brand Reputation Management:** Brand Reputation Management is concern about managing your reputation in market. Opinions from customers or any other parties can damage or enhance your reputation. Brand Reputation Management (BRM) is a product and company focused rather than customer. Now, one-to-many conversations are taking place online at a high rate. That creates opportunities for organizations to manage and strengthen brand reputation. Now Brand perception is determined not only by advertising, public relations and corporate messaging. Brands are now a sum of the conversations about them. Sentiment analysis helps in determining how company's brand, product or service is being perceived by community online.

- **Government:** Sentiment analysis helps government in assessing their strength and weaknesses by analyzing opinions from public. For example, "If this is the state, how do you expect truth to come out? The MP who is investigating 2g scam himself is deeply corrupt". this example clearly shows negative sentiment about government. Whether it is tracking citizens' opinions on a new 108 system, identifying strengths and weaknesses in a recruitment campaign in government job, assessing success of electronic submission of tax returns, or many other areas, we can see the potential for sentiment analysis.

- **Summarizing Reviews:** With the massive popularity of e-commerce sites and online shopping there has been a total paradigm shift of how people make their purchase decisions. Before deciding to go for a particular product most of us rely on the reviews of the users on these sites. A sentiment analysis system can be of great help here as it can collect all the reviews of a particular product and present us with a concise summary of the opinions expressed therein.

- **Detecting Hate Messages in Forums:** With a sentiment analysis system different Web forums can be monitored for detecting flames (overly heated or antagonistic messages) (E. Spertus, 1997 and M. Yang et al., 2012) so that timely action such as removal of content or banning of the user propagating such messages can be taken. It is also possible to identify and flag individuals having a terrorist mind set (J. Brynielsson et al., 2012).

- **Voting Advice Applications:** These applications can help voters decide which political party to vote for depending on their election manifestos, past performances, public policies as well as the perception of other voters.

- **Monitoring Political Campaigns:** The political parties cannot stay away from the public opinion in the virtual world. Political parties in many countries including US and India use sentiment analysis systems for monitoring the public perception of their prime candidates especially during election campaigns.

- **e-Governance:** Sentiment analysis can prove to be really beneficial for automatic analysis of public opinion about Government policies and regulations. Thus leading to better governance.

Challenges of Sentiment Analysis

Sentiment Analysis is the computational study of affect, opinions, and sentiments expressed in text viz. blogs, editorials, newspaper articles and reviews of products, movies and books. General challenges in the research of sentiment analysis are:

- **Noise (abbreviations, slangs):** Noise on the web is increasing day by day. Abbreviations, slangs, emotions are commonly used by people for ease of use but for language processing, these contribute towards the increase in complexity.
- **Unstructured Data:** Web contains a large amount of unstructured data. Same entity is represented by different forms (Pushpa R. Suri et al., 2010). The sources of web varies from web documents, journals, books, health records, internal files of an industry, companies logs, multimedia platforms, texts, videos, audios, images etc. So, this diversity in the sources of data and different formats increases the complexity (Mikhail Bautin et al., 2008).
- **Contextual Information:** Actual sense of the text varies from domain to domain; this property is referred as contextual property. So, based on the context, the behaviour of the word changes.
- **Word Sense Disambiguation:** One word may have multiple meanings. This concept also affects the polarity of the word. For example-In English word "good" have multiple senses according to the usage in a particular sentence (Melville et al., 2009).
- **Language Constructs:** Different styles in a language lead to different challenges. Some of the challenges while dealing with English language are as under:
- **Word order:** for identifying the subjective nature of the text, arrangements of words in a sentence play an important role. In English language, there is a fixed order set by grammatical rules i.e. subject is followed by verb which is further followed by object.
- **Morphological Variations:** The concept of morphological variables states that information is fused in the words.
- **Handling Spelling Variations:** As in Punjabi language, one word can possess many spellings, so this lead to high complexity. It becomes complex

to process all the variants a single word. This problem is also faced during training the model.

- **Lack of resources:** Lack of tools, resources, corpora lead to great struggle while doing sentiment analysis for Indian languages.

- **Problem of Language:** In SA and sentiment mining, English language is very much utilized due to its accessibility (W. Medhat, 2014). Reviews given by clients could be in language other than English (German, Italic, Arabic, Urdu and so on). Therefore, to handle each language according to its coordination is a crucial job.

- **Fake Opinion:** It is related to unauthentic instruction. Some fake reviewer posts reviews which misguide the users by giving them false positive or negative sentiments identified with any article. How to check the accessibility and quality of the review being trustworthy is a major problem (Haseena Rahmath, 2014).

- **Temporal Relations:** The season of audits might be significant for analysis of sentiments. The commentator may feel that Windows Vista is great in 2008, however now he may have negative supposition in 2009 in view of Windows 7. So, evaluating this sort of assessments that are shifted with interval may recover the exhibition of the analyzed framework. This causes to watch if a specific item gets enhanced with time, or individuals change their conclusion about an item.

- **Sarcastic Sentences:** Content may have ironic and sarcastic words. For instance, "What an extraordinary vehicle, it quit working in the subsequent day." In such case, positive words can have negative feeling of importance. Ironic and sarcastic sentences can be difficult to distinguish which can prompt incorrect conclusion mining.

- **Grouping Synonyms:** Many occasions content contains various words having same significance. So, such word ought to be distinguished and bunch together for classification based on accuracy. It is a troublesome undertaking to recognize these words, as individuals frequently utilize various words to portray a similar component. For instance, "voice" and "sound" both allude to a similar element in telephone survey.

- **Thwarted Expectations:** Some content contains sentences beginning with various setting which has diverse significance toward the end. For instance, "The cast was bad, on-screen characters performed ineffectively, however I loved it." In above survey the last sentence makes the entire audit positive. In the event that term recurrence considered the above articulations would arrange as negative because of increasingly negative words in survey.

- **Asymmetry in Availability of Software:** Software which are used to perform mining tasks are costly. Currently these are affordable only to large industries and ministry. It is away from the commoner's assumption (Haseena Rahmath, 2014).

- **Lack of Proper Data:** The major challenge of the emotion detection is the fulfillment of proper data. Organizations need to maintain unlimited data sources to get prosecutable judgment. So, lack of proper data may lead to disorganized outcome. j) Geographical Variations: Various countries and regions use particular assertion and slang, even within the similar language. Large numbers of services only fulfill in English, ignoring the other languages spoken in the world. While a few services consolidate dictionary slang, they cannot keep up with developments in street slang.

- **Co-referential Resolution:** This kind of goals is the issue of recognizing what a noun or a pronoun phrase alludes to. For instance, "We viewed the film and went to eat dinner; it was terrible." What does "It" allude to? Co-referential goals might be valuable for the theme/perspective- based mining.

- **Coreference resolution:** Coreference resolution is the problem of identifying what a pronoun, or a noun phrase refers to. For example, "We watched the movie and went to dinner; it was awful." What does "It" refer to? Coreference resolution may be useful for the topic/aspect based sentiment analysis. Coreference resolution may improve the accuracy of opinion mining.

- **Requirement of World Knowledge:** Knowledge about worlds' facts, events, people are often required to correctly classify the text. Consider the following example (A. Joshi et al., 2011), "Casablanca and a lunch comprising of rice and fish: a good Sunday" The system without world knowledge classifies above sentence as positive due to the word "good", but it is an objective sentence because Casablanca is the name of the famous movie.

- **Domain Considerations:** The accuracy of sentiment classification can be influenced by the domain of the items to which it is applied. The reason is that the there are many words whose meaning changes from domain to domain. For example (B. Pang et al., 2008), "Go read the book." This sentence has positive sentiment in book domain while it indicates negative sentiment for movie domain.

- **Negation:** In traditional text classification small differences between two pieces of text don't change the meaning very much. In Sentiment analysis, however, "the movie was great" is very different from "the movie was not great". Negation handling is a difficult task in sentiment analysis as it reverses the polarity. Negation also expresses by sarcasm and implicit sentences which doesn't contain any negative words.

- **Review Spam Detection:** On product review site, many people write fake reviews, called review spam, to promote their products by giving undeserving positive opinions, or defame their competitors' products by giving false negative opinions. The opinion spam identification task has great impacts on industrial communities. If the opinion provided services contain large number of spams, they will affect the users' experience. Furthermore, if the user is cheated by the provided opinion, he will never use the system again.

Tools for Sentiment Analysis

For analyzing the customer view point from written text and emoticons, a number of tools are available (Alessia D'Andrea et al., 2015). The tools used for the sentiment analysis are discussed in Table 2.

Table 2. Tools for sentiment analysis

Tools for Sentiment Analysis	Description
NLTK	The mechanism of Natural Language Tool Kit provides processing tools for certain languages (J. K. Rout et al., 2018). This kind of toolkit involves the processes like sentiment analysis, data mining, data scraping, machine learning, and many other tasks of language processing. It provides a platform for modelling of the Python programs in order to work with human based data language which provides an easy interface corresponding as WordNet, in conjunction with libraries of text processing for tokenization, stemming, parsing, tagging, and classification (S Padmaja et al., 2013).
Tweet NLP	It represents the collection of certain tools for performing NLP tasks in connection to the Twitter's conversational language (M. M. Fouad et al., 2018). Tweet NLP includes hierarchical word clusters, a tokenizer, POS tagger, dependency parser. The POS tagger forms a significant tool for many applications of NLP for modelling feature vectors for a specified classifier. The Tweet NLP based tagger presented an accuracy level maintained above 93%.
Scikit-Learn	This basically represents a framework for Python programming language offering large machine learning models as well as the tools for data analysis and pre-processing. It provides state-of-art applications for large machine learning models with its aim to pay particular attention to consistent API, good type of documentation, and good performance. Such type of documentation provides a simplified structure for both the experienced and inexperienced type of readers to search the deep information and to take an over-view of the topic, respectively.
Pandas	It represents an open source library which provides high-level of data performance of data structures, and it involves the analysis of data for Python programming language. It involves different tools for effective writing and reading of data between distinct textual file formats and in-memory structures of data like comma-separated value-based files.
CRF Suite	It is an implementation based on a classifier named Conditional Random Fields (CRF) sequence. Such a classifier is presented in C++ programming language. The parameter C1 and C2 forms the input parameters for each of the CRF classifier for the settlement of L1 and L2 normalization levels coefficients, respectively.
Mechanical Turk	The Amazon Mechanical Turk represents a marketplace which requires human intelligence methodology for their work (Alessia D'Andrea et al., 2015). It basically helps in performing large tasks based on human intelligence providing large workforce. It is a useful tool for annotating large tweet number manually that may be positive or negative one.
Google Alert	This is an easy and convenient approach to monitor search queries. By using this approach user will receive regular email updates on particular topic or entity. It is a powerful tool for finding latest trend.
Weka	Weka is a collection of machine learning algorithms for data mining tasks (Sahayak Varsha et al., 2015). The algorithms can either be applied directly to dataset. It is an open source tool and mainly used for text classification in to different categories.
Rapid Miner	Rapid miner is an effective tool which allow user to perform data analysis task. In aspect-based analysis it can be used to find sentiments. Business can use it to increase customer satisfaction by focusing on enhancing certain aspects of their products and services. It is an open source tool and can analyze big data.
Facebook Insights	If a trade's Facebook page has more than 30 likes then it can take profit of Facebook Insights. With the help of Facebook Visions, brands are able to see their number of viewers, number of likes and dislikes. It also allows you to view daily active users and permit you to know your social media fans more appropriately.
Google Analytics	It permits occupation to find what about their brand is attracting users and how they can take advantage of it. Google Analytics allows to see the exact number of visitors that have found ones website and which exact terms they type in search engines. It will help organization to scale their rank high.

CONCLUSION AND FUTURE RESEARCH DIRECTIONS

Sentiment Analysis can be used for analyzing opinions in blogs, articles, Product reviews, Social Media websites, Movie-Review websites where a third person can narrates the views. Different types of features and classification algorithms may be combined for efficient analysis. The interest in languages other than English in this field is growing as there is still a lack of resources and researches concerning these languages. The most common lexicon source used is WordNet which exists in languages other than English. Building resources, used in Sentiment Analysis tasks, is still needed for many natural languages. Information from micro-blogs, blogs and forums as well as news source, is widely used in Sentiment Analysis recently. This media information plays a great role in expressing people's feelings, or opinions about a certain topic or product. Using social network sites and micro-blogging sites as a source of data still needs deeper analysis. There are some benchmark data sets especially in reviews like IMDB which are used for algorithms evaluation. This chapter reveals that the hybrid algorithm significantly improve the accuracy of predicting review helpfulness in restaurant business domain. This approach is an innovative technique that combines the different machine learning algorithms in predicting restaurant reviews. This chapter provides new insight on sustainable economic development by developing sustainable marketing strategies to maximize restaurant industry's performance growth. After analyzing the chapter, it is apparent that applying sentiment analysis to excavate the vast quantity of data has become a significant research problem. The techniques and algorithms used for sentiment analysis have made good progress, but a lot of challenges in this field remain unsolved. More future research can be done for solving these challenges.

REFERENCES

Alena, N., Helmut, P., & Mitsuru, I. (2010). Recognition of Affect, Judgment, and Appreciation in Text. *Proceedings of the 23rd international conference on computational linguistics (Coling 2010)*, 806–814.

Bautin, M., Vijayarenu, L., & Skiena, S. (2008). International Sentiment analysis for news and blogs. *Proceedings of the International Conference on Weblogs and Social Media (ICWSM)*.

Bolshakov & Gelbukh. (2004). *Comput Linguis: Models, Resources, Applications*. Academic Press.

Brynielsson, J., Horndahl, A., & Johansson, F. (2012). *Analysis of Weak Signals for Detecting Lone Wolf Terrorists. In European Intelligence & Security Informatics Conference*. EISIC.

Chowdhary. (2012). *Natural Language Processing*. Academic Press.

D'Andrea, A., Ferri, F., Grifoni, P., & Guzzo, T. (2015). Approaches, Tools and Applications for Sentiment Analysis Implementation. *International Journal of Computers and Applications*, *125*(3), 26–33. doi:10.5120/ijca2015905866

Fang, X., & Zhan, J. (2015). Sentiment analysis using product review data. *Journal of Big Data*, *2*(5), 1–14.

Fouad, M. M., Gharib, T. F., & Mashat, A. S. (2018). Efficient Twitter Sentiment Analysis System with Feature Selection and Classifier Ensemble. *International Conference on Advanced Machine Learning Technologies and Applications (AMLTA2018)*, *723*, 516–527.

Joshi, A., Balamurali, A. R., Bhattacharyya, P., & Mohanty, R. (2011). C-feel-it: a sentiment analyzer for microblogs. *Proceedings of ACL: Systems Demonstrations, HLT '11*,127–132.

Joshi, M., Prajapati, P., Shaikh, A., & Vala, V. (2017). A Survey on Sentiment Analysis. *International Journal of Computers and Applications*, *163*(6), 34–38. doi:10.5120/ijca2017913552

Li & Wu. (2010). Using text mining and sentiment analysis for online forums hotspot detection and forecast. *Decision Support Systems Archive*, *48*(2), 354-368.

Li, S., & Tsai, F. (2011). Noise control in document classification based on fuzzy formal concept analysis. *IEEE International Conference on Fuzzy Systems (FUZZ)*, 2583-2588. 10.1109/FUZZY.2011.6007449

Ligthart, A., Catal, C., & Tekinerdogan, B. (2021). Systematic reviews in sentiment analysis: A tertiary study. *Artificial Intelligence Review*, *54*(7), 4997–5053. Advance online publication. doi:10.100710462-021-09973-3

Medhat, W., Hassan, A., & Korashy, H. (2014). Sentiment analysis algorithms and applications : A survey. *Ain Shams Engineering Journal*, *5*(4), 1093–1113. doi:10.1016/j.asej.2014.04.011

Melville & Gryc. (2009). Sentiment Analysis of Blogs by Combining Lexical Knowledge with Text Classification. *KDD '09: Proceedings of the 15th ACM SIGKDD international conference on Knowledge discovery and data mining*, 1275-1284.

Moreo, A., Romero, M., Castro, J. L., & Zurita, J. M. (2012). Lexicon-based comments-oriented news sentiment analyzer system. *Expert Systems with Applications, 39*(10), 9166–9180. doi:10.1016/j.eswa.2012.02.057

Mouthami, Devi, & Bhask. (2013). Sentiment Analysis and Classification Based On Textual Reviews. *Information Communication and Embedded Systems (ICICES),* 271-276.

Mudinas, Zhang, & Levene. (2012). Combining Lexicon and Learning based Approaches for Concept-Level Sentiment Analysis. *Journal of American Society,* 1-8.

Nikil Prakash, T., & Aloysius, A. (2020). Applications, Approaches, and Challenges in Sentiment Analysis. *International Research Journal of Modernization in Engineering Technology and Science, 02*(07), 910–915.

Padmaja, S. (2013). Opinion Mining and Sentiment Analysis –An Assessment of Peoples' Belief: A Survey. *International Journal of Ad hoc Sensor & Ubiquitous Computing, 4*(1), 21–33. doi:10.5121/ijasuc.2013.4102

Pang, B., & Lee, L. (2008). Opinion mining and sentiment analysis. *Foundations and Trends in Information Retrieval, 2*(1-2), 1–135. doi:10.1561/1500000011

Priss, U. (2006). *Formal concept analysis in information science.* Presented at the annual review of information science and technology. 10.1002/aris.1440400120

Rout, J. K., Choo, K. K. R., Dash, A. K., Bakshi, S., Jena, S. K., & Williams, K. L. (2018). A model for sentiment and emotion analysis of unstructured social media text. *Electronic Commerce Research, 18*(1), 181–199. doi:10.1007100660-017-9257-8

Spertus, E. (1997). Smokey: Automatic recognition of hostile messages. *Proceedings of the 14th National Conference on Artificial Intelligence and 9th Innovative Applications of Artificial Intelligence Conference,* 1058-1065.

Suman, J. S. (2017). Sentiment Analysis of Tweets using Support Vector Machine. *International Journal of Computer Science and Mobile Applications, 5*(10), 83–91.

Suri, P. R., & Taneja, H. (2010). Object Oriented Information Computing over WWW. *International Journal of Computer Science Issues, 7*(3), 38–41.

Turney, P. (2002). Thumbs Up or Thumbs Down? Semantic Orientation Applied to Unsupervised Classification of Reviews. *Proceedings of the 40th Annual Meeting of the Association for Computational Linguistics (ACL),* 417-424.

Umar, S., & Maryam, F. A. (2018). Sentiment Analysis Approaches and Applications: A Survey. *International Journal of Computers and Applications*, *181*(1), 1–9. doi:10.5120/ijca2018916630

Vapnik, V. (1995). *The Nature of Statistical Learning Theory*. Springer-Verlag. doi:10.1007/978-1-4757-2440-0

Varsha, S., Shete, V., & Pathan, A. (2015). Sentiment analysis on twitter data. *International Journal of Innovative Research in Advanced Engineering*, *2*(1), 178–183.

Vishal, A. (2016). Sentiment Analysis of Twitter Data: A Survey of Techniques. *International Journal of Computers and Applications*, *139*(11), 5–15. doi:10.5120/ijca2016908625

Wang, Z., Victor, J. C. T., & Chin, H. C. (2014). *Enhancing Machine Learning Methods for Sentiment Classification of Web Data*. Springer International Publishing. doi:10.1007/978-3-319-12844-3_34

Wille, R. (1982). Restructuring lattice theory: an approach based on hierarchies of concepts. In *I. Rival* (pp. 445–470). Reidel. doi:10.1007/978-94-009-7798-3_15

Yang, M., & Chen, H. (2012). Partially supervised learning for radical opinion identification in hate group web forums. *IEEE International Conference on Intelligence and Security Informatics*, 96-101. 10.1109/ISI.2012.6284099

Yue, L., Chen, W., Li, X., Zuo, W., & Yin, M. (2019). A survey of sentiment analysis in social media. *Knowledge and Information Systems*, *60*(2), 617–663. doi:10.100710115-018-1236-4

Zhai, Z., Bing, L., Hua, X., & Hua, X. (2011). Clustering Product Features for Opinion Mining. *Proceedings of WSDM'11*, 347-354.

Zhang, Ghosh, Dekhil, & Liu. (2011). *Combining Lexicon-based and Learning-based Methods for Twitter Sentiment Analysis*. HP Laboratories.

Zhang, W., Xu, H., & Wan, W. (2012). Weakness Finder: Find product weakness from Chinese reviews by using aspects based sentiment analysis. *Expert Systems with Applications*, *39*(11), 10283–10291. doi:10.1016/j.eswa.2012.02.166

KEY TERMS AND DEFINITIONS

Aspect-Based Level: The aspect-based level approach carries both the document level and the sentence level analyses.

Document Level: The document level approach is to classify whether the whole document expresses as positive or negative sentiment.

Domain Specific: The main problem experienced by information retrieval and emotion analysis is the domain dependent nature of words.

Lexicon-Based Approach: The basic concept of this approach respites an idea that the significant part of education involves understanding and produce lexical phrases as chunks.

Machine Leaning Approach: Machine learning is a subset of computer science that developed from the study of pattern acknowledgement and computational study theory in artificial intelligence.

Pandas: It represents an open source library which provides high-level of data performance of data structures, and it involves the analysis of data for Python programming language.

Rapid Miner: Rapid miner is an effective tool which allow user to perform data analysis task. In aspect-based analysis it can be used to find sentiments.

Recommendation Systems: It is provided to the users for providing their views. This system also provides the development of a great corpus.

Sentence Level: Sentence level approach goes to the sentences to determine whether the sentence communicated as positive, negative, or neutral opinion. Usually, neutral means no opinion.

Sentiment Analysis: Sentiment analysis is the automated mining of attitudes, opinions, and emotions from text, speech, and database sources through natural language processing.

Chapter 2
A Survey on Building Recommendation Systems Using Data Mining Techniques

Rajab Ssemwogerere

iD https://orcid.org/0000-0002-9786-8898
Islamic University in Uganda, Uganda

Wamwoyo Faruk
Makerere University, Uganda

Nambobi Mutwalibi

iD https://orcid.org/0000-0001-6822-616X
Islamic University in Uganda, Uganda

ABSTRACT

Classification is a data mining technique or approach used to estimate the grouped membership of items on a basis of a common feature. This technique is virtuous for future planning and discovering new knowledge about a specific dataset. An in-depth study of previous pieces of literature implementing data mining techniques in the design of recommender systems was performed. This chapter provides a broad study of the way of designing recommender systems using various data mining classification techniques of machine learning and also exploiting their methodological decisions in four aspects, the recommendation approaches, data mining techniques, recommendation types, and performance measures. This study focused on some selected classification methods and can be so supportive for both the researchers and the students in the field of computer science and machine learning in strengthening their knowledge about the machine learning hypothesis and data mining.

DOI: 10.4018/978-1-7998-8413-2.ch002

INTRODUCTION

In today's era of the internet and fast-growing web social media technologies, many web retail businesses like Amazon, and eBay, social media network programs like Facebook, Twitter, LinkedIn, and YouTube, entertainment web platforms like Netflix, Pandora, and Waze that defines the best route have evolved (Briciu & Briciu, 2021). This has also massively increased the amount of information online (Mahadik et al., 2020). Due to this factor, individuals find a challenging time to skim the information about the desired products in a short period. To cater to this challenge, Recommender systems were developed and implemented into most e-commerce websites to efficiently tailor products and services to customers (Ahmadian et al., 2020; Chehal et al., 2020). Additionally, the massively increased amount of information online factor has made RSs so tremendous in today's world and our daily lives. Regularly more and more RSs evolve basing on the textual review, comparative opinion, user ratings, purchase patterns, user profiles, among others (Gupta & Dave, 2020).

A Recommender System is a program that filters information based on user preferences, interests, likes, dislikes, and ratings of the preferred item, builds a user profile, and then predicts whether the user will prefer the item or not (Anandhan et al., 2018; Jannach et al., 2020). Commonly, there are four approaches available for generating personalized recommendation systems, they include content-based (CB) filtering, collaborative (CF) filtering, knowledge-based (KB) filtering, and hybrid-based (HB) filtering (Hernández-Nieves et al., 2020). Under the CB filtering approach, the recommendation of items is based on content similarities such as the features and preferences, for example, a movie recommender system on NetFlix recommending other movies with the same actor(s) to a user (Shu et al., 2018; Wu et al., 2018). CF filtering approach is the most prominent approach used on the web (Schafer et al., 2007). It uses the known likings of a group of users to make recommendations or predictions of the unknown likings for other users (Su & Khoshgoftaar, 2009). HB approach combines CB and CF approaches and solves almost all the problems encountered in the two methods (Barros et al., 2020). Like all other recommender system approaches, the KB approach doesn't base on the rating of other user ratings (Burke & systems, 2000). Its judgments are independent of individual tastes. The most common kind of recommendation system is a web application with which a user interacts with. This web application presents to a user a list of items from which a user selects an item to receive more details about that.

For example, from a catalog of many items or products in the database that wouldn't seemingly fit into a webpage, it is necessary to select a subset of items from the database to display to the user. E-commerce website applications display a page containing a list of products, then the user can select a product to see more details about the product if possible proceeds to purchase the product.

Recommender systems use various techniques and software-related tools to learn user profiles, make suggestions for specific items for the user, and predict the users' future behaviors, and also help users find new items (Jannach et al., 2020). Suggestions are defined as the power of decision-making that can be adopted by websites already implementing recommender systems on choosing some specific items. The specific items may comprise several lists of products which include; textbooks, movies, news articles, videos, or songs among others. To recommend products to users, these systems learn from several factors. These factors may include demographics of the user, previous user buying behavior, among others to predict the future user behavior or recommend specific items to a user that are thought to be so valuable from among a list of items available in an item set.

RSs design is based on four stages which include; Data collection, data storage, data analysis, and data recommendation (Cui et al., 2020). Following the general high-level architecture of a recommendation system shown below in figure 1, data from the users is collected on a specific website, or applications using explicit and implicit techniques, then stored in either a relational database or non-relational database to be processed by the machine learning algorithm, finally this information is reallocated back to the database to its final destination depending on the compilation directives, it is then passed and analyzed by the recommendation engine.

Figure 1. Shows a high-level architecture of a recommendation system

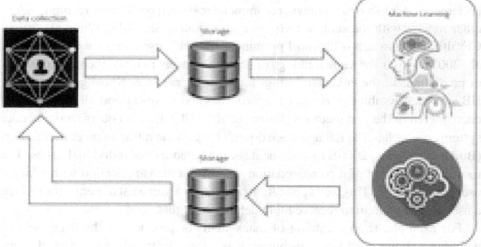

Content-Based Approach

The CB method analyzes item descriptions to identify items that are of particular interest to the user (Pazzani & Billsus, 2007). It deals with the user profiles that were created initially. The profile contains information about a user, information containing the likes and dislikes, tastes, and preferences about a specific item. CB relies on two different kinds of background data (set of users and a set of keywords), typically uses keywords, tags, and weights to describe items, and also uses them during the information retrieval (Felfernig et al., 2014; Sridevi et al., 2016). From this stage, abstract features can be generated using a vast of algorithms like the most commonly known Term Frequency times Inverse Document Frequency (TF-IDF). The basic approach of the CB during the recommendation process is, it compares the items already rated by the known user with the new items that have not yet been rated by the user and draws a similarity between these items (Shu et al., 2018). Then highly-rated items will be recommended to a user.

Figure 2. Illustrates a content-based recommendation system

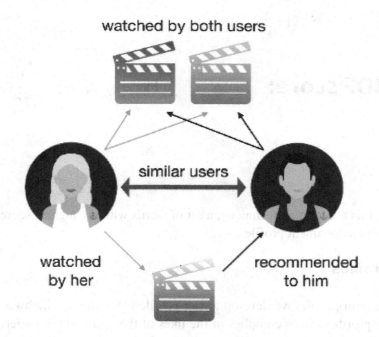

Item Representation

When designing a RS using a CB approach, we start with a user and find a set of items that a user likes using implicit and explicit methods. For example, we can look at the items that the user has rated highly and a set of items that the user has purchased, and then we build an item profile. An item profile defines a description of the item or a set of features about an item, or a collection of records representing important features of the item. In case we are building an item profile that recommends user news articles, we can use a text mining technique TF-IDF.

Figure 3.

$$TF_{ij} = \frac{f_{ij}}{\max_k f_{kj}}$$

$$IDF_i = \log \frac{N}{n_i}$$

TF-IDF score: $w_{x,y} = tf_{x,y} \times \log\left(\frac{N}{df_x}\right)$

TF-IDF

Using this text mining technique, a set of words with the highest scores will be picked from a document profile.

User Profiles

From the item profile, we develop a user profile (Melville & Sindhwani, 2010). This user profile defines complies of the likes of the user and the preferred items the user likes. The user profile is obtained by taking the average Once the user profile is obtained, it is matched against the catalog and recommends other items to the user. When building a user profile using this approach, several data mining classification techniques can be utilized such as KNN to reveal the hidden interests of users from a large amount of data to provide useful recommendations. Content-based systems share in common, first, means for describing the items that may be recommended, second, means for creating a profile of the user describing types of items the user likes, and third, means of comparing items to the user profile to determine what to recommend (Pazzani & Billsus, 2007). After the profile has been created, it is automatically updated basing on the feedback presented by the user. When recommending items to the user, the key step is to take a pair of user and item profiles then figure out the rating for that user. The angle α is the angle between a pair of two vectors. The angle between the pair of two vectors is then estimated using the cosine formula.

Figure 4.

$$\text{similarity} = \cos(\theta) = \frac{A \cdot B}{\|A\|\|B\|} = \frac{\sum_{i=1}^{n} A_i B_i}{\sqrt{\sum_{i=1}^{n} A_i^2}\sqrt{\sum_{i=1}^{n} B_i^2}},$$

We compute the cosine similarity between the user and all the items in the catalog. Then items with the highest cosine similarity are recommended to the user.

Recommendation Algorithms

A model of users' preferences created from the history of the user in form of classification. Classification algorithms are a key component when designing any RS because they formulate a function that models each of the user's interests (Malviya, 2020; Shani & Gunawardana, 2011). The researcher presents several classification machine learning algorithms designed to work on both structured and high-dimensional spaced data.

The formulated function predicts whether the user would be interested in the item given a new item and the user learning model (Shani & Gunawardana, 2011). Some ML classification algorithms formulate a function that provides an estimated probability that the user might need the unseen product which can later be used to sort the list of recommendations to be displayed to the user. While others directly predict a numerical value such as the degree of interest.

K-Nearest Neighbor (KNN) algorithm

This is a supervised machine learning technique that can solve classification problems. Its closest neighbor is measured concerning the value of k. This value defines the average nearest neighbors that need to be examined to describe a specific class of a sample data point. This algorithm assumes that similar items always exist in proximity, following the proverb ***"Birds of the same feathers flock together."*** The KNN algorithm has one major challenge. It becomes remarkably slower as the volume of the data increases (Malviya, 2020). KNN captures the idea of similarity or closeness of items defined by the distance metric known as Euclidean Distance between two points on a graph which can be computed (Yang & Jin, 2006). This is expressed in the formula below.

Figure 5.

$$d(p, q) = d(q, p) = \sqrt{(q_1 - p_1)^2 + (q_2 - p_2)^2 + \cdots + (q_n - p_n)^2}$$

Figure 6.

$$d(\mathbf{p}, \mathbf{q}) = \sqrt{\sum_{i=1}^{n}(q_i - p_i)^2}$$

Figure 7.

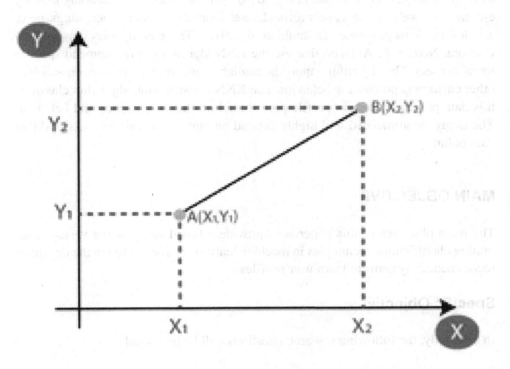

Where:

- *p, q* denotes the two points in Euclidean n-space
- q, p_i denotes Euclidean vectors starting from the initial point of the space.
- *n* denotes the n-space

The KNN technique is categorized into structure-based KNN and structure-less KNN (Bhatia, 2010). The Structure-based KNN deals with the basic structure of the data that has less mechanism with the training data samples, and the structure-less KNN category, the entire data is categorized into sample data point and training data point (Bhatia, 2010). The distance is computed between these data points to obtain the point with the smallest distance known as the nearest neighbor (Soofi et al., 2017). This classification algorithm best learns by comparison between the test dataset and training data set on a basis of similarity between the two datasets (Malviya, 2020).

The KNN algorithm is used in recommender systems that are provided with enough computing resources to solve problems that have solutions that depend on identifying similar items (Chae et al., 2018). This algorithm is commonly used by e-commerce websites on a user profile dataset about the recent movies, songs, news articles, or items purchased (Sohrabi et al., 2012). These companies may include Pandora, Netflix, or Amazon that use the KNN algorithm to recommend specific items to users. The algorithm inputs the available customer data and compares it to other customers purchasing behavior. The KNN classification algorithm classifies this data point as a certain profile point based on their experience and behavior. The items recommended will highly depend on how the algorithm classified that data point.

MAIN OBJECTIVE

The main objective of this paper is to provide a broad study of the various data mining classification techniques in machine learning implemented in the design of recommender systems to learn user profiles.

Specific Objectives

In this study, the following research questions will be answered.

1. What recommendation approaches are mostly used in designing the current Recommendation systems?
2. What are the data mining techniques used in designing the current Recommendation systems?
3. What are the recommendation types used in designing the current Recommendation systems?

Significance of the Study

This study enabled the researcher to fully develop usefully predictive models with good predictive results.

Challenges of Recommender Systems

The main challenge for inaccurate predictive user behaviors by the recommender systems was the use of improper variables.

LITERATURE REVIEW

In 2018, Juan et al. 2018 designed an experiment that caters to both suppliers' and buyers' demands and psychological status for the long-term interests of all enterprises between the suppliers and buyers (Du & Jing, 2017). They formulated a new collaborative and clustering filtering technique that recommends suppliers for the buyers in the supply chain management to improve the efficiency of the whole supply chain and reduce the total cost of the supply chain. This technology was based on a user behavior analysis method to optimize a recommendation engine to business to a business platform to achieve a win-win situation between suppliers and buyers meeting their needs. Immediately after training the recommendation algorithm, the recommended results based on the users' historical behavior and collaborative filtering were efficient, so quick, and accurate as compared with the traditional supplier recommendation mechanism.

They could solve the accompanying problems like the cold start problem that is based on the users' historical score of the product, and the data-sparse problem that is used to generate relatively a sparse scoring matrix that could challenge the chances of scoring accurate predictions.

Bushra et al. 2019, proposed a recommendation system that recommends hotels to travelers based on the hotel features and guest type for a personalized recommendation (Ramzan et al., 2019). The system could handle heterogeneous data using the big data Hadoop platform, then recommends a hotel class based on guest type using ambiguous rules. Performing different experiments over the real-world datasets, the values of precision, recall, and F-measure were obtained and computed. The obtained results were discussed in terms of improved accuracy and response time. These results were far more significant than the traditional approaches.

Experimental Evaluation

To evaluate the strength of recommendation-based techniques. The researcher compared the results using different parameters and reported a relative improvement over the k-nearest neighbor approaches and hybrid approaches.

Dataset

In our experiments, we used a publicly available MovieLens 100K Dataset (Harper & Konstan, 2015). This MovieLens 100k dataset is a stable standard dataset with 100,000 ratings given by 943 users for 1682 movies, with each user having rated at least 20 movies. All ratings are integer values ranging from 1 to 5, where 1 is the lowest rating (disliked / negative rating), and 5 is the highest rating (liked / positive rating). This dataset consists of the movies.csv, links.csv, ratings.csv, and tags.csv files that hold data about the movies, the links, the ratings, and the tags given by users to the movies they watched and rated.

Figure 8. Illustrates five movies.csv head

Out[2]:

	movieId	title	genres
0	1	Toy Story (1995)	Adventure|Animation|Children|Comedy|Fantasy
1	2	Jumanji (1995)	Adventure|Children|Fantasy
2	3	Grumpier Old Men (1995)	Comedy|Romance
3	4	Waiting to Exhale (1995)	Comedy|Drama|Romance
4	5	Father of the Bride Part II (1995)	Comedy

Figure 9. Illustrates five rating.csv head

Out[3]:

	userId	movieId	rating	timestamp
0	1	1	4.0	964982703
1	1	3	4.0	964981247
2	1	6	4.0	964982224
3	1	47	5.0	964983815
4	1	50	5.0	964982931

Figure 10. Illustrates five tags.csv head

Out[4]:

	userId	movieId	tag	timestamp
0	2	60756	funny	1445714994
1	2	60756	Highly quotable	1445714996
2	2	60756	will ferrell	1445714992
3	2	89774	Boxing story	1445715207
4	2	89774	MMA	1445715200

We then compute the TF and IDF values. To obtain these values we group the movies and tags, count, rename and finally drop the duplicates We then multiply them together to obtain the TF*IDF score.

*Figure 11. Illustrates the five TF*IDF score head*

Out[9]:

	movieId	tag	tf-idf
0	60756	funny	5.622700
1	60756	Highly quotable	2.719331
2	60756	will ferrell	8.686268
3	89774	Boxing story	3.196453
4	89774	MMA	3.196453

We then calculate the unit vector by dividing the TF and IDF value with the vector length of the particular movie. We then return the movieId, tag, TF*IDF, vect_length, and the tag_vec.

Figure 12.

Out[12]:

	movieId	tag	tf-idf	vect_length	tag_vec
0	60756	funny	5.622700	10.887728	0.516425
1	60756	Highly quotable	2.719331	10.887728	0.249761
2	60756	will ferrell	8.686268	10.887728	0.797804
3	89774	Boxing story	3.196453	5.368248	0.595437
4	89774	MMA	3.196453	5.368248	0.595437

Now we calculate the unique values for the ratings and the user Ids, having ratings greater or equal to 3 (positive rating). So the user profile will receive recommendations based on the ratings of the movies. We calculate the user_tag (feature) preference for each user.

Figure 13.

Out[16]:

	tag	tag_pref	user
0	animation	0.279565	89
1	Disney	1.235981	89
2	funny	0.811149	89
3	original	0.368530	89
4	Pixar	1.692234	89

We then calculate the cosine similarity between the vectors and finally print those recommendations best for the specific user. In our study, we used user 89 as our case study.

Figure 14. Illustrates the 10 best recommendations for user 89 TF*IDF score head

```
Out[21]:
```

	user	movieId	rating
82	89	2295.0	0.292864
3	89	62.0	0.186961
67	89	1357.0	0.186961
77	89	2070.0	0.186961
131	89	6377.0	0.183781
22	89	594.0	0.180987
23	89	595.0	0.180987
24	89	596.0	0.180987
26	89	616.0	0.180987
46	89	1022.0	0.180987

Popularity-Based Approach

This approach recommends items based on the popularity of the item itself (X. Chen & Zhang, 2003). It's normally considered primitive because it directly depends on popular items that are recommended often with high popularity (C.-M. Chen et al., 2016; Lai et al., 2019; Majid et al., 2013). This approach is based on the review of the item itself and what the user likes and excludes the users or opinions. The systems built with this approach have less diversity in their recommendations than the CB and CF recommendation approaches (Lops et al., 2019).

For a popular-based system, first, an item profile is created for each item. An item profile is a collection of records representing important features of the item (Al Fararni et al., 2020). It consists of some characteristics of an item that are easily discovered. Moreover, item features need to be classified by their characteristics so the recommender will find similar items and provide a correct classification. The behavior of any user will depend directly on their sociology (Fatemi & Rezaei-Moghaddam, 2020), also in other words the popularity of the items or products that the model could recommend will depend directly on some factors of the user in terms of attraction, superiority, or liking (well-liked, situation better looking found, what best iPhone is available on the market? who might sell the iPhone?). At this point, we have filtered our sample to know its popularity.

There are many approaches to compute the popular-based recommender. But depends on the kind of item being evaluated. If working with the documents or news articles the best approach is to use the TF-IDF. The TF-IDF metric is the best numerical statistic that is intended to reflect how important a word is to a document in a collection (Romadon et al., 2020). It is commonly used in text mining using information retrieval or modeling to calculate the weight factor. The TF is referred to as the term frequency, which is the proportion of occurrences a term t appears in a document to the total number of terms in the document (Jalilifard et al., 2020). The IDF is also referred to as the inverse document frequency. It is the inverse of the proportion of the total number of documents that contain the term t (Robertson, 2004).

Collaborative Filtering-Based Recommender System

This recommendation approach filters information based on comparisons between an item and a user profile (Sharma et al., 2017). Its approach is based on customers' behaviors, activities, and preferences to predict what customers will like based on their similarity to orders. For example when a user likes product x on amazon, and product y likes to buy products from eBay then person x may like eBay as well.

Approaches of Collaborative Filtering

Like many machine learning techniques, a recommender system makes predictions based on the user's historical behaviors (Gupta & Dave, 2020). Specifically, it predicts user's preferences on a set of items based on the experience (Du & Jing, 2017). There are two approaches to the collaborative filtering technique in which the row changes depending on the approach (Cui et al., 2020; Du & Jing, 2017).

Figure 15.

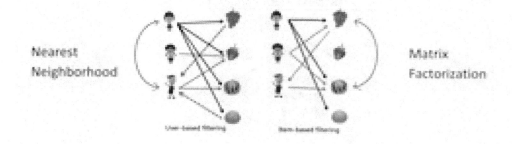

1. Nearest Neighborhood-Based CF Algorithm

The main idea is to find the most similar users to the nearest neighborhood and rate the ratings on all reviews of an item as the prediction of ratings of this item for targeting users (Aggarwal, 2016; Chae et al., 2018). We assume that users are familiar with the same kind of content when they give the same item a similar rating.

2. Matrix Factorization CF Approach

This algorithm lets us assume what the user will like for example in an illustration below, there are four users and there is one to whom we want to recommend the movie. The Matrix movie is the previously watched movie by a couple of more users well as the others have just one view. The matrix system shows that the recommender system will suggest the movie will be any of the matrix series since it's the most-watched. Several challenges are faced under CF such as scalability, data sparsity, and diversity (Bokde et al., 2015).

Figure 16.

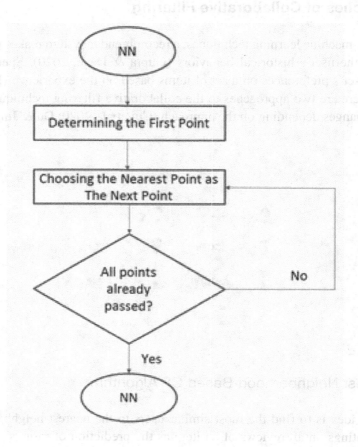

Figure 17.

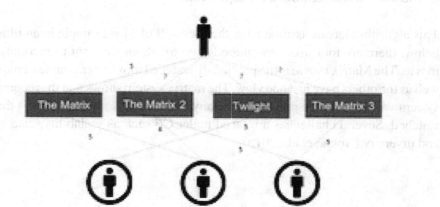

Exploring the Required Functions

The main key idea behind collaborative filtering is that similar users share the same interest in similar items, and those similar items are liked by a user. The usage of this utility matrix is that m users like n items and filling the cells with the ratings are reduced. There are two methods of collecting reviews or opinions; explicit and implicit methods (Nehe & Nawathe, 2020). The explicit method is hard to correct as they require additional input from the users. And the implicit data is easier to gather in large quantities without any input from the users, the aim is to change user behaviors into user preference.

User-Based CF

The user-based CF systems share the same writing patterns with the activity user and they use ratings to calculate predictions from their other users. The major aim of the user-based CF is to compute user similarity and can be archived by using Pearson correlation and cosine similarity (Akama et al., 2020). Pearson correlation shows the similarity based on how the ratings by common users for the appearance of items deviate from the average reviews for those items (Wang & Fu, 2021).

Figure 18.

$$u_{ik} = \frac{\sum_j (V_{ij} - V_i)(V_{kj} - V_k)}{\sqrt{\sum_j (V_{ij} - V_i)^2 \sum_j (V_{kj} - V_k)^2}}$$

The cosine similarity algorithm is also known as the vector view similarity, it computes two items and their ratings as vectors to define the similarity between them by calculating the angle between them (Lin, 2020).

Figure 19.

$$\cos\left(u_i, u_j\right) = \frac{\sum_{k=1}^{m} V_{ik} V_{jk}}{\sqrt{\sum_{k=1}^{m} (V^2)_{ik} \; \sum_{k=1}^{m} (V^2)_{jk}}}$$

Item-Based CF

This approach was invented by amazon to address the scalability challenges with user-based filtering (Dubey et al., 2018). When the number of selling items is fewer than the number of users, the item-item similarities can be computed offline and accessed more dynamically (Shi et al., 2008).

Implementation of CF Recommender Systems

The researcher explored the internet movie database (IMDb) formula to determine the weighted rating and calculate the score. IMDb is an online database of information related to films, television programs, home videos, video games, internet streams that include some casts (Dodds, 2006). This IMDb evaluates approximately 250,000 items of datasets. The IMDb weighted rating formula is shown below, where R is the average for the movie (mean) which equals the rating of the movie, v is the number of votes for the movie which equals to the votes, m is the minimum votes required to be listed in the top-rated list which is 25,000 for the IMDb webpage, and c is the mean vote across the whole report.

Figure 20.

$$WR = \left(\frac{v}{v+m} * R\right) + \left(\frac{m}{v+m} * C\right)$$

This formula aids to calculate the rating of our databases to evaluate their scores and later construct the recommender system. To evaluate a recommender system we need to calculate the predictions for all the ratings in the test set, these calculations are done using the utility matrix. The graph in the figure below shows how the implementation of the matrix was used, and how the CF was implemented from the IMDb formula. The process was iterative for the N quantity of users or items to predict the final resource in each case.

Figure 21. Illustrates the implementation of the IMDb formula

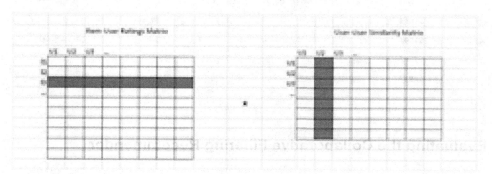

Applying the CF Algorithm to the IMDbs Dataset

The researcher implemented the IMDb formula to determine the score of the CF recommender. Obtained the mean vote *c* as 5.61 out of 10, the minimum vote *m* as 160. Filtered out the qualified movies and obtained 27. Progressed and computed the metric for each movie by defining the weighted rating, then sorted out the movies with the values of the score in ascending order. Lastly, print out the top 10 qualified movies by their titles as shown in the figure below. Then the top 10 ranked movies would be recommended to the user.

Figure 22. Illustrates the 10 qualified movies score by titles with the implementation of the IMDb formula in the CF recommendation system

Out[110]:

	title	vote_count	vote_average	score
522	Schindler's List	4436.0	8.3	8.206638
1639	Titanic	7770.0	7.5	7.462032
4766	Harry Potter and the Philosopher's Stone	7188.0	7.5	7.459025
4863	The Lord of the Rings: The Fellowship of the Ring	8892.0	8.0	7.957900
5814	The Lord of the Rings: The Two Towers	7641.0	8.0	7.950149
7900	The Lord of the Rings: The Return of the King	8226.0	8.1	8.052649
10554	Harry Potter and the Goblet of Fire	5758.0	7.5	7.449124
11008	Pirates of the Caribbean: Dead Man's Chest	5360.0	7.0	6.960093
11567	Superman Returns	1429.0	5.4	5.421972
11827	Pirates of the Caribbean: At World's End	4627.0	6.9	6.857156

Evaluating the Collaborative Filtering Recommender

The results were obtained with the implementation of the CF recommender. The results in the figure just above show the top 10 movies with at least 90% than the rest of the other movies in the dataset. But there is a discrepancy in the number of votes and we wanted to calculate *m* with the highest possible percentage to obtain a close recommendation. Moreover, the filter we selected after the movie needs to have a home page is peaky because the viewer can go and visit the website and it will increase the interaction between the weak viewers, the movie, and the recommender encouraging the user to join for implicit feedback. This gives us a hint for the probability of the next movie the user will like to watch. The Figure shows the most voted movies of the dataset. If we make a curve at the end of the top count or each movie, we observe that the Longtail phenomena apply. The head is far from the central part of the chart because of the popularity. However, this doesn't happen when we are using our recommender, the curve is very close to one another as we applied some filters at the beginning and the distribution is not dispersed. Some movies have fewer votes that are required to be at the top. In the area above the curve of the long tail, we notice that some good products were less popular finding them harder to recommend to the user. This makes it necessary for the system that can recommend those movies that are less popular but probably more likely to be watched by the user.

Figure 23.

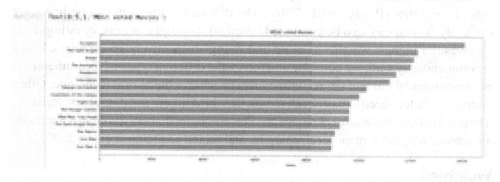

We can use the CF recommenders for very large datasets. This is simply because it lets the user use a user-item matrix. Additionally, when new movies are included it increases the diversity as it introduces new recommendations to the user. Using this kind of recommender is fantastic because the attendance of other users watching the same kind of content tends to increase. The CF also discovers the latent association between the users and the items.

Hybrid-based recommender system

This approach is a combination of two or multiple filtering techniques like merging collaborative filtering, and content-based filtering or also adding on the knowledge-based model (Barros et al., 2020).

Figure 24: Illustrates a hybrid-based recommendation system.

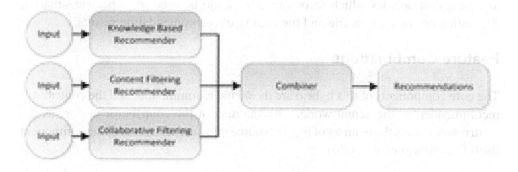

The main challenge of this approach is that it combines all the challenges of other approaches (Pandya et al., 2016). The different output will still be linear for the analysis, and can also be combined based on its weight, scores, or ratings as it receives the highest weights as close and ratings respectively.To achieve a better recommender system, we combine and merge the different types of recommenders. So we combined CB and CF recommenders to achieve the hybrid technique. Other additional factors need to be considered such as the domain, and data characteristics. The different hybridization techniques are; Feature augmentation, feature combination, switching, weighted, meta-level, cascade, and mixed (Al Fararni et al., 2020).

Weighted

The components can produce a recommendation score by combining two or more recommendation systems, then computes the weighted sums of their scores (Al Fararni et al., 2020).

Mixed

This hybrid relies on the margin of multiple ranges of the list onto one (Al Fararni et al., 2020). It combines the results of completely various recommender systems at the level of the user interface where results from different techniques are presented together.

Switching

It is based on the selection of confidence and criteria because it might have components that have different performances in different situations. Switching hybrids require an oracle that decides which recommender should be used in a specific situation depending on the user profile and the quality of recommendation results.

Feature Combinations

The core components of this hybrid are the actual recommender and the contributor recommender, as the actual works with the data of the contributor in one, as the contributor injects the features of the one source into another source of the component itself (Al Fararni et al., 2020).

Feature Augmentation

This hybrid technique belongs to the monolithic hybrid design that can be used to integrate many recommendation algorithms and also applies more complex transformation steps.

Cascade

This hybrid is similar to the Feature augmentation techniques because it works on the first model and makes additional candidates with the older models refine their scores. It is based on a sequenced order of techniques.

Meta-level

This meta-level hybridization technique uses the contributing recommender as input for the actual one. One recommender system builds a model that is exploited by the principal recommender to make recommendations (Amini et al., 2014).

Hybrid Recommender – Workflow

Here we need to understand the logic behind the hybrid filtering technique. The workflow for the implementation of our hybrid recommender is defined in four steps. In step 1, we shall take in a movie title and a user as input. In step 2 we shall use the content-based model to compute the twenty-five most similar items. At step 3 the computation needs to be done to predict the ratings that the user will give for the twenty-five titles obtained in the previous step. Finally, in step 4 our hybrid recommender will return the top ten movies with the highest predicted ratings.

CATEGORIZATIONS OF HYBRIDIZATION RECOMMENDATION

The categorization is divided into three main types

1. Monolithic Hybrids

These use a single recommendation component that is based on Featurecombination and Feature augmentation, and at the same time distributed content-based collaborative filtering which is where the content features additional ratings are created and recommendations on research papers where suggestions are interpreted as collaborative recommendations.

Figure 25.

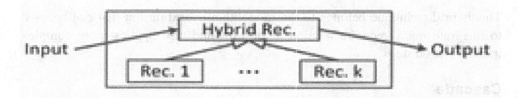

2. Parallelized hybrids

Its outputs depend exist on the existing implementations combined at the same time. It has a least invasive design monolithic hybrid, and the weights can be learned dynamically. Their main strategy is to employ several recommenders side by side and employ specific mechanisms to aggregate their inputs. It has three specific strategies switching, weighted, and mixed hybrids.

Figure 26.

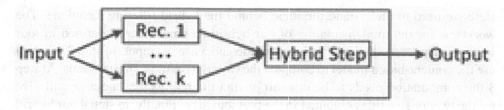

3. Pipelined Hybrids

The main idea of this design is that one recommender preprocesses some input for subsequent recommender making the possibility to work in cascade. The main strategy is to implement a staged process, in which the techniques are built-in in sequence on each other before the final one computes the recommendation for the final user. It has three main specific strategies; cascade, meta-level, combination of (meta-level and cascade).

Figure 27.

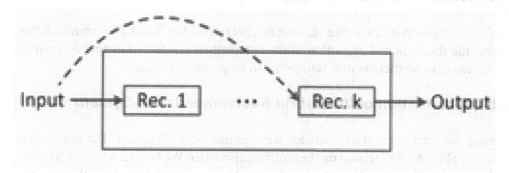

ALGORITHM IMPLEMENTATION FOR HYBRID RECOMMENDER SYSTEM

The road map for building this hybrid recommender is almost more similar to the CF algorithm. First, we compute the cosine similarity. We then compute the Singular Value Decomposition (SVD) for collaborative filtering recommender. We shall build title to ID and ID to title mappings. We will then workout on the relevant metadata of the movies. We will then extract some IDs and assign them to the datasets then sort, filter, and then return recommendations.

SVD for Collaborative Filtering

This is one of the factorization algorithms for collaborative filtering used to find a low-dimension model that maximizes the log-likelihood of observed ratings in recommendation systems (Zhang et al., 2005).

The researcher then got the top N recommendations for each user by retrieving the top ten items with the highest rating prediction for each user in the dataset. The researcher first trained an SVD on the whole dataset and then predicted all the ratings for both the user and the item. Lastly, retrieved the top ten predictions for each user.

Figure 28.

$$A_{nxp} = U_{nxn} S_{nxp} V^T_{pxp}$$

3rd Winner – Netflix Algorithm

This is another code implementation of the SVD algorithm. This CF recommendation was the third optimal algorithm in the competition conducted to find an optimal algorithm to predict the user ratings based on previous reviews.

Implementation of the Hybrid Recommendation System

First, we need to build a CF model, we then use the SVD model. The next step is to calculate the SVD based on the collaborative filter. We build a function, a reader then we pass then data. We calculate the hybrid recommender function. We compute the predicted ratings using the SVD filter, sort the movies by the predicted rating, and then return the ratings. When we call the created function with the userId and a specific movie by name, a list of recommended movies for the user is returned.

Figure 29.

Out[8]:

	title	vote_count	vote_average	year	id	est
4173	Minority Report	2963.0	7.1	2002	180	3.155891
7562	The Book of Eli	2207.0	6.6	2010	20504	2.878143
7208	Replicant	93.0	5.0	2001	10595	2.798160
6442	Déjà Vu	1519.0	6.6	2006	7551	2.772988
5580	The Three Lives of Thomasina	12.0	6.8	1963	15081	2.768000
7948	Stake Land	290.0	6.2	2010	52015	2.765156
8207	Looper	4777.0	6.6	2012	59967	2.742064
7901	Super 8	2496.0	6.6	2011	37686	2.737892
7826	I Am Number Four	1608.0	5.9	2011	46529	2.663714
5824	Fortress	171.0	5.7	1992	12066	2.649633

Evaluating the Hybrid Recommender System

Under the hybrid recommendation approach, both users watching the same movie obtain different recommendations such as the content and order, because the listing is made of old similar movies to the search, it shows off the content-based filtering implementation and the other hand the different order encountered was proportionally performed by the collaborative filtering recommender. Recommendation systems power most of the social media, e-commerce websites. They provide incredible value to the site owners and their users. However, they have some criticisms and downsides. We can analyze a slightly larger dataset and even try different types of recommendations, depending on where your customer is in his journey. If the recommendation is supplementary, the techniques need to differ completely for every viewer. Feeding personal information to the recommender system results in better recommendation services. The feedback plays an extremely important role while implementing recommenders, but it has some downsides. Sometimes the users are unwilling to provide feedback on recommender systems because they are concerned about data privacy issues.

Therefore, the recommender system should be built to increase the trust among the users. It should be noted that the collaborative filtering technique, the user data including the ratings is being stored in a database which can lead to data misuse. Therefore, to lick up the approach that we have implemented is combining the collaborative and content-based filtering to make predictions based on the weighted average of those recommenders.

Additional Hybrid Algorithms

The interleaved algorithm forms the recommendation list to suggest to the entire users by alternating item predicted of the CF and one of the CB. SimComb algorithm is a weighted average algorithm in which the item similarity values are computed as a linear combination between the content-based and the collaborative similarities. FFA, similarity injection KNN, and non-normalized cosine algorithms.

CONCLUSION

We can use CF for very large datasets because it lets us use the user-item matrix but let to the cold start problem when included in the movies. It also has a very good benefit to increase the diversity as we can introduce near recommendations to the user where we got the long tail phenomena that unintentionally does the opposite. Also, we can assume that one user can share some movies with very good feedback, but to make up that rating to the opponents, so the data can easily\be manipulated. It is necessary to take extra caution when measuring the dataset and the kind of similarity of the recommendation that we can predict while using this recommender. It is fantastic as the number of users watching the same kind of content tends to increase and this is by far the strongest advantage of this recommender as it discovers the latent association between the users and the items.

REFERENCES

Aggarwal, C. C. (2016). Neighborhood-based collaborative filtering. In *Recommender systems* (pp. 29–70). Springer. doi:10.1007/978-3-319-29659-3_2

Ahmadian, S., Joorabloo, N., Jalili, M., Ren, Y., Meghdadi, M., & Afsharchi, M. (2020). A social recommender system based on reliable implicit relationships. *Knowledge-Based Systems*, *192*, 105371. doi:10.1016/j.knosys.2019.105371

Akama, S., Kudo, Y., & Murai, T. (2020). Neighbor Selection for User-Based Collaborative Filtering Using Covering-Based Rough Sets. In *Topics in Rough Set Theory* (pp. 141–159). Springer. doi:10.1007/978-3-030-29566-0_9

Al Fararni, K., Aghoutane, B., Riffi, J., Sabri, A., & Yahyaouy, A. (2020). Comparative Study on Approaches of Recommendation Systems. In *Embedded Systems and Artificial Intelligence* (pp. 753–764). Springer. doi:10.1007/978-981-15-0947-6_72

Amini, M., Nasiri, M., & Afzali, M. (2014). *Proposing a new hybrid approach in movie recommender system*. Academic Press.

Anandhan, A., Shuib, L., Ismail, M. A., & Mujtaba, G. (2018). *Social media recommender systems: review and open research issues*. Academic Press.

Barros, M., Moitinho, A., & Couto, F. M. (2020). Hybrid semantic recommender system for chemical compounds. *European Conference on Information Retrieval*, 94–101.

Bhatia, N. (2010). Survey of nearest neighbor techniques. *ArXiv Preprint ArXiv:1007.0085*.

Bokde, D., Girase, S., & Mukhopadhyay, D. (2015). Matrix factorization model in collaborative filtering algorithms: A survey. *Procedia Computer Science*, *49*, 136–146. doi:10.1016/j.procs.2015.04.237

Briciu, V.-A., & Briciu, A. (2021). Social Media and Organizational Communication. In Encyclopedia of Organizational Knowledge, Administration, and Technology (pp. 2609–2624). IGI Global.

Burke, R. (2000). *Knowledge-based recommender systems*. Academic Press.

Chae, D.-K., Lee, S.-C., Lee, S.-Y., & Kim, S.-W. (2018). On identifying k-nearest neighbors in neighborhood models for efficient and effective collaborative filtering. *Neurocomputing*, *278*, 134–143. doi:10.1016/j.neucom.2017.06.081

Chehal, D., Gupta, P., & Gulati, P. (2020). Implementation and comparison of topic modeling techniques based on user reviews in e-commerce recommendations. *Journal of Ambient Intelligence and Humanized Computing*, 1–16.

Chen, C.-M., Tsai, M.-F., Lin, Y.-C., & Yang, Y.-H. (2016). Query-based music recommendations via preference embedding. *Proceedings of the 10th ACM Conference on Recommender Systems*, 79–82. 10.1145/2959100.2959169

Chen, X., & Zhang, X. (2003). A popularity-based prediction model for web prefetching. *Computer*, *36*(3), 63–70. doi:10.1109/MC.2003.1185219

Cui, Z., Xu, X., Fei, X. U. E., Cai, X., Cao, Y., Zhang, W., & Chen, J. (2020). Personalized recommendation system based on collaborative filtering for IoT scenarios. *IEEE Transactions on Services Computing*, *13*(4), 685–695. doi:10.1109/TSC.2020.2964552

Dodds, K. (2006). Popular geopolitics and audience dispositions: James Bond and the internet movie database (IMDb). *Transactions of the Institute of British Geographers*, *31*(2), 116–130. doi:10.1111/j.1475-5661.2006.00199.x

Du, J., & Jing, H. (2017). Collaborative Filtering-Based Matching and Recommendation of Suppliers in Prefabricated Component Supply Chain. *International Conference on Applications and Techniques in Cyber Security and Intelligence*, 128–139.

Dubey, A., Gupta, A., Raturi, N., & Saxena, P. (2018). Item-Based Collaborative Filtering Using Sentiment Analysis of User Reviews. *International Conference on Application of Computing and Communication Technologies*, 77–87. 10.1007/978-981-13-2035-4_8

Fatemi, M., & Rezaei-Moghaddam, K. (2020). Sociological factors influencing the performance of organic activities in Iran. *Life Sciences, Society and Policy*, *16*(1), 1–16. doi:10.118640504-020-00098-z PMID:32390089

Felfernig, A., Jeran, M., Ninaus, G., Reinfrank, F., Reiterer, S., & Stettinger, M. (2014). Basic approaches in recommendation systems. In *Recommendation Systems in Software Engineering* (pp. 15–37). Springer. doi:10.1007/978-3-642-45135-5_2

Gupta, S., & Dave, M. (2020). An Overview of Recommendation System: Methods and Techniques. In *Advances in Computing and Intelligent Systems* (pp. 231–237). Springer. doi:10.1007/978-981-15-0222-4_20

Harper, F. M., & Konstan, J. A. (2015). The movielens datasets: History and context. *Acm Transactions on Interactive Intelligent Systems (Tiis)*, *5*(4), 1–19.

Hernández-Nieves, E., Hernández, G., Gil-González, A.-B., Rodríguez-González, S., & Corchado, J. M. (2020). Fog computing architecture for personalized recommendation of banking products. *Expert Systems with Applications*, *140*, 112900. doi:10.1016/j.eswa.2019.112900

Jalilifard, A., Caridá, V., Mansano, A., & Cristo, R. (2020). Semantic sensitive TF-IDF to determine word relevance in documents. *ArXiv Preprint ArXiv:2001.09896.*

Jannach, D., Manzoor, A., Cai, W., & Chen, L. (2020). A survey on conversational recommender systems. *ArXiv Preprint ArXiv:2004.00646.*

Lai, C.-H., Lee, S.-J., & Huang, H.-L. (2019). A social recommendation method based on the integration of social relationship and product popularity. *International Journal of Human-Computer Studies*, *121*, 42–57. doi:10.1016/j.ijhcs.2018.04.002

Lin, K.-S. (2020). A case-based reasoning system for interior design using a new cosine similarity retrieval algorithm. *Journal of Information and Telecommunication*, *4*(1), 91–104. doi:10.1080/24751839.2019.1700338

Lops, P., Jannach, D., Musto, C., Bogers, T., & Koolen, M. (2019). Trends in content-based recommendation. *User Modeling and User-Adapted Interaction*, *29*(2), 239–249. doi:10.100711257-019-09231-w

Mahadik, K., Wu, Q., Li, S., & Sabne, A. (2020). Fast distributed bandits for online recommendation systems. *Proceedings of the 34th ACM International Conference on Supercomputing*, 1–13. 10.1145/3392717.3392748

Majid, A., Chen, L., Chen, G., Mirza, H. T., Hussain, I., & Woodward, J. (2013). A context-aware personalized travel recommendation system based on geotagged social media data mining. *International Journal of Geographical Information Science*, *27*(4), 662–684. doi:10.1080/13658816.2012.696649

Malviya, A. (2020). *Machine Learning: An Overview of Classification Techniques*. Academic Press.

Melville, P., & Sindhwani, V. (2010). Recommender systems. Encyclopedia of Machine Learning, 1, 829–838.

Nehe, M. P. B., & Nawathe, A. N. (2020). *Aspect based sentiment classification using machine learning for online Reviews*. EasyChair.

Pandya, S., Shah, J., Joshi, N., Ghayvat, H., Mukhopadhyay, S. C., & Yap, M. H. (2016). A novel hybrid based recommendation system based on clustering and association mining. *2016 10th International Conference on Sensing Technology (ICST)*, 1–6.

Pazzani, M. J., & Billsus, D. (2007). Content-based recommendation systems. In *The adaptive web* (pp. 325–341). Springer. doi:10.1007/978-3-540-72079-9_10

Ramzan, B., Bajwa, I. S., Jamil, N., Amin, R. U., Ramzan, S., Mirza, F., & Sarwar, N. (2019). An intelligent data analysis for recommendation systems using machine learning. *Scientific Programming, 2019*, 2019. doi:10.1155/2019/5941096

Robertson, S. (2004). Understanding inverse document frequency: On theoretical arguments for IDF. *The Journal of Documentation, 60*(5), 503–520. doi:10.1108/00220410410560582

Romadon, A. W., Lhaksmana, K. M., Kurniawan, I., & Richasdy, D. (2020). Analyzing TF-IDF and Word Embedding for Implementing Automation in Job Interview Grading. *2020 8th International Conference on Information and Communication Technology (ICoICT)*, 1–4.

Ben Schafer, J., Frankowski, D., Herlocker, J., & Sen, S. (2007). Collaborative filtering recommender systems. In *The adaptive web* (pp. 291–324). Springer. doi:10.1007/978-3-540-72079-9_9

Shani, G., & Gunawardana, A. (2011). Evaluating recommendation systems. In *Recommender systems handbook* (pp. 257–297). Springer. doi:10.1007/978-0-387-85820-3_8

Sharma, R., Gopalani, D., & Meena, Y. (2017). Collaborative filtering-based recommender system: Approaches and research challenges. *2017 3rd International Conference on Computational Intelligence & Communication Technology (Cict)*, 1–6.

Shi, X., Ye, H., & Gong, S. (2008). A personalized recommender integrating item-based and user-based collaborative filtering. *2008 International Seminar on Business and Information Management, 1*, 264–267.

Shu, J., Shen, X., Liu, H., Yi, B., & Zhang, Z. (2018). *A content-based recommendation algorithm for learning resources*. Academic Press.

Sohrabi, B., Mahmoudian, P., & Raeesi, I. (2012). A framework for improving e-commerce websites usability using a hybrid genetic algorithm and neural network system. *Neural Computing & Applications, 21*(5), 1017–1029. doi:10.100700521-011-0674-7

Soofi, A. A., & Awan, A. (2017). *Classification techniques in machine learning: applications and issues*. Academic Press.

Sridevi, M., Rao, R. R., & Rao, M. V. (2016). *A survey on recommender system*. Academic Press.

Su, X., & Khoshgoftaar, T. M. (2009). *A survey of collaborative filtering techniques.* Academic Press.

Wang, H., & Fu, W. (2021). Personalized learning resource recommendation method based on dynamic collaborative filtering. *Mobile Networks and Applications*, 26(1), 473–487. doi:10.100711036-020-01673-6

Wu, C.-S. M., Garg, D., & Bhandary, U. (2018). Movie recommendation system using collaborative filtering. *2018 IEEE 9th International Conference on Software Engineering and Service Science (ICSESS)*, 11–15.

Yang, L., & Jin, R. (2006). Distance metric learning: A comprehensive survey. *Michigan State Universiy*, 2(2), 4.

Zhang, S., Wang, W., Ford, J., Makedon, F., & Pearlman, J. (2005). Using singular value decomposition approximation for collaborative filtering. *Seventh IEEE International Conference on E-Commerce Technology (CEC'05)*, 257–264. 10.1109/ICECT.2005.102

Chapter 3
A Survey on Sentiment Analysis Techniques for Twitter

Surabhi Verma
National Institute of Technology, Kurukshetra, India

Ankit Kumar Jain
(iD) https://orcid.org/0000-0002-9482-6991
National Institute of Technology, Kurukshetra, India

ABSTRACT

People regularly use social media to express their opinions about a wide variety of topics, goods, and services which make it rich in text mining and sentiment analysis. Sentiment analysis is a form of text analysis determining polarity (positive, negative, or neutral) in text, document, paragraph, or clause. This chapter offers an overview of the subject by examining the proposed algorithms for sentiment analysis on Twitter and briefly explaining them. In addition, the authors also address fields related to monitoring sentiments over time, regional view of views, neutral tweet analysis, sarcasm detection, and various other tasks in this area that have drawn the researchers' attention to this subject nearby. Within this chapter, all the services used are briefly summarized. The key contribution of this survey is the taxonomy based on the methods suggested and the debate on the theme's recent research developments and related fields.

DOI: 10.4018/978-1-7998-8413-2.ch003

1. INTRODUCTION

Internet and social media has changed how people share their opinions. Blog entries, online discussion boards, product review website act as a significant interpersonal dependency. Friends and family counselling has served a decision tool in previous years before any new purchase. The opinion of others is a definite go to in case of decision making. Nonetheless, the online analysis is being looked at in recent years before any decision is made. Customers or consumers rely heavily on web-based information that is accessible through many shopping channels, internet directories, forums, tweets, etc. Before purchasing any product or accessing any service. If one is ordering a product from a website for e-commerce or going to a restaurant to have dinner or watching a film in the cinema, we still consider other customers before enjoying the product and/or the facilities (Akhtar, Gupta, Ekbal, & Bhattacharyya, 2017). If we want to make an online / offline transaction, what will we do initially? We visit various blogs and forums to see if people chat about it. We have seen some online shops selling what we are looking for. We read via the feedback and opinions written or shared by many people on the product and online store. It is only after a sufficient number of comments that we know whether or not to make the order. Analysis of sentiments is a concept that involves several activities such as the extraction of feelings, classification of feelings, classification of subjectivity, summation of opinions and spam opinion detection (Sahoo & Gupta, 2020). This seeks to examine emotions, behaviours, emotional views, etc. about factors such as goods, people, concepts, organizations and services. The increasing importance of sentiment analysis correlates with social media growth including ratings, forums, conversations, blogs, microblogs, Facebook and social networks (Clarizia, Colace, Pascale, Lombardi, & Santaniello, 2019). The massive quantity of data produced makes the social media content impossible to interpret or to summarize. The majority of users write their opinions, social media blogs, ecommerce sites etc. For individuals, the industry, the government and research, this content is very important for decision-making. Mining is a hot area of study under natural language processing for this emotion interpretation and viewpoint.

Twitter sentiment analysis program has a wide range of implementations on a number of the fields described below. Sentiment Analysis aims to achieve different targets, including public opinion in the form of business research, political activity, film revenue forecasting, consumer satisfaction assessment and more. Some of them are listed below:

- **Business**: It allows marketing firms to formulate and frame new approaches, evaluate their consumer feeling for products or brands and use their input in order to refine and enhance the product edition (Yadollahi, Shahraki, & Zaiane, 2017).

- **Politics**: It is used in politics to track political perspectives, opinions, schemes and to draw the relative diagram of policies framed and implemented at the level of the citizens. Assessing the masses' thoughts helps the government body detect consistency and incoherence between statements and actions at government level . All that can be done through Twitter sentiments analysis, from shaping political outcomes to knowing the opinion of the common masses in relation to a particular scheme.

- **Public behaviour**: The tweet ocean can be used to track and evaluate social events, to identify potentially hazardous circumstances and to represent citizens' behaviour at ground level (Tayal & Yadav, 2017).

The rapidly spreading existence of online content has also turned opinions online into a very valuable commodity. Twitter is a dominant social media site. People tweet different subjects, from everyday occurrences to major incidents. Twitter with more than million users is a rich source of knowledge for organizations and people who are involved in preserving and enhancing their credibility politically, economically or socially (Sahoo & Gupta, 2019). The organization uses Sentiment Analysis in order to track different social media sites. Twitter Sentiment Analysis (TSA) is a growing activity whose purpose is to identify the opinions and feelings expressed in text, created by a human parity (Liu, Hu, & Cheng, 2005). However, it is difficult to obtain these huge quantities of data because of the massive quantities of data produced. The viewpoints about a subject are contained within the data and so it is almost difficult to look at a variety of sources and produce valuable data background. It thus provides the researchers with a pathway to invest and establish approaches that can automatically detect the text's polarity in order to effectively mine information from the excess data. Moreover, sentiment analysis is not trivial. The shortness of these messages, the constraint on the length of up to 140 characters and the casual existence of social media sites messages, the usage of new words like slang abbreviation, URLs, emoticons etc. These factors along with inadvertent punctuation and improper spellings make extracting people's views and feelings more complex (Giachanou & Crestani, 2016). The proposed method for sentiment analysis considers all these characteristics in order to achieve a better result.

Figure 1. Typical Process for Sentiment Analysis

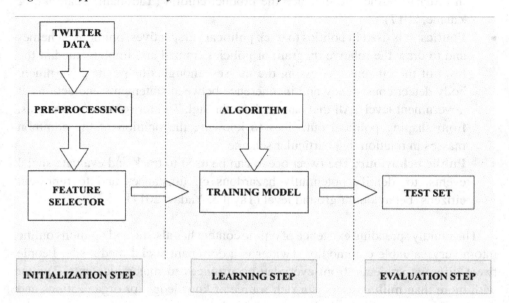

Therefore, it is a common field for NLP and Data Mining to classify subjective attitudes in the broad social databases. TSA is working on the formal approach Machine Learning introduces (Pang, Lee, & Vaithyanathan, 2002; Taboada, Brooke, Tofiloski, Voll, & Stede, 2011). Figure 1 shows the typical process for sentiment classification. First, tweets from the Twitter API are retrieved. The data obtained may be labelled (classified) as well as unlabelled. The labelled data serves as information for training. The extracted data is in the form of raw data, and needs pre-processing. The pre-processing steps include data cleaning, noise elimination in the form of redundant information to assess the sentence polarity further defined as positive, negative and neutral. There is a lot of work going on in the field of analysing sentiments, and especially on Sentiment Analysis. This provides the need for a survey report to provide a short summary of the strategies suggested and reflect on recent developments in the field. The survey is focussed on sentiment analysis as an approach, its types and applications.

This survey gives an overview of the Twitter Sentiment Analysis region, including recent trends. Initially, it sorts the studies discussed based on a methodology that involves the use of machine learning. Researchers and newcomers can therefore get a panoramic view of the field in particular. The solutions are also objectively discussed based on their benefits and drawbacks. Secondly, the discussion focuses on Sentiment Analysis fields, which have gained an interest in research. Thirdly, this survey addresses various tools widely used. In creating sentiment lexicons for

Twitter, we synopsize and define the available appraisal data sets, describing the development of Twitter results. This study describes and addresses many open challenges and suggestions for studies into the future.

The rest of the chapter is organised as follows. Section 2 gives an overview of the popular microblogging site Twitter. Section 3 discusses the evaluation parameters that helps in keeping a check on how good one's model is for sentiment analysis. Section 4 presents the steps for Sentiment Analysis. Section 5 highlights the levels of Sentiment Analysis algorithms. Section 6 discusses methods used for sentiment analysis. Section 7 summarizes some of the Sentiment Analysis tools. Section 8 presents some standard datasets available for Twitter Sentiment Analysis. Section 9 discusses the significance of Sentiment Analysis. Section 10 points out some of the limitations of sentiment analysis. Section 11 discusses the open issues and challenges. The paper is then summarised with a conclusion in section 12.

2. TWITTER OVERVIEW AND RELATED RESEARCH

Twitter is a global microblogging network that allows brief messages to be submitted and received, called tweets. This can be called tweeting when Tweets are shared by users. The tweets then reach millions of viewers and can be gathered or interpreted as their response. Twitter posts can be up to 140 characters long and can include links to websites and resources relevant to them. Members on Twitter carry on from other people. An individual can see their tweets in their Twitter account, following someone. One elects to pursue individuals and organizations of common academic and personal interests. Someone can build one's own tweets, and retweet details that others have tweeted. Retweeting means information can be swiftly and efficiently shared with large no people. Users can submit or share tweets, videos, photos, photographs, emoticons, quotations, songs and more. It has thus become increasingly popular among celebrities, sports stars, politicians, students, policy makers. It is commonly used by mobile users who don't want to read the lengthy contents on the computer because of the snappy nature of tweets (Jain & Gupta, 2019).

Many of the most common uses of Twitter are:

- Helps to encourage analysis through links to various blog posts, journal articles and news reports .
- To reach many people quickly via tweets and retweets.
- To follow the work of other industry experts.
- In building ties with experts and other backers.
- To stay up to date with the latest news and trends and quickly share them with everyone.

- Reaching international markets.
- Check for input and suggestions on your job.
- Follow up and engage in case debates, such as conferences where one cannot attend in person.
- To share one 's opinions on a certain culture, economic or political question.

It is not all about "breaking the cake," as other people believe! This involves the electronic exchange of links to other issues, exchanging ideas and opinions and debating current affairs. Twitter also helps people communicate in private short formats without their messages being published. It acts as a gold miner for the national, social and economic interests of organizations and individuals who sustain and improve their power and prestige (Jain, Sahoo, & Kaubiyal, 2021). It is difficult to manually pass all information by the unprecedented amount and range of content generated by users. To order for a product or service to be impartial, however all comments must be compiled and read. It involves the task to systematically review all tweets, taking into account the tremendous amount of time and energy. Consequently, tools and strategies need to be built to allow users to gather the required data from the analysis set. After going over what prominent critics and peers have about the product / service, most buying decisions in the virtual environment are made. That is why businesses now have to look at and interpret what people chat about on the internet. Reviews and only reviews are becoming really critical from a company's viewpoint. Therefore, an audit of feedback and ratings cannot be ignored by a client. Such feedback, thoughts and reviews are known as "sentiment data" and it is known as "Sentiment Data Analysis" or "Sentiment Analysis" to determine whether the feedback and reviews are positive or negative. Thereby, came the need of Sentiment Analysis. Further we will refer it as TWITTER SENTIMENT ANALYSIS.

Sentiment Analysis can be described as a process which, via Natural Language Processing (NLP), automatically extracts attitudes, beliefs, views and emotions from texts, tweets and databases (Khan, et al., 2016). Study of emotion includes the grouping of views in texts into categories such as "positive" or "weak" It is also known as analysing subjectivity, mining of opinion and extraction of evaluations.

The terms viewpoint, feeling, opinion and belief are used synonymously but they vary.

- Opinion: A conclusion open to dispute (because different experts have different opinions).
- View: subjective opinion.
- Belief: deliberate acceptance and intellectual assent.
- Sentiment: opinion representing one's feelings.

An example for terminologies for Sentiment Analysis is as given below,

SENTENCE= Film story was faint and boring.
Sentiment HOLDER= Reviewer
OBJECT= Book
FEATURE = script
OPINION= boring
OVERALL POLARITY= Negative.

Sentiment Analysis is a well-established sequence of tasks aimed at evaluating the polarity of view reflected in a specific user review (Akhtar, Gupta, Ekbal, & Bhattacharyya, 2017). In general, polarity can, depending on the feeling conveyed in a review, be positive, negative or neutral. Twitter serves a huge platform for sentiment analysis. Text Sentiment Analysis is deriving opinions and views from the texts. The automated method of determining whether a section of text includes factual or perceptions and may also establish the polarity of the texts' feelings. The purpose of the Twitter classification of sentiments is to automatically evaluate whether the polarity of feelings is negative or positive. Some of the case studies related to the topic are mentioned below:

(Pak & Paroubek, 2010) suggested a model for the objective, positive and negative categorization of tweets. By collecting Twitter tweets, they have created a Twitter corpus and automatically recorded the tweets using emoticons. This corpus has been used to build a feeling classification using a Naive Bayes multinomial method which uses features such as N-grams and POS tags. The training set was less effective as it only includes tweets with emoticons.

(Go, Huang, & Bhayani, 2009) proposed a technique for evaluating twitter data feelings using remote control that included tweets that acted as noisy labels. With Naive Bayes, MaxEntropy and SVM they build their models. They had as their usable space unigrams, bigrams and part of speech tagging. He claimed that SVM surpasses other versions and the unigram is better.

(Bifet & Frank, 2010) used Firehouse API streaming information from Twitter, which provided all app messages that are publicly accessible in real-time. Multinomial naive Bayes, stochastic gradient descent, were experimented with. They came to a conclusion that the SGD-based model was better than the rest when used with a suitable learning rate.

(Davidov, Tsur, & Rappoport, 2010) sought to make the twitter-defined tweet updates a sentiment-type classification using punctuation, individual words, n grams and trends as distinctive characteristics categories which were then merged into a single sentiment-classification feature matrix. They used K-Nearest Neighbour strategy for assigning sentiment marks by generating a feature vector in the train and check collection for all scenario.

(Turney, 2002) used a sentimental analysis method which does not consider relationships between words and a document as just a combination of words. This method was used for sentiment analysis. The feelings for the entire document have been decided by each word and the emotions are connected with other aggregation functions.

(Liu & Zhang, 2012) have identified the mining opinion problem for the first time. They have assessed the definition the key technical issues which need to be addressed to identify some major mining projects which have been studied and their representative techniques in the research literature. Moreover, issue of spam opinion detection or fake reviews have also been discussed for evaluating the utility or accessibility of customer reviews (Sahoo & Gupta, 2021; Kaubiyal & Jain, 2019).

(Xia, Xu, Yu, Qi, & Cambria, 2016) used the paradigm of the Sentiment Classification Ensemble that was accomplished by integrating different collections of features and classification processes. In their work, they use two types of functional sets, part-speaking and word associations, and three basic classifiers (Naive Bayes, Maximal Entropy and Vector Support Machines). They adopted ensemble methods including a set mix, a weighted mix and a mixture of meta-classification to describe sensation and gain greater precision.

3. EVALUATION METRICS FOR SENTIMENT ANALYSIS

Twitter Sentiment Analysis can be seen as a classification method, because tweets essentially have to be categorized as positive, negative or neutral. Table 1 presents some list of parameters that need to be evaluated on.

Table 1. Various parameters used for sentimental analysis

Parameter	Description
Total sentiment score	Total no of positive tweets – Total number of negative tweets
Sentiment Score (T_j)	$\sum w_i$ (sum of all word score)
Pos	No of tweet signifying positive sentiment
Neg	No of tweet signifying negative sentiment
Pos_true	positive tweets correctly analysed by the tool
Neg_true	negative tweets correctly analysed by the tool
Pos_false	positive tweets which are incorporated false by the analysed tool
Neg_false	negative tweets which are incorporated false by the analysed tool

DP (POLARITY OF THE DOCUMENT): The overall document turns out to be positive, negative or neutral.

$$DP = \frac{pos}{pos + neg} \times 100 \tag{1}$$

PRECISION: Precision is the fraction of positive observations correctly predicted to the total positive observations forecasted.

$$Precision = \frac{pos\_true}{pos\_true + neg\_false} \tag{2}$$

RECALL(r): The proportion of positive cases expected to be positive. It can also be stated as the number of relevant tweets that were actually retrieved.

$$Recall = \frac{pos\_true}{pos\_true + pos\_false} \tag{3}$$

ACCURACY: Evaluation of the appropriate tweets identified during extraction. It tests how much the system assessed makes the accurate predictions. The percentage of true forecasts divided by the total number of forecasts.

$$Accuracy = \frac{pos\_true + neg\_true}{pos\_true + neg\_true + pos\_false + neg\_false} \tag{4}$$

F_SCORE: The calculation of recall and precision is not enough to get the overall accuracy. A combination of the two is more appropriate to evaluate the performance of the methods.

$$F\_score = \frac{2pr}{p + r} \tag{5}$$

4. STEPS OF SENTIMENT ANALYSIS

The basic steps of Sentiment Analysis can be jotted as follows:

STEP 1: The textual data is divided into its constituent element, such as sentences, token and speech sections.

STEP 2: Identify each sentiment bearing phase and component.

STEP 3: Attribute each sentence and component to a sentiment score (-1 to +1).

STEP 4: Calculate the overall polarity of the document.

STEP 5: Combine scores with multi - dimensional sentiment analysis.

STEP 6: Sentiments can be categorized as Positive, Negative or Neutral.

The sentiment with positive emotions include all consumptions such as likes, comments and shares etc.

Figure 2 shows the general model for sentiment analysis. The detailed explanation is as follows.

Figure 2. General Model for Sentiment Analysis

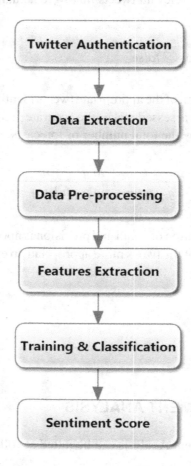

4.1. Twitter Authentication

Twitter can be regarded as a data repository. Unlike other social media sibling sites, it shows tweets to be entirely public and taken. In addition, the Twitter data is accurate and precise. Twitter's API helps one to do complicated queries, such as pulling each tweet on a specific subject over the last twenty minutes or pulling non-retweeted tweets from a certain consumer (Giachanou & Crestani, 2016). Authentic Twitter developer account supports this process by supplying only the authentication keys that pull the data further and run python script on those. Twitter lets us mine every user's data using either Twitter API or Tweepy. The details would be derived from consumer tweets (Go, Bhayani, & Huang, 2009). The first thing to do is get the consumer key, consumer password, development key and Twitter developer permission password conveniently accessible to-customer. Such keys can assist the authentication of the API.

Twitter allows us to use Twitter API or Tweepy to mine any user's data. The details would be derived from consumer tweets. The first thing to do is get the consumer key, consumer password, development key and Twitter developer permission password conveniently accessible to-customer. These keys will help the authentication API.

4.2. Data Extraction

The data is pulled from Twitter in the form of tweets. The dataset can be both labelled and unlabeled (Giachanou & Crestani, 2016). Labelled data is a term for pieces of data identified with one or more labels marking those properties or attributes, or classifications or configuration properties in them. The labeled data comprises of unlabeled data which contains a features, description or label. So, e.g. A picture is mentioned in a labeled image dataset as it is a photograph of a cat and is a photograph of a dog. Unlabeled data is data taken from nature or generated by humans to discover the scientific processes behind it. Many unlabeled data examples may include images, audio files, videos, news stories, tweets, x-rays, etc. The main concept is that the data features have no explanation, label, tag, class or name. The data directly extracted from Twitter can be called as raw data (Zhang, Ghosh, Dekhil, Hsu, & Liu, 2011; Khan, et al., 2016). The raw data are very prone to incoherence and redundancy. Thereby data needs to be pre-processed, which is the step3.

4.3. Pre-processing and Tokenisation of Data

One cannot explicitly move on data derived from Twitter, also known as raw data. Raw data information is vulnerable to incoherence and duplication. Data quality is also a major consideration for the approach to machine learning (Singh & Kumari,

2016). Good data consistency has to be obtained to achieve correct results for the sentiment analysis process. As well as the main data, the data extracted from Twitter is filled with noise, redundant amounts of information. Therefore, specific steps such as eliminating noisy, meaningless data, translating to lower case, punctuation and extra white space to be omitted from the start and end of tweets.

Tokenisation is the method of converting text into symbols until it becomes vectors. Filtering out unnecessary tokens is easier too. For example, a text in paragraphs, or words in sentences. Phrases or word types are divided into phrases called tokens. Such tokens are important to better monitor and evaluate emotions.

4.4. Feature Extraction

Upon tokenisation, the dataset collected still has distinctive properties. The extraction stage for function involves extracting aspect (adjective) from the data collection. This adjective also classifies whether the emotion is positive or negative and eventually defines the sentence's polarity. The major pillars of feature extraction are the counting of positive and negative hashtag, part of speech tagging (post-tag), special keywords, presence of negation emotion, number of positive keywords and number of negative keywords. The relevant specific features of Twitter are hashtags and emoticons. The emoticons may be either positive or negative. Various emoticons bear various weights. Positive emoticons bear a '1' weight and negative emoticons bear a "-1" weight. We maintain a negative list of keywords, a positive list of keywords and a list of various terminology that represent negation. Adjective, adverb, or verb is a relevant part of speech. Such a specific part of speech is specified in terms of its importance in deciding sentiments. Thus, the feature vector consists of 8 related elements (Singh & Kumari, 2016). The 8 features used include the speech tag, special keyword, presence of negation, the emoticon, the number of positive keywords and the negative number of keywords.

4.5. Training and Classification

Supervised learning is an essential tool for solving issues of classification. The classification is conducted with Naïve Bayes, Vector Support System, and Maximum Entropy after constructing a function matrix (Pang, Lee, & Vaithyanathan, 2002; Pang & Lee, 2004).

4.6. Sentiment Score

The tweets will be labelled as either positive, negative or neutral. If the no. of positive tweets is greater than (>) no of negative tweets then the sentiment score of the overall document is positive else negative.

5. LEVELS OF SENTIMENT ANALYSIS

Sentiment Analysis is related to the field of Natural Language Processing. It is a big suitcase of NLP problems. Sentiment Analysis occur at three different levels, depending on how much granularity or detail a model or decision procedure is taken into account, namely sentence analysis, document analysis and the sentiment level analysis. Figure 3 showcases the levels of Sentiment Analysis. On the basis of granularity, the sentiment analysis is divided into three levels such as the sentence level analysis, document level analysis and aspect based analysis.

Figure 3. Levels of sentiment Analysis on the basis of Granularity

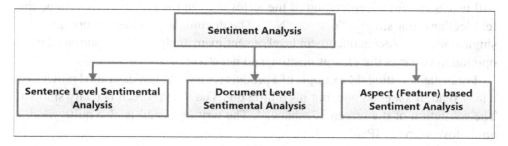

5.1. Sentence-level Sentiment Analysis

The sentences level is taken into consideration if there is to get a more detailed interpretation of the various views shared in the text on individuals. This form of emotion analysis excludes words that have no views and decides if their viewpoint is good or negative. A sentence level defines a sentence as either factual or subjective. Subjective means to have an opinion. It is allocated to a class otherwise overlooked because it is subjective.

As for the sentence level, it classifies it in positive and negative opinions if a sentence is subjective. Thus, it categorizes sentiment expressed in every sentence. Sentiment Analysis (SA) approaches to sentence and document level may find only one feeling in a sentence or document. In (Pang, Lee, & Vaithyanathan, 2002), the authors have used classification algorithms such as Naive Bayes, Maximum Entropy, and Help vector machine compare of that text classification of the feeling of film reviews approaches. They explain the comparatively poor methods performance as a result of Sentiment Analysis requiring a deeper understanding of the document being analysed.

In (Morinaga, Yamanishi, Tateishi, & Fukushima, 2002), the authors allocated sentiment to terms but relied on quantitative details such as word association levels or statistical forecasts. In (Matsumoto, Takamura, & Okumura, 2005), the authors of the paper recognize the word order and syntactic relationships among words are absolutely essential in the classification of sentiments, and is therefore crucial and cannot be discarded. They create a dependency tree for every sentence and then prune them to construct a Category subtree.

5.2. Document-Level Sentiment Analysis

Opinions are often subjective terms that reflect the thoughts, perceptions or opinions of individuals in relation to an object or event. Some blogs or forums try to express their views through reviews and comments. If opinion is expressed in a review, it will take a careful interpretation of the terms used in the review to determine the real feelings, not simply "Yes" or "No". The document provides an opinion of a single opinion holder at document level of sentiment analysis. Here, one can define opinion in two specific classes positive and negative:

For instance, citing the example of a product review: "A few days ago I purchased a new IPad. It's a good one, but it's a little big. The touch screen is really smooth. The resolution of the screen is enhanced. The writing pencil is also quite good. I am in love with the IPad.

The subjective opinion is said to be constructive in terms of the words or phrases used in the analysis (nice, fine, great, love). Objective views are calculated with a scale of 4 or 5 stars, positive and negative 1 or 2 stars. In (Pang, Lee, & Vaithyanathan, 2002), the author proposes a fairly full state of the art focused on the applications and Sentiment Analysis issues. They mentioned the techniques used to solve each problem. In (Abdulla, Ahmed, Shehab, & Al-Ayyoub, 2013), the author introduces in his book a synthesis of plays in the analysing sentiment. It updates the granularity introduced by (Pang, Lee, & Vaithyanathan, 2002) and distinguishes three analytical levels: text, paragraph, and degree of aspect.

The fundamental task of classifying document-level analysis is to deal with the extraction of opinion baring words from comments, and to detect the polarity of these perceived terms (Liu & Zhang, 2012). Based on these words, the program determines whether a positive or negative opinion has been expressed on this subject in general. The compilation and interpretation of opinions from these sentences will further categorize such subjective sentences as positive or negative.

5.3. Aspect (Feature) Based Sentiment Analysis

The analysis of the document and sentence level works well when it refers to a unified entity. In certain instances, though, people talk of things with multiple characteristics or attributes. Aspect based SA can find different feelings with related target terms in a text. It can identify opinion tuples consisting of target term, target (aspect) and objective feeling.

Categorizing the positive and negatives of this review hides the valuable information about the product. Therefore, the Aspect based Sentiment Analysis focuses on the recognition of all sentiment expressions within a given document and the aspects to which the opinions refer. Table 2 presents example of a restaurant reviews, aspect terms and their sentiment polarities

Table 2. Example of a restaurant reviews, aspect terms and their sentiment polarities

Sr.no	REVIEWS	ASPECT TERM	POLARITY
1.	The hotel staff is amazing	Hotel staff	positive
2.	The noodles taste heaven	Noodles taste	positive
3.	The menu is concised, but the food is good	Menu, food	Negative, positive
4.	The ambience is just okk.	ambience	Neutral (conflict)

Aspect-based SA function can be categorised into three major subtasks as extraction of aspect and opinion, analysis of emotion lexicon and description of opinion (Taboada, Brooke, Tofiloski, Voll, & Stede, 2011). Opinion summarization is a presentation in qualitative (Liu, Hu, & Cheng, 2005) or quantitative fashion of the extracted aspects and the polarity of their opinion words. The most critical and difficult task of them all is the aspect and opinion extraction process, studied by most researchers compared to the other tasks.

6. APPROACHES FOR SENTIMENT ANALYSIS

There are two basic approach to Sentiment Analysis (Yadollahi, Shahraki, & Zaiane, 2017). One is lexicon based approach and the other is machine learning based approach. A variation of the two known as hybrid approach is also a very common method of evaluating emotions. Table 3 displays the description of methods used in a tabular format.

Table 3. A short summarized view of the methods used for sentiment analysis

Sr. No	Technique	Description	Strength	Weakness
1.	Lexicon Based Approaches (Feizollah, Ainin, Anuar, Abdullah, & Hazim, 2019) (Al-Smadi, Qawasmeh, Al-Ayyoub, Jararweh, & Gupta, 2018) (Da Silva, Hruschka, & Hruschka Jr, 2014)	Use lexicons of emotion, lexicons of feelings are sets of annotated and pre-processed expressions of feeling. Words that characterize the speaker 's positive, negative and neutral mood are given sentiment values.	No training is required.	Precision, accuracy is dependent on lexical resources. Quantified no of lexicon terms and limited sensation orientation.
2.	Machine Learning Based Approaches (Pang, Lee, & Vaithyanathan, 2002) (Go, Bhayani, & Huang, 2009)	Using machine learning algorithms and linguistic function to label the text as positive, negative or neutral.	For a particular purpose or context, the model can be designed.	It may be costly to collect labelled data for preparation.
3.	Hybrid Approaches (Zhang, Ghosh, Dekhil, Hsu, & Liu, 2011) (Tayal & Yadav, 2017) (Akhtar, Gupta, Ekbal, & Bhattacharyya, 2017)	Combination of both	Incorporates the best of both	Different kinds of datasets can vary the accuracy

Figure 4 displays the taxonomy of Sentiment Analysis on the basis of approaches used for its evaluation. Primarily there are three approaches namely lexicon, machine learning and hybrid approach which can be further categorised.

Figure 4. Taxonomy of sentiment analysis

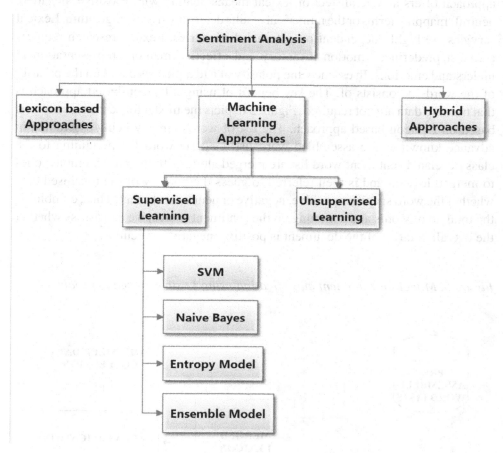

6.1. Lexicon Based Approaches

Lexicon Based approaches make use of the lexicon tools available. It uses Bag of Words approach for examination of sentiment. This methodology does not take into account the closeness of the individual terms that serves as a significant drawback for other approaches such as machine learning. Here the feeling of each word is evaluated and identified with the terms that are already described in the dictionary. Maximum number of positive and negative terms are determined and the total document polarity is determined. In the Lexicon method, a dictionary built from the semantic orientation of the terms or phrases inside a text is measured as instructions. This approach to classifying feelings is based on the understanding that the polarity of a text piece can be achieved based on the polarity of the words it contains. This approach offers an overall feel of lexical means dealing with (positive, negative, neutral) mapping terms or the numerical results determined by an algorithm. Lexical services are highly dependent on external dictionaries. Lexical research requires a robust predefined emotion inventory and effective memory representation to understand emotions. In essence, the polarity of a text piece is based on the polarity of the words it consists of. The key benefit of using a lexicon-based approach is that training data are not required. Figure 5 depicts the model for sentiment analysis based on Lexicon based approach. The list of words already being assembled in advance known as pre-assembled word list. Generic word list pertaining to the class of related sentiment word list are merged along with the pre-assembled ones to merged lexicon and is then referred to guess the polarity of the tokenised data whether the word specifies positive, negative or neutral sentiment. Thus, combining the total no of words and summing up the sentiment scores, we can assess whether the overall polarity of the document is positive, negative or neutral.

Figure 5. Model for sentiment classification using Lexicon based approach

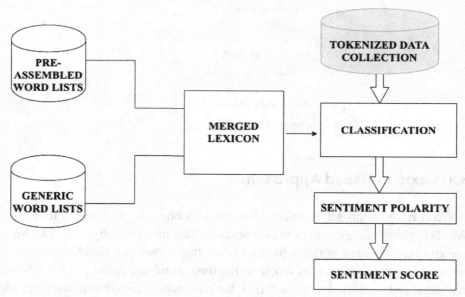

Thus, Lexicon based approach is one of the widely based approach for Sentiment Analysis. Generally, machine learning for Sentiment Analysis is more preferable but many studies have suggested that in many cases lexicon approach has performed well than machine learning approach. It inferred that Lexicon-based approach is superior not only to the accuracy, timing, recall and F-measurement approach, but also to the reduction of time and effort. Table 4 displays a short tabular format of some of the significant works done on this approach.

Table 4. Short Summary of some papers that uses lexicon based methods

Sr. No	Author	Description	Strength	Limitations
1.	(Taboada, Brooke, Tofiloski, Voll, & Stede, 2011)	The paper outlines a method focused on lexicons to extract emotions from text. The Semantic Orientation (SO-CAL) calculator uses term dictionaries with noted semantic orientation (polarity and strength), including improvement and rejection main subject.	The presence of dictionary ensured consistency and reachability worked well on blog posts, game reviews.	The method does not aim at full linguistic analysis.
2.	(Melville, Gryc, & Lawrence, 2009)	In this paper, the author has presented a standardized framework in which one can use context lexical information in terms of word class associations, and use any available training sets to refine this information for different domains.	Background level information can be used to refine for available training examples.	Labelled examples can't be explored in related domains.
3.	(Kanayama & Nasukawa, 2006)	This work presented by the author focusses on a non-supervised method of constructing lexicons for polar clauses that express positive or negative features in a particular context.	No manual training required and the precision of polarity reached up to 94%.	Restricted to narrow domains.
4.	(Neviarouskaya, Prendinger, & Ishizuka, 2011)	In this paper, the author discusses methods of producing and scoring a new feeling lexicon SentiFul. WordNet 's algorithm was expanded for the automatic generation of new sentiment-related compounds using SentiFul.	Synonyms and antonyms relation established well.	Not able to identify well defined patterns.

The pre-assembled word lists formed after breaking of line into various words and grouping them together along with the generic word list forms a merged lexicon. The tokenised data collection and the merged data collection if formed together to calculate the no of positive, negative and neutral words. After doing all these steps, the data is then grouped into set of sentiments classifying them as positive, negative or neutral.

The lexicon based approach is also known as symbolic techniques. Having a pre-annotated dictionary with pre-defined words and a sentiment sore assigned to them is easy but has its disadvantages in many aspects.

Disadvantages of Lexicon Based Approaches

1. There are no efficient and non-context-based opinion words system, for example. A 'small' word can intend a positive or negative opinion about the function of the product due to its history and meaning. There is no way of understanding the semantical orientation of a context without prior awareness of the product function.
2. Cannot cope with many contrasting terms in a paragraph.

Lexicon Based approaches further classified into Corpus Based and Dictionary based approaches.

6.1.1. Corpus Based Approaches

The lexicon based approaches find co-occurrences patterns of words to determine the sentiments of words or phrases. Corpus Based method deals with a seed list of opinion terms and uses other terms of opinion in a broad corpus to help identify opinion words with context-specific orientation. Paper (Musto, Semeraro, & Polignano, 2014) addresses all Arabic-language approaches to SA. As the number of Arabic and Arabic Lexicons available for SA is small, the paper starts with the creation of a handwritten dataset and then takes the reader through comprehensive steps in the construction of the lexicon. Experiments are carried out in the various stages of this process to track and compare changes to the accuracy of the device.

6.1.2. Dictionary Based Approaches

The lexicon based approaches use synonyms and antonyms in popular lexicon dictionary like WordNet to determine word sentiments based on a set of seed opinion words. It can be used to collect information on links and connections between words, such as synonyms and antonyms. Lexicon-based dictionaries can be manually created as defined in this article (Stone, Dunphy, & Smith, 1966; Tong et al., 2001) or automatically, with the aid of seed words (Turney & Littman, 2003) to extend the list of terms. A significant part of the lexicon based work was performed on adjectives as markers of textual semantic orientation (Hatzivassiloglou & McKeown, 1997; Taboada, Brooke, Tofiloski, Voll, & Stede, 2011).

6.2. Machine Learning Based Approaches

The paradigm of machine learning is best known because of the text richness of Twitter. The prevalence of short slang terms, along with phrases represented as emoticons, numerous expressions and hashtags makes manual labelling difficult, thereby paving the way for machine learning to develop.

Machine learning is an algorithm that enables the learning of computers by means of artificial intelligence. This usually results in the projection of a set of data into an algorithm which provides information on the properties of the data and helps it to predict certain data it might encounter in the future since virtually all non-random data contain patterns and require computers to generalizes. It enables the prediction of unseen data to happen. The computer trains a model to generalize what it determines are the important aspects of the data.

Sentiment Analysis by machine learning is a method that automates the mining of documents, phrases, tweets and databases through natural language processing for opinions, views and emotions (NLP). The methodology of machine learning uses a training set and a classification test set. The training set comprises the input vector and the associated class labels. The test set is used by predicting the class labels to validate the model. It is often referred to as study of subjectivity, mining of opinion and extraction of judgments. Some of the approaches suggested for dealing with TSA are based on a machine learning classifier trained in various tweet apps. Naïve Bayes (NB), Maximum Entropy (MaxEnt), Support Vector Machines (SVM) are some of the strongest classifiers (Giachanou & Crestani, 2016). The supervised learning is an important technique for solving classification problems. Various classifiers:

6.2.1. Naïve Bayes Method

The Naïve Bayes method is a probabilistic classifier which uses a number of documents to learn patterns. This applies text to the list of terms in the correct category for classification of the paper. This implies the interfaces are mutually exclusive. The Naïve Bayes classifier utilizes all features in the vector functions and analyses them separately since they are equally independent. The conditional probability for Naïve Bayes can be defined as:

$$P\left(X|y_j\right) = \Pi_{i=1}^{m} P(x_i|y_j) \tag{6}$$

Where 'X' is the feature defined as $X=\{x1,x2,\ldots..xm\}$ and yj is the class label. Specific independent functions like emoticons, emotional keywords, counts of positive and negative keywords, counts of positive and negative hashtags are used to efficiently define Naïve Bayes (Gamallo & Garcia, 2014). Because it does not acknowledge the relationship between characteristics. Therefore, the connections between part of a voice tag, emotional keyword and negation cannot be used. In (Parikh & Movassate, 2009), the author has analysed how the naïve Bayes method is better than the entropy based model.

6.2.2. SVM Classifier (Support Vector Machines)

The SVM analyses data, identifies decision boundaries and uses computational kernels (Linear, Sigmoid, polynomial). This classification uses a wide classification margin and tries to create a large difference between two classes. SVM uses a discriminative function defined as:

$$g\left(X\right) = \omega^{T} \varnothing\left(X\right) + b \tag{7}$$

Where X is the feature vector, 'w' is the vector of weights and 'b' is the vector of bias of Non-linear mapping from input space to large-size function space. On the training set 'b' are immediately trained. Linear classification kernel is used here. This creates a wide division between two groups. In (Li & Li, 2013) the author used SVM as a classifier of sentiment polarity. He had developed a system that enables a compact numerical overview of views of micro-blog platforms by defining and retrieving the topics listed in user inquiries. The opinions then collected are categorized by SVM. Two SVM multiclass approaches were employed, Single-machine multi-class SVMs and comments are categorized.

6.2.3. Maximum Entropy Classifier

In Maximum Entropy, a probabilistic classifier is one of an exponential model family. Like the classification of Naïve Bayes, this do not presume that the features are conditionally independent. Because of this minimum assumption that the maximum entropy classifier is used when the conditional independence of features cannot be assumed. This is used especially in the problem of text classification where our features are usually words that obviously are not independent (Go, Bhayani, & Huang, 2009). This classifier tries to maximize the entropy of the system by estimating the conditional distribution of the class label. The conditional distribution is defined as:

$$P_\lambda \left(y | X \right) = 1 / Z \left(X \right) \exp \left\{ \sum_i \lambda_i f_i \left(X, y \right) \right\} \tag{9}$$

'X' is the feature vector and 'y' is the class label. Z(X) is the normalization factor and λ_i is the weight co-efficient. $f_i(X,y)$ is the feature vector which is defined as

$$f_i \left(X, y \right) = \{ {}^{1, \, X = x_i \, and \, y = y_i}_{0, \, otherwise} \tag{10}$$

The relation between parts of speech tag, emotional keyword and negation are utilized effectively for classification.

6.2.4. Ensemble Classifier

The approach for machine learning that helps improve performance through the combination of multiple models. This approach enables better predictive performance than a single model. The individual decisions of the different classifiers (weighted or unweighted approach) are combined in some way to identify new instances. This uses the attributes of all the common classifications to achieve the best classification. In (Xia, Zong, & Li, 2011), the author has applied ensemble approaches like fixed combination, weighted combination and Meta-classifier combination for sentiment classification and obtained better accuracy. Table 5 presents summary of various machine learning approaches used for TSA.

Table 5. Description of some papers using Machine Learning Approach

Sr.no	Author	Description	Strength	Limitations
1.	(Pang & Lee, 2004)	The author evaluated by comparing several classifiers on movie reviews and gave insight and understanding in the analysis of sentiments and opinion mining.	Outperforms human produced baselines in comparison to Lexicon based approach.	The method doesn't perform well on topic based categorization.
2.	(Go, Bhayani, & Huang, 2009)	The author has researched Bigram and POS. They also omitted emoticons from their classification training data when compared to Naive Bayes, MaxEntropy, SVM.	Accuracy is 80% when trained with emoticon data.	The method may be further evaluated for trigram approach.
3.	(Barbosa & Feng, 2010)	The author proposes a framework in which sentiments are automatically detected by Twitter messages (tweets) and recognise certain features of the writing of tweets and meta-information of the words that make up those messages.	The solution is effective in case of biased and noisy data.	The method doesn't perform fine grained analysis on antagonistic sentiments.
4.	(Sarlan, Nadam, & Basri, 2014)	In this review, a sentiment analysis is designed that collects a significant number of tweets. Customer viewpoints are categorized as positive and negative by tweets as seen in the tarpaulin graph and the html tab.	Able to analyse data on vast number of tweets.	The method gets restricted to Linux server or LAMP.

6.3. Hybrid approaches

The integration of machine learning and lexical strategies to obtain better precision and complexity results when testing against SVM, Naïve Bayes and other classification systems is known as Hybrid approach (Rashid, Hamid, & Parah, 2019). It is the best of the two methods popular for sentiment analysis (Rashid, Hamid, & Parah, 2019). This approach was to incorporate the knowledge extracted from the rule based method as features into the classifier. Figure 6 displays the architecture of hybrid model. In general, the hybrid approach implements two stages of Sentiment Analysis. First by checking the polarity terms of a current set of words in the Lexicon dictionary and then by teaching the computer algorithm through the polarities of the first Lexicon (Tan, Wang, & Cheng, 2008). The tweet score that is calculated in the Lexicon based method was added in the feature used in the machine learning approach. For the optimum results, a hybrid approach is the combination of machine learning and lexicon-based approach, which usually produces better results. Both approaches have their respective advantages and disadvantages, and recent research shows that both methods are mutually complimentary. In the hybrid approach, both statistical learning and a knowledge based approach have been demonstrated to outperform many of the existing methods that use only one type of method. Table 6 summarizes some of the work done on sentiment analysis using Hybrid Model.

Figure 6. Hybrid Model for sentiment analysis

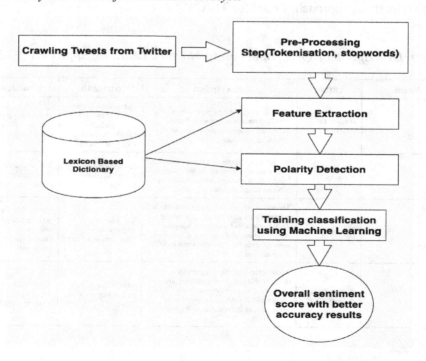

Table 6. A brief summary of research papers using hybrid model

Sr.no	Author	Description	Strength	Limitations
1.	(Zhang, Ghosh, Dekhil, Hsu, & Liu, 2011)	The framework first uses an entity-level approach based on a lexicon analysis of feelings. A classifier is then equipped to classify the entities in the tweets newly discovered.	High Precision (The ratio of correctly predicted observations to the total predicted).	Low Recall (The fraction of positive instances that were predicted to be positive.
2.	(Mittal, Agarwal, Agarwal, Agarwal, & Gupta, 2013)	The author suggests the use of a three-stage hierarchical model for opinion extraction, to mark the tweets with predetermined terms with strong positive or negative feelings.	Helps in product analysis before purchase	Not able to handle sarcasm and discourse relations.
3.	(Tayal & Yadav, 2017)	A sentiment analysis method called SENTI-METER has been used by the author in this post. Unbiased twitters have been collected for this particular campaign and were able to achieve	84.47% accuracy by using a unigram machine learning method as compared with manual tagging.	Bi gram model couldn't be explored
4.	(Lalji & Deshmukh, 2016)	Sentiment analysis is performed by looking for the polarity terms already predefined in the dictionary of lexicons and the next stage level by assessing the machine learning algorithm by the polarity provided by lexicon at first stage.	Combining the best of supervised learning approach without la- belled data.	The quality of sentiment lexicon is highly depended on some bias resources

7. TWITTER SENTIMENT ANALYSIS TOOLS

Many tools to interpret sentiments in short informal social media texts have been developed in recent years. The tools included free systems built in academic environments, commercial API applications that include a monthly subscription and some NLP literature algorithms (Ahmed Abbasi & Dhar, 2014). The analysed tools can be categorised into two: stand-alone and trained workbench tools. The stand-alone solutions use text processing models which can automatically be embedded in "out- of-the-box" unlabelled documents, including API-based deals and others that can be installed as desktop applications (Ahmed Abbasi & Dhar, 2014).

1. **Senti-strength**: Senti-Strength is a common autonomous *Stand-alone tool* to evaluate sentiment. It uses a lexicon of emotion to assign negative and positive text phrases. The sentence level scores can be added to determine sentence or

document level polarities. The unsupervised learning essence of this method makes it possible for any data set to apply.

2. **Sentiment 140**: This *Stand-alone tool* uses a qualified classifier for machine learning, based on a broad Twitter corpora. The tool uses n-grams in word and speech tag and a maximum entropy-based computer analysis classification.

3. **EWGA (Entropy Weighted Genetic Algorithm)**: This *Trained work-bench tool* model uses entropy-weighted genetic algorithm to effectively select the output of a feature sub- set as the functional value within the genetic algorithms for the sentiment classifications.

4. **BPEF (Bootstrap Parametric Ensemble Framework)**: This *Trained Workbench tool* incorporates a bootstrap parametric ensemble framework. Tens of thousands of one- to-one binary classifiers have been created to exploit various data set combinations and classifiers of machine learning.

8. STANDARD DATASETS AVAILABLE FOR TWITTER SENTIMENT ANALYSIS

While it is possible to crawl, and download a large number of tweets through Twitter APIs, it is difficult to use such data for scientific analysis, Twitter does not enable the redistribution of collected tweets, and this is also the case for annotated tweet datasets. Numerous assessment databases were developed because of TSA's increasing popularity. The datasets typically contain a range of Twitter-crawled tweets along with the feeling of tweets. Following are the some standard Data-sets available for TSA:

Sanders Twitter Sentiment Corpus (Ziegelmayer & Schrader, 2012): The tweets are listed by hand and are comprised of four Twitter search terms: @apple, google, Microsoft and # Twitter. Sentiments extracted from the tweets are classified and broadly categorised into: only 570 positive and 654 negative tweets were tested positive, neutral, optimistic and pessimistic.

Stanford Twitter Sentiment Corpus (Go, Huang, & Bhayani, 2009): This dataset consists of 1600,000 tweets from a scraper testing the Twitter API. The scraper continuously sends a question to the positive emotion and at the same time a direct answer to the negative emotion. Upon deleting retweets, one gets multiple tweets with positive emoticons and numerous tweets with negative emoticons, repetitive tweets and emotional prejudices.

Obama Mccain Debate (Omd) (Shamma, Kennedy, & Churchill, 2009): This data collection was made of 3,238 tweets that came along First debate in September 2008 on US presidential news. The scores for the tweets were compiled using the

Amazon Mechanical Turkte. Each tweet has been deemed to be positive, bad, mixed," other" (tweets cannot be evaluated).

9. SIGNIFICANCE OF SENTIMENT ANALYSIS

Sentiment Analysis is Natural Language Processing task where your system needs to test texts feeling based on training data set. For the microblogging platform Sentiment Analysis is a vital tool for research and business applications. Understanding the emotions of individuals is essential for business, as customers can express emotions more freely than ever before. Through collecting customer feedback dynamically from survey responses to social media interaction marketers will listen attentively to their customers and customize goods and services to suit their needs. Machine learning processes help to extract useful conclusions about human behaviour by understanding human sentiment and understanding of human writings.

Analysis of feelings is also crucial for effective media analysis, as it helps us to get an insight of those issues of wider public opinion. The overall customer experience is quick to reveal. It lets data analysts gage public sentiment inside big companies, perform pronounced market analysis, track brand and company credibility and appreciate consumer perception.

10. LIMITATION OF SENTIMENT ANALYSIS

Sentiment Analysis is a common way of interpreting what public opinion is toward a particular company or product. It does, though have its own challenges and limitations that can be overcome if used effectively. The brevity of messages (tweets cannot reach more than 140 characters) and the casual existence of texts on social media websites, the use of slang abbreviations, new words, URLs, etc. The users of such social media platforms write very informally and a lot of slang and abbreviations are usually found in the texts. Slang is one of the types of language comprising of forms and idioms which are considered not to be very formal and precisely confined to a group of people. Abbreviations are a minimized form of a sentence term. These words and phrases have to be replaced to impute their meaning in order to be interpreted correctly (stemming in a part of the sentiment analysis which words are reduced to their actual base meaning).

These factors together with the improper punctuation and incorrect spellings make it more complex to extract people's opinions and feelings. TSA operates on the systematic approach adopted by the machine learning system first by extracting tweets from the Twitter API. The pre-processing portion which involves cleaning up data by eliminating noise in the form of irrelevant information and then going through the classifier to infer the polarity of positive, negative or neutral tweets. However, some algorithms are complicated and may not produce very insightful results. But on a broader aspect Sentiment Analysis is an excellent way to get unbiased opinions from customers about several things. It helps a company in lot of aspect especially when it comes to marketing and advertising or market research.

11. OPEN ISSUES AND CHALLENGES

A significant amount of research has been done over the past decade in Sentiment Analysis and it continues to grow rapidly in new directions. Most of this work involved designing more reliable classifiers, usually with supervised machine learning algorithms and a series of functionality. Surveys provide summaries of the various automated classifiers, attributes, and emotion datasets. In this chapter, we address some of the remaining challenges, questions that have not been adequately explored, and new problems arising from new Sentiment Analysis. We are still debating strategies to address these issues. The objective is to provide practitioners and researchers with insights into the latest developments in the field and encourage further work in the varied problem landscape, particularly in areas that are comparatively less addressed. Some of the major issues are following:

Data Sparseness: Data sparsity is largely due to the wide range of informal textual characteristics on Twitter. It is really important to deal with data sparsity, as it can affect the performance of TSA. In (Saif, He, & Alani, 2012) the author has investigated data sparsity reduction. We assume, however, that this issue needs to be explored further given the importance of reducing the data sparsity. Sparse data is a critical factor in the overall success of a standard system classification have demonstrated, due to the vast number of irregular terms found in tweets, that Twitter data are sparser than other data types (for example, film review data) (Saif, He, & Alani, 2012).

Multi-Lingual Content: The fact that it depends heavily upon language is a big difficulty in sentiment analysis. Language specific are the terms embedding, feelings lexicon, and even annotated details. Tweets are released in a wide range of languages and are often used in the same tweet in more than one language. Few researchers have, however, attempted to tackle multilingual TSA (Can, Ezen-Can, & Can, 2018). It is a relevant area of study that needs to be further explored to tackle multilingual TSA.

Sarcasm Detection: Sarcasm, both humorous and negative, plays a significant role in human social interaction. Sarcasm is "a sharp, bitter, or cutting expression or remark". The use of irony to mock or convey contempt (SINGH, 2019). For example: Such a great book that I never even thought of reading it. The word great may signify it to be a positive sentence but the emotion is negative. The identification of sarcasm is not so investigated. However, some of the researchers worked on this topic. Sarcasm detection is required to improve the results of the Sentiment Analysis.

Data-Set Problems: There is no specific data set for use in the research and assessment of implicit aspect retrieval. The lack of common public data sets opens the doors to the development of publicly accessible uniform data sets (Tubishat, Idris, & Abushariah, 2018). Another difficulty found in the study is that most of the works are in English and Chinese. In the implied dimension of extraction other languages are also unemployed (Tubishat, Idris, & Abushariah, 2018). One potential future path is to hybridize several methods to address individual drawbacks by benefiting from each included technique.

Domain Dependence: Across multiple contexts, the same sentence or phrase may have different meanings (Peddinti & Chintalapoodi, 2011). For example, in the field of film, drama, etc., the word 'unpredictable' is optimistic, but when the same word is used in the sense of a steering vehicle, then it has a negative.

12. CONCLUSION

The research interests in analysing tweets according to their articulated sentiments have increased in recent years. It is due to the vast number of messages shared on Twitter every day which provide important public information on many subjects. In this chapter, we include a survey and comparative analysis of Sentiment Analysis (opinion mining) techniques, including lexicon-based and machine learning based and hybrid approaches, as well as cross-domain and cross-lingual methods and some measurements. Research findings indicate that machine learning methods such as SVM and Naive Bayes are of the highest quality and can be considered as the simple learning methods, whereas in some cases lexicon based methods are very successful, requiring little effort in the human labelled text. The survey also focuses on common sentiment analysis tools and standard data sets available.

REFERENCES

Abdulla, N. A., Ahmed, N. A., Shehab, M. A., & Al-Ayyoub, M. (2013). *Arabic sentiment analysis: Lexicon-based and corpus-based. In 2013 IEEE Jordan conference on applied electrical engineering and computing technologies*. AEECT.

Ahmed Abbasi, A. H., & Dhar, M. (2014). Benchmarking twitter sentiment analysis tools. *Proceedings of the Ninth International Conference on Language Resources and Evaluation (LREC'14).*

Akhtar, M. S., Gupta, D., Ekbal, A., & Bhattacharyya, P. (2017). Feature selection and ensemble construction: A two-step method for aspect based sentiment analysis. *Knowledge-Based Systems, 125,* 116–135. doi:10.1016/j.knosys.2017.03.020

Al-Smadi, M., Qawasmeh, O., Al-Ayyoub, M., Jararweh, Y., & Gupta, B. (2018). Deep Recurrent neural network vs. support vector machine for aspect-based sentiment analysis of Arabic hotels' reviews. *Journal of Computational Science, 27,* 386–393. doi:10.1016/j.jocs.2017.11.006

Barbosa, L., & Feng, J. (2010). Robust sentiment detection on twitter from biased and noisy data. *Coling 2010,* 36-44.

Bifet, A., & Frank, E. (2010). Sentiment knowledge discovery in twitter streaming data. *International conference on discovery science.*

Can, E. F., Ezen-Can, A., & Can, F. (2018). *Multilingual sentiment analysis: An RNN-based framework for limited data.* Retrieved from arXiv preprint arXiv:1806.04511

Clarizia, F., Colace, F., Pascale, F., Lombardi, M., & Santaniello, D. (2019). Sentiment Analysis in Social Networks: A Methodology Based on the Latent Dirichlet Allocation Approach. In *11th Conference of the European Society for Fuzzy Logic and Technology (EUSFLAT 2019),* (pp. 241-248). Academic Press.

Da Silva, N. F., Hruschka, E. R., & Hruschka, E. R. Jr. (2014). Tweet sentiment analysis with classifier ensembles. *Decision Support Systems, 66,* 170–179. doi:10.1016/j.dss.2014.07.003

Davidov, D., Tsur, O., & Rappoport, A. (2010). Enhanced sentiment learning using twitter hashtags and smileys. *Coling 2010.*

Feizollah, A., Ainin, S., Anuar, N. B., Abdullah, N. A., & Hazim, M. (2019). Halal Products on Twitter: Data Extraction and Sentiment Analysis Using Stack of Deep Learning Algorithms. *IEEE Access: Practical Innovations, Open Solutions, 7,* 83354–83362. doi:10.1109/ACCESS.2019.2923275

Gamallo, P., & Garcia, M. (2014). Citius: A NaiveBayes Strategy for Sentiment Analysis on English Tweets. *Proceedings of the 8th International Workshop on Semantic Evaluation.* 10.3115/v1/S14-2026

Giachanou, A., & Crestani, F. (2016). Like it or not: A survey of twitter sentiment analysis methods. *ACM Computing Surveys, 49*(2), 1–41. doi:10.1145/2938640

Go, A., Bhayani, R., & Huang, L. (2009). Twitter sentiment classification using distant supervision. CS224N project report, Stanford.

Go, A., Huang, L., & Bhayani, R. (2009). Twitter sentiment analysis. *Entropy (Basel, Switzerland)*, 17.

Hatzivassiloglou, V., & McKeown, K. (1997). Predicting the semantic orientation of adjectives. In *35th annual meeting of the association for computational linguistics and 8th conference of the European chapter of the association for computational linguistics*, (pp. 174-181). Academic Press.

Jain, A. K., & Gupta, B. B. (2019). Feature Based Approach for Detection of Smishing Messages in the Mobile Environment. *Journal of Information Technology Research*, *12*(2), 17–35. doi:10.4018/JITR.2019040102

Jain, A. K., Sahoo, S. R., & Kaubiyal, J. (2021). Online social networks security and privacy: comprehensive review and analysis. *Complex & Intelligent Systems*, 1-21.

Kanayama, H., & Nasukawa, T. (2006). Fully automatic lexicon expansion for domain-oriented sentiment analysis. In *Proceedings of the 2006 conference on empirical methods in natural language processing*, (pp. 355-363). 10.3115/1610075.1610125

Kaubiyal, J., & Jain, A. K. (2019). A feature based approach to detect fake profiles in Twitter. In *Proceedings of the 3rd International Conference on Big Data and Internet of Things* (pp. 135-139). ACM. 10.1145/3361758.3361784

Khan, M. T., Durrani, M., Ali, A., Inayat, I., Khalid, S., & Khan, K. H. (2016). Sentiment analysis and the complex natural language. *Complex Adaptive Systems Modeling*, *4*(1), 1–19. doi:10.118640294-016-0016-9

Lalji, T., & Deshmukh, S. (2016). Twitter sentiment analysis using hybrid approach. *International Research Journal of Engineering and Technology*, *3*(6), 2887–2890.

Li, Y. M., & Li, T. Y. (2013). Deriving market intelligence from microblogs. *Decision Support Systems*, *55*(1), 206–217. doi:10.1016/j.dss.2013.01.023

Liu, B., & Zhang, L. (2012). A survey of opinion mining and sentiment analysis. In *Mining text data* (pp. 415–463). Springer. doi:10.1007/978-1-4614-3223-4_13

Liu, B., Hu, M., & Cheng, J. (2005). Opinion observer: analyzing and comparing opinions on the web. In *Proceedings of the 14th international conference on World Wide Web*, (pp. 342-351). 10.1145/1060745.1060797

Matsumoto, S., Takamura, H., & Okumura, M. (2005). Sentiment classification using word sub-sequences and dependency sub-trees. In Pacific-Asia conference on knowledge discovery and data mining, (pp. 301-311). Academic Press.

Melville, P., Gryc, W., & Lawrence, R. D. (2009). Sentiment analysis of blogs by combining lexical knowledge with text classification. In *Proceedings of the 15th ACM SIGKDD international conference on Knowledge discovery and data mining* (pp. 1275-1284). ACM. 10.1145/1557019.1557156

Mittal, N., Agarwal, B., Agarwal, S., Agarwal, S., & Gupta, P. (2013). A hybrid approach for twitter sentiment analysis. In *10th international conference on natural language processing (ICON-2013)*, (pp. 116-120). Academic Press.

Morinaga, S., Yamanishi, K., Tateishi, K., & Fukushima, T. (2002). Mining product reputations on the web. In *Proceedings of the eighth ACM SIGKDD international conference on Knowledge discovery and data mining*, (pp. 341-349). 10.1145/775047.775098

Musto, C., Semeraro, G., & Polignano, M. (2014). A Comparison of Lexicon-based Approaches for Sentiment Analysis of Microblog Posts. DART@ AI* IA, 59-68.

Neviarouskaya, A., Prendinger, H., & Ishizuka, M. (2011). SentiFul: A lexicon for sentiment analysis. *IEEE Transactions on Affective Computing*, 2(1), 22–36. doi:10.1109/T-AFFC.2011.1

Pak, A., & Paroubek, P. (2010). Twitter as a corpus for sentiment analysis and opinion mining. LREc, 10, 1320-1326.

Pang, B., & Lee, L. (2004). *A sentimental education: Sentiment analysis using subjectivity summarization based on minimum cuts.* Retrieved from arXiv preprint cs/0409058

Pang, B., Lee, L., & Vaithyanathan, S. (2002). *Thumbs up? Sentiment classification using machine learning techniques.* Retrieved from arXiv preprint cs/0205070

Parikh, R., & Movassate, M. (2009). *Sentiment analysis of user-generated twitter updates using various classification techniques.* CS224N Final Report.

Peddinti, V. M., & Chintalapoodi, P. (2011). Domain adaptation in sentiment analysis of twitter. *Workshops at the Twenty-Fifth AAAI Conference on Artificial Intelligence.*

Rashid, M., Hamid, A., & Parah, S. A. (2019). Analysis of Streaming Data Using Big Data and Hybrid Machine Learning Approach. In Handbook of Multimedia Information Security: Techniques and Applications (pp. 629-643). Springer. doi:10.1007/978-3-030-15887-3_30

Sahoo, S. R., & Gupta, B. B. (2019). Hybrid approach for detection of malicious profiles in twitter. *Computers & Electrical Engineering, 76*, 65–81. doi:10.1016/j. compeleceng.2019.03.003

Sahoo, S. R., & Gupta, B. B. (2020). Classification of spammer and nonspammer content in online social network using genetic algorithm-based feature selection. *Enterprise Information Systems, 14*(5), 710–736. doi:10.1080/17517575.2020.17 12742

Sahoo, S. R., & Gupta, B. B. (2021). Real-time detection of fake account in twitter using machine-learning approach. In *Advances in computational intelligence and communication technology* (pp. 149–159). Springer. doi:10.1007/978-981-15-1275-9_13

Saif, H., He, Y., & Alani, H. (2012). Semantic sentiment analysis of twitter. In *International semantic web conference* (pp. 508-524). Springer.

Sarlan, A., Nadam, C., & Basri, S. (2014). Twitter sentiment analysis. In *Proceedings of the 6th International conference on Information Technology and Multimedia* (pp. 212-216). IEEE. 10.1109/ICIMU.2014.7066632

Shamma, D. A., Kennedy, L., & Churchill, E. F. (2009). Tweet the debates: understanding community annotation of uncollected sources. *Proceedings of the first SIGMM workshop on Social Media*, 3-10. 10.1145/1631144.1631148

Singh, D. (2019, July 3). *Sarcasm Detection: Step towards Sentiment Analysis*. Retrieved January 22, 2021, from https://towardsdatascience.com/sarcasm-detection-step-towards-sentiment-analysis-84cb013bb6db/

Singh, T., & Kumari, M. (2016). Role of text pre-processing in twitter sentiment analysis. *Procedia Computer Science, 89*, 549–554. doi:10.1016/j.procs.2016.06.095

Stone, P. J., Dunphy, D. C., & Smith, M. S. (1966). *The general inquirer: A computer approach to content analysis*. M.I.T. Press.

Taboada, M., Brooke, J., Tofiloski, M., Voll, K., & Stede, M. (2011). Lexicon-based methods for sentiment analysis. *Computational Linguistics, 37*(2), 267–307. doi:10.1162/COLI_a_00049

Tan, S., Wang, Y., & Cheng, X. (2008). Combining learn-based and lexicon-based techniques for sentiment detection without using labeled examples. *Proceedings of the 31st annual international ACM SIGIR conference on Research and development in information retrieval*, 743-744. 10.1145/1390334.1390481

Tayal, D. K., & Yadav, S. K. (2017). entiment analysis on social campaign "Swachh Bharat Abhiyan" using unigram method. *AI & Society, 32*(4), 633–645. doi:10.100700146-016-0672-5

Tong, Evangelista, M., Parsons, A. B., Xu, H., Bader, G. D., Pagé, N., Robinson, M., Raghibizadeh, S., Hogue, C. W. V., Bussey, H., Andrews, B., Tyers, M., & Boone, C. (2001). Systematic genetic analysis with ordered arrays of yeast deletion mutants. *Science, 294*(5550), 2364–2368. doi:10.1126cience.1065810 PMID:11743205

Tubishat, M., Idris, N., & Abushariah, M. A. (2018). Implicit aspect extraction in sentiment analysis: Review, taxonomy, oppportunities, and open challenges. *Information Processing & Management, 54*(4), 545–563. doi:10.1016/j. ipm.2018.03.008

Turney, P. D. (2002). *Thumbs up or thumbs down? Semantic orientation applied to unsupervised classification of reviews.* Retrieved from arXiv preprint cs/0212032

Turney, P. D., & Littman, M. L. (2003). Measuring praise and criticism: Inference of semantic orientation from association. *ACM Transactions on Information Systems, 21*(4), 315–346. doi:10.1145/944012.944013

Xia, R., Xu, F., Yu, J., Qi, Y., & Cambria, E. (2016). Polarity shift detection, elimination and ensemble: A three-stage model for document-level sentiment analysis. *Information Processing & Management, 52*(1), 36–45. doi:10.1016/j. ipm.2015.04.003

Xia, R., Zong, C., & Li, S. (2011). Ensemble of feature sets and classification algorithms for sentiment classification. *Information Sciences, 181*(6), 1138–1152. doi:10.1016/j.ins.2010.11.023

Yadollahi, A., Shahraki, A. G., & Zaiane, O. R. (2017). Current state of text sentiment analysis from opinion to emotion mining. *ACM Computing Surveys, 50*(2), 1–33. doi:10.1145/3057270

Zhang, L., Ghosh, R., Dekhil, M., Hsu, M., & Liu, B. (2011). *Combining lexicon-based and learning-based methods for Twitter sentiment analysis.* HP Laboratories, Technical Report.

Ziegelmayer, D., & Schrader, R. (2012). Sentiment polarity classification using statistical data compression models. In *2012 IEEE 12th international conference on data mining workshops* (pp. 731-738). IEEE.

Chapter 4

Role of Social Media in the COVID-19 Pandemic:
A Literature Review

Kriti Aggarwal
Chandigarh College of Engineering and Technology, India

Sunil K. Singh
ⓘD https://orcid.org/0000-0003-4876-7190
Chandigarh College of Engineering and Technology, India

Muskaan Chopra
Chandigarh College of Engineering and Technology, India

Sudhakar Kumar
Chandigarh College of Engineering and Technology, India

ABSTRACT

Today, social networks and media have become an integral part of everyone's daily existence. The rising popularity of social media has increased tenfold during the times of COVID-19 when people were forced to isolate following social distancing norms. Between July 2020 and July 2021, active social users grew to 520 million. The COVID-19 crisis has resulted in the usage of digital platforms not only for entertainment purposes but also for educational and corporate reasons. Hence, the spread of information has increased excessively on every social media platform. This has resulted in an equal rise of false information. The term infodemic was widely introduced during COVID-19 to explain the harmful effects of misinformation through social media. The chapter, hence, argues that the advantages of social media surpasses the dangers of misinformation. It discusses the role of COVID-19 in digitalization and how social media has helped in provision of various industries.

DOI: 10.4018/978-1-7998-8413-2.ch004

INTRODUCTION

Today, social media is one of the most widely used interactive technologies. Social media has not only made creation and exchange of information simple, but has also paved a way for people to share and develop their career interests and ideas. It has become a medium of expression through quickly building networks and virtual communities (Kietzmann & Kristopher, 2021; Obar & Wildman, n.d.). Social media consumers from all over the world actively use web-based applications and software to use social media sites. This has become possible only due to the widespread use of electronic devices like computers, mobiles, and smartphones etc.

Social media development began with rudimentary platforms (Kirkpatrick, 2011). GeoCities, established in November 1994, was one of the first social networking sites. It was followed by Classmates.com in December 1995 and soon afterwards, SixDegrees.com in May 1997 (NGAK, 2011). Unlike instant-messaging and chat clients, SixDegrees was the first online company that served people using their real names instead of bots (Kirkpatrick, 2011). It allowed registered people to maintain profiles, friend lists, and school affiliations. As a result, SixDegrees was regarded as the very first social networking site, according to various media channels like CBS News (NGAK, 2011).

However, social media has altered the way we all connect with one another on the internet. It has enabled us to learn what is occurring in the world in real time, to interact with one another and keep in contact with long-distance acquaintances, and to have access to an infinite quantity of knowledge at our fingertips. In many ways, social media has enabled many people to connect with others online, making the world appear more approachable.

The use of social media has further flourished during the last few years. The onset of the COVID-19 pandemic has led to a rapid consumption of social media services. It has now become an integral and popular communication tool for information generation, consumption and dissemination. Today, more than 3.8 billion people, worldwide, use social media (Kemp, 2020). Researchers have found that even though continents like America and Europe have ubiquitous social media usage, after pandemic scenarios have changed. Today, Asian nations such as Indonesia are at the top of the list of social media users (Social Media: What Countries Use It Most & What Are They Using?, 2019). A rise in the usage of social media can be seen via Figure 1. In only a short time, the number of users has increased from 3.59 billion to 4.48 billion.

Figure 1. A rise in social media users during May 2019 till October 2019 (in billions)

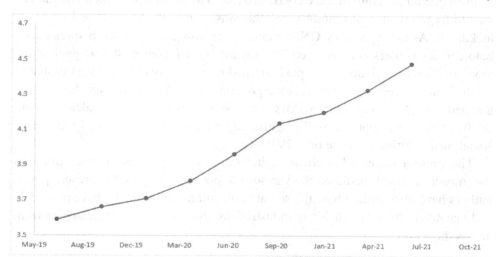

Despite rising social media usage, various researchers find it difficult to categorise social media based upon features and usage. When it comes to these services, a wide range of inbuilt and stand-alone features can be found that vary from application to application (Tuten, Tracy L.; Solomon, Michael R., 2018; Aichner, T.; Grünfelder, M.; Maurer, O.; Jegeni, D., 2021). However, it is possible to define similarities between all the services. One of the most important points defining social media is the fact that they are interactive Web 2.0 and Internet-based applications.Andreas M. Kaplan and Michael Haenlein, 2010, The Law Commission, 2018Most of these services allow user generated content. This could include short text like posts or comments. This can also include digital media like pictures and videos. The majority of content circulated on social media includes data that was generated during online interactions. This content flow is the lifeblood of social media applications (Kaplan Andreas M., Haenlein Michael, 2010). One of the attractive aspects of social media is that it allows users to create service-specific profiles (The Law Commission, 2018). Overall, use of social media platforms increases user engagement and makes them visible online. It has allowed people to build communities and expand their networks in just a few clicks (The Law Commission, 2018).

Despite all of the advantages and utility, academics have begun to refer to social media as an infodemic. The word infodemic (WHO Situation Report 13; Zarocostas, J., 2020) was coined during covid-19 to describe the dangers of spreading misinformation. This concept was widely seen during the management phase of disease outbreaks (W.H. Director, 2020; Mendoza, et. al. 2010; Starbird, K., et. al. 2014). Many researchers raised concerns that an infodemic could result in an even greater speedup in the COVID process. The influence of social media can lead to fragmentation of opinions, and this was seen in the case of the Lombardy lockdown. As anticipated by CNN, rumours regarding the lockdown spread even before official orders were received. This resulted in an increased state of panic in the town. Before the lock-down, people crammed trains and airports to flee Lombardy for the southern regions, hampering the government's effort to manage the diseases and perhaps spreading infection. (M. Cinelli, W. Quattrociocchi, A. Galeazzi, et al., 2020).Thus, it is important to distinguish and understand the uses and misuses of social media during the time of COVID-19.

The present paper talks about digitalization during times of pandemic and the impact of social media on the various sectors of society. In the present paper, authors have also studied how the social applications and services have positively and negatively impacted different industries by studying various researchers from across the world.

DIGITALIZATION IN COVID-19 PANDEMIC

Due to social distancing conventions and countrywide lockdowns, the Covid-19 epidemic has inevitably resulted in an increase in the usage of digital technology. People and organisations all around the world have had to adapt to new methods of doing business and living (Rahul De', Neena Pandey, Abhipsa Pal, 2020). The impact of Covid-19 can be seen in almost all major sectors of the economy. These sectors are listed in Figure 2.

Increased Engagement

Social media has allowed increased engagement of people more than ever. During COVID-19, when in-person and social interactions have become limited, statistics show that social media engagement has increased by up to 61 percent during the initial wave of the pandemic (Nicole Fullerton, 2021). For many people, social media has become a path to the outer world, especially as they seek ways to keep connected and entertained.

Beyond the question, the study of the present communication truth is concerned with comprehending every occurrence in terms of the influence it has on social networks (Pérez-Escoda, A. et. al., 2020). The most well-known method of gathering data in the twentieth century was to sit in front of the television, buy daily newspapers, or listen to radio data releases.In the twenty-first century, it is more common to input search keywords into an internet browser on any electronic device (Secretariat, 2020). Social media platforms have evolved into persistent media stream stages that connect with nearly 50% of the total population, effectively competing with the media and writers as members in the data correspondence measure (Ballesteros C, 2019, Pérez-Soler S., 2017).

Figure 2. Sectoral Impact of Covid-19
Source: Mihir Gandhi, 2020

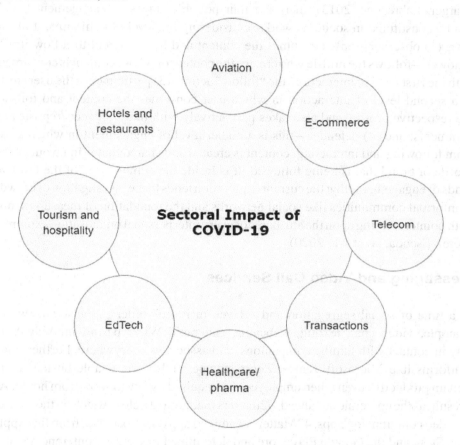

Within the framework of social network research, new related words have emerged that offer conceptual support and symbolic meaning to the phenomena, elucidating the number of audiences that the networks assemble around certain profiles. When faced with a crisis, the increased demand for information produces an unmeasurable anxiety for knowledge, which allows for the establishment of interaction with health experts who have a presence in social networks (Pérez-Soler S., 2017). As a theoretical clarification for the phenomenon, commitment infers the gigantic following of explicit profiles, and from a mental angle, it infers an intuitive and co-inventive experience as a reaction to an improvement like Covid-19, regarding an article, i.e., a profile that turns into a correspondence data referent (Wolter L.-C., et. Al., 2017)

The investigation of engagement has been drawn nearer from numerous perspectives as a multidimensional wonder that clarifies different kinds of responsibilities, and it has developed in pertinence with the development of associations by means of social networks. According to the previous work done by Barger and Labrecque (Barger, Labrecque, 2013), there are four possible stages of engagement which can be constituted in social networks, considering the level of commitment of the user: (1) observer—only consumes the content and has no intent to follow it; (2) follower—follows the profile who creates the content or whose content is consumed, with the first level of interaction, the "follow" action; (3) participant—the user shifts to a second level of interaction in which user consumes the content and follows the respective profile, and also takes part actively with likes, retweets/reposts and comments; and (4) defender—this is a higher level of engagement in which aside from following and interacting, content is created and shared that is in favour of the profile or brand that is being followed. It is inside the combination of the last two kinds of engagements that the current exploration tends to the investigation of crowds in informal communities like social networks and the foundation of measurements, with pointers relying upon the attributes of every interpersonal organisation explored. (Pérez-Escoda, A. et.Al., 2020)

Messaging and Video Call Services

In a time of social segregation and "Haven in Place" orders, advancements, for example, video chat, texting, webcams, and rapid Wi-Fi permit individuals to stay in contact with family, companions, and associates everywhere. Furthermore, platforms like Microsoft Teams, Zoom, Skype, and others enable businesses to remain productive even when employees are required by law to work from home. As a result, as the epidemic advanced, 42matters maintained a close watch on the growth of video conferencing apps. 42Matters examined app download data from the Apple App Store and the Google Play Store and determined that video conferencing apps are popular. Video conferencing programmes had 58 million downloads in March 2020, a figure that was 23 times higher than in January 2020. Zoom was the most downloaded video conferencing application on the planet. Zoom represented 8 out of each 10 video conferencing application downloads in March 2020.

Media companies like Lifesize, Inc., Google LLC, Microsoft Corp., LogMeIn, Inc., RingCentral, Inc., Zoho Corp., StarLeaf Ltd., Communications, Inc., and others are among the key businesses involved in the market. These firms see the pandemic scenario as a way to boost their growth while also assisting the nation through the crisis. Market participants provide their services to businesses and government entities for free or at a low cost.

For instance, in March 2020, Zoom Video Communications, Inc., a California-based remote conferencing administration firm, offered free admittance to video conferencing innovations for K-12 schools in the midst of the COVID-19 issue. Furthermore, the company's stock price has risen in recent months, as investors are certain that the infection will enhance demand for Zoom's video conferencing goods, as shown in Figure 3. (Impact of COVID 19 on the Video Conferencing Market, 2020) (Perez, S, 2020).

Figure 3. Increase in number of users of Video conferencing platforms

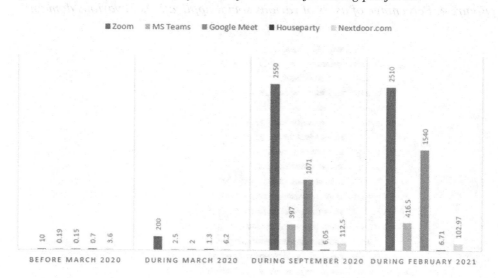

Increase in Digitalization (Online Transitions)

Physical transactions are almost out of date due to the contact-spread of COVID-19. Digital transactions in India have seen an exponential increase as compared to paper money. The Covid-19 epidemic has accelerated the digitalized way of payments and hence has also increased the digital development of the industry. Aside from broadening the use of technology in payments, the epidemic has fueled the growth of digital forms of payment, driving the country toward 'less-cash' or cashless alternatives (Our Bureau, 2021) by promoting the use of Net Banking, NEFT, IMPS,

UPI etc. Leading ventures like PayTM, Google Pay, PhonePe, etc. have also seen a boom in their growth.

USE OF SOCIAL MEDIA FOR VARIOUS PURPOSES

Social media is being used for almost every purpose today, from networking to education to news and information circulation. Whatsapp, Inc has also proposed a new option of inbuilt payment with the messaging app. The figure 4 shows the percentage of users of various social applications in various domains.

Figure 4. Percentage of users of various social applications in various domains.

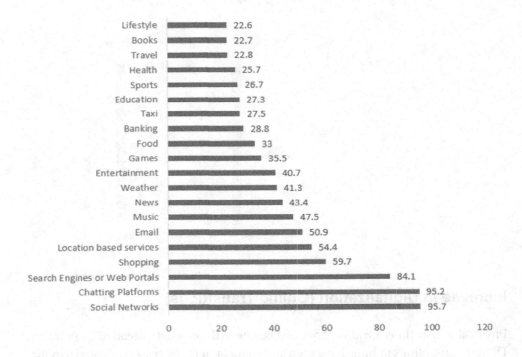

Social networking has the highest mark of 95.7%, preceding it, there are other applications like e-commerce, education, sports, gaming, food, entertainment, Banking and Transactions, Music, Taxis, GPS etc.

Mental Health & social media

Anxiety and tension have also been exacerbated by an abundance of disinformation on social media. During the epidemic, the transmission of potentially dangerous information grew so pervasive that several sites, including Facebook and Twitter, began identifying and, in some cases, deleting content that was not founded on facts. Despite these attempts, social media users continue to be inundated with pictures, stories, and messages that propagate disinformation and add to an already heightened sense of anxiety.

The impact of this knowledge may be highly distressing, especially when users try to make sense of their own emotions in relation to the social and political concerns of the previous year.

At the onset of the epidemic, there was an obvious need for enhanced connectivity. Screenshots of Zoom parties and new challenges, such as the #see10do10 pushup challenge, demonstrated that users wanted to stay active while adjusting to a new, shared world. However, pandemic-related problems have decreased, and social media feeds are returning to many of the same old hazards that have made them tough for mental health for years, such as disinformation and poorly altered pictures. These exaggerated depictions have an effect on users, particularly those who use social media more often. People who have social anxiety, for example, are already predisposed to the harmful effects of social media.

In terms of social media usage, the weekly hourly rate for high-and low-informational social media was more than 20 and 15 hours, respectively. Pleasure, the positive emotion, was shown to be substantially lower than the other four bad emotions (Christopher E. et. al., 2021).

The consequences of excessive screen usage extend well beyond individuals suffering from social anxiety. Because the epidemic reduces possibilities for in-person connection, many people feel less connected than they did before the pandemic, despite their aspirations to utilise social media to connect more. In fact, psychologist Melissa G. Hunt, PhD, assistant director of clinical training in Penn's Psychology department, discovered that social media use increased sadness and loneliness in the first experimental research of Facebook, Snapchat, and Instagram use.

Online Business and Social Media- Social Commerce

Social media is an important part of people's lives all around the world. As more nations industrialise and Wi-Fi becomes more widely available, even the most rural people are taking the time to utilise and set up social media accounts. Currently, more than half of the world's population uses some form of social media. With 4.2 billion users globally, the typical user spends more than two hours each day on social media sites. Even the tiniest businesses have a compelling reason to have a basic social media presence. According to the 2021 Sprout Social Index, 86% of customers who follow a brand on social media choose that brand over a rival (Salvador Ordorica, 2021). Currently, the majority of businesses and organisations rely on digital advertising and marketing strategies since internet marketing looks to be more successful and efficient than traditional types of advertising and marketing.

Since it is generally cheap and permits associations to pass on a message to clients and customers while additionally connecting with their partners, online correspondence by means of web-based media is one of the most broadly utilised and valuable instruments for item advancement. (Hancu-Budui, et. al., 2020). Communication through modern technology increases the likelihood of purchase. Therefore, it makes sense to present products on social networks. Their examinations find that online media is the most powerful business among 21 sorts of business (Cinelli, M., Quattrociocchi, W., Galeazzi, A. et al., 2020; Korenkova et al., 2020). The examinations have furthermore demonstrated the differentiation between the more established and more energetic ages (Y and Z) in seeing a wide range of net publicity. The older generation (Gen X) perceives advertisements as being more intrusive (e.g., pop-ups on the web) than younger generations. This additionally applies to social media and different kinds of on-line advertising. This could be because of the reality that more youthful people who spend greater time online are more familiar with advertising. During the COVID-19 pandemic, there had been many regulations on establishing hours or the whole closure of retail (particularly at some point of the lockdown), which caused an intensification of on-line shopping. As per the portal Criteo, 44% of Italian consumers (31% of them from era Y and Z) downloaded a buying utility to their cell phone throughout the lockdown, which became promoted via social marketing (26%), TV marketing (16%), or became recommended through the use of every other utility (15%). In this context, we investigated whether or not the respondents opt for buying via e-stores and stores that have been designed for them via means of the social community as a part of marketing and advertising or that have been promoted on TV, radio, or the web (within the length of time after the outbreak of the COVID-19 pandemic and the following creation of a restriction on establishing hours of whole store closure) (Ali Taha V, 2021).

Integrating ecommerce with social media is powerful. It allows purchasers to look at manufacturers through social content and discover merchandise they might otherwise no longer search for on an ecommerce platform. Social trade applies to various buying scenarios, starting from product search, influencers and cellular pay. In addition, China's wildly famous social media platform WeChat is closely making an investment in its ecommerce pursuits with the booming social trade mini-software that draws international manufacturers starting from Sephora and Nike to Gucci and

Armani. WeChat mini-packages are lightweight sub-apps used by manufacturers to benefit the marketplace and promote seamlessly within the larger WeChat platform.

Social media systems provide social capabilities for manufacturers and outlets to create interactive, shareable, and immersive campaigns that assist new product launches in going viral. For instance, group-shopping for deals, on-line mini-video games and interactive demanding situations can improve the client experience. This rapidly expanding social commerce market is expected to reach nearly $315. five billion US by the end of 2021 (Franklin Chu, 2020).Group-shopping for and WeChat-primarily based totally social trade exceeds 90% of the entire marketplace percentage for social trade. The coronavirus pandemic expanded the wide variety of clients who've established social trade as a brand new norm for purchasing and incorporated it into their everyday lives (Franklin Chu, 2020)

Gaming and Entertainment Through Social Media

Virtual entertainment is one of the most popular industries today and is slowly displacing traditional media. Over the last decade, video rental firms have gone out of business as services like Netflix have made movie rental more convenient (It's Curtains for Blockbuster Stores, 2017). Cable and satellite television businesses are frequently in similar circumstances. YouTube TV, a new service, was launched in March 2017. The announcement sparked debate over how the service would stack up against existing cable and satellite services (YouTube TV Gets Ready to Take on Cable, 2017). When looking at the stock market, firms that supply cable or satellite services have seen declining share values, but firms like Netflix have shown significant growth (Stock Comparison: Compare DISH Network Corporation (DISH) to Other Stocks, 2017).

Online social entertainment combines entertaining interactive functionality and content such as real-time video streaming, multi-player gaming, music, and video chat communications. These elements are additionally enhanced by web-based media administrations, for example, social charting, executives, audits, appraisals, gatherings, and geolocation alternatives.It fills in as the establishment for a more vivid, animating, intelligent, and friendly substance utilisation experience (David, 2011).

The existence of computer games is not a new concept. They have been around since the 1950s. Although video games were not commercially accessible until 1971, they captivated the hearts of programmers and common computer fans. While single-player games flourished prior to the widespread use of the Internet, online communication and chat rooms were highly popular in the 1980s. These chat rooms were called Internet Relay Chat or IRC. After the popularity of IRCs, the 1990s witnessed a boost in Instant Messaging or IM services and applications. Almost 50 years have passed since the invention of games, and virtual games are more popular than ever before (Bankov and Boris, 2019).

With the rising popularity of online social networks such as Instagram, Facebook, and Twitter, an increasing number of games have made their way onto the social media platforms (Aki Järvinen, 2009). Facebook applications draw millions of users on a regular basis, and game apps routinely rank in the top ten of the platform's popularity rankings.

Through the Internet's increasing strength as a medium for entertainment, communication, information exchange, and dissemination, a new era has begun. Years have passed, and internet gaming has experienced a number of modifications. The gaming business no longer caters to a certain age group or client category. Gaming has evolved into a viable method of networking and community development. Gamers utilise it for a variety of purposes: (Piplani S, 2020)

- Disseminating comprehensive information regarding the latest game updates
- Investigating how other players are completing a challenging level
- I'm looking for feedback and suggestions for game changes.

Gamers use social media to form groups and effectively communicate with one another (Piplani S., 2020).Gaming contention on social media platforms continues to perform consistently. This is because it includes all of the necessary components that make it attractive and easy for people. These components are briefed below (Mangan, 2020):

- Relatability-Social media platforms allow people to share their wins and losses with other gamers online. This increases the relatability factor in virtual games.
- Enhanced Visuals-Inclusion of social media platforms like YouTube has allowed real-time sharing of games in video formats. Not only does it capture the attention of people, it also makes it more interesting and sensational.
- Collaboration and sharing: Sharing game promo codes and trailers has become a trend on social media platforms like Facebook. This has increased social media engagement as well. Especially during the times of COVID-19, sharing and collaboration between people is one of the most attractive features of virtual games.

Education and Digital Learning Through Social Media

Education through social media platforms is not a recent concept. Social media allows students to create, share and modify course materials and information via different formats like text, video, pictures or audio formats. The concept originated as the result of technological advancements which allowed this new type of virtual learning to become a reality. Social media is one of the best education advancements that have occurred for the purpose of collaborative discovery and engagement. Fig 5 shows the different ways social media allows collaborative learning.(Selwyn, 2012).

Figure 5. Social media for Collaborative Learning
Source: Ansari et. al, 2020

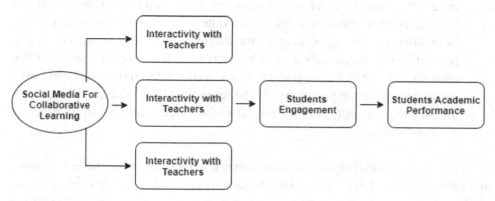

The social media phenomenon emerged in 2005, after the emergence of Web2.0. Today, it can be described as "a collection of Internet-based apps" that are built on the conceptual and technological underpinning of web 2.0. (Kaplan & Haenlein, 2010). Students can use mobile devices and social media to access course materials and related resources as well as to engage with colleagues and mentors. (Cavus & Ibrahim, 2008, 2009; Richardson & Lenarcic, 2008).

The opportunities provided by social media in terms of education can be categorised into two sections, jobs & research and second is digital learning.

- **Construction of Jobs & Research Opportunities:** Remote working and collaboration via mediating technology, rather than face-to-face, is not new (O'Leary et al., 2002), but it was formerly the province of a few who were physically far or chose a different lifestyle. Lockdowns triggered by COVID-19 quickly converted a large section of the population into remote employees. Social media or social networking sites are recognised as important online resources. They provide additional networking chances for job searchers by providing a variety of communication channels and personalised networking platforms. Furthermore, social networking sites are regarded as a significant medium for human resource experts to effectively and efficiently advertise jobs and gather information about job searchers (Nikolaou, 2014).

- **Digital Learning & Online Education:** Social media can be useful for any academic institution. (Greenhow, 2011a, 2011b). Researches show that almost 90% of the school going students consistently use internet out of which at least 75% [population is teenagers using social online networking sites for digital learning (DeBell & Chapman, 2006; Lenhart, Arafeh, & Smith, 2008; Lenhart, Madden, & Hitlin, 2005). This number has only grown in recent years. An older survey done by the researchers in three different US universities confirmed that appropriate use of social media can result in creation of new opportunities for the learners (Gikas & Grant, 2013). According to a literature survey done by (Liu et al., 2009), it was found that even back in 2009, blogs, podcasts were some of the most commonly used social networking applications. At the same time (Hovorka and Rees, 2009) investigated the application of several social media platforms in information systems courses.

Incorporating social media into classes may not only make them more interesting and even enjoyable, but it may also teach students vital and widespread professional skills such as communication, cooperation, community, convergence, and creativity (Friedman, Linda & Friedman, Hershey, 2013). The figure 6 demonstrates how social media is being used for various purposes in education. Teaching and learning won't be anymore associated with the physical presence of the teacher or the student. They can be taken up online like broadcasting, using a Facebook page for updates and alerts.

Social media has the potential to democratise education and improve the participation of all parties involved in the education of young Indians. It also has the potential to increase job opportunities and research in the country. It has already rocked the entertainment, political, industrial, and professional worlds; now it may be fully utilised for the benefit of our children, our future. This is one of the most practical ways to increase the accessibility and affordability of digital education. In the post-pandemic world, no realistic discussion of digital education can avoid including social media. Social media and digital education are here to stay, and innovations will continue to connect the two to deliver greater results in 2021 and beyond (Shashank Pandey, 2021).

Figure 6. Application of social media in Education

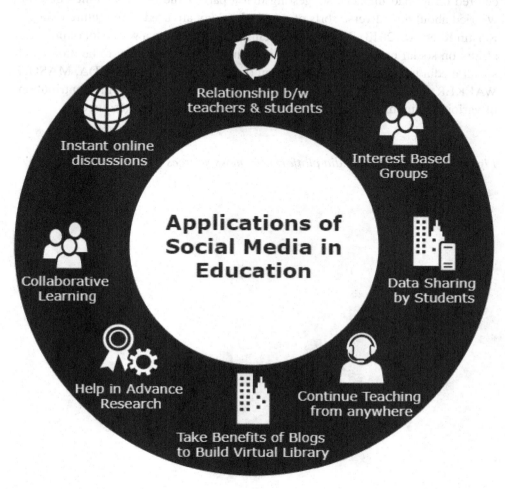

News and Media Through Social Media

Information

The social media feed is made of a combination of personal and public postings, and information is intertwined with all varieties of activities. What humans are exposed to is influenced in part by the behaviour of their fellow networkers (Annika Bergström & Maria Jervelycke Belfrage, 2018).Possibly the most distinguished function of information intake nowadays is the sheer quantity of facts that customers are exposed to. Using nanotechnology as an example, a study was carried out that studied tweets from Twitter and discovered that a few 41% of the discourse about nanotechnology centred on its bad impacts, suggesting that a part of the general public could be worried about how diverse sorts of nanotechnology are used in the future (Runge, Kristin K. et. Al., 2013). Most human beings are exposed to a whole lot of political affairs on social media. Younger human beings have a tendency to be more avid social media information customers than their elders (NAMI SUMIDA, MASON WALKER, AND AMY MITCHELL, 2019). The figure 7 shows the contribution of various social media applications and platforms used as news sources.

Figure 7. Use of social media platforms as news sources (in % age)

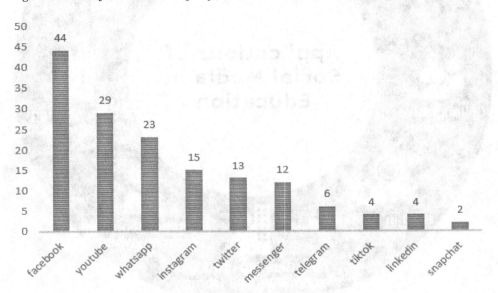

Infodemic of Misinformation and Cybercrime

In the course of the Covid19 pandemic, most universities had to switch to "emergency online learning". At the same time, scientists were looking for ways to combat "infodemia," a wave of misinformation that is spreading around the world, affecting social media and political life, and undermining efforts to cope with the pandemic (Christian Scheibenzuber, Sarah Hofer, Nicolae Nistor, 2021). Social networks like Facebook and Twitter have contributed significantly to the spread of rumors, conspiracy theories, hatred, xenophobia, racism and prejudice. In the news, researchers around the world have made significant efforts to create and share research articles, models, and datasets on COVID19. (Mohamed Seghir Hadj Ameur, Hassina Aliane, 2021) introduced an "AraCOVID19MFH", a COVID19 fake news and hate speech detection record in Arabic with manual annotations and multiple tags. The remedies and dangers it offers have inundated almost every country (Gupta, A, 2022).

As registrations of new covid cases reported by all countries began to rise, an avalanche of fake news began to fill all major social media applications, particularly Facebook, WhatsApp, and Twitter. COVID19 was checked for facts and this Corpus was shared with the community. This resulted in 1,500 tweets with 1,274 false claims and 226 partially false claims. In addition, many researchers have found that false claims spread faster than partially false claims (Sahoo, S. R., & Gupta, B. B. 2020, 2021).

In times of crisis, cybersecurity is vital. Figure 8 shows the security level of various social media applications (Zhang & Gupta, 2018).

Figure 8. Security level of various social media applications
Source: Zhang & Gupta, 2018

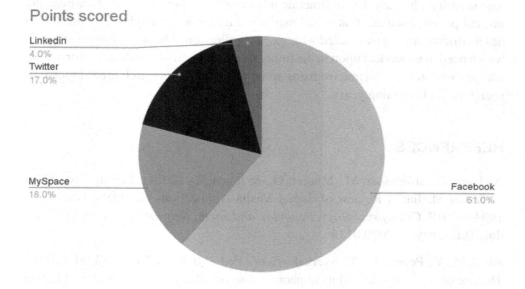

Since then, there has been an increase in incidents warning of phishing emails with attachments and links everywhere. Children are easy prey for cyber criminals as they often fail to differentiate between the real and the virtual world. Thus, a there is a need of proper education for operating social media. (UN tackles 'infodemic' of misinformation and cybercrime in COVID-19 crisis, 2020).

CONCLUSION

In today's era, social media plays a very important role in the daily life of almost every individual. The global digital growth from July 2020 to July 2021 has increased in huge numbers. The total number of unique mobile phone users has increased by 117 million, the number of internet users has increased by 257 million, and the increase in both has resulted in a boom increase in active social media users. It has increased by 520 million! The COVID-19 crisis has given rise to the use of digital media for educational as well as corporate purposes. The authors have studied the impact of social media on digitalization. The authors have also been briefed about various applications of social media in different sections of society. The present paper also mentions the use cases studied by various researchers from across the world. Covid-19, being a contagious disease, has given a boost to online or cashless transactions by the means of net banking, UPI, etc. Keeping all the above factors in mind, the authors also came across the drawbacks of the same in the form of data security, phishing, frauds, unethical hacking and other practices. However, the present paper concludes that social media is a major need in today's world. It also has its disadvantages associated with major applications like fake news, fraud, etc., which need to be worked upon in the future. Identification of fraudulent information and prevention of Infodemic remains some of the major research areas in term of social media in coming years.

REFERENCES

Aichner, T., Grünfelder, M., Maurer, O., & Jegeni, D. (2021). Twenty-Five Years of Social Media: A Review of Social Media Applications and Definitions from 1994 to 2019. *Cyberpsychology, Behavior, and Social Networking, 24*(4), 215–222. doi:10.1089/cyber.2020.0134

Ali Taha, V., Pencarelli, T., Škerháková, V., Fedorko, R., & Košíková, M. (2021). The use of social media and its impact on shopping behavior of Slovak and Italian consumers during COVID-19 pandemic. *Sustainability, 13*(4), 1710. https://doi.org/10.3390/su13041710

An Integrated Marketing Communications Perspective on Social Media Metrics. (n.d.). Available online: https://papers.ssrn.com/sol3/papers.cfm?abstract_id=2280132

Ansari, J. A. N., & Khan, N. A. (2020). Exploring the role of social media in collaborative learning the new domain of learning. *Smart Learn. Environ, 7,* 9. doi:10.1186/s40561-020-00118-7

Ballesteros C. (2019). *El índice de engagement en redes sociales, una medición emergente en la comunicación académica y organizacional.* Academic Press.

Bankov, B. (2019). *The Impact of Social Media on Video Game Communities and the Gaming Industry.* Academic Press.

Beaudoin & Hong. (2021). Emotions in the time of coronavirus: Antecedents of digital and social media use among Millennials. *Computers in Human Behavior, 123.* doi:10.1016/j.chb.2021.106876

Bergström, A., & Jervelycke Belfrage, M. (2018). News in Social Media. *Digital Journalism, 6*(5), 583–598. doi:10.1080/21670811.2018.1423625

Bouarara, H. A. (2021). Recurrent Neural Network (RNN) to Analyse Mental Behaviour in Social Media. *International Journal of Software Science and Computational Intelligence, 13*(3), 1–11.

Bureau, O. (2021, May 27). *Covid-19 pandemic fuelled digital payments modes: RBI annual report.* @businessline. https://www.thehindubusinessline.com/money-and-banking/covid-19-pandemic-fuelled-digital-payments-modes-rbi-annual-report/article34657571.ece

Cavus, N., & Ibrahim, D. (2008). *A mobile tool for learning English words.* Retrieved from http://libezproxy.open.ac.uk/login?url=http://search.ebscohost.com/login.aspx?direct=true&db=eric&AN=ED504283&site=ehost-live&scope=site

Cavus, N., & Ibrahim, D. (2009). M-learning: An experiment in using SMS to support learning new English language words. *British Journal of Educational Technology, 40*(1), 78–91.

Chaudhary, P., Gupta, B. B., & Yamaguchi, S. (2016, October). XSS detection with automatic view isolation on online social network. In *2016 IEEE 5th Global Conference on Consumer Electronics* (pp. 1-5). IEEE.

Chen, T. Y., Chen, Y. M., & Tsai, M. C. (2020). A Status Property Classifier of Social Media User's Personality for Customer-Oriented Intelligent Marketing Systems: Intelligent-Based Marketing Activities. *International Journal on Semantic Web and Information Systems, 16*(1), 25–46.

Chu, F. (2021, February 10). *Social Commerce is leading the future of ecommerce.* Digital Commerce 360. https://www.digitalcommerce360.com/2021/02/10/social-commerce-is-leading-the-future-of-ecommerce/

Cinelli & Quattrociocchi. (2020). The COVID-19 social media infodemic. *Sci Rep, 10*, 16598. doi:10.1038/s41598-020-73510-5

David, C. (2011). *How Traditional Entertainment Can Use Social Media.* GigaOm. Retrieved 2011-06-19. https://gigaom.com/2011/05/10/how-traditional-entertainment-can-use-social-media/

De', R., Pandey, N., & Pal, A. (2020). Impact of digital surge during Covid-19 pandemic: A viewpoint on research and practice. *International Journal of Information Management.* doi:10.1016/j.ijinfomgt.2020.102171

DeBell, M., & Chapman, C. (2006). *Computer and internet use by students in 2003.* Statistical analysis report. NCES 2006-065. National Center for education statistics.

Friedman, L., & Friedman, H. (2013). Using Social Media Technologies to Enhance Online Learning. *Journal of Educators Online., 10.* Advance online publication. doi:10.9743/JEO.2013.1.5

Fullerton, N. (2020). *Instagram vs. Reality: The Pandemic's Impact on Social Media and Mental Health.* https://www.pennmedicine.org/news/news-blog/2021/april/instagram-vs-reality-the-pandemics-impact-on-social-media-and-mental-health

Gikas, J., & Grant, M. M. (2013). Mobile computing devices in higher education: Student perspectives on learning with cellphones, smartphones & social media. *Internet and Higher Education Mobile, 19,* 18–26. doi:10.1016/j.iheduc.2013.06.002

Greenhow, C. (2011a). Online social networks and learning. *On the Horizon, 19*(1), 4–12.

Greenhow, C. (2011b). Youth, learning, and social media. *Journal of Educational Computing Research, 45*(2), 139–146. https://doi.org/10.2190/EC.45.2.a

Gupta, A. (2022). An Exploratory Analysis on the Unfold of Fake News During COVID-19 Pandemic. In *Smart Systems: Innovations in Computing* (pp. 259–272). Springer Singapore.

Gupta, S., & Gupta, B. B. (2017). Detection, avoidance, and attack pattern mechanisms in modern web application vulnerabilities: Present and future challenges. *International Journal of Cloud Applications and Computing, 7*(3), 1–43.

Hadj Ameur, M. S., & Aliane, H. (2021). Aracovid19-MFH: Arabic covid-19 multi-label fake news & hate speech detection dataset. *Procedia Computer Science, 189,* 232–241. https://doi.org/10.1016/j.procs.2021.05.086

Hancu-Budui, A., Zorio-Grima, A., & Blanco-Vega, J. (2020). Audit Institutions in the European Union: Public Service Promotion, Environmental Engagement and COVID Crisis Communication through Social Media. *Sustainability, 2020*(12), 9816.

Hovorka, D., & Rees, M. J. (2009). Active collaboration learning environments: The class of Web 2.0. *20th Australasian Conference on Information Systems: ACIS 2009.*

It's Curtains for Blockbuster Stores. (2013, Nov. 13). *ABC News.*

Järvinen, A. (2009). Game Design for Social Networks. *Proceedings of the 2009 ACM SIGGRAPH Symposium on Video Games - Sandbox '09.* doi:10.1145/1581073.1581088

Kaplan & Haenlein. (2010). Users of the world, unite! The challenges and opportunities of social media. *Business Horizons, 53*(1), 61. doi:10.1016/j.bushor.2009.09.003

Kaplan, A. M., & Haenlein, M. (2010). Users of the world, unite! The challenges and opportunities of social media. *Business Horizons, 53*(1), 59–68.

Kemp, S. (2020, January 30). *Digital 2020: 3.8 billion people use social media.* We Are Social. https://wearesocial.com/blog/2020/01/digital-2020-3-8-billion-people-use-social-media

Kietzmann, J. H., & Kristopher, H. (2021, May-June). Social media? Get serious! Understanding the functional building blocks of social media. *Business Horizons, 54*(3), 241–251. doi:10.1016/j.bushor.2011.01.005

Kirkpatrick, D. (2011). *The Facebook effect: The real inside story of Mark Zuckerberg and the world's fastest-growing company.* Academic Press.

Korenkova, M., Maros, M., Levicky, M., & Fila, M. (2020). Consumer Perception of Modern and Traditional Forms of Advertising. *Sustainability, 2020*(12), 9996.

Lenhart, A., Arafeh, S., & Smith, A. (2008). *Writing, technology and teens.* Pew Internet & American Life Project.

Lenhart, A., Madden, M., & Hitlin, P. (2005). *Teens and technology.* Washington, DC: Pew Charitable Trusts.

Liu, M., Kalk, D., Kinney, L., & Orr, G. (2009). Web 2.0 and its use in higher education: A review of literature. *World Conference on E-learning in Corporate, Government, Healthcare, and Higher Education (ELEARN).*

Mangan, T. (2020, September 6). *5 Social Media Marketing Strategies For Video Games* [web log]. http://blog.hellosocial.com.au/blog/5-social-media-marketing-strategies-for-video-games

Market Research Reports - Welcome. (n.d.). https://www.researchandmarkets.com/reports/5013565/impact-of-covid-19-on-the-video-conferencing?utm_source=dynamic&utm_medium=BW&utm_code=bpftq7&utm_campaign=1379168%2B-%2BImpact%2Bof%2BCOVID-19%2Bon%2Bthe%2BVideo%2BConferencing%2BMarket%2C%2B2020&utm_exec=joca220bwd

Mendoza, M., Poblete, B., & Castillo, C. (2010). Twitter under crisis: Can we trust what we RT? *Proceedings of the first workshop on social media analytics* 71–79.

Ngak, C. (2011, July 6). *Then and now: A history of social networking sites.* CBS News. https://www.cbsnews.com/pictures/then-and-now-a-history-of-social-networking-sites/

Nisa, Z. U. (2021, January 9). *The role of Social Media in Education: 2021.* ITSABUZAR. https://itsabuzar.net/role-of-social-media-in-education/

Noor, S., Guo, Y., Shah, S. H. H., Nawaz, M. S., & Butt, A. S. (2020). Research synthesis and thematic analysis of twitter through bibliometric analysis. *International Journal on Semantic Web and Information Systems*, *16*(3), 88–109.

ObarJ. A.WildmanS. (n.d.). Social media definition and the governance challenge: An introduction to the special issue. *Telecommunications Policy*, 745–750. doi:10.1016/j.telpol.2015.07.014

Ordorica, S. (2021, August 30). *Council post: Why your business needs a multilingual social media presence.* Forbes. https://www.forbes.com/sites/forbesbusinesscouncil/2021/08/30/why-your-business-needs-a-multilingual-social-media-presence/?sh=53aceeac27f6

Organization, W. H. (2020). *Director-general's remarks at the media briefing on 2019 novel Coronavirus on 8 February 2020.* https://www.who.int/dg/speeches/detail/director-general-s-remarks-at-the-media-briefing-on-2019-novel-coronavirus---8-february-2020

Perez, S. (2020). Video conferencing apps saw a record 62m downloads during one week in March. *Tech Crunch.* https://techcrunch.com/2020/03/30/videoconferencing-apps-saw-a-record-62m-downloads-during-one-week-in-march/

Pérez-Escoda, A., Jiménez-Narros, C., Perlado-Lamo-de-Espinosa, M., & Pedrero-Esteban, L. M. (2020). Social Networks' Engagement During the COVID-19 Pandemic in Spain: Health Media vs. Healthcare Professionals. *International Journal of Environmental Research and Public Health*, *17*(14), 5261. https://doi.org/10.3390/ijerph17145261

Pérez-Soler, S. (2017). *Periodismo y Redes Sociales*. Claves Para la Gestión de Contenidos Digitales. Editorial UOC.

Piplani, S. (2020, April 13). *Is Online Gaming The New Social Media?* [web log]. https://blog.synclarity.in/marketing/is-online-gaming-the-new-social-media

PricewaterhouseCoopers. (n.d.). *Impact of the COVID-19 outbreak on digital payments*. PwC. https://www.pwc.in/consulting/financial-services/fintech/dp/impact-of-the-covid-19-outbreak-on-digital-payments.html

Richardson, J., & Lenarcic, J. (2008). Text Messaging as a Catalyst for Mobile Student Administration: The "Trigger" *Experience. International Journal of Emerging Technologies & Society*, *6*(2), 140–155.

Runge, K. K., & Yeo, S. K. (2013). Tweeting nano: How public discourses about nanotechnology develop in social media environments. *Journal of Nanoparticle Research*, *15*(1), 1381.

Sahoo, S. R., & Gupta, B. B. (2020). Classification of spammer and nonspammer content in online social network using genetic algorithm-based feature selection. *Enterprise Information Systems*, *14*(5), 710–736.

Sahoo, S. R., & Gupta, B. B. (2021). Multiple features based approach for automatic fake news detection on social networks using deep learning. *Applied Soft Computing*, *100*, 106983.

Scheibenzuber, C., Hofer, S., & Nistor, N. (2021). Designing for fake news literacy training: A problem-based undergraduate online-course. *Computers in Human Behavior*, *121*, 106796. https://doi.org/10.1016/j.chb.2021.106796

Scheibenzuber, C., Hofer, S., & Nistor, N. (2021). Designing for fake news literacy training: A problem-based undergraduate online-course. *Computers in Human Behavior*, *121*, 106796. https://doi.org/10.1016/j.chb.2021.106796

Selwyn, N. (2012). Making sense of young people, education and digital technology: The role of sociological theory. *Oxford Review of Education*, *38*(1), 81–96.

Shahi, G. K., Dirkson, A., & Majchrzak, T. A. (2021). An exploratory study of covid-19 misinformation on Twitter. *Online Social Networks and Media*, *22*, 100104. doi:10.1016/j.osnem.2020.100104

Sharma, Y., Bhargava, R., & Tadikonda, B. V. (2021). Named Entity Recognition for Code Mixed Social Media Sentences. *International Journal of Software Science and Computational Intelligence*, *13*(2), 23–36.

Social Media: What Countries Use It Most & What Are They Using? (2019, January 31). *Digital Marketing Institute*. https://digitalmarketinginstitute.com/blog/social-media-what-countries-use-it-most-and-what-are-they-using

Starbird, K., Maddock, J., Orand, M., Achterman, P. & Mason, R. M. (2014). Rumors, false flags, and digital vigilantes: Misinformation on twitter after the 2013 Boston marathon bombing. *IConference 2014 Proceedings*.

Stock Comparison: Compare DISH Network Corporation (DISH) to Other Stocks. (2017, Mar. 13). NASDAQ.com.

Sumida, N., Walker, M., & Mitchell, A. (2019, December 31). *The role of social media in news*. Pew Research Center's Journalism Project. https://www.pewresearch.org/journalism/2019/04/23/the-role-of-social-media-in-news/

Técnica, S. (2020, February 29). *Coronavirus. Por Qué La comunicación tradicional no sirve*. Inicio - Asociación Nacional de Informadores de la Salud. http://www.anisalud.com/index.php?option=com_content&view=article&id=5741

The Law Commission. (2018). Abusive and Offensive Online Communications: A Scoping Report. *WHO Situation Report 13* https://www.who.int/docs/default-source/coronaviruse/situation-reports/20200202-sitrep-13-ncov-v3.pdf?sfvrsn=195f4010_6

Times of India Blog. (2021, February 5). https://timesofindia.indiatimes.com/blogs/voices/outlook-for-2021-the-evolution-of-social-media-and-the-role-it-can-play-in-the-future-of-education/

Tuten, T. L., & Solomon, M. R. (2018). *Social media marketing*. Sage.

United Nations. (n.d.). *Un tackles 'infodemic' of misinformation and cybercrime in covid-19 crisis*. Author.

United Nations. (n.d.). https://www.un.org/en/un-coronavirus-communications-team/un-tackling-%E2%80%98infodemic%E2%80%99-misinformation-and-cybercrime-covid-19

Wang, H., Li, Z., Li, Y., Gupta, B. B., & Choi, C. (2020). Visual saliency guided complex image retrieval. *Pattern Recognition Letters*, *130*, 64–72.

ways to use social media for Education. (2021, March 31). *Sprout Social*. https://sproutsocial.com/insights/social-media-for-education/

Wolter L.-C., Chan-Olmsted S., Altobelli C.F. (2017). *Understanding video engagement on global service networks—The case of Twitter users on mobile platforms*. Dienstleistungen 4.0.

YouTube TV Gets Ready to Take on Cable. (2017, Mar. 8). *KTLA*.

Zarocostas, J. (2020). How to fight an infodemic. *Lancet, 395*, 676.

Zhang, Z., & Gupta, B. B. (2018). Social media security and trustworthiness: Overview and new direction. *Future Generation Computer Systems, 86*, 914–925.

Zhang, Z., Jing, J., & Wang, X. (2020). A crowdsourcing method for online social networks security assessment based on human-centric computing. *Human-Centric Computing and Information Sciences, 10*, 1–19.

Chapter 5
Data Mining Approaches for Sentiment Analysis in Online Social Networks (OSNs)

Praneeth Gunti
National Institute of Technology, Kurukshetra, India

Brij B. Gupta
National Institute of Technology, Kurukshetra, India

Elhadj Benkhelifa
Staffordshire University, UK

ABSTRACT

IoT technology and the widespread usage of public networking platforms and apps also made it possible to use data mining in extracting useful perspectives from unorganised knowledge. In the age of big data, opinion mining may be applied as a valuable way in order to classify views into various sentiment and in general to determine the attitude of the population. Other methods to OSA have been established over the years in various datasets and evaluated in varying conditions. In this respect, this chapter highlights the scope of OMSA strategies and forms of implementing OMSA principles. Besides technological issues of OMSA, this chapter also outlined both technical problems regarding its production and non-technical issues regarding its use. There are obstacles for potential study.

DOI: 10.4018/978-1-7998-8413-2.ch005

INTRODUCTION

Nowadays, there is a massive volume of data coming in, and every day it rises. The rapid advances in data analytics technology have contributed to the production of big data (Addo-Tenkorang, 2016). Furthermore, extensive data has been rendered possible by technologies. People are technologically smart of wearable technology systems, networking devices, and Internet or social network apps. For instance, businesses are profiting from collecting sales data because of the growing amount of transactional data. Various networked sensors are installed in cell phones, smart energy metres, cars, and manufacturing robots. Breakthroughs of Internet technology and sensors have rendered the Internet of Things (IoT) feasible. With the advent of social networking and mobile phones, people can communicate to build an extensive digital archive. For example, Twitter has many users producing 175 million messages every day(Yasin, 2014). Correspondingly, the space used to hold one second of a Video capture is 2000 times greater than a simple document. Besides, International Data Company's information stated that the world produced around 14ZB of knowledge in 2014. By 2022, the volume of data we make is projected to hit 50ZB; nearly half of it will be textual data produced by social networking, such as Facebook, Twitter, and smartphone immediate communication applications like Facebook and Whatsapp. Five hundred million messages are being delivered each day, and 40 million are posted every day. About 4.3 billion updates and 5.75 billion likes are shared on Facebook every day. Information will begin to arrive regardless of the rise in emerging technology.

The unrestricted use of computational information and enormous exchange of information added significantly to big data analysis. Big data and market analytics apply to two parts: big data and analytics. Big Data is valuable because it is entirely beyond human capacity to store, maintain, and interpret it. Big data is distinguished by a large number, range, and velocity. Volume reflects the amount of information that uses a significant range of documents. For e.g., some instances are Wal-Mart generates data around 2.5 Petabytes of data, Tesco generates data of about 1.5 billion pieces of information each month, and Dell maintains information storage that can handle data around 1.5 million records a day. Knowledge is a significant source of variation (Davenport, 2013).

The origins may involve sensors, social media platforms, online applications, smartphones, and other portable devices. The data may be in either structured data such as SQL or unstructured such as XML. Velocity shows how knowledge is readily gathered and provided through various channels. The data may be produced occasional, regular, and in real-time. Analytics relates to a firm's willingness to utilise mathematics, finance, calculus, chance, and optimisation to help them. Companies in most industries are highly data-oriented and gather data from a broad range of sources (Misra, 2014). Big data poses numerous problems for the enterprise because of its sophistication. First, you'll need to have data storage with a massive amount of data. Another need is to develop methods to work with a large volume of input data in many ways (Batty, 2014). It is critical to design scalable data storage to collect and retrieve practical knowledge with performance. High-speed networking can use less power while transmitting the results. The second task is to disseminate knowledge through multiple networks for collecting vast volumes of data from various databases in a fair amount of time. To address this problem, cloud infrastructure programming is employed. Besides all the concerns we already listed, another concern is privacy, protection, and implementation. We usually rely on the views of others when making a decision. We depended on friends and family to send us positive or poor recommendations before the Internet. The Internet is a valuable platform to check for thoughts and experiences to complete the task. The number of opinions and feedback on the Web has significantly improved over the past five years, and they're quickly reachable to strangers on the site. Text mining and sentiment processing face difficulties like categorising documents with feedback or specifically opinionated messages, detecting the sentiments of the texts, and summarising the sentiment data. The purpose of this study is to:

- Find and coordinate details relevant to the production of sentiment methodology.
- Conversations on the challenges relating to the creation of sentiment methodology. These problems would be the focus of more study.

A Description in Text Mining and Analysis

In this era of big data, we might analyse to explain the significance of the data in a document, picture, or video format. Text mining is among the ancestors of text processing. Natural language processing utilises text mining methods to retrieve content from records. Text analytics, close to text mining, work with far broader information to retrieve and produce valuable non-trivial details and expertise. Text mining/analytics is first used for two reasons. The first aim is to survey the public's views about everything. Sentiment analysis involves a large volume of textual information to classify individuals' perceptions, feelings, opinions, and feelings. The second aim of web surveys is to determine people's opinions on an item, occurrence, individual, organisation, or subject. Text mining is a natural language processing activity that utilises an algorithmic strategy to differentiate popular viewpoints and categorise them into optimistic, harmful, or neutral contexts. The computing technologies of text mining/analytics have been expanded to several other fields; as well as the implementations are evolving with the expansion of big data.

Summary of the Mining and Sentiment Research Opinion

A perception corresponds to the personal responses to the current in the context. Sentiment analysis is often focused on the algorithmic. An opinion is a person's or group's impression of a specific issue. Also, like emotion research, opinion mining is based on machine algorithm. (Zaslavsky, 2013)(Qazi, 2017) argued that opinion might be divided into three major categories. The most common approach to test a commodity is daily opinion. Comparative views aid in confirming relationships between several separate individuals, and this is valuable for strategic intelligence. But there are missing scholarly studies on defining comparable sentences used for the contrast of different persons. There has been a notable introduction of viewpoint mining in the area of science. It will be used for company knowledge and e-learning problems. This is an excellent idea for expanding the popularity of online forums.

Sentiments involve emotions, beliefs, behaviours, perceptions, decisions, and feelings. This result was routinely collected through traditional scientific techniques (Quigley, 2007). She used the personal tone of describing her thoughts and emotions. However, the emotions may be evaluated in the machine learning techniques through a lexicon-based method. Recently, sentiment analysis has concentrated on various methods, including speech and video, rather than a study that focused on texts in unimodality. Text mining addressed many NLP subtasks, such as object retrieval aspect identification, subjectivity detection, defined object identification and sarcasm detection.

The key goal of sentiment analysis is to demonstrate people's thoughts regarding a good or service. It offers knowledge that is helpful for both consumers and suppliers. Both maker and consumers view summaries as more important than thorough criticism. Opinion research may be beneficial on both sides of reaching a legal judgement. At this period, the effect these scientific resources have on humans remains enigmatic. There has been an insistence on methods at the detriment of new techniques. This work intends to explore the role of the "human factor" in emotion analysis and opinion mining. To meet our goal, we will analyse the related theories that have examined all methods of learning.

This chapter has a variety of valuable aspects. First, the critical subject of the chapter is to concentrate the research of perception mining and sentiment analysis on both technological and non-technical problems. The second is focusing on possible opportunities for study by searching for development areas of use. The paper contains details on various data databases that prospective scholars will use in perception mining and sentiment analysis experiments.

The remainder of the document is structured as described. The dissertation contains the analysis methods included in this article. Finally, we point out the effects of our analysis. The paper illustrates the most widely used dataset in literature. Later parts address various approaches of sentiment analysis and demonstrate their applicability. Finally, the research highlights the emerging transparent complexities of big data sentiment processing.

METHODOLOGY

The key aim of this chapter is to examine the sentiment analysis methods of text mining on implementations of individual text analysis. This research seeks to put forward results of applications in the community. The research in the analysis is a systematic literature examination. A systematic review is a systematic comparison of what has been achieved in the past. This "sharpen" form of research renders the systemic assessments distinct from the conventional review.

(Zhang, 2017) suggested a comprehensive multimedia networking site trinity method, designed the algorithm for an enhanced hybrid suggestion by combining interactive filters and content-based suggestions and created the CyVOD working prototype. Mobile multimedia DRM modes are added to the network, including offline and online. Managing digital ownership is accomplished by digital content encryption and secured access rights. In addition, security protocols are introduced that validate user identification to prevent unauthorised users from transmitting their digital content maliciously. Compared with the only content-driven approaches, the enhanced hybrid proposed methodology used in CyVOD has upgraded the performance.

The continuing violations of social networking protection entitle the organisations to protect the knowledge exchanged across the network. Any breach of security explicitly hinders the organisation's economic development (Zhang, 2018)(Gupta, 2018). The social network may be studied by analysing the actions of the person or collective of their consumers. Users of the Internet must be aware of the vulnerabilities to their personal and financial records.

(Al-Qurishi, 2018) offers an online social network protection system named SybilTrap. It's a semi-monitored graphic strategy, which uses a random step with absorbing states to spread valid labels via the social media network graph.

To allocate social users to evaluation tasks concerning the safety and confidence of online social networks reliably and efficiently (Zhang, 2020), the usage of situational knowledge and history data by evaluating user-defined role assign variables and their characteristics and user tasks is analysing. Therefore, a task allocation system for multitudes evaluation was established, and a task algorithm focused on human-centred computational abstraction was proposed by(Zhang, 2020).

RELATED WORKS

Our approach first reviews relevant literature on social networks, privacy, and trust management, then classifies the results into three main groups.

OSN Privacy and Security

Online social networks (OSNs) provide new ways of engagement and information exchange but simultaneously produce challenges such as copyright management, the use of audiovisual media, and the safeguarding of confidentiality via picture. Presently, commercial OSNs allow users to regulate access to shared data in a multiuser setting without adding advanced methods to safeguard data privacy. (Chaudhary, 2020) also proposed XSS detection techniques using automatic view isolation.In (Gupta, 2018) computational intelligence paradigms are brought into the areas of privacy and security for social media platforms.In light of these issues, the solution to secure data access in multiuser scenarios suggested by (Hongxin, 2012) is a logical description like an access control mechanism. Here on the idea of community-centric role-interaction based access control (CRiBAC), the study authors recommended using community-centric property-based access control (CPMAC) to improve collaboration in huge networking sites. A preliminary model has shown on Facebook to assess the viability of the concept. In addition, two real-life situations have demonstrated the application of the instance. Security and privacy in web applications(Gupta, 2016)(Gupta 2017), IoT devices (Tewari 2017) is very important and should be addressed so that the information and the transactional data is secured.

Additionally, OSNs confront a significant issue due to the violation of private rights as well as suppliers or illegal users. Issues about user privacy may be addressed using a P2P-OSN framework developed by (Raji, 2014) that consists of configuring privacy options across social activities and enabling adaptive methods for determining the status of shared information. To provide distribution of restricted access, this system connects the accessibility of distributed data on P2P-OSN. We created a transmission route method on the idea of prediction to keep material secure in social platforms. It is implemented and tested in the actual social network to verify the approach's efficiency and effectiveness. (Fogues, 2015)found that despite the immense growth in social media user populations over the last several years, the benefits currently provided by SNS platforms like Facebook and Twitter have been eclipsed by the risk of self data leakage and security breach. In their study, they identified all of the privacy risks, as well as the mechanisms needed to limit these risks. Big data, which is available on social networks, include personal details which may be gathered and used by other organisations for profit, according to Viejo Alexandre and others(Viejo,

2016). Current solutions primarily utilise access control measures to ensure personal and private data is secure but do not enable users to differentiate between sensitive and confidential data. Social networking providers may find existing methods to be impractical because of their participation. They offered a novel solution to deal with the issue caused by this shortcoming. A separate software module may be created to improve existing social media networks' privacy protection, which doesn't rely on the platform. This is an automated test for user-released sensitive data to find clearance mechanisms for it. For another thing, it is capable of reading customers' security credentials and utilise them to set content releasing proprietors' access rights, which means enabling the wide accessibility of sensitive material that needs privacy and security. The practical application of this technology to two worldwide social networks, Twitter and PatientsLikeMe, has been completed.

Social Networks--Trust Management

It is essential to trust the community of users on social networks. A strong OSN network requires a trust evaluation methodology that is accurate. A quantitative metric called group compactness was proposed by (De Meo, 2014), and others. This technique is optimised as well, with an algorithm built to do so. A suggested trust model and evaluation technique have been developed tailored for digital social media (Zhang, 2013). In addition, there is also a significant study on whether or not one can accurately anticipate another person's trustworthiness. Analysis of the trust configuration is the basis of the conventional method.

Nevertheless, according to sociological research and people's views, it is noticed that individuals from the same social group have the same tendencies of behaviour and preferences. Joint social network mining (JSNM) by combining diverse social networks has been developed by (Huang, 2013) to handle auxiliary information usage in trust assessment. Moreover, studies on the development of internet faith are complicated by the paucity of reliable data access. For this research, a technique based on ideas in sociology was suggested. Recently, Pasquale and his co-authors (De Meo, 2014)(Agreste, 2015) indicated that understanding group formation and the evolution of topological structure must be put into practice since both are key aspects of social structure development. But, the trust connection between users is critical for community development. They suggested a technique for quantifying group robustness and then assessed how similar and trustworthy members are.

Additionally, they came up with a new algorithm to significantly improve the technique. Using centrality measures to demonstrate the benefits of their new approach empirically, they introduced Prosper, Ciao, and Epinion as examples of social networks. Whether intentional or not, the overlapping between users has the potential to affect network structure in many ways. Once that's done, the big issue is to figure out how to establish or substantiate trustworthiness. To put it another way, when under such circumstances, trust implication has an essential function to play in socialising (smartphone) consumers. The results of a study done by(Chen, 2015) determined that in the case of social networking websites that include overlapping communities, trust relations may be inferred using fuzzy community. The process known as the Kappa-Fuzzy Trust is in operation. Additionally, researchers created a fuzzy implicit social network to evaluate the community system of a complicated system with degree kappa. Lastly, researchers conducted many simulation-based studies to assess the critical functionalities of Kappa-Fuzzy Trust.

MINING OF THE SOCIAL BIG DATA: FUNDAMENTAL PRINCIPLES

The data obtained by social networks is named social big data. These details are recognised by the wide number, the disturbance that produced (Spam) and the complex component (changing message every day) (Barbier, 2011). Users and their members may be identified by their network connections (due to ties here between clients), the non-structural existence (attributable to the duration of the posts needed by some micro-blogging, the occurrence of grammatical errors and others), as well as the absence of comprehensiveness(Tang, 2013). The features of social Big Data render them distinct from many other data to which existing simple data mining techniques can be implemented. For spinning the same kind of data, numerous approaches, strategies and procedures are required. We introduce social networking mining over the next segment; then, we address the perception mining-based analysis.

Social Network Mining

A novel, complex image recovery model driven by visual salinity is described by (Wang, 2020). Social media mining is the study and retrieval of valuable knowledge from social networking sites. There are six study problems from(Gundecha, 2012): group analysis or identification, opinion mining and sentiment analysis, suggestion, analysis of impact, dissemination or transmission of knowledge, and confidentiality. (Mukkamala, 2014) assumes that perhaps the Social Big Data is composed of two sections, social relationships and social information. The very first aspect of social networking is described by social networks, where nodes reflect consumers of social media and ties identify their relationships. The second aspect is the details shared on the platform. The social material is defined by linguistic transactions in media platforms (topics, keywords, sentiments expressed, etc.). (Tang, 2014) focuses the research on consumer info, social connections and media. (Tang, 2014)splits social network data analysis into three categories: Social networking mines centred on user details, like group identification, user identification and spam filtering, as well as the social networking processing, focused on interaction among humans such as link prediction, relationship's intensity estimation and relationship's estimate. We intend to merge two classifications on social network mining proposed by (Gundecha, 2012) and (Tang, 2014). The model matched the data well (Guellil, 2015).

Figure 1. The grouping of numerous research problems that have emerged as a consequence of social network mining

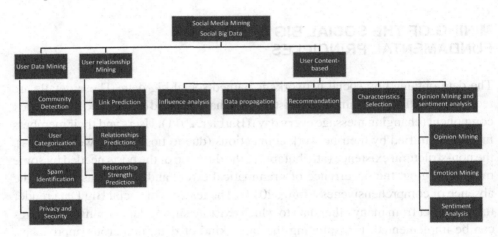

In Figure 1, data mining has been categorised into three groups, namely the extraction of users' data, interactions with users and information produced by clients. The four critical objectives for extracting user information are group discovery, categorisation of users, spam filtering and stability. The detection will be to pull out tacit categories. Users are categorised similarly to the same characteristics and habits. In spam identification, social media network consumers are also checked for the mailing lists they are subscribed to. Protection is described as the need to safeguard the belongings yourself. To predict the interactions among the connections between clients, three main testing problems are recognised; prediction of links, prognostication of connections and estimation of the intensity of partnerships. This connection prediction attempts to say client pairs that they can be linked. Relationship estimation aims to find the relations between the people. The estimation of the partnership intensity aims to find the importance of the relationship and determination of the interdependence between users(Tang, 2014). Five primary research issues to mining the content created by users include: The below was the objective study for the above: This research aimed to establish the ties between the people. There is an emphasis on how the knowledge can propagate across social networking. This is to suggest new links or acquaintances to customers. Feature collection seeks to classify the specific characteristics of social network data(Tang. 2012). Opinion mining and sentiment analysis is one approach to establish awareness of the unspoken emotions of people. Considering the exponential increase in knowledge sharing through social networking and the rich information on views, attitudes and thoughts, sentiment analysis is generating a lot of attention in the science world. We are going to discuss social network mining in the next segment.

Opinion Mining and Sentiment Research

Two related but separate study fields are perception mining and sentiment analysis. The dividing line between natural language processing, artificial intelligence and text mining has always been blurred and will begin to overlap. They can be achieved at three stages of discourse: text level, sentence level and feature level. To identify feelings shared by the writers in all sentences in a text, they use Microsoft Word. The first step is to decide the arbitrary sentence(Valakunde, 2013). Extraction of sentences or records in the first aspect stage addresses aspect level. As a result, the sentences are classified about certain features on specific dimensions. Over the following pages, we will be discussing the definition of subjectivity, element and object.

We recognised two patterns in connection with both the opinion mining and sentiment study through the literature research. On the other side, many studies have looked at this topic and reported mixed findings. Concerning these general aspects, this also researches emotion mining. We discuss three study fields of social network extraction.

1. **Opinion mining:** According to (Liu, 2012), opinion is a significant element that affects human behaviour. Opinion mining requires processing thoughts, perceptions, and assessments—the previous memory to a commodity, service, agency or individual. For starters, we should acknowledge the efficiency of standby time, display performance, etc. (Zhang, 2014) for the model mobile phone. As per(Rafea, 2013)(Shahheidari, 2013), opinion mining is a study field involving retrieving the prevailing bias of a source context. Based on the meanings and our various interpretations, three major practises are synonymous with opinion mining. This perspective needs to be modelled to allow it. The second aspect is to offer a potential opinion to help your proposal (the individual who expressed the opinion). For this study, we feel that it is

essential to examine the ambiguity of a text. This is accurate, and it includes truth and viewpoint.

2. **Emotion Mining:** Emotion is an emotional condition that causes psychological improvement. The emotion mining may be split into three groups based on the meaning. You can determine to the degree the document includes optimistic or harmful feelings. The second party explains text that involves feelings and text which don't. The third division reflects the kinds of feelings people have.

3. **Sentiment Analysis:** To assess the emotional and sentimental contents and distinguish them into good, neutral or negative. (Bhuta, 2014) analyses global contact focused on four stages: data acquisition, pre-processing, examination and recognition of valuable information.

Study works on sentiment analysis primarily take data through past projects or automated repository. A pre-treatment phase can involve several activities like sentence segmentation, lemmatisation, word spotting, POS tagging as well as N-gram analysis.

The bulk of academic research introduces the word "sentiment analysis" instead of "sentiment classification" to describe the third stage of the sentiment analysis method. (Zheng, 2019) provides an intimacy-based security approach that doesn't invade users' privacy in social networks. As a phase of that effort, we have used "classification." The crucial role in sentiment analysis, as per (Colace, 2013)(Karamibekr, 2012) (Zhang, 2019), is sentiment classification. Categorisation procedures may be achieved using three machine learning methods: controlled, unsupervised, or combination. A controlled technique uses a named sample to teach a sentiment classifier. Unsupervised techniques are using lexical and syntactic methods oriented. Hybrid methods utilise a mixture of two established precedents-based strategies. The information produced by sentiment analysis may be either specific or scientific. Awareness in public is among those who have researched the community studied. Technical expertise applies to the different methods that are being utilised.

Hybrid learning is focused on a sentiment vocabulary to help build an algorithm. Others use a predetermined database of trends for text categorisation like Alchemy API and Google prediction (Mukkamala, 2014)(Singh, 2013).

The majority of the work concerned with information transfer focuses on knowledge creation. Firstly, the writers have used a collection of distinct clusters in their work. The writers in the (Akaichi, 2013) describe a mixture of styles of functions. These works expose different techniques or creative forms of generating intelligence. We find only one report on information generation(Ngoc, 2014). This methodology retains a tally of both favourable and derogatory reviews on various sites. In (Sharma, 2021) for code mixed social media sentences a Named Entity Recognition is used.

METHODS

In this portion, we address typical approaches for conducting sentiment analysis. This method begins with target defining and finishes with successfully applying sentiment analysis (Shayaa, 2018). Big data is derived from single or several sources and then applies emotion analysis to the analysis findings. The subsequent move is to use unique opinion analysis techniques to uncover insight into this broad corpus's organisation. The general opinion review takes place in the manner in Figure 2. We then state how sentiment analysis is normally performed. First of all, the core method starts from the aggregation of the data from social network outlets. Note that the data gathered would make sense to the project. If the organisation needs to get their data, keywords would be "important to get data". Of course, the object of the sentiment analysis should be to decide the related terms relating to Singaporean culture. The next phase would be pre-processing the data to eliminate noise and unconnected information. The development of a sentiment analysis framework should accompany this. Machine learning approaches usually include unsupervised methods of testing. In addition, the developed sentiment framework is extended to proven data to explore the latest techniques in big data. Sentiment analysis systems are described in the subsequent sections of this chapter.

Figure 2. The sentiment analysis approach in general

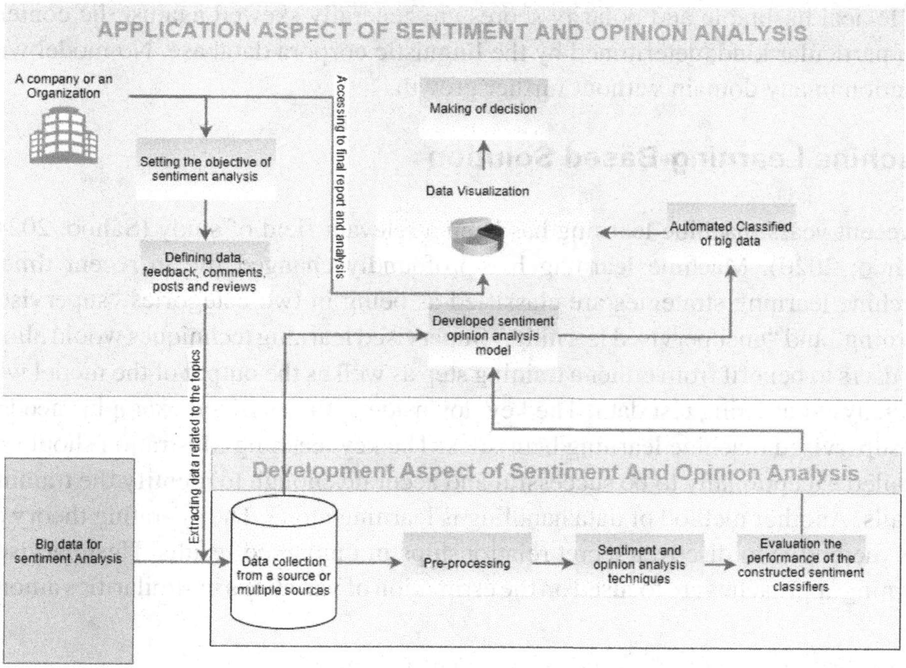

Keyword-Based Grouping

In this way, this website may distinguish between a positive and negative word like pleasant, joyful, pleased, miserable, unhappy, frightened, and uninterested. The biggest downside to keyword-based categorisation is the complexity of categorising nullified terms and polar words since the method relies heavily on surface elements. A popular shortcoming is that this method depends on apparent polarity. However, a post can sometimes convey a sense that is not clear polarity terms (Cambria, 2013).

Lexicon-Based Grouping

Lexicon-based methods generate collections of terms classified as positive or negative polarisation, with a polarity score given for each word. The lexicon is being used to approximate the general sentiment of a given statement or message. One noteworthy aspect of the system is that it may not require training samples. The lexicon-based approach is commonly utilised in traditional texts such as reviews, websites, and posts. The conventional mining methods cannot apply to social data because big data is derived from social networking platforms. The primary explanation why social networking networks impact adolescents is the unorganised format and complex form of expression. Even if this methodology overcomes other categorisation approaches, it still has potential for development. The postings of particular meanings confuse the feedback score calculation at the exact moment. The second downside is that the lexical hashtable and polarity scores are generally skewed against the content of a particular kind, determined by the linguistic corpora database. No model will function in any domain without further growth.

Machine Learning-Based Solution

In recent years machine learning has been a relevant field of study (Sahoo, 2021) (Sahoo, 2020). Machine learning has profoundly changed life in recent times. Machine learning strategies are classified as being in two categories "supervised learning" and "unsupervised learning." Supervised learning techniques would allow the users to benefit from either a training step as well as the output of the model will be analysed utilising test data. The key downside is the artificial examples needed for supervised machine learning heuristics. The key teaching illustration should be detailed exceptionally to be successful and accurate enough to identify the training details. Another method of data handling is learning alone. The operating theory of this method is to discover secret relationships in unmarked results. Unsupervised learning approaches are focused on the estimation of variations in similarities among data. For e.g., it determines the k-means wherein the correlation among the data is determined based on proximity measurements, including the Euclidean distance.

Algorithms for Machine Learning

There are several widely employed sentiment analysis techniques in machine learning.

Artificial Neural Network (ANN)

ANN is a statistical method for modelling the operations of the human brain (McCulloch, 1943). It is focused on an Artificial Dynamic Framework that is focused on some decentralised infrastructure. ANN utilises very tightly knit "artificial neurons" to handle vast volumes of data and display data (Grossi, 2007).(Bouarara, 2021) used RNN to analyse the Human mental state in the social platform, which got great results.

These organised structures may conform to a particular intent and form. There are numerous artificial neural networks used for different issues. Their implementation has also been found for linear problems (Boulesteix, 2012). The dilemma has too many facets, such as studying pattern recognition, modelling memory, and envisioning a complex structure. In certain instances, networks run in either a controlled or unmonitored manner. The guided learning will have either input and output. The device integrates the information into the computations to feed the results. In unsupervised testing, only feedback is given to the network, and the system is utilised to identify natural aggregation for a dataset irrespective of extrinsic restriction. The framework must be able to make choices about which functionality to implement to process the data correctly.

Random Forest

Random Forests is an analysis and categorisation system. In the latest times, there has been collective learning, a process in which multiple classifiers are employed, and aggregate results are collected. For the grouping, the most used classifications for trees are enhancing and packing. The latter suggested a more straightforward way to bag RF trees by introducing the layers with various forms of randomness. In language models, the classifier is used as a split criterion such that the total group prediction likelihood improves (DGI). Besides, it chooses the separating vector from a dynamically selected set of predictors. The approach uses bootstrap projection, and each assumption is eventually obtained by popular vote.

Help Vector Machine

Support vector machines were known to be general learning machines. Standard linear trigger methods are the ones that are learned. Through the usage of several essential features, polynomial algorithms may be utilised. Originally SVM was meant for the classification problem, but later its implementations were expanded into multiclass categorisation. There have been two known methods for multiclass SVM's. In this chapter, the genetic method applies the first application to manage the optimisation construct.

John Holland invented the genetic method in 1970. Marvin Minsky, in his book "The Society of Mind", introduced this theory in 1976. Genetic Algorithm (GA) has drawn broad scientific interest in recent years (Sivanandam, 2008). Improvement has gained attention in academic fields owing to its range of applications in computer science, institutional research, architecture, administration, and related fields. There are plenty of benefits of this strategy, including its content, reliability and its usefulness in economic situation.

Genetic Algorithms are adaptive optimisation methods. Their creation is focused on the tenets of evolution and natural selection. The scientific approach ranges from genetic modification to artificial intelligence-related technology. The emerging methodology is often able to discover how multiple associations occur in a piece of evidence.

Naive Bayes

Naïve Bayes (NB) classification model has often been seen in several supervised machine learning situations. It is known to be a data processing instrument. This is built on a basic rule of the likelihood for analysing data. The NB algorithm is commonly applicable to numeric results. This system is quick, easy to understand, and fast for categorisation. It takes small data to practise and then is be utilised to estimate the attributes for model evaluation.

Decision Tree

The decision tree (DT) categorisation was helpful in correctly classifying activities. This decision tree is straightforward to grasp—the hierarchical interpretation of classifiers developed by the decision tree. The model is created of vertices, sides, and connections. An extensive range of classifiers is used in different implementations. There have been problems that specific classifiers can't integrate all kinds of combinations of information, like noise as the tree gets more extensive and higher. Overfitting is a significant issue for machine learning algorithms. With the inclusion of details, the nature of an image gets blurred. One proposed workaround for this issue is to choose the random forest algorithm, which tends to identify patterns accurately.

K-Nearest Neighbour Algorithm (KNN)

KNN algorithm requires statistical simulation focused on supervised learning. It conducts a non-parametric process that compares all occurrences using computing methods, including Euclidean distance.

Combination Classifier

A graded voting system for prediction consolidates the group of models a fusion of several classifiers wherein their judgments. This categorisation approach is included in the group vote classification.

TRENDS IN OPINION MINING AND SENTIMENT RESEARCH

Opinion Mining and Sentiment Research is being utilised in several different sectors. LUCC has been incorporated in various fields such as hospitals, the finance industry, sports, governance, travel and tourism, and culture. Any of the latest implementation fields will be discussed in this portion.

Healthcare

(Korkontzelos, 2016) implemented the Emotion Analysis Functionality that improved the ADR Process. This experiment aims to see if sentiment analysis features will enable us to find ADR notes. There are several peer-reviewed ADR articles linked to drugs contained in this Twitter and Regular Power site. And sentiment analysis characteristics are introduced into the framework to determine whether it's successful in finding ADR mentions. The findings suggest that sentiment analysis methods can identify ADR and may serve as a drug safety method in the coming years.

(Rodrigues, 2016) used SentiHealth-Cancer to research the mindset of people with cancer. The key purpose of the research is to reveal the mental state of Brazilian people with cancer in the Portuguese language forum. In addition, the comments obtained from two cancer groups on Facebook are examined. The findings indicate this emotion analysis method exceeded other methods in all lab studies concerning cancer. In(Kim, 2016)looked at the pattern in representation and sentiment in various media outlets. This research embraced newspapers and Twitter as outlets of knowledge. The goal of the study is to review the impact of methods to lessen the

Ebola virus outbreak. The report reviewed about 16,189 news stories to about 1006 separate outlets, and 7,106,297 tweets were performed. In addition, the experiment examined how Twitter and media outlets acted differently on social issues. This shows that Twitter is a very short-lasting way of disseminating news and knowledge.

Financial Field

(Hai, 2015) neural network model integrates particular topics contributing to the firm's success. Both past performance set and attitude data sets are being utilised to compare the usefulness of the design. Geographical market prices of 18 firms through Yahoo Finance were derived, and the attitude of the customers, conversation relevant to the administration of the company and several unique incidents were derived from the chat forum. And three generates different price, individual sentiment and sentimental analysis and LDA- based system, JST- based approach and integral part sentiment. The expected stock price is nearly 2% higher while considering opinion. The accuracy of the market price forecast is about 10% higher than the conventional process.

However, (Luo and Meesad, 2016) have worked on forecasting stock market movements, but the research concentrated on identifying emotion in stock quotes to minimise potential socialisation bias. The above model includes the help vector machine with spatial characteristics. For the trial, 4,622 tweets were obtained through Topsy.com. The SVM existed stronger than most other machine learning algorithms such as Naïve Bayes and KNN. Besides, the design focused on SVM identification with combined function selection is more reliable for forecasting stock market change by utilising bootstrapping. The precision of reverse socialisation discrimination also strengthened with the addition of its linear SVM classifier.

(Chen, 2016) et al. studied the correlation between popular sentiments and the stock price reform of China. The repository for this analysis is on Weibo, a social networking forum. Originally, Jieba is often was using to define and describe the seven primary emotions in the language. Market perception is highly affected by volatility in stock markets in the region. The research shows that neural network models would forecast the stock price movements.

Politics

In research by (Ceron, 2014) participants were questioned what subjects could be used in the political debates on social networking sites. This analysis focuses on analysing the general opinion of the web visibility of numerous Italian lawmakers and representatives in the year 2011. The research employed the approach of categorising and studying tweets. Social networking networks is well capable of the forecasting election result. This research highlights the social network datagram analytics capacity to foresee what will happen in the future.

Alfaro et al. combined controlled and unmonitored machine learning for automated sentiment detection for forum topics in (Alfaro, 2016). The analysis used posts on workers and college weblogs to assess the structure. The test showed that SVM is greater than k-NN despite accuracy. However, it is possible to boost the accuracy by combining both SVM and k-NN. Centred on the work by (Alfaro, 2016), one may assume that it would apply to numerous government, regulatory and economic matters. For example, LuCC may be used to review feedback on a company's goods and facilities and connect it to its marketing activities.

Hospitality and Tourism

(Philander and Zhong, 2016) explored emotion analysis with relation to Las Vegas as a research sample. This review used Twitter to illustrate the use of sentiment classification as a cheap and quick method of collecting consumer concerns about merchandise and ventures. Using Twitter info, a sentiment lexicon model was built to translate tweets. Analysing social opinion data was used to assess the success of various businesses for various periods. There is a substantial degree of association between the sentiment score and other data points. The results demonstrate that Twitter includes broad, specific, and indirect viewpoint against people's perceptions against Las Vegas resources.

(Rodolfo, 2015)used text feedback intending to incorporate sentiment analysis across multiple methods. First, hotel bookings were obtained from the Travel Advisor platform. Then, evaluations were taken as optimistic or pessimistic through means of three sentiment analysers.

This may be analysed that both classifiers can be matched with the corresponding ranking from consumers. Next, the results of all three matrices are evaluated with actual scores and identified complicated methodologies which, centred on hybrid enhancement and recursive deep learning, were more robust in efficiency relative to the basic Naïve Bayesian process. This is helpful in transportation platforms because it offers a summarisation and consolidation of views of travellers and expert views on travel platforms.

Additional Domain Fields

(Chung and Zeng, 2016) studied the patterns on social networking sites on US immigration and border security by way of the device iMood. For the trial, about 909,0350 tweets were analysed based on 300,000 users' emotions. Given the evidence revealed by the study, there have been substantial shifts in sentiment and opinion. This will provide a framework for policy decisions in response to popular opinion.

(Liang, 2015) utilised a multidimensional opinion study on the purchases of smartphone devices to forecast remarks produced online. Comments relevant to productivity and improved quality of 80 iOS applications are collected from the app store. Thus, app purchases are fully guided by product and service efficiency and have a relatively good influence on their assessments.

(Kim, 2013) used social media to forecast a film's popularity. First, researchers looked at 200 separate video screeners from YouTube to decide how movies were rated for the experiment. Next, the marketing property details of the selected movies were retrieved from the International Movie Database (IMDB) and box office web pages, and these movies were divided into various groups. The findings show that mixing viewer feedback with marketing assets will affect box office success.

(Zhou, 2016) and co-workers used multi-grained sentiment analysis methodology in interpreting customers' actions in various regions of China. The analysis was carried out on consumers who own digital image, cell phone and tablet devices. The research also uncovered fascinating results, such as that American clients are honest and unabashed in voicing their beliefs. On the other hand, Chinese clients are considered to use subtle gestures much of the time. Furthermore, as American clients enjoyed item information and inner features rather than physical characteristics, the shoppers of China gave more importance to external than inner qualities.

Being informed and understanding the items are essential for shopping online. Facebook feedback of the brands Nokia and Zalando were experimentally measured. The research used the Bayesian consensus strategy to accumulate views from various locations to make a shared judgement. This would make buying online more straightforward and quicker. The writers have claimed that suppliers or dealers will profit from taking input and expectations from the purchasers.

CONCLUSION AND FUTURE RESEARCH DIRECTIONS

Some significant results may be concluded from the systematic review of reported OMSA publications from 2000 to 2016. More studies were posted on sentiment assessment since 2015. The value of sentiment analysis is a proper fit for the growth of online social networking use, like Facebook, forums, Tweets, etc. We already have connections to large volumes of excitable data and can be utilised to help grasp various topics. Moreover, 80% of data from social media can be intercepted for analytic use.

Monitoring tools will research a single 140-character message and give a sentiment value to a certain tweet. A sentiment score is structured to analyse if the tweet appears optimistic, negative, or neutral. Opinions on labels and other items are typically collected by data mining. In addition, information regarding goods and services is generally obtained by reading the documents. These figures suggest that people tend to convey their emotions rather than express their real opinions on social networking networks.

There is an array of studies into determining forms of emotion analysis. Much of the problems arise from utilising machines rather than people. Main practises in advertising also control the applications pursued by the finance, healthcare, and hospitality & tourism sectors. Further studies of machine translation and sentiment analysis in democratic governance are common and ongoing. Collective information may be valuable in issues surrounding management and strategy.

Twitter apps control the majority of the databases used in OMSA. This is also associated with the rise of opinion research in which much of the insight is collected from social networking such as Facebook, Instagram, Twitter, and Tumblr. Earlier, it has been seen as a knowledge spreading network instead of as a social media forum. This study forecasts that top consumers are actors and others who draw the masses media's attention. Twitter often has the purpose of being an investor sentiment tool. This has expanded the reach of hacking to individuals in politics and public service. This messaging could be able to raise market share, create buzz and sell more goods.

REFERENCES

Addo-Tenkorang, R., & Helo, P. T. (2016). Big data applications in operations/supply-chain management: A literature review. *Computers & Industrial Engineering*, *101*, 528–543. doi:10.1016/j.cie.2016.09.023

Agreste, S., De Meo, P., Ferrara, E., Piccolo, S., & Provetti, A. (2015). Trust networks: Topology, dynamics, and measurements. *IEEE Internet Computing*, *19*(6), 26–35.

Akaichi, J. (2013, September). Social networks' Facebook'statutes updates mining for sentiment classification. In *2013 International Conference on Social Computing* (pp. 886-891). IEEE.

Al-Qurishi, M., Rahman, S. M. M., Alamri, A., & Mostafa, M. A., Al-Rubaian, et al. (2018). SybilTrap: A graph-based semi-supervised Sybil defense scheme for online social networks. *Concurrency and Computation*, *30*(5), e4276.

Alfaro, C., Cano-Montero, J., Gómez, J., Moguerza, J. M., & Ortega, F. (2016). A multi-stage method for content classification and opinion mining on weblog comments. *Annals of Operations Research*, *236*(1), 197–213.

Barbier, G., & Liu, H. (2011). Data mining in social media. In *Social network data analytics* (pp. 327–352). Springer.

Barbosa, R. R. L., Sánchez-Alonso, S., & Sicilia-Urban, M. A. (2015). Evaluating hotels rating prediction based on sentiment analysis services. *Aslib Journal of Information Management*.

Batty, M., Axhausen, K. W., Giannotti, F., Pozdnoukhov, A., Bazzani, A., Wachowicz, M., Ouzounis, G., & Portugali, Y. (2012). Smart cities of the future. *The European Physical Journal. Special Topics, 214*(1), 481–518. doi:10.1140/epjst/e2012-01703-3

Bhuta, S., Doshi, A., Doshi, U., & Narvekar, M. (2014, February). A review of techniques for sentiment analysis Of Twitter data. In *2014 International conference on issues and challenges in intelligent computing techniques (ICICT)* (pp. 583-591). IEEE.

Bouarara, H. A. (2021). Recurrent Neural Network (RNN) to Analyse Mental Behaviour in Social Media. *International Journal of Software Science and Computational Intelligence, 13*(3), 1–11.

Boulesteix, A. L., Janitza, S., Kruppa, J., & König, I. R. (2012). Overview of random forest methodology and practical guidance with emphasis on computational biology and bioinformatics. *Wiley Interdisciplinary Reviews. Data Mining and Knowledge Discovery, 2*(6), 493–507.

Cambria, E., Schuller, B., Xia, Y., & Havasi, C. (2013). New avenues in opinion mining and sentiment analysis. *IEEE Intelligent Systems, 28*(2), 15–21.

Ceron, A., Curini, L., Iacus, S. M., & Porro, G. (2014). Every tweet counts? How sentiment analysis of social media can improve our knowledge of citizens' political preferences with an application to Italy and France. *New Media & Society, 16*(2), 340–358.

Chaudhary, P., Gupta, B. B., Choi, C., & Chui, K. T. (2020, December). XSSPro: XSS Attack Detection Proxy to Defend Social Networking Platforms. In *International Conference on Computational Data and Social Networks* (pp. 411-422). Springer.

Chen, S., Wang, G., & Jia, W. (2015). κ-FuzzyTrust: Efficient trust computation for large-scale mobile social networks using a fuzzy implicit social graph. *Information Sciences, 318*, 123–143.

Chen, W., Cai, Y., Lai, K., & Xie, H. (2016, January). A topic-based sentiment analysis model to predict stock market price movement using Weibo mood. In Web Intelligence (Vol. 14, No. 4, pp. 287-300). IOS Press.

Chung, W., & Zeng, D. (2016). Social-media-based public policy informatics: Sentiment and network analyses of US Immigration and border security. *Journal of the Association for Information Science and Technology*, *67*(7), 1588–1606.

Colace, F., De Santo, M., & Greco, L. (2013, September). A probabilistic approach to tweets' sentiment classification. In *2013 Humaine Association Conference on Affective Computing and Intelligent Interaction* (pp. 37-42). IEEE.

Davenport, T. H., & Dyché, J. (2013). Big data in big companies. *International Institute for Analytics*, *3*, 1–31.

De Meo, P., Ferrara, E., Rosaci, D., & Sarné, G. M. (2014). Trust and compactness in social network groups. *IEEE Transactions on Cybernetics*, *45*(2), 205–216.

Fogues, R., Such, J. M., Espinosa, A., & Garcia-Fornes, A. (2015). Open challenges in relationship-based privacy mechanisms for social network services. *International Journal of Human-Computer Interaction*, *31*(5), 350–370.

Grossi, E., & Buscema, M. (2007). Introduction to artificial neural networks. *European Journal of Gastroenterology & Hepatology*, *19*(12), 1046–1054.

Guellil, I., & Boukhalfa, K. (2015, April). Social big data mining: A survey focused on opinion mining and sentiments analysis. In *2015 12th international symposium on programming and systems (ISPS)* (pp. 1-10). IEEE.

Gundecha, P., & Liu, H. (2012). Mining social media: a brief introduction. *New directions in informatics, optimization, logistics, and production*, 1-17.

Gupta, B. B., Sangaiah, A. K., Nedjah, N., Yamaguchi, S., Zhang, Z., & Sheng, M. (2018). *Recent research in computational intelligence paradigms into security and privacy for online social networks (OSNs)*. Academic Press.

Gupta, S., & Gupta, B. B. (2016). JS-SAN: Defense mechanism for HTML5-based web applications against javascript code injection vulnerabilities. *Security and Communication Networks*, *9*(11), 1477–1495.

Gupta, S., & Gupta, B. B. (2017). Detection, avoidance, and attack pattern mechanisms in modern web application vulnerabilities: Present and future challenges. *International Journal of Cloud Applications and Computing*, *7*(3), 1–43.

Gupta, S., Gupta, B. B., & Chaudhary, P. (2018). Hunting for DOM-Based XSS vulnerabilities in mobile cloud-based online social network. *Future Generation Computer Systems*, *79*, 319–336. doi:10.1016/j.future.2017.05.038

Hu, H., Ahn, G. J., & Jorgensen, J. (2012). Multiparty access control for online social networks: Model and mechanisms. *IEEE Transactions on Knowledge and Data Engineering*, *25*(7), 1614–1627.

Huang, J., Nie, F., Huang, H., Tu, Y. C., & Lei, Y. (2013). Social trust prediction using heterogeneous networks. *ACM Transactions on Knowledge Discovery from Data*, *7*(4), 1–21.

Karamibekr, M., & Ghorbani, A. A. (2012, December). Sentiment analysis of social issues. In *2012 International Conference on Social Informatics* (pp. 215-221). IEEE.

Kim, D., Kim, D., Hwang, E., & Choi, H. G. (2013). A user opinion and metadata mining scheme for predicting box office performance of movies in the social network environment. *New Review of Hypermedia and Multimedia*, *19*(3-4), 259–272.

Kim, E. H. J., Jeong, Y. K., Kim, Y., Kang, K. Y., & Song, M. (2016). Topic-based content and sentiment analysis of Ebola virus on Twitter and in the news. *Journal of Information Science*, *42*(6), 763–781.

Korkontzelos, I., Nikfarjam, A., Shardlow, M., Sarker, A., Ananiadou, S., & Gonzalez, G. H. (2016). Analysis of the effect of sentiment analysis on extracting adverse drug reactions from tweets and forum posts. *Journal of Biomedical Informatics*, *62*, 148–158.

Li, J., & Meesad, P. (2016). Combining sentiment analysis with socialization bias in social networks for stock market trend prediction. *International Journal of Computational Intelligence and Applications*, *15*(01), 1650003.

Liang, T. P., Li, X., Yang, C. T., & Wang, M. (2015). What in consumer reviews affects the sales of mobile apps: A multifacet sentiment analysis approach. *International Journal of Electronic Commerce*, *20*(2), 236–260.

Liu, B. (2012). Sentiment analysis and opinion mining. *Synthesis Lectures on Human Language Technologies, 5*(1), 1-167.

McCulloch, W. S., & Pitts, W. (1943). A logical calculus of the ideas immanent in nervous activity. *The Bulletin of Mathematical Biophysics*, *5*(4), 115–133.

Misra, A., Sharma, A., Gulia, P., & Bana, A. (2014). Big data: Challenges and opportunities. *International Journal of Innovative Technology and Exploring Engineering*, *4*(2), 41–42.

Mukkamala, R. R., Hussain, A., & Vatrapu, R. (2014, September). Fuzzy-set based sentiment analysis of big social data. In *2014 IEEE 18th International Enterprise Distributed Object Computing Conference* (pp. 71-80). IEEE.

Ngoc, P. T., & Yoo, M. (2014, February). The lexicon-based sentiment analysis for fan page ranking in Facebook. In *The International Conference on Information Networking 2014 (ICOIN2014)* (pp. 444-448). IEEE.

Nguyen, T. H., Shirai, K., & Velcin, J. (2015). Sentiment analysis on social media for stock movement prediction. *Expert Systems with Applications, 42*(24), 9603–9611.

Philander, K., & Zhong, Y. (2016). Twitter sentiment analysis: Capturing sentiment from integrated resort tweets. *International Journal of Hospitality Management, 55*, 16–24.

Qazi, A., Tamjidyamcholo, A., Raj, R. G., Hardaker, G., & Standing, C. (2017). Assessing consumers' satisfaction and expectations through online opinions: Expectation and disconfirmation approach. *Computers in Human Behavior, 75*, 450–460. doi:10.1016/j.chb.2017.05.025

Quigley, M. (Ed.). (2007). *Encyclopedia of information ethics and security*. IGI global. doi:10.4018/978-1-59140-987-8

Rafea, A., & Mostafa, N. A. (2013, May). Topic extraction in social media. In *2013 International Conference on Collaboration Technologies and Systems (CTS)* (pp. 94-98). IEEE.

Raji, F., Jazi, M. D., & Miri, A. (2014). PESCA: A peer-to-peer social network architecture with privacy-enabled social communication and data availability. *IET Information Security, 9*(1), 73–80.

Rodrigues, R. G., das Dores, R. M., Camilo-Junior, C. G., & Rosa, T. C. (2016). SentiHealth-Cancer: A sentiment analysis tool to help detecting mood of patients in online social networks. *International Journal of Medical Informatics, 85*(1), 80–95.

Sahoo, S. R., & Gupta, B. B. (2020). Classification of spammer and nonspammer content in online social network using genetic algorithm-based feature selection. *Enterprise Information Systems, 14*(5), 710–736.

Sahoo, S. R., & Gupta, B. B. (2021). Multiple features based approach for automatic fake news detection on social networks using deep learning. *Applied Soft Computing, 100*, 106983.

Shahheidari, S., Dong, H., & Daud, M. N. R. B. (2013, July). Twitter sentiment mining: A multi domain analysis. In *2013 Seventh International Conference on Complex, Intelligent, and Software Intensive Systems* (pp. 144-149). IEEE.

Sharma, Y., Bhargava, R., & Tadikonda, B. V. (2021). Named Entity Recognition for Code Mixed Social Media Sentences. *International Journal of Software Science and Computational Intelligence*, *13*(2), 23–36.

Shayaa, S., Jaafar, N. I., Bahri, S., Sulaiman, A., Wai, P. S., Chung, Y. W., ... Al-Garadi, M. A. (2018). Sentiment analysis of big data: Methods, applications, and open challenges. *IEEE Access: Practical Innovations, Open Solutions*, *6*, 37807–37827.

Singh, V. K., Piryani, R., Uddin, A., & Waila, P. (2013, March). Sentiment analysis of movie reviews: A new feature-based heuristic for aspect-level sentiment classification. In *2013 International Mutli-Conference on Automation, Computing, Communication, Control and Compressed Sensing (iMac4s)* (pp. 712-717). IEEE.

Sivanandam, S. N., & Deepa, S. N. (2008). Genetic algorithms. In *Introduction to genetic algorithms* (pp. 15–37). Springer.

Tang, J., Chang, Y., & Liu, H. (2014). Mining social media with social theories: A survey. *SIGKDD Explorations*, *15*(2), 20–29.

Tang, J., Hu, X., & Liu, H. (2013). Social recommendation: A review. *Social Network Analysis and Mining*, *3*(4), 1113–1133.

Tang, J., & Liu, H. (2012, April). Feature selection with linked data in social media. In *Proceedings of the 2012 SIAM International Conference on Data Mining* (pp. 118-128). Society for Industrial and Applied Mathematics.

Tewari, A., & Gupta, B. B. (2017). A lightweight mutual authentication protocol based on elliptic curve cryptography for IoT devices. *International Journal of Advanced Intelligence Paradigms*, *9*(2-3), 111–121.

Valakunde, N. D., & Patwardhan, M. S. (2013, November). Multi-aspect and multi-class based document sentiment analysis of educational data catering accreditation process. In *2013 International Conference on Cloud & Ubiquitous Computing & Emerging Technologies* (pp. 188-192). IEEE.

Viejo, A., & Sánchez, D. (2016). Enforcing transparent access to private content in social networks by means of automatic sanitization. *Expert Systems with Applications*, *62*, 148–160.

Wang, H., Li, Z., Li, Y., Gupta, B. B., & Choi, C. (2020). Visual saliency guided complex image retrieval. *Pattern Recognition Letters*, *130*, 64–72.

Yasin, A., Ben-Asher, Y., & Mendelson, A. (2014, October). Deep-dive analysis of the data analytics workload in cloudsuite. In *2014 IEEE International Symposium on Workload Characterization (IISWC)* (pp. 202-211). IEEE. 10.1109/IISWC.2014.6983059

Zaslavsky, A., Perera, C., & Georgakopoulos, D. (2013). *Sensing as a service and big data*. arXiv preprint arXiv:1301.0159.

Zhang, L., & Liu, B. (2014). Aspect and entity extraction for opinion mining. In *Data mining and knowledge discovery for big data* (pp. 1–40). Springer.

Zhang, X. L., He, X. Y., Yu, F. M., Liu, L. X., Zhang, H. X., & Li, Z. L. (2019). Distributed and personalised social network privacy protection. *International Journal of High Performance Computing and Networking*, *13*(2), 153–163.

Zhang, Z., & Gupta, B. B. (2018). Social media security and trustworthiness: Overview and new direction. *Future Generation Computer Systems*, *86*, 914–925. doi:10.1016/j.future.2016.10.007

Zhang, Z., Jing, J., & Wang, X. (2020). A crowdsourcing method for online social networks security assessment based on human-centric computing. *Human-centric Computing and Information Sciences*, *10*, 1–19.

Zhang, Z., Sun, R., Zhao, C., Wang, J., Chang, C. K., & Gupta, B. B. (2017). CyVOD: A novel trinity multimedia social network scheme. *Multimedia Tools and Applications*, *76*(18), 18513–18529. doi:10.100711042-016-4162-z

Zhang, Z., & Wang, K. (2013). A trust model for multimedia social networks. *Social Network Analysis and Mining*, *3*(4), 969–979.

Zheng, H., He, J., Zhang, Y., Wu, J., & Ji, Z. (2019). A mathematical model for intimacy-based security protection in social network without violation of privacy. *International Journal of High Performance Computing and Networking*, *15*(3-4), 121–132.

Zhou, Q., Xia, R., & Zhang, C. (2016). Online shopping behavior study based on multi-granularity opinion mining: China versus America. *Cognitive Computation*, *8*(4), 587–602.

Chapter 6
Sentiment Analysis and Summarization of Facebook Posts on News Media

Yin-Chun Fung
Hong Kong Metropolitan University,
Hong Kong

Gary Hoi-Kit Cheung
Hong Kong Metropolitan University,
Hong Kong

Lap-Kei Lee
Hong Kong Metropolitan University,
Hong Kong

Chak-Him Tang
Hong Kong Metropolitan University,
Hong Kong

Kwok Tai Chui
Hong Kong Metropolitan University,
Hong Kong

Sze-Man Wong
Hong Kong Metropolitan University,
Hong Kong

ABSTRACT

Social media has become part of daily life in the modern world. News media companies (NMC) use social network sites including Facebook pages to let net users keep updated. Public expression is important to NMC for making valuable journals, but it is not cost-effective to collect millions of feedback by human effort, which can instead be automated by sentiment analysis. This chapter presents a mobile application called Facemarize that summarizes the contents of news media Facebook pages using sentiment analysis. The sentiment of user comments can be quickly analyzed and summarized with emotion detection. The sentiment analysis achieves an accuracy of over 80%. In a survey with 30 participants including journalists, journalism students, and journalism graduates, the application gets at least 4.9 marks (in a 7-point Likert scale) on the usefulness, ease of use, ease of learning, and satisfaction with a mean reliability score of 3.9 (out of 5), showing the effectiveness of the application.

DOI: 10.4018/978-1-7998-8413-2.ch006

1. INTRODUCTION

Social media life with mobile apps has belonged to most humans these days. Social media such as Facebook and Twitter facilitates people to get connected because of their popularity (Zúñiga et al., 2012). In April 2021, Facebook was ranked as the most popular social network site (SNS) worldwide (Statista, 2021). Facebook page (or simply page) is universally applied by many different types of organizations with their special purposes. Under the trend of page, every company branches a team to concentrate on maintaining pages for spreading its journals to and interacting with the public.

SNS has a pro-social effect that helps people get news and encourages individuals' social capital and improves their civic engagement and political participation (Zúñiga et al., 2012). News media companies (NMC) report their journals to the public through periodical publication and broadcasting. Meanwhile, NMC has applied page as a platform to reach their audience and make them connected. NMC shares posts with the abstract of their journals or discussion topics of social issues on their pages. It helps their followers to keep in touch with news, and brings opportunities for them to give opinions, express feelings, and start discussions. It is beneficial to reflect the views from different issues since both NMC and the public can listen to the voices from the public. Public expression also leads NMC to continue to make valuable journals. Pages may help to keep news values and then benefit NMC, the public, and the societies.

The NMC can listen to the voices of their page followers efficiently so that they have ideas on how they should report while keeping news values. News should be accurate and objective, and also be concise, clear, and balanced (Wahl-Jorgensen & Hanitzsch, 2009). With the help of summarized contents, NMC has their directions to report transferable journals for their audience.

Their followers' horizons can be broadened to see what social issues happen and different aspects in their communities exist. It encourages them to be humbler and more responsible for their societies. It is attractive for the public to care about issues from their neighborhood to the world. They will be more confident to share their thoughts, try to understand others, and think more for justice, without following the trend blindly or being selfish. Different classes of people and government officials are counted as individuals of the public. SNS use for news encourages individuals' willingness to join and participate in civic and political activities (Zúñiga et al., 2012).

The convenience of the Internet encourages people to express themselves. However, NMC or the public can't listen to too many voices and think objectively within a limited time. It is cost-ineffective to be performed humanly. There are many pages analytic tools that are useful for NMC pages to realize their followers. Even though, none of them is beneficial for keeping news values because they are mainly for profit-making and purely-popularity-boosting purposes. To keep news values and improve people's social participation in the limited technology environment these days, summarizing the contents of news-media-related pages with the use of keeping news values and the advantages of prosocial effect coupled with Natural Language Processing (NLP) becomes a trend (Abu-Salih et al., 2021).

NLP is an area of computer science used for research and application. It enables computers to understand and manipulate natural language text or speech. It is available to use NLP to process statements such as posts and comments from the user. Most NLP algorithms are machine learning algorithms. NLP automatically learns the rules by analyzing a set of examples, instead of applying a large set of hard-coding rules for the processing, and making a static inference (Cambridge & White, 2014). There are two sub-topics of NLP that are beneficial to summarizing the contents of news-media-related pages.

Sentiment analysis (SA) is one of the NLP techniques to detect the main aspects of the entity and to estimate how positive or negative the opinions are on average (sentiment) of the texts per aspect (Pavlopoulos, 2014). There are three main levels of sentiment analysis: document level, sentence level, and aspect level (Mir & Usman, 2015). There are several usages of SA on social media such as detecting cyberbullying (Zhao et al., 2016), finding malicious (Lippman et al., 2016), and detecting terrorism (Azizan & Aziz, 2017).

SA enables businesses to use less time and human resources for processing large data from the Internet. The process data usually is text and it includes the opinions on the social media website. Using sentiment analysis can reduce the resource spending on processing the data because SA can automatically process the data by the machine. Although the accuracy of using SA is less than human, it is better to process a large amount of data at the same time.

This book chapter presents an application called Facemarize that helps to summarize the contents of news-media-related pages with the advantages of prosocial effect coupled with Natural Language Processing (NLP). Section 2 will review the functionality and limitations of existing applications or software. Section 3 presents the details of our application and compares its functionality with those reviewed in Section 2. Section 4 gives the evaluation results, including the precision, recall, F-score, and accuracy of the sentiment analysis function and the findings from a user survey. Finally, Section 5 concludes the book chapter and suggests future works.

2. EXISTING APPLICATION

There are existing applications that provide summarization and sentiment analysis of social media platforms. They mainly provide quantified results on a post that are usually the index for chasing the ranking of popularity, but it is not the main responsibility of NMC. For understanding the public, qualified results are important. The sentimental status of the posts and comments can be sorted by entities generated from the Natural Language Understanding (NLU) API. NLU means stated above is "to accomplish human-like language processing". The choice of the word 'processing' is very deliberate and should not be replaced with 'understanding' (Liddy, 2001). It helps users to find out the expression of the public faster and easier. In this section, we will explore four of those applications.

Facebook Insights[1]. Facebook Insights enables any user to view the data from the fans page once they have over 30 fans. It provides the details about your post such as the post, comment, and engagement of the post. The engagement metrics can be shown on the overview or for each post, users can know what type of content is popular. Although Facebook Insights can access the post from Facebook, it is missing an analytic function to let the user quickly know this comment generally is explaining what emotion. However, users can only analyze their page. The service does not allow analyzing other Pages.

Sociograph.io[2]. It is third-party software that you can analyze any page for free. The software shows some data on a page like the comments given below the post. It also shows the average number of reactions, shares, and comments per post, the average is calculated by the software. The types of the post and the top posts also can show on the software. Those functions can be chosen in a time frame. The software does not provide a huge amount of the types of data to operate even the layout of showing the operation result is quite pretty. The data getting from Facebook is less and unsuitable for the NMC page. However, Sociograph.io does not include sentiment analysis. The interface of their application is more likely for the professional user because the interface has many alternative functions, and it is not suitable for rookie users.

Opinion Crawl[3]. It makes use of sentiment analysis to process the text. The user needs to input the data into the web page and the result will be shown. This website represents the result in both text and graphics. The service provides the user with a single word and the system will return the analysis result. Those functions are useful in daily life. But the page needs to input the data one by one, the data is also input by the user, and it is not related to Facebook.

Apache OpenNLP[4]. It is a Java library for NLP, developed under the Apache license. NLP, as a domain, deals with the interaction between computers and human language. The goal of OpenNLP is to enable computers to extract meaning from the natural language. It supports tasks such as tokenization, sentence segmentation, part-of-speech tagging, etc. The Apache OpenNLP will only return the sentiment of the post instead of regulating by the user.

3. DESIGN OF OUR APPLICATION

Under the trend of using mobile applications, we developed a mobile application called Facemarize that applied different NLP technologies discussed above into one new product with pre-defined aspects about social issues. Users need to use their Facebook account to log into Facebook and then they can select a Facebook Page for analysis (Fig. 1). Once a Page is selected, users can see all the posts of the page, sorted by time or popularity (Fig. 2).

When the user selected a post, the analysis result will be shown. The analyzing steps are provided by the IBM Watson Tone Analyzer that generates a score of the emotion of the post and comments. The first part of the summary shows the sentiment analysis of the post. User can't view the result in a larger word and the NLP API usually return the result in numeric, which is not very readable to the user. Therefore, three categories (positive, neutral, and negative) are shown to the users for representing the result. A pie chart showing the percentage of the result is also included for an easy and fast understanding of the result. The second part of the summary is the emotion mining of the post. Users can filter comments by the 'joy', 'anger', 'fear', and 'sad' emoticons. (Fig. 3).

Figure 1. Login with Facebook Account (left) and select a Facebook Page for analysis (right)

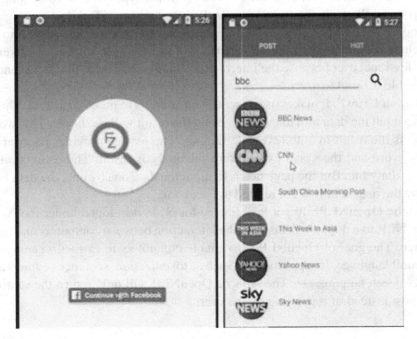

Figure 2. Selecting Post by time (left) or popularity (right)

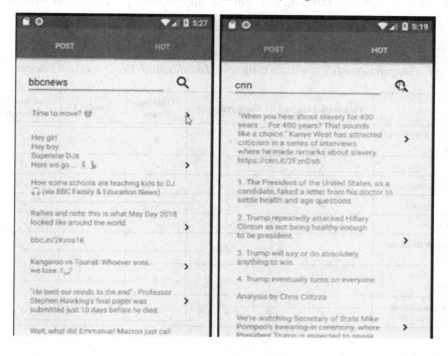

Figure 3. Analysis result of a post

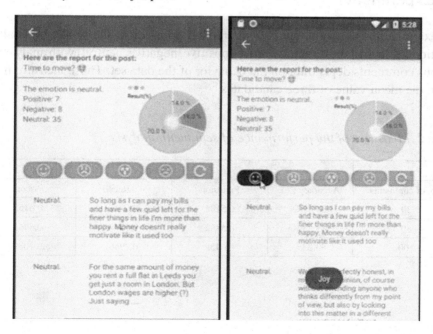

Here is a summary table on the functionality of our app compared with other social media analytical tools in the market.

Table 1. Comparison of different existing social media analytical tools and Facemarize

	Facebook Insights	Sociograph.io	Opinion Crawl	OpenNLP	Facemarize (Our App)
Access Facebook's data	✓	✓	x	✓	✓
SA	x	x	✓	✓	✓
Emotion detection	x	x	✓	x	✓
Recent posts	✓	✓	✓	x	✓
Hot posts	✓	✓	✓	x	✓
A graph to show data	✓	✓	✓	x	✓
Simple User Interface	x	x	x	x	✓
Unsophisticated summary	✓	x	x	x	✓

4. EVALUATION

4.1 Experiments

We examine the precision, recall, F-score, and accuracy of the sentiment analysis function for each of the three categories (positive, negative, neutral) with analysis for various comments depending on the behavior of the data set. These measurements are in the mean value of three candidates.

Table 2. Measures of the performance of sentiment analysis

	Mean			
No. of comments	Accuracy (%)	Precision	Recall	F-score
30	81.11%	0.5185	0.6926	0.6155
50	83.33%	0.5882	0.8078	0.6961
100	83.33%	0.6458	0.7966	0.7089

Table 3 below shows how much the candidates differ from the mean value for the group.

Table 3. Standard deviation (3 candidates) about the performance of Sentiment Analysis

No. of comments	Standard deviation			
	Accuracy (%)	Precision	Recall	F-score
30	0.1171	0.2313	0.2517	0.2405
50	0.1007	0.2121	0.1528	0.1940
100	0.0252	0.1183	0.0255	0.0652

The accuracy of the emotional opinion mining function for each category (joy, anger, fear, sad) with analysis for various comments depending on the behavior of the data set.

Table 4. Accuracy and standard deviation of analyzing comments with emotion detection

No. of comments	Accuracy (1)	Accuracy (2)	Accuracy (3)	Average accuracy	Standard deviation
30	86.67%	86.67%	90.00%	87.78%	0.0192
50	88.00%	80.00%	90.00%	86.00%	0.0529
100	85.00%	81.00%	87.00%	84.33%	0.0306

4.2 User Survey

We conducted a user survey on 30 participants including journalists, and journalism students, and journalism graduates. The survey was based on the USE Questionnaire (Lund, 2001). The original survey has 4 sub-scales and 30 items. We extracted 4 to 10 items out of each category and formed a scale of 30 items. Interviewees will give a score from 1 to 7 to represent their satisfaction with a different aspect of the app. There are 5 more questions on the identity and background information of the interviewee which are used to calculate the reliability score.

The reliability score checks if the data provided by the interviewee is reliable or not. It is scored according to the identity, awareness, and experience according to their feedback. For the score of Awareness and Experience, they are given according to the answer of interviewees and are scored from 1 to 5. The reliability score is calculated as:

Reliability Score = Identity Score × 0.45 + Awareness × 0.275 + Experience × 0.275

Table 5. 4 categories and 30 items in the questionnaire

Usefulness	Ease of Use	Ease of Learning	Satisfaction
1. It helps me get the trend of the societies on an objective way. 2. It helps me glance what the public feel and think. 3. It is useful. 4. It will be a tool applied in my life. 5. It makes the things I want to accomplish easier to get done. 6. It saves me time to get the atmosphere of the society/world. 7. It meets my needs. 8. It does everything I would expect it to do. 9. It inspires journalists to report journals with news values. 10. It encourages to bring prosocial effect.	11. It is easy to use. 12. It is user-friendly. 13. It requires the fewest steps possible to accomplish what I want to do with it. 14. It is flexible. 15. Using it is effortless. 16. I can use it without written instructions. 17. I don't notice any inconsistencies as I use it. 18. Both occasional and regular users would like it. 19. I can use it successfully every time.	20. I learned to use it quickly. 21. I easily remember how to use it. 22. It is easy to learn to use it. 23. I quickly became skillful with it.	24. I am satisfied with it. 25. I would recommend it to a friend. 26. It is fun to use. 27. It works the way I want it to work. 28. It is wonderful. 29. I feel I need to have it. 30. It is pleasant to use.

Table 6. Structures of the conducted questionnaire

Question Number	Section
31	Interviewee's Identity
32 to 35	Interviewee's Awareness of news and the views of the public; and their Experience of using social media for hearing the voices of the public

Table 7. The weighting of different measuring sections

	Identity	Awareness	Experience
Weight	0.45	0.275	0.275

Table 8. Default score for different identities

	Journalist	Journalist student/ graduate	Other
Identity Score	5	4	3

The means scores of all measurements are near the rank of 5. It indicates that all requirements can satisfy the users. The survey has acceptable reliability since the mean reliability score is 3.9 out of 5.

Table 9. Statistics about users' feedback on Facemarize

Variable	N	Mean	Std Dev	Minimum	Maximum
Usefulness	30	4.95	1.472547434	1.00	7.00
Ease of Use	30	5.09	1.15648583	3.00	7.00
Ease of Learning	30	5.02	1.4209964	2.00	7.00
Satisfaction	30	4.90	1.505950752	1.00	7.00

Table 10. Results of the reliability of the survey

	Mean	Min	Max
Reliability Score	3.90	3.00	4.45

5. CONCLUSION AND FUTURE WORK

Along with the popularity of applying Facebook Page, news media companies have also created pages to share their journals frequently for reaching their audience. It provides platforms for their visitors to share views on social issues and therefore journalists and the public may hear many different voices. However, everyone can only receive a limited number of stances from different commenters in many comments. Even though there are many powerful existing tools for summarizing Facebook Page's content, none of them is news-media-related or helpful for hearing from others.

In this chapter, we developed an Android app for journalists and the public to see summaries of news-media page's content. The summaries are about the recent posts, hot posts, and their comments.

Through the app, users may choose one existing news-media page to read all messages of its recent and hot posts. They may select a message to see the summary of that post. The summary will talk about the ratio of the commenters' sentiments and comments mined on different emotional aspects. Therefore, users may grasp how the overall voices on a post are. Meanwhile, we apply a simple user interface so that it is easy for users to understand how to use the app and the presentation of summaries.

In terms of the limitation of our app, the text analyzing functions cannot find the proper sentiments or emotions of the ironic comments' sentiments. The wording of ironic comments is usually the opposite of the exact mood of commenters. Also, the summaries provided by our app are not complete enough to represent the voices of the public. Even if it can cover all comments on every Facebook Page's post, the voices of the non-cyber users or other social media networks are still missed.

To improve the functionalities and the features of the app, future work implementation and maintenance are vital. Covering the news-media posts from other different social media networks will make the app more complete since more voices will be covered. To enhance the summarized results to be more concise and representative of the reality, auto grouping all posts from different platforms into a variety of social issues should be proposed. It may provide recent issues, hot issues, and a summary of the comments on any issue. Also, other kinds of aspects for doing emotion mining are needed. Since the comments are not always only talking about commenters' emotions on the news; other aspects about the quality of news and the reliability of the news agency should be included. Then, the comment processing function should support other languages in colloquial form like Cantonese. It may improve the practicality of the app.

REFERENCES

Abu-Salih, B., Wongthongtham, P., Zhu, D., Chan, K. Y., Rudra, A., Abu-Salih, B., ... Rudra, A. (2021). Sentiment Analysis on Big News Media Data. *Social Big Data Analytics: Practices, Techniques, and Applications*, 177-218.

Azizan, S. A., & Aziz, I. A. (2017). Terrorism detection based on sentiment analysis using machine learning. *Journal of Engineering and Applied Sciences (Asian Research Publishing Network)*, *12*(3), 691–698.

Cambria, E., & White, B. (2014). Jumping NLP curves: A review of natural language processing research. *IEEE Computational Intelligence Magazine*, *9*(2), 48–57. doi:10.1109/MCI.2014.2307227

Lippman, R. P., Weller-Fahy, D. J., Mensch, A. C., Campbell, W. M., Campbell, J. P., Streilein, W. W., & Carter, K. M. (2017, March). Toward finding malicious cyber discussions in social media. *Workshops at the Thirty-First AAAI Conference on Artificial Intelligence*.

Lund, A. M. (2001). Measuring usability with the use questionnaire 12. *Usability Interface, 8*(2), 3-6.

Mir, J., & Usman, M. (2015). An effective model for aspect based opinion mining for social reviews. *2015 Tenth International Conference on Digital Information Management (ICDIM)*, 49-56. 10.1109/ICDIM.2015.7381851

Pavlopoulos, I. (2014). *Aspect Based Sentiment Analysis* (Ph.D. thesis). Department of Informatics, Athens University of Economics and Business.

Statista. (2021). *Global social networks ranked by number of users 2021*. Retrieved July 29, 2021, from https://www.statista.com/statistics/272014/global-social-networks-ranked-by-number-of-users/

Tran, Y. H., & Tran, Q. N. (2017, December). Estimating public opinion in social media content using aspect-based opinion mining. In *International Conference on Mobile Networks and Management* (pp. 101-115). Springer.

Wahl-Jorgensen, K., & Hanitzsch, T. (2009). *The Handbook of Journalism Studies*. Routledge. doi:10.4324/9780203877685

Zhao, R., Zhou, A., & Mao, K. (2016). Automatic detection of cyberbullying on social networks based on bullying features. *Proceedings of the 17th international conference on distributed computing and networking*. 10.1145/2833312.2849567

Zúñiga, H. G., Jung, N., & Valenzuela, S. (2012). Social Media Use for News and Individuals' Social Capital, Civic Engagement and Political Participation. *Journal of Computer-Mediated Communication*, *17*(3), 319–336. doi:10.1111/j.1083-6101.2012.01574.x

ENDNOTES

[1]   https://www.facebook.com/business/insights/
[2]   https://sociograph.io/
[3]   http://www.opinioncrawl.com/
[4]   https://opennlp.apache.org/

Chapter 7
An Improved Cross–Domain Sentiment Analysis Based on a Semi–Supervised Convolutional Neural Network

Lap-Kei Lee
Hong Kong Metropolitan University,
Hong Kong

Kwok Tai Chui
Hong Kong Metropolitan University,
Hong Kong

Jingjing Wang
Hong Kong Metropolitan University,

Hong Kong

Yin-Chun Fung
Hong Kong Metropolitan University,
Hong Kong

Zhanhui Tan
Hong Kong Metropolitan University,
Hong Kong

ABSTRACT

The dependence on Internet in our daily life is ever-growing, which provides opportunity to discover valuable and subjective information using advanced techniques such as natural language processing and artificial intelligence. In this chapter, the research focus is a convolutional neural network for three-class (positive, neutral, and negative) cross-domain sentiment analysis. The model is enhanced in two-fold. First, a similarity label method facilitates the management between the source and target domains to generate more labelled data. Second, term frequency-inverse document frequency (TF-IDF) and latent semantic indexing (LSI) are employed to compute the similarity between source and target domains. Performance evaluation is conducted using three datasets, beauty reviews, toys reviews, and phone reviews. The proposed method enhances the accuracy by 4.3-7.6% and reduces the training time by 50%. The limitations of the research work have been discussed, which serve as the rationales of future research directions.

DOI: 10.4018/978-1-7998-8413-2.ch007

1. INTRODUCTION

Internet has become one of the most important tools in our daily life, with the ever-increasing penetration rate. It exceeded 60% this year according to Statista (Statista, 2021). The use of Internet relies more heavily on smartphones compared with computers attributable to the mobility and weight. During pandemic (COVID-19), we have witnessed the escalation of the penetration rate of internet for leisure and online shopping to maintain social-distancing and prevent the outbreak of the pandemic (Chang, & Meyerhoefer, 2021). More and more users begin to use online services, whom tend to read and share review comments on products. Before adding the items into shopping bag, it is often for one to consider the following criteria (i) review comments from other buyers; (ii) reputation of sellers; and (iii) price and quality. Particularly, the review comments contain complex and valuable information which can be effectively analysed via natural language processing (NLP) and artificial intelligence (AI). The research topic is known as sentiment analysis.

The contents can be generally categorized into 3-class, positive, neutral, and negative. In addition, multiple sources, as cross domains could be considered to enhance the analysis. In this chapter, the formulation tackles with 3-class cross-domain sentiment analysis.

1.1 Literature Review

Companies have realized that user-generated contents are useful. However, proper algorithms are needed to be implemented for the analysis. Sentiment analysis has recently received attention which drives various research groups to conduct systematic literature review (Do, Prasad, Maag, & Alsadoon, 2019; Hajiali, 2020; Yadav, & Vishwakarma, 2020). The focus of this chapter is sentiment analysis for product review.

Two network architectures were proposed for the 2-class (positive and negative) sentiment analysis of Amazon reviews (Zhao et al., 2017). The first architecture was constructed by weakly-supervised deep embedding (WDE) and convolutional neural network (CNN) whereas the second merged WDE and long short-term memory (LSTM). Performance evaluation was carried out based on the dataset containing 12k strong labeled and 1.1 million weak labeled reviews. The WDE-LSTM architecture slightly outperforms the WDE-CNN architecture. Both of them increase the accuracy by 3.4-21.7% compared with 11 existing approaches such as CNN-weak, CNN-rand11m, CNN-rand, sentiment-specific word embedding, Naive Bayes enhanced support vector machine, support vector machine, and Lexicon.

More than 14k 2-class reviews for 27 airlines were analyzed using word count analysis, frequency analysis, and topic modeling (Kwon, Ban, Jun, & Kim, 2021).

The word count analysis relied on word cloud where keywords of large font size were mentioned more frequent. The top 100 keywords were analyzed in frequency analysis. Majorly, they can be categorized into countries, positive expressions, and negative expressions. Regarding topic modeling, six topics have been highlighted namely staff service, Singapore airline, seat comfort, seat class, entertainment, and in-flight meal.

Continuous Naïve Bayes learning was proposed which integrated the ideas of domain adaptation, new-domain incremental learning, and old-domain knowledge storage (Xu, Pan, & Xia, 2020). Five 2-class datasets, each with 2000 samples, were considered on the review comments for kitchen, elec, DVD, book, and movie. The research studies are two-fold, cross-domain and domain-specific sentiment classification. The corresponding accuracies were ranged 74.8-77.5% and 82.2-85.6%, respectively.

The work (Riaz, Fatima, Kamran, & Nisar, 2019) extended the sentiment analysis on the 1.2M Amazon reviews in the topics of video surveillance devices, TVs, tablets, smartphones, and cameras. The strength of the keywords was measured to determine the level of expressions. K-means clustering was adopted to group relevant keywords. A trial and error approach was used to find out optimal value of the number of clusters K.

A parallel-based framework was proposed to incorporate CNN and LSTM/BiLSTM for 2-class sentiment analysis (Li, Zhu, Shi, Guo, & Cambria, 2020). Sentiment padding was used instead of zero padding. It differs from traditional idea of feature extraction by CNN plus prediction model by LSTM/BiLSTM. Results with tourism dataset suggested that CNN-LSTM outperformed CNN-BiLSTM, with accuracy 95% versus 91.3%.

Sentiment analysis of hotels' reviews was studied with support vector machine and deep recurrent neural network (Al-Smadi, Qawasmeh, Al-Ayyoub, Jararweh, & Gupta, 2018). The results may differ from our thought with shallow learning outperformed deep recurrent neural network in terms of accuracy (9.7-94.6%) but with a longer training time (2.1 to 5.3 times). One of the possible reason is that deep learning is easier to be overfitted and support vector machine is not computationally efficient in high-dimensional feature space.

There are other recommended readings such as mental health analysis via social media usage (Bouarara, 2021), social media sentences analysis via named entity (Sharma, Bhargava, & Tadikonda, 2021), code-mixed bilingual-phonetic-text sentiment classification (Singh, & Sachan, 2021), security challenges and solutions (Gou, Yamaguchi, & Gupta, 2017), trinity multimedia social network (Zhang et al., 2017), attack pattern mechanisms in web applications (Gupta, & Gupta, 2017), online social network (Gupta, Gupta, & Chaudhary, 2018), scale-free social network

(Chui & Shen, 2019), and online social network using automatic view isolation (Chaudhary, Gupta, & Yamaguchi, 2016, October).

1.2 Limitations of Existing Works

There are three major limitations in existing works:

- The major portion of research articles focuses on 2-class sentiment analysis which does not fully match the nature of opinions/expressions that carries positive, neutral, and negative strengths. Also, it is worth noting that some of the words and phrases in the target domain rarely or even do not exist in the source domain. The polarity of a word may change in different domains. As a results, typical algorithms for sentiment analysis are prone to sensitive variation in word representation.
- The training time and complexity of the model increase along with the size of the dataset. A scalable and manageable algorithm is sought for to manage the ever-increasing number of available data.
- The accuracy of the sentiment analysis in small-scale datasets could be further improved where there exist tremendous amount of data in various domains.

1.3 Research Contributions

To address the abovementioned limitations, we have proposed a semi-supervised CNN approach to enhance the accuracy and reduce time complexity of the three-class cross-domain sentiment analysis. The research contributions of our work is summarized as follows:

- The proposed algorithm enhances the accuracy by 4.3-7.6% compared with baseline CNN model.
- The proposed algorithm reduces the training time by 50% compared with baseline CNN model.

1.4 Organization of the Chapter

This chapter is organized as follows. Section 2 presents the methodology of the semi-supervised convolution neural network. This is followed by the performance evaluation and analysis using three cross-domain datasets. In Section 4, future research directions are discussed. Finally, a conclusion is made in Section 5.

2. METHODOLOGY

The overview of the proposed methodology is summarized in Figure 1. First, we use the similarity label method to handle the labelled input source domain and the unlabelled target domain. It converts the data into vector space. The similarity method helps reducing the training time of the model. Frequency-inverse document frequency (TF-IDF) and latent semantic indexing (LSI) are adopted to calculate the similarity between the source domain and the target domain. These help in improving the accuracy of the sentiment analysis model. For instance, some labelled source domain data is randomly selected. The similarity between sentences is calculated. If a sentence from target domain has high similarity score with a sentence from source domain, an indication of high possibility that they share identical sentiment. Thus, the unlabelled sentence is labelled using the label from the labelled sentence.

A semi-supervised CNN model is trained with the source domain data and the data that labelled by the similarity label method. With the trained model, the label of the target domain data can be predicted. If a sentence is labelled with a high probability, we use it as a real label. This technique is also known as pseudo labelling. To fine-tune the model, pseudo labelling is repeated for several epochs until the increase of accuracy (testing) becomes saturated or the model gets over-fitting. Finally we use the model for sentiment analysis which predicts if a sentence is positive, negative or neutral.

Figure 1. Overview of the proposed semi-supervised CNN model

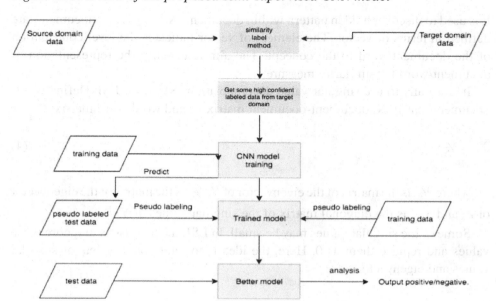

2.1 TF-IDF

The technique is comprised of two parts (i) TF: For every corpus, the number of occurrence for a word is measured. As a corpus is contributed by various documents, each document and its words could have a distinct TF; and (ii) IDF: It is a measure of how rarely a word occurs in a document. A higher count indicates the word is rare. The TF-IDF value for word i and document j is computed by:

$$TFIDF_{ij} = TF(i,j) \times IDF(i) \tag{1}$$

$$TF(i,j) = \frac{f_{ij}}{Total\,words\,in\,document\,j} \tag{2}$$

$$IDF(i) = \log_2\left(\frac{Total\,number\,of\,doucments}{documents\,with\,word\,i}\right) \tag{3}$$

Where word i and document j has frequency f_{ij}.

2.2 LSI

It is used to discover hidden pattern within document. All words and documents are defined in terms of vector. The element of vector indicates the level contribution of the document/word to the concept. The aim is to unify the representation of document/word for similarity measure.

It is usually to use singular value decomposition (SVD) for LSI. Define word-document matrix X, document-document matrix Y, and word-word matrix Z.

$$X = \frac{1}{2}_Y \cdot \sum_Y \frac{1}{2}_Z \tag{4}$$

where $\frac{1}{2}_Y$ is the matrix of the eigenvector of Y, $\frac{1}{2}_Z$ is the matrix of the eigenvector of Z, and $\sum_Y$ is the diagonal matrix of the singular values of Y.

Some of the singular values may be small. In LSI, the practise is to ignore those values and replace them as 0. Here, the idea is to retain only N sets of singular values and eigenvectors.

2.3 Semi-supervised CNN

Figure 2 summarizes the architecture of the CNN model. As preliminary study, we have tested a few sets of hyperparameters as a simple fine-tuning for the CNN model. We chose the following setting: one embedding layer, one convolutional layer, one max-pooling, one dropout, and one fully connected layers, as well as one softmax activation function. The embedding layer is used to represent words in form of dense vector, i.e. words are projected into a vector form. Convolutional layer applies convolution to the inputs which are activated to feature map. Summarized the most activated presence of a feature, max-pooling layer can down sample feature map. The dropout layer randomly dropouts some nodes to reduce generalization error and thus overfitting. The softmax activation function normalizes the outputs. Besides, there are three filters in the CNN model with sizes 2, 3, and 4, respectively.

Figure 2. Architecture of the semi-supervised CNN

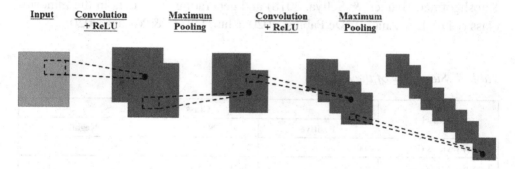

2.4 Summary of the Tools

We have highlighted the tools for the implementation.

- Python 3.6 is adopted.
- MXNet framework is employed to support machine learning and CNN algorithms.
- Gensim library is used to build vector space, TF-IDF, and LSI models.
- Regular expression and Numpy library are used for data processing.
- GPU service is provided by Paperspace for cloud service.

3. PERFORMANCE EVALUATION AND ANALYSIS

3.1 Datasets

The datasets, Beauty Reviews (B), Toys Reviews (T), and Phone Reviews (P) are retrieved from Amazon reviews datasets which there are review content and the rating score. The reviews with 4-5 star are labelled as positive, likewise, 3 star for neutral and 1-2 star for negative. The datasets are defined as three-class datasets. Table 1 summarizes the sample size of each class of the dataset. There could be an issue of class-imbalance in which the classification bias towards the majority class, i.e., the classification accuracy is statistically higher in majority class (Li, Tang, Shang, Mathiak, & Cong, 2020; Pasupa, Vatathanavaro, & Tungjitnob, 2020). Weighting has been introduced to reduce the dominance in majority classes, in our cases, positive and negative classes are majority and neutral class is minority (Fernando, & Tsokos, 2021; Li, Zhao, Sun, Yan, & Chen, 2020). There are other possible approaches like reducing the data in the majority class (Johnson, & Khoshgoftaar, 2019; Leevy, Khoshgoftaar, Bauder, & Seliya, 2018) and generating more data in the minority class (Chui, Liu, Zhao, & De Pablos, 2020; Chui, Lytras, & Vasant, 2020).

Table 1. Summary of the datasets

Dataset	Class		
	Positive	Neutral	Negative
Beauty reviews (B)	4000	2000	4000
Toys reviews (T)	3500	2000	2900
Phone reviews (P)	3600	2000	3600

3.2 Results

The formulations of the cross-domain sentiment analysis are three-fold, T to B, B to T, and P to T. We have compared our proposal with the baseline CNN model and results are shown in Table 2. The ranges of the accuracies are 64.6-67.4% and 67.4-72.5% in baseline CNN model and our work, respectively. Therefore, the results reveal that our work outperforms the baseline model by 4.3-7.6%.

Analysis is also made to study the effect of similarity method. We compare our works that with and without similarity method. By removing the similarity method, the accuracy of the model could be further enhanced by 1%. However, another goal of the research study is to lower the time complexity in training of the CNN model.

Using similarity method, the training time is reduced by about 50%. As a result, the significant reduction in training time of model using similarity method is much worthy compared with the small reduction in classification accuracy.

Table 2. Results of TF-IDF and LSI-based CNN model

Cross-domain	Accuracy of the model (%)	
	Baseline CNN model	Proposed TF-IDF and LSI-based CNN model
T to B	67.1	70.4
B to T	67.4	72.5
P to T	64.6	67.4

4. DISCUSSION OF FUTURE RESEARCH DIRECTIONS

There is room for further improvement in the cross-domain sentiment analysis. In this section, the discussion of future research directions is presented in two perspectives (i) accuracy-oriented in the research topics of small-scale datasets, incremental learning, and transfer learning; and (ii) time complexity-oriented.

4.1 Small-Scale Datasets

The nature of some datasets (including those in this research) is small-scale due to costly data collection process, initial dataset, limiting resources, etc. Although deep learning algorithms have received attention in enhancing the accuracy of the classification models using large-scale (even big data) datasets, most of those algorithms such as the category of deep neural network algorithms, tends to overfit with small-scale datasets (Nash, Drummond, & Birbilis, 2018; Yamashita, Nishio, Do, & Togashi, 2018).

Some recent research works have suggested the adoption of deep support vector machine (deep SVM) which reduces the issue of overfitting with small-scale datasets (Chui, Lytras, & Liu, 2020; Li, Zhang, Li, Su, Wang, & Chen, 2019; Okwuashi, & Ndehedehe, 2020). Nonetheless, this brings to other topics like feature extraction and kernel selection. For feature extraction, the feature vector can be constructed based on experts' knowledge in the application or manage by CNN (Le et al., 2021). Regarding kernel selection, multiple kernel learning (Gu, Chanussot, Jia, & Benediktsson, 2017) or customized kernel (Wang, Zhong, Adeli, Wang, & Liu,

2018) could be advanced techniques to enhance the performance compared with typical kernels (Achirul Nanda, Boro Seminar, Nandika, & Maddu, 2018).

4.2 Incremental Learning

The size of product review datasets is increasing as time flies, given the fact that more and more Internet users share review after purchasing or using the products. The trained sentiment analysis model could be updated with newly available data (Elshakankery, & Ahmed, 2019). The rationale is updating the hyperparameters without retraining the model in order to get rid of the lengthy training period.

There is an emergent variant of incremental learning that supports online learning that could update the model in real-time (Nallaperuma et al., 2019). Typical algorithms that support incremental learning are SVM, Learn++, artificial neural networks, decision trees. The problem becomes more complicated and computational-hungry if we extend the model to a deep architecture. Fog (Chaudhary, Gupta, Chang, Nedjah, & Chui, 2021) and cloud computing (Gupta, Agrawal, Yamaguchi, & Sheng, 2020) are reliable solutions to support computational-intensive algorithms.

4.3 Transfer Learning

Borrowing the trained models from another application (similar data type) or other datasets (same data type) via transfer learning is a potential solution to obtain a quick implementation of deep learning model in our desired application (Zhuang et al., 2020). Some of the hyperparameters are updated to customize into our goal.

Alternatively, we may combine our model with the trained model to obtain a superior performance because it is usually the best idea to use the data (our application) as much as possible and mimic the others (to take the advantages). This is also known as ensemble learning (Zhang, Miao, Wang, & Zhang, 2019). Various challenges have been reported in the following review articles (Adegun, & Viriri, 2021; Dong, Yu, Cao, Shi, & Ma, 2020).

4.4 Time Complexity

Apart from the accuracy-oriented topics in 4.1-4.3, the time complexity to train the model is important as a tradeoff between computational recourses and time. The higher the computing-power, the smaller the training time is. Indeed the idea of transfer learning helps in the reduction of time, however, ultimately we still need more time when we add-on the technique of ensemble learning.

Various works have proposed the solutions to lower the training time of deep learning models, for instance, introduction of autoencoder to convolutional neural network (Wang, Zhao, & Wang, 2019), dimensionality reduction of feature vector (Ke, Zheng, Yang, & Chen, 2017), hierarchical feature compression by tensor-train decomposition (Zhang, Yang, Chen, & Li, 2018), and adaptive dropout with distribution function for faster convergence (Zhang, Yang, Chen, P., & Bu, 2019).

5. CONCLUSION

In this chapter, an improved cross-domain sentiment analysis algorithm is proposed based on TF-IDF and LSI-based semi-supervised CNN algorithm. Results have revealed an improvement of accuracy by 4.3-7.6% compared with baseline model. As a tradeoff of small accuracy decrement with the adoption of similarity method, the training time has been reduced by about 50%. Thus, similarity method can be chosen based on the importance of accuracy and training time. When computing resource is limited, similarity method should be adopted. We have realized various limitations of the research study and thus suggesting four research topics namely small-scale dataset, incremental learning, transfer learning, and time complexity, to further enhance the accuracy and reduce the training time of the classification model for cross-domain sentiment analysis.

REFERENCES

Achirul Nanda, M., Boro Seminar, K., Nandika, D., & Maddu, A. (2018). A comparison study of kernel functions in the support vector machine and its application for termite detection. *Information (Basel)*, *9*(1), 5. doi:10.3390/info9010005

Adegun, A., & Viriri, S. (2021). Deep learning techniques for skin lesion analysis and melanoma cancer detection: A survey of state-of-the-art. *Artificial Intelligence Review*, *54*(2), 811–841. doi:10.100710462-020-09865-y

Al-Smadi, M., Qawasmeh, O., Al-Ayyoub, M., Jararweh, Y., & Gupta, B. (2018). Deep Recurrent neural network vs. support vector machine for aspect-based sentiment analysis of Arabic hotels' reviews. *Journal of Computational Science*, *27*, 386–393. doi:10.1016/j.jocs.2017.11.006

Bouarara, H. A. (2021). Recurrent Neural Network (RNN) to Analyse Mental Behaviour in Social Media. *International Journal of Software Science and Computational Intelligence*, *13*(3), 1–11. doi:10.4018/IJSSCI.2021070101

Chang, H. H., & Meyerhoefer, C. D. (2021). COVID-19 and the demand for online food shopping services: Empirical Evidence from Taiwan. *American Journal of Agricultural Economics, 103*(2), 448–465. doi:10.1111/ajae.12170

Chaudhary, P., Gupta, B. B., Chang, X., Nedjah, N., & Chui, K. T. (2021). Enhancing big data security through integrating XSS scanner into fog nodes for SMEs gain. *Technological Forecasting and Social Change, 168*, 120754. doi:10.1016/j. techfore.2021.120754

Chaudhary, P., Gupta, B. B., & Yamaguchi, S. (2016, October). XSS detection with automatic view isolation on online social network. In *2016 IEEE 5th Global Conference on Consumer Electronics* (pp. 1-5). IEEE. 10.1109/GCCE.2016.7800354

Chui, K. T., Liu, R. W., Zhao, M., & De Pablos, P. O. (2020). Predicting students' performance with school and family tutoring using generative adversarial network-based deep support vector machine. *IEEE Access: Practical Innovations, Open Solutions, 8*, 86745–86752. doi:10.1109/ACCESS.2020.2992869

Chui, K. T., Lytras, M. D., & Liu, R. W. (2020). A generic design of driver drowsiness and stress recognition using MOGA optimized deep MKL-SVM. *Sensors (Basel), 20*(5), 1474. doi:10.339020051474 PMID:32156100

Chui, K. T., Lytras, M. D., & Vasant, P. (2020). Combined generative adversarial network and fuzzy C-means clustering for multi-class voice disorder detection with an imbalanced dataset. *Applied Sciences (Basel, Switzerland), 10*(13), 4571. doi:10.3390/app10134571

Chui, K. T., & Shen, C. W. (2019). Tolerance analysis in scale-free social networks with varying degree exponents. *Library Hi Tech, 37*(1), 57–71. doi:10.1108/LHT-07-2017-0146

Do, H. H., Prasad, P. W. C., Maag, A., & Alsadoon, A. (2019). Deep learning for aspect-based sentiment analysis: A comparative review. *Expert Systems with Applications, 118*, 272–299. doi:10.1016/j.eswa.2018.10.003

Dong, X., Yu, Z., Cao, W., Shi, Y., & Ma, Q. (2020). A survey on ensemble learning. *Frontiers of Computer Science, 14*(2), 241–258. doi:10.100711704-019-8208-z

Elshakankery, K., & Ahmed, M. F. (2019). HILATSA: A hybrid Incremental learning approach for Arabic tweets sentiment analysis. *Egyptian Informatics Journal, 20*(3), 163–171. doi:10.1016/j.eij.2019.03.002

Fernando, K. R. M., & Tsokos, C. P. (2021). Dynamically weighted balanced loss: Class imbalanced learning and confidence calibration of deep neural networks. *IEEE Transactions on Neural Networks and Learning Systems*, 1–12. doi:10.1109/TNNLS.2020.3047335 PMID:33444149

Global internet penetration rate as of April 2021, by region. (2021). *Statista*. Retrieved 3 August 2021 Online https://www.statista.com/statistics/269329/penetration-rate-of-the-internet-by-region/

Gou, Z., Yamaguchi, S., & Gupta, B. B. (2017). Analysis of various security issues and challenges in cloud computing environment: a survey. In Identity Theft: Breakthroughs in Research and Practice (pp. 221-247). IGI Global. doi:10.4018/978-1-5225-0808-3.ch011

Gu, Y., Chanussot, J., Jia, X., & Benediktsson, J. A. (2017). Multiple kernel learning for hyperspectral image classification: A review. *IEEE Transactions on Geoscience and Remote Sensing*, *55*(11), 6547–6565. doi:10.1109/TGRS.2017.2729882

Gupta, B. B., Agrawal, D. P., Yamaguchi, S., & Sheng, M. (2020). Soft computing techniques for big data and cloud computing. *Soft Computing*, *24*(8), 5483–5484. doi:10.100700500-020-04766-2

Gupta, S., & Gupta, B. B. (2017). Detection, avoidance, and attack pattern mechanisms in modern web application vulnerabilities: Present and future challenges. *International Journal of Cloud Applications and Computing*, *7*(3), 1–43. doi:10.4018/IJCAC.2017070101

Gupta, S., Gupta, B. B., & Chaudhary, P. (2018). Hunting for DOM-Based XSS vulnerabilities in mobile cloud-based online social network. *Future Generation Computer Systems*, *79*, 319–336. doi:10.1016/j.future.2017.05.038

Hajiali, M. (2020). Big data and sentiment analysis: A comprehensive and systematic literature review. *Concurrency and Computation*, *32*(14), e5671. doi:10.1002/cpe.5671

Johnson, J. M., & Khoshgoftaar, T. M. (2019). Survey on deep learning with class imbalance. *Journal of Big Data*, *6*(1), 1–54. doi:10.118640537-019-0192-5

Ke, J., Zheng, H., Yang, H., & Chen, X. M. (2017). Short-term forecasting of passenger demand under on-demand ride services: A spatio-temporal deep learning approach. *Transportation Research Part C, Emerging Technologies*, *85*, 591–608. doi:10.1016/j.trc.2017.10.016

Kwon, H. J., Ban, H. J., Jun, J. K., & Kim, H. S. (2021). Topic modeling and sentiment analysis of online review for airlines. *Information (Basel)*, *12*(2), 78. doi:10.3390/info12020078

Le, D. N., Parvathy, V. S., Gupta, D., Khanna, A., Rodrigues, J. J., & Shankar, K. (2021). IoT enabled depthwise separable convolution neural network with deep support vector machine for COVID-19 diagnosis and classification. *International Journal of Machine Learning and Cybernetics*, 1–14. PMID:33727984

Leevy, J. L., Khoshgoftaar, T. M., Bauder, R. A., & Seliya, N. (2018). A survey on addressing high-class imbalance in big data. *Journal of Big Data*, *5*(1), 1–30. doi:10.118640537-018-0151-6

Li, F., Tang, H., Shang, S., Mathiak, K., & Cong, F. (2020). Classification of heart sounds using convolutional neural network. *Applied Sciences (Basel, Switzerland)*, *10*(11), 3956. doi:10.3390/app10113956

Li, K., Zhang, R., Li, F., Su, L., Wang, H., & Chen, P. (2019). A new rotation machinery fault diagnosis method based on deep structure and sparse least squares support vector machine. *IEEE Access: Practical Innovations, Open Solutions*, *7*, 26571–26580. doi:10.1109/ACCESS.2019.2901363

Li, T., Zhao, Z., Sun, C., Yan, R., & Chen, X. (2020). Adaptive channel weighted CNN with multisensor fusion for condition monitoring of helicopter transmission system. *IEEE Sensors Journal*, *20*(15), 8364–8373. doi:10.1109/JSEN.2020.2980596

Li, W., Zhu, L., Shi, Y., Guo, K., & Cambria, E. (2020). User reviews: Sentiment analysis using lexicon integrated two-channel CNN–LSTM family models. *Applied Soft Computing*, *94*, 106435. doi:10.1016/j.asoc.2020.106435

Nallaperuma, D., Nawaratne, R., Bandaragoda, T., Adikari, A., Nguyen, S., Kempitiya, T., De Silva, D., Alahakoon, D., & Pothuhera, D. (2019). Online incremental machine learning platform for big data-driven smart traffic management. *IEEE Transactions on Intelligent Transportation Systems*, *20*(12), 4679–4690. doi:10.1109/TITS.2019.2924883

Nash, W., Drummond, T., & Birbilis, N. (2018). A review of deep learning in the study of materials degradation. *NPJ Materials Degradation*, *2*(1), 1-12.

Okwuashi, O., & Ndehedehe, C. E. (2020). Deep support vector machine for hyperspectral image classification. *Pattern Recognition*, *103*, 107298. doi:10.1016/j.patcog.2020.107298

Pasupa, K., Vatathanavaro, S., & Tungjitnob, S. (2020). Convolutional neural networks based focal loss for class imbalance problem: A case study of canine red blood cells morphology classification. *Journal of Ambient Intelligence and Humanized Computing*, 1–17. doi:10.100712652-020-01773-x

Riaz, S., Fatima, M., Kamran, M., & Nisar, M. W. (2019). Opinion mining on large scale data using sentiment analysis and k-means clustering. *Cluster Computing*, *22*(3), 7149–7164. doi:10.100710586-017-1077-z

Sharma, Y., Bhargava, R., & Tadikonda, B. V. (2021). Named Entity Recognition for Code Mixed Social Media Sentences. *International Journal of Software Science and Computational Intelligence*, *13*(2), 23–36. doi:10.4018/IJSSCI.2021040102

Singh, S. K., & Sachan, M. K. (2021). Classification of Code-Mixed Bilingual Phonetic Text Using Sentiment Analysis. *International Journal on Semantic Web and Information Systems*, *17*(2), 59–78. doi:10.4018/IJSWIS.2021040104

Wang, J., Zhong, D., Adeli, H., Wang, D., & Liu, M. (2018). Smart bacteria-foraging algorithm-based customized kernel support vector regression and enhanced probabilistic neural network for compaction quality assessment and control of earth-rock dam. *Expert Systems: International Journal of Knowledge Engineering and Neural Networks*, *35*(6), e12357. doi:10.1111/exsy.12357

Wang, W., Zhao, M., & Wang, J. (2019). Effective android malware detection with a hybrid model based on deep autoencoder and convolutional neural network. *Journal of Ambient Intelligence and Humanized Computing*, *10*(8), 3035–3043. doi:10.100712652-018-0803-6

Xu, F., Pan, Z., & Xia, R. (2020). E-commerce product review sentiment classification based on a naïve Bayes continuous learning framework. *Information Processing & Management*, *57*(5), 102221. doi:10.1016/j.ipm.2020.102221

Yadav, A., & Vishwakarma, D. K. (2020). Sentiment analysis using deep learning architectures: A review. *Artificial Intelligence Review*, *53*(6), 4335–4385. doi:10.100710462-019-09794-5

Yamashita, R., Nishio, M., Do, R. K. G., & Togashi, K. (2018). Convolutional neural networks: An overview and application in radiology. *Insights Into Imaging*, *9*(4), 611–629. doi:10.100713244-018-0639-9 PMID:29934920

Zhang, Q., Yang, L. T., Chen, Z., & Li, P. (2018). A tensor-train deep computation model for industry informatics big data feature learning. *IEEE Transactions on Industrial Informatics*, *14*(7), 3197–3204. doi:10.1109/TII.2018.2791423

Zhang, Q., Yang, L. T., Chen, Z., Li, P., & Bu, F. (2018). An adaptive dropout deep computation model for industrial IoT big data learning with crowdsourcing to cloud computing. *IEEE Transactions on Industrial Informatics, 15*(4), 2330–2337. doi:10.1109/TII.2018.2791424

Zhang, Y., Miao, D., Wang, J., & Zhang, Z. (2019). A cost-sensitive three-way combination technique for ensemble learning in sentiment classification. *International Journal of Approximate Reasoning, 105*, 85–97. doi:10.1016/j.ijar.2018.10.019

Zhang, Z., Sun, R., Zhao, C., Wang, J., Chang, C. K., & Gupta, B. B. (2017). CyVOD: A novel trinity multimedia social network scheme. *Multimedia Tools and Applications, 76*(18), 18513–18529. doi:10.100711042-016-4162-z

Zhao, W., Guan, Z., Chen, L., He, X., Cai, D., Wang, B., & Wang, Q. (2017). Weakly-supervised deep embedding for product review sentiment analysis. *IEEE Transactions on Knowledge and Data Engineering, 30*(1), 185–197. doi:10.1109/TKDE.2017.2756658

Zhuang, F., Qi, Z., Duan, K., Xi, D., Zhu, Y., Zhu, H., Xiong, H., & He, Q. (2020). A comprehensive survey on transfer learning. *Proceedings of the IEEE, 109*(1), 43–76. doi:10.1109/JPROC.2020.3004555

Chapter 8
Detection of Economy–Related Turkish Tweets Based on Machine Learning Approaches

Jale Bektaş
Mersin University, Turkey

ABSTRACT

Conducting NLP for Turkish is a lot harder than other Latin-based languages such as English. In this study, by using text mining techniques, a pre-processing frame is conducted in which TF-IDF values are calculated in accordance with a linguistic approach on 7,731 tweets shared by 13 famous economists in Turkey, retrieved from Twitter. Then, the classification results are compared with four common machine learning methods (SVM, Naive Bayes, LR, and integration LR with SVM). The features represented by the TF-IDF are experimented in different N-grams. The findings show the success of a text classification problem is relative with the feature representation methods, and the performance superiority of SVM is better compared to other ML methods with unigram feature representation. The best results are obtained via the integration method of SVM with LR with the Acc of 82.9%. These results show that these methodologies are satisfying for the Turkish language.

1. INTRODUCTION

Social media such as Twitter makes interpersonal communications more effective with the aid of virtual platforms. Today, the internet has become a global forum where people can freely express and share their ideas. However, this situation has brought along some problems. It may be difficult for users to get through this

DOI: 10.4018/978-1-7998-8413-2.ch008

excessive information as anyone can upload exorbitant amounts of information, be it consciously or unconsciously.

Social media makes the communication of people with each other more effective with the use of virtual platforms. Microblogs such as Twitter, a type of social network, are used by professionals to share information and news. Twitter is a popular Microblog service that quickly disseminates information about any incident happening anywhere on the world. Jost et al. (2018) discusses that such personal records on social networks provide valuable and useful information for social psychology, marketing intelligence, and opinion mining research. Prabowo & Thelwall (2009) discuss that it is important to examine the content of the data collected from social media to derive meaningful information through classification research.

In social media studies, the techniques of data mining and text mining are used in the analysis of textual information (Surjandari et al., 2015). The core of these statistical methods consist of text mining techniques, which use such parameters as: author recognition, text classification, sentiment analysis, and opinion mining (Hemmatian et al., 2019).

The process of text analysis can be summarised as follows. First, the informational content of the document is transformed into a structure form in a vector space model. In fact, most text mining techniques are based on the idea that any document can be represented with bag-of-words projection in accordance with its term group (Karthikeyan et al., 2019). According to this projection, each *i* document of the collection is represented as a *N*-dimensional vector and the document is shown as $V_i = \left\{ w\left(t_{i1}\right), \ldots, w\left(t_{ij}\right), \ldots, w\left(t_{iN}\right) \right\}$. According to this projection, *N* determines the number of terms, and $w\left(t_{ij}\right)$ determines the weight of t_j term in document *i*.

This way of thought can improve upon by tweaking the parameters by introducing new operations so that the text mining may specialise in specific goals. The introduction of operations, such as: accommodating terms for machine learning (ML) techniques by transforming them into numeric features (i.e. weights), linguistic analysis techniques, indexing, statistical techniques, filtering terms via particular keywords, feature extraction, future selection (this subject will scale down in high-dimension datasets and it is highly important for the selection of attributions that will contribute to the study the most) and text summarization are some of the examples that help with the optimization the process (Sharma & Jain, 2019). Next, data mining and ML algorithms are applied to classify documents in vector space projections, grouping or building regression models.

2. RELATED WORKS

There exists a variety of ML algorithms and they all have a potential to show high speed, high performance operations. Thus, ML has been a go to strategy for a variety of researchers. In a study of comparative analysis for phishing detection, the objective is to train ML algorithms by categorizing the hyperlink specific features (Jain & Gupta, 2019), and it is found that more than 98.4% Accuracy is achieved in the logistic regression classifier. Furthermore, Ouaguid et al. (2018) lay out a framework consisting of two blockchains that allows the analysis of the desired permissions in an Android application, and acts as the registry for permissions. Lastly, Gou et al. (2017) provide a comparative analysis with ML for security threats and attacks in cloud computing and various solutions to deal with these problems.

To obtain useful information from text classification studies conducted by ML methods and with reference to current approaches of social media and internet use, Natural Language Processing (NLP) techniques were examined. Since optimizing a variety of parameters, SVM and Naïve Bayes in NLP have proven to get the best results supported in many previous articles. In this context, it has been observed that ML methods are more successful when compared with lexicon-based methods (Hailong et al., 2014). There is a sentiment analysis based classification study in which comments of Turkish films are used as data sources in Kaya et al. (2012). On that dataset, the binary classification (Positive, Negative) is carried out by SVM, and finally Acc with the 85% success rate is achieved. Agarwal et al. (2011) perform sentiment analysis of tweets. Two or three categories classification tasks are applied by using Naive Bayes, SVM, Maximum Entropy methods by combining data through bi-gram and unigram. In another study, sentimental analysis of Turkish news reports is executed by Demirsöz & Özcan (2017). Naive Bayes has the highest performance with 85.8% Acc. At the same time, Hayran & Sert (2017) utilize feature representation with fusion and the Turkish tweet dataset consists of 16000 positive and 16000 negative emotions are tested by using SVM. In a different study, Karcioğlu & Aydin (2019) use two different data sets, English and Turkish Twitter feeds, where BOW and Word2Vec models are conducted. As a result, 65.62% success is achieved by using linear SVM and logistic regression. Vural & Cambazoğlu (2013) observe the positive and negative comments which have the 85% success when analysing Turkish news reports. When the sentiment analysis studies over Twitter messages are considered, there are studies which use both dictionary-based and ML methods, and result in 75.2% and 85% Accuracy respectively. Ahmad et al. (2017) conduct some studies on various ML and hybrid techniques such as Maximum Entropy, Stochastic Gradient Descent, Random Forest, and Multinomial Naive Bayes with twitter data streams for sentiment analysis. Hassonah et al. (2020) propose to use SVM classifier integrating with ReliefF dimension reduction method in one framework in which the number of features are reduced by up to 96.85% from the original feature set. From these results it can be said that this framework yields in more accurate results in long-lasting experiments.

Conducting NLP for the Turkish language is a lot harder than conducting it for other Latin-based languages such as English. Turkish is a language that has many affixes that alter the meaning of the base word, resulting in innumerable number of conjugations of the simplest of verbs, and even nouns. The suffixes used in the Turkish language can lead to the words even changing meaning which adds another dimension to the existing problem. Therefore, revealing the type of suffixes precisely during the analysis is important for success on the one hand, and emphasizes how troublesome the NLP process which has an excessive number of affixes and conjugations (Boynukalin & Karagoz, 2013). Kirelli & Arslankaya (2020) carry through a study on 30,000 random Turkish tweets to perform a classification sentiment analysis. This analysis compares the results to the benchmarks in other datasets to get further verification of its Accuracy. Karahoca et al. (2019) propose to use five different ML methods (SVM, random forests, boosting, maximum entropy, and artificial neural networks) to classify the sentiments of the posts on Twitter.

Based on such studies examined in the literature, the aim of this study is to examine the profiles of 13 economists who are expert in their fields in Turkey and to analyse their tweets shared from 23-06-2019 to 31-12-2019 and classify these tweets if they are of economic interest or not.

3. SYSTEM MODEL AND METHODS

3.1. Dataset

The tweets shared between 23-06-2019 and 31-12-2019 by particular Turkish economists who have shown success in their fields have been included. These Tweets were then examined by the data analysis experts and the ones related with economy were tagged. The profile information and the number of tweets shared by each economist included in the study are given in Figure 1.

Figure 1. Tweet Statistics of Economists

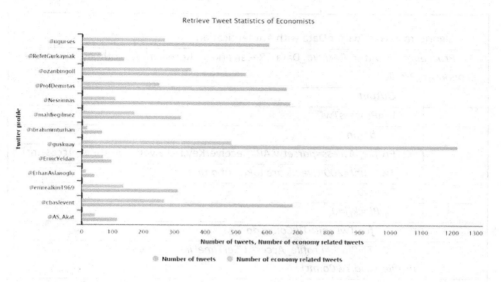

3.2. The Process of Data Retrieving from Twitter

Bonzanini (2016) proposes to open the Authorization protocol which is used to retrieve data from social media platforms. With the use of Python programming language, the obtained tweets are imported into a Pandas library with a .csv format. Twitter API (Application Programming Interface) is created primarily for retrieving tweets. API is an interface that allows any application to interact with other applications. Thus, Python programming language is used as a medium for data extraction and analysis. Jupyter Notebook interface is used to run the texts on the Python codes that were pulled. In addition, Tweepy, WordCloud, Twython and Pandas libraries were used. Finally, the Rapidminer program is used to classify and visualize the data. The Twitter application is developed which uses the new authorized Twitter API account given in Algorithm 1. Necessary permissions (Consumer Key and Consumer Secret) are obtained to access the tweets shared by economists. Detailed Python codes were gives as Appendix.

Algorithm 1, the twitter profile of an economist is entered and the date range when the data is intended to be retrieved is input. A loop is created to retrieve data. As a result of the loop, the first 200 tweets are checked. This step takes the computer some time to process this data and when it finishes computing, it will proceed to the next step. The data retrieved from Twitter is checked according to the pre-set criteria and then assigned to a new queue given in Algorithm 2.

Algorithm 1: Get Twitter Data with Authentication

Algorithm 1: Get Twitter Data with Authentication	
Procedure Twitter_Receive_Data (ReceiverKey, ReceiverInf, AuthKey, AccessInf, *Economist_Profile*)	
	Output
	WhProcessTw
	begin
	Profile_Access=parsetw.API(ReceiverKey,ReceiverInf,AuthKey,AccessInf)
	TwCount=200 tweets are taken at a time..
	TwId=0
	TwBlock[]=0
	for *TwLimit>TwCount* **do**
	TwBlock=Profile_Access.USerTimeLine(Economist_Profile,TwId,TwCount)
	The tweets obtained in groups are passed through the criteria in the sent function and made suitable for processing.
	[IslemTw,TwId]=ProcessTwFilter(TwBlock,TwId)
	WhProcessTw= WhProcessTw.Append (ProcessTw)
	TwCount+=200
	End
	End

Algorithm 2 is a module where the tweets are filtered in terms of whether they are between the date range determined as a criterion as well as where the tweets are checked whether they are the main tweets or not. Make sure that the tweets are not retweets (retweets are not taken into account) and that they do not contain the "@R" character group. Tweets collected by grouping on a profile basis are stored in separate files. Collected data is saved as a .csv file.

Algorithm 2: Filtering Tweets By Criteria

Algorithm 2: Filtering Tweets By Criteria	
Procedure ProcessTwFilter (TwBlock,TwId)	
	Output
	ProcessTw, TwId
	begin
	Tw_Start_Date="24.06.2019"
	Tw_End_Date="31.12.2019"
	for *Tweet ∈ TwBlock* ***do***
	If Tweet.Status<>Retweet and "@R" not in Tweet
	If Tweet.CreationDate>Tw_Start_Date and
	Tweet.CreationDate<Tw_End_Date
	ProcessTw= ProcessTw.Append (Tweet)
	End
	End
	End
	TwId=TwBlock[maxid]
	end

3.3. Pre-process of Twitter Data

Before analysing the tweets shared by economists with ML methods, it is necessary to pass through the pre-processing a stage with text mining tools. Text mining is an ever-evolving method of analysis that is associated with gathering information from natural language texts in a meaningful way. Another task of text mining is to process and extract information from texts that are communicating information or thoughts based on real transactions. While it is generally used to analyse large-scale natural language texts, it is also included in analytical studies when extracting information from lexical usage patterns. Following the steps, the pre-process procedures were completed, and a word list was built. In this step Han et al. (2015) propose cleaning, merging, reduction and transformation techniques to be used when analysing the data. Relevant analyses are applied to the pre-processed data.

Mostafa (2013) uses the Tokenization process which divides the texts according to the determined criteria. In the transform cases process, all letters are turned into lower cases. The Stopwords process is filtering the common redundant words. In the stepping process, compares the similarity between the words. Then, derivational and inflexional suffixes are cleaned. In the Filter tokens step, the words longer than three characters are taken into the word list. In the data retrieved from Twitter, if there are "#", "@" and URL addresses, they were analysed after cleaning these characters. TF-IDF is a method that determines how much a *Term* is important in the document. The next step for the dataset is the preparation for the TF-IDF association, which assigns the data the most appropriate classifier. The methodological sequence that is employed in the study is shown in Figure 2.

Figure 2. Overview of the pre-processing frame on a sample tweet

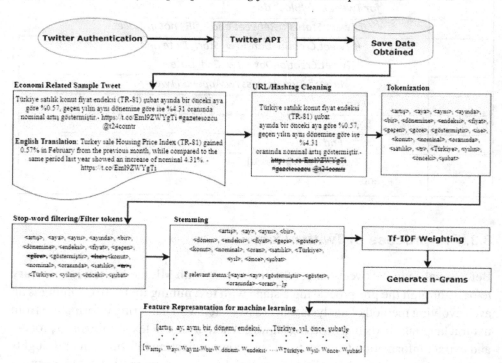

3.3.1. N-Gram Feature Representations

N-grams can be singular words that pass more frequently in texts than other words that pass in the text, as well as words that are possible by using phrases consisting of bigram, trigram or more words together. Terms can be repeated separately in a text very often, but when viewed individually, they can also be caused by the fragmentation of binary term expressions. In these cases, n-gram analysis will reveal how many times binary term expressions are seen. In n-gram analysis, the n value refers to how many words the phrase consists of (Awwalu et al. 2019, Schonlau et al. 2017). In addition, grams with $n=1$ are called unigram, n-grams with $ne=2$ are called bigram, n-grams with N=3 are called trigram. Feature definitions were prepared by extracting n-gram samples at the level of $n=1$, $n=2$ and $n=3$ based on the texts in this study. When these phrases are examined and the resulting feature definitions are analysed separately, an idea of the general framework can be obtained.

3.4. THE SELECTION OF CLASSIFIER

3.4.1. Naive Bayes Classifier

Naive Bayes classification which is used by Wikarsa & Thahir (2015) is a supervised learning method that includes learning technique based on Bayes theorem. The assumption that the learning algorithm is based on is the independence of the feature of data items. Since there is a strong meaningful relationship between the words chosen as tokens, Çoban et al. (2015) propose this assumption, in particular to text classification, does not align with the nature of this relationship. In spite of this, the approach could be applied to text categorisation and the performance will be satisfactory.

When text which has d number of features is coded to a numerical vector with d dimension, it is denoted as $a_1, \ldots\ldots, a_d$. The probability of quality a_i, is the x_i value in the C_k category. $P\left(a_i = x_i \mid C_k\right)$ is expressed as the quality of x_i value's equivalent in the $P\left(x_i \mid C_k\right)$ likelihood. If the feature vector is defined as $x = \left[x_1, x_2 \ldots.. x_d\right]$, the likelihood of feature vector C_k is defined as the multiplication of the values with the equation below Eq.1.

$$P\left(x \mid C_k\right) = P\left(x_1 \mid C_k\right).sP\left(x_d \mid C_k\right) = \prod_{i=1}^{d} P\left(x_i \mid C_k\right) \tag{1}$$

The Bayesian classifier begins the training process with the probabilities of the input vector and identifies the causal relationships between the features. Then, it classifies the data items according to their probability at the end of the training; these are often referred to as maximum probability learning. In the learning process, Naive Bayes calculates the probabilities of individual feature values and requires linear complexity proportional to the number of features.

3.4.2. Logistic Regression

The main purpose of Binay Logistic Regression Analysis is to examine the causality relationship between independent variables, as in other regression methods. The goal is to create an acceptable model that defines the relationship between the result variable and explanatory variables that will provide the best harmony using the least variables Abbe et al. (2016). LR is a regression analysis method that can predict the result of a variable in a limited class as in Gökçe et al. (2014). By giving an input vector and output variables, LR can be adapted to a likelihood principle that can predict the possibility of result. This possibility will be p if, $\gamma_i = 1$, *1-p* if, $\gamma_i = 0$.

$$L\left(\varnothing\right) = \prod_{i=1}^{n}\left(p_i\right)^{\gamma_i}\left(1 - p_i\right)^{\left(1-\gamma_i\right)} \tag{2}$$

Mathematical calculation of log value of the equation is considered to be more practical. Log-likelihood can be defined with the equation below. It is maximized by $\varnothing$ variance which is named as the maximum likelihood prediction.

$$lnln\,L\left(\varnothing\right) = \sum_{i=1}^{n}\left(y_i lnln\,p_i + \left(1 - \gamma_i\right)lnln\left(1 - p_i\right)\right) \tag{3}$$

3.4.3. Support Vector Machines- Kernel Selection(SVM-K)

SVM is a ML method which is used in classification and based on the strategy that determines dual borders parallel to each other in the new space is used in the study of Li et al. (2019). The limitation of forming decision boundaries in SVM is the maximization of the margin between the two linear boundaries. The training data in SVM is defined as dots in the vector space. It was chosen to assign the training samples into two classes, *A* and *B*, in advance. If *n* training sample is considered to be used for training, each *i* = 1,..., n is member of either class *A* or class *B*. Hyperplane separation theorem is applied.

$$\omega^T x \geq \gamma, \tag{4}$$

Here $x \in R^N$ corresponds to feature vector, and $\omega \epsilon\ R^N$, $\gamma \in \left\{-1,1\right\}$ corresponds to classification categories of samples. To solve ω and γ it is necessary to apply the linear SVM optimization formula below.

$$\text{minimize} \frac{1}{2}\|\omega\|^2 + Ce^T y \tag{5}$$

where $\omega \epsilon\, IR^N$, $\gamma \epsilon\, IR^N$, $y \epsilon\, IR^N$

SVM has a lot of potential in the analysis and classification of data. It can be used with different kernel options such as Radial Basis and Polynomial Kernel in Shastry et al. (2017). It was deemed better to use the Polynomial Kernel for its strong potential. For the Polynomial Kernel, Pearson expanse parameters (σ,ω) are important components. In this study, σ and ω parameters were set to 0.1. The Polynomial Kernel function is shown in Eq.6.

$$\frac{((x.y)+1)^d}{\sqrt{((x.x)+1)^d((y.y)+1)^d}} \tag{6}$$

3.4.4. Support Vector Machines - Integration of Logistic Regression (SVM-LR)

The support vectors are defined as the data points which are closest to the Hyperplane x_j. The signed distances are calculated with the formula in the vector ω and b value shows bias.

$$\omega^T = \left[\left(\sum_1^j \alpha_j x_j\right)^T b\right], \tag{7}$$

Depending on the complexity of the data, instances that cannot be linearly separated are simulated by looking at the relational properties of features in high dimensional space. This is how the hyperplane is determined between classes.

$$f(x) = sign\left[\sum_i \alpha_i y_i \phi(x).\phi(x_i) + b\right] \tag{8}$$

During the training stage of SVM, it is assumed that the training samples are assigned to two pre-determined classes as a representation and are cumulatively represented by a fixed value, such as n. "n" is a member one of the two classes x_i, $i = 1, \ldots$. We have a separating regulation of the form of $\omega^T x$.

Here, $x \in R^N$ is represented as attribute vector; and $É \in R^N$, and $\gamma \in \{-1, 1\}$ refer to the labels of the classes of the samples. The main aim is to find optimal E and ^{3}. Therefore, the SVM problem must be transformed to a linear approach by the following equations, such as Eq.10.

$$minimize \frac{1}{2}\omega^2 + Ce^T y, \tag{10}$$

where $\omega \in IR^N$, $\gamma \in IR^N$

Separating hyperplane is obtained by E and ^{3} calculation. Support vectors which are the closest to the hyperplane are considered and data point are determined as Hyperplane x_j. The Equation 11. is used to compute the signed distances in vector d ("*b*" refers to the bias).

$$d^T = \left[\left(\sum_j \alpha_j x_j \right)^T b \right], \tag{11}$$

Boundary line samples include the linear decision surface with the widest gap, with parametric adjustment. The *C* parameter, which is the most important of these parameters and directs it to linear projection, for example, a positive value higher than 10 and 10 is selected and then mapped to a much higher-dimensional attribute field for the linear kernel. This structure requires a device with a good infrastructure to perform transformation with strong mathematical projection.

The signed distances on hyperplanes must be calculated for each instance of K in the dataset, and a vector $d = (d_{k, 1}, \dots d_{k, n})$ with *D* dimensions must be obtained in the output. The *D* vector is then set to be presented to the LR model, and the likelihood values are calculated by comparing the responses to the SVM models.

3.4.4.1. Ensemble Framework Based on LRA and SVM

Bektaş & Ibrikci (2017) propose the process which starts with the regularisation of the *C* parameter. The operation of the flow takes place in the sequence numbered below. Then, the results are analysed in a separate manner.

1.   SVM classifier is constructed. Therefore, the feature representation D term frequency matrix defined by TF-IDF is presented to the model. When SVM models that were both trained and tested using cross-validation were created, the linear kernel was selected.

2. The performance of end-classifiers will be affected by the selection of statistical models for LRA at an important degree. It is necessary to increase the number of iterations and regulate the soft margin parameter in order to construct the model when encountering a dataset that cannot be linearly partitioned. In this case, changing the kernel structure changes the structure of the framework, so the linear kernel should also be preferred.

3. The datasets which include unigram, bigram, and trigram feature representations that classification is possible with linear kernel selection.

4. The average distance of support vectors is calculated based on the margin distances around the hyperplane. The average value is considered the threshold value.

5. Estimation probabilities for all samples are calculated using the logistic regression model. The data instance is treated as a positive class value when the probability value is greater than the threshold value that is considered the average distance.

3.5. Visualization

Data visualization is the method that allows the obtained intangible information to be interpreted through the use of graphics. It also allows more complex or scattered data to be perceived easily. Gallagher et al. (2019) use WordCloud that is one of the data visualization methods in data mining. It is a figure which is created in different colours and patterns in response to the word frequency. As a result, the most frequent words in the tweets were visualized using the WordCloud method. Wordclouds add ease of interpretation to the stacked word list. When the term is sorted by frequency, the most commonly used terms stand out more in a WordCloud.

4. EXPERIMENTAL RESULTS

It is really difficult to determine the amount of data required to build a stable model, and the complexity and size of the data directly affect the performance of the chosen learning task. In order to classify the economy tweets, Naive Bayes, Logistic Regression, SVM with Polynomial kernel selection, and SVM which is used by Karcioğlu & Aydin (2019). Another method that is used to integrate with Logistic regression, has been compared according to many performance criteria. In Table 1, the correct classification rates obtained by these four classifiers on Twitter messages with different feature sets and n-gram trials are presented.

Table 1. Tweet classification accuracies for ML methods according to feature representation

Feature representation	Classification Algorithms			
	Naive Bayes	Logistic Regression	SVM+Kernel	SVM+LR
unigram	0.747	0.731	0.820	**0.829**
bigram	0.695	0.671	0.769	0.781
trigram	0.623	0.608	0.710	0.718

When represented by the unigram feature set, it is observed that the use of SVM+LR method as the classification algorithm reached the highest value with 82.9% Acc. The unigram model was discovered to give better results, as in Mostafa (2013). Overfitting problems can be experienced with bigram and trigram models because adding more features makes it easier for the model to overfit a small dataset. Hence, other performance evaluations according to the unigram feature set are presented in Table 2.

As a result of our experiments, it is seen that the performance of SVM is noticeably higher than the other two models, both with the choice of using a kernel and with Logistic Regression integration. In the use of SVM + Logistic Regression, sensitivity is the most successful with 0.918 and with SVM polynomial kernel selection, Sensitivity ranks second with 0.911.

Table 2. Tweet classification performances for ML methods

	ACC	F-Measure	Sensitivity	Specificity	Precision	Recall	AUC
Naive Bayes	0.747	0.776	0.759	0.730	0.795	0.759	0.648
Logistic Regression	0.731	0.753	0.710	0.759	0.804	0.710	0.704
SVM+Kernel	0.820	0.861	0.911	0.706	0.812	0.911	0.900
SVM+LR	**0.829**	**0.861**	**0.918**	0.715	**0.816**	**0.918**	**0.901**

The words that emerged as a result of the analysis made were visualized using WordCloud in Figure 3.

Figure 3. WordCloud of 5477 tweets obtained according to the presented unigram feature representation

The changes related to the AUC values that were obtained according to the validation data are presented in Figure 4. The ROC evaluation is included in the graph separately for each method.

Figure 4. The ROC and ROC(threshold) evaluations of four methods are given respectively

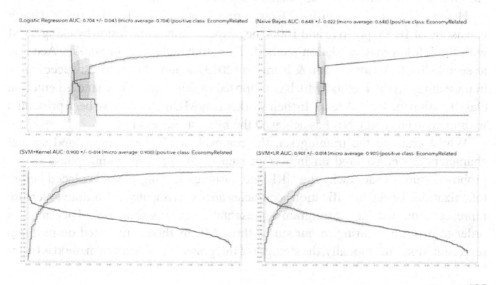

The transactions of 5477 tweets were analysed with the application of the binary classification process (economy-related/ economy-unrelated. General purpose is to find out if the tweets shared by economists are of economic interest or not.

4.1. Comparative Performance Analysis

Social media studies on the Turkish language with ML techniques are given in Table 3 according to their success rate. It is a good idea to take these methods which yield a high success rate and compare it to the study that was carried out, and see which one of the methods is better. Other methods which yielded varying success rates were also taken into account in order to get an overall view of the efficiency of the proposed method. Kaya et al. (2012) utilizes SVM and Naive Bayes and study sentiment classification of Turkish political news and achieve an 76.54% Acc rate. Vural et al. (2013) use lexicon-based methods by using a corpus of Turkish movie reviews with known polarities. This study achieves an 74.63% Acc rate. Kirelli & Arslankaya (2020) design a NLP (word stemming), N-gram (K-NN, SVM) methodology and challenge to solve the sentiment analysis problem for Turkish tweets about global warming and climate change. Çoban et al. (2015) utilize ML methods including SVM, Naive Bayes, Multinomial Naive Bayes, and KNN. The aim of this study is to classify social media data such as blogs, Twitter and Facebook. Shepherd et al. (2015) attains an Acc of 65.79%. Karcioğlu & Aydin (2019) utilizes linear SVM model and logistic regression for classification of labeled data in English and Turkish Twitter feeds with Word2Vec model. Karcioğlu & Aydin (2019) attains an Acc of 65.62%. Karahoca et.al (2019) uses five ML methods which include SVM, Random forest, Neural Networks and Turkish Tweet sentiment analysis is studied on brief emotion descriptions. This study achieved a 54% Acc rate.

Hayran & Sert (2017) utilizes feature representation on Turkish tweet dataset consisting of 16000 positive and 16000 negative emotions and tested by using SVM with the k-fold cross validation method. This study achieved an 80.05% Acc rate as seen in Table 3. Boynukalin & Karagoz (2013) achieved the closest success rate in their study to the method which is proposed in this study. They studied emotion classification for Turkish texts. In their work, many ML methods have been presented with many trials and CNB has achieved the highest success rate.

Whilst creating the training set, the removal of all the symbols and special characters are considered an important step in the pre-processing phase in the proposed study. That is why the URL and hashtag cleaning phase is placed before tokenization. Tweet classification accuracies are experimented according to feature representation and then a unigram representation is superimposed. Therefore, in order to avoid overfitting in our study, three ML methods are tested on unigram representation. Additionally, the strength of integrated classification method is better seen by using Linear SVM model and logistic regression for classification. Thus we can see that this framework can be used in the training of a text dataset with a complex language and still provide good results.

Table 3. NLP studies in Turkish Language

	Year	Methodology	Purpose	Best Acc(%)
Proposed framework		SVM+LR	Preprocess frame is conducted with proposed methodology.	82.9
Boynukalin & Karagoz	2013	Complement Naive Bayes (CNB)	Emotion classification for Turkish texts.	80.39
Hayran & Sert	2017	SVM classifier	Feature representation with fusion are utilized and the Turkish tweet dataset consists of 32000 emotions are tested .	80.05
Kaya et al.	2012	SVM and Naive Bayes	Sentiment classification of Turkish political news	76.54
Vural et al.	2013	Lexicon-based methods	A corpus of Turkish movie reviews with known polarities.	76
Kirelli & Arslankaya	2020	NLP (word stemming), N-gram (K-NN,SVM)	Turkish tweets about global warming and climate change	74.63
Çoban et al.	2015	ML methods include SVM, Naive Bayes, Multinomial Naive Bayes and KNN	Classification on social media such as Blogs, Twitter, and Facebook.	65.79
Karcioğlu & Aydin	2019	Linear SVM model and logistic regression for classification	Classification of labeled data in English and Turkish Twitter feeds with Word2Vec model.	65.62
Karahoca et.al	2019	Five ML methods include SVM,Random forest, Neural Networks	Turkish Tweet sentiment analysis on brief emotion descriptions.	54

5. CONCLUSION

Social media makes the communication of people with each other more effective on virtual platforms. Microblogs such as Twitter, a type of social network, are used by professionals to share information and news. Twitter is a popular Microblog service that quickly disseminates information about any incident happening anywhere on the world. It is therefore important to examine the content of the data collected from social media to have meaningful information in classification researches. In social media studies, the techniques of data mining and text mining are used in the analysis of textual information. There are statistical methods within the core of text mining techniques and these techniques are used in the fields such as author recognition, text classification, sentiment analysis, and opinion mining.

Text classification is one of the most useful methods for social media monitoring studies. This study aims to construct a general frame in Python programming language that acts as a gateway for classification of the tweets which are economy-related. Twitter API (Application Programming Interface) is created primarily for retrieving tweets. API is an interface that allows any application to interact with other applications. Python programming language is used for data extraction and analysis. Jupyter Notebook interface is used to run the texts and Python codes we pulled. In addition, Tweepy, WordCloud, Twython and Pandas libraries are used. Finally, the Rapidminer program is used to classify and visualize the data. According to specific date range filtering operation, 7731 tweets shared by the 13 famous economists in Turkey are retrieved from Twitter by using the constructed frame. By using text mining techniques, term weighting values were calculated in accordance with the linguistic approach and adapted to machine learning techniques. Some of the text mining processes are the tokenization process which divides the texts according to the determined criteria, the Stopwords process which filters the common redundant words, and the stepping process which measures the similarity of words. The derivational and inflexional suffixes are cleaned. Filtering tokens, in this step, the words This is a starting point and a specific frame on building up the next steps.

In this study, some limitations were encountered during the process. First of all, when creating the dataset, the limited data extraction permission has prolonged the process and caused the algorithms to be created in an iterative structure. Another issue is that during the tagging process of the tweets, the topics covered a wide compass and required detailed analysis. Problems related to Turkish language structure required different N-gram trials of our tests. Solutions for these problems were offered by detecting them early on and proposing workarounds. Moreover, via the basic methods used in text classification, a binary classification is made on the messages obtained from the Twitter environment, and the success rate obtained in the studies using basic methods in the literature for Turkish is achieved. After the pre-processing step, the classification results of tweets with five different common machine learning methods (Support Vector Machines (SVM), Naive Bayes, Logistic Regression (LR) with kernel selection and LR to SVM) were compared. The features represented by the Term Frequency-IDF (TF-IDF) weighting model were tested in different N-Gram feature representation techniques and visualized with WordCloud. The effect of the overall framework on the classification results were investigated.

The results showed that, in order to increase the success rate of a text classification problem in Turkish language, the order of pre-processing methods and feature representation methods should be applied. According to the findings obtained from the experiments in this study, it has revealed that Twitter messages can be classified by ML methods and there exists a performance difference between SVM compared to other ML methods with unigram feature representation. The best result is obtained via the integration method of SVM with LR with a success rate of 82.9% Acc; followed by using a SVM + Polynomial kernel with a success rate of 82.0%. Instead of using a powerful machine learning technique such as SVM alone, integrated use of a powerful analysis method such as LR in text mining seems to increase the success rate. These results show that methodology is satisfying for the Turkish language.

REFERENCES

Abbe, A., Grouin, C., Zweigenbaum, P., & Falissard, B. (2016). Text mining applications in psychiatry: A systematic literature review. *International Journal of Methods in Psychiatric Research*, *25*(2), 86–100. doi:10.1002/mpr.1481 PMID:26184780

Agarwal, A., Xie, B., Vovsha, I., Rambow, O., & Passonneau, R. J. (2011, June). Sentiment analysis of twitter data. In *Proceedings of the workshop on language in social media (LSM 2011)* (pp. 30-38). Academic Press.

Ahmad, M., Aftab, S., Muhammad, S. S., & Ahmad, S. (2017). Machine learning techniques for sentiment analysis: A review. *Int. J. Multidiscip. Sci. Eng*, *8*(3), 27.

Awwalu, J., Bakar, A. A., & Yaakub, M. R. (2019). Hybrid N-gram model using Naïve Bayes for classification of political sentiments on Twitter. *Neural Computing & Applications*, *31*(12), 9207–9220. doi:10.100700521-019-04248-z

Bektaş, J., & Ibrikci, T. (2017, February). Hybrid classification procedure using SVM with LR on two distinctive datasets. In *Proceedings of the 6th International Conference on Software and Computer Applications* (pp. 68-71). 10.1145/3056662.3056717

Bonzanini, M. (2016). *Mastering social media mining with Python*. Packt Publishing Ltd.

Boynukalin, Z., & Karagoz, P. (2013). Emotion analysis on Turkish texts. In *Information Sciences and Systems, 264* (pp. 159–168). Springer.

Çoban, Ö., Özyer, B., & Özyer, G. T. (2015, May). Sentiment analysis for Turkish Twitter feeds. In *2015 23nd Signal Processing and Communications Applications Conference (SIU)* (pp. 2388-2391). IEEE. 10.1109/SIU.2015.7130362

Gallagher, C., Furey, E., & Curran, K. (2019). The application of sentiment analysis and text analytics to customer experience reviews to understand what customers are really saying. *International Journal of Data Warehousing and Mining, 15*(4), 21–47. doi:10.4018/IJDWM.2019100102

Gökçe, O. Z., Hatipoğlu, E., Göktürk, G., Luetgert, B., & Saygin, Y. (2014). Twitter and politics: Identifying Turkish opinion leaders in new social media. *Turkish Studies, 15*(4), 671–688. doi:10.1080/14683849.2014.985425

Gou, Z., Yamaguchi, S., & Gupta, B. B. (2017). Analysis of various security issues and challenges in cloud computing environment: a survey. In Identity Theft: Breakthroughs in Research and Practice (pp. 221-247). IGI Global. doi:10.4018/978-1-5225-0808-3.ch011

Hailong, Z., Wenyan, G., & Bo, J. (2014, September). Machine learning and lexicon based methods for sentiment classification: A survey. In *2014 11th web information system and application conference* (pp. 262-265). IEEE.

Han, E. J., & Sohn, S. Y. (2015). Patent valuation based on text mining and survival analysis. *The Journal of Technology Transfer, 40*(5), 821–839. doi:10.100710961-014-9367-6

Hassonah, M. A., Al-Sayyed, R., Rodan, A., Ala'M, A. Z., Aljarah, I., & Faris, H. (2020). An efficient hybrid filter and evolutionary wrapper approach for sentiment analysis of various topics on Twitter. *Knowledge-Based Systems, 192*, 105353. doi:10.1016/j.knosys.2019.105353

Hayran, A., & Sert, M. (2017, May). Sentiment analysis on microblog data based on word embedding and fusion techniques. In *2017 25th Signal Processing and Communications Applications Conference (SIU)* (pp. 1-4). IEEE. 10.1109/SIU.2017.7960519

Hemmatian, F., & Sohrabi, M. K. (2019). A survey on classification techniques for opinion mining and sentiment analysis. *Artificial Intelligence Review, 52*(3), 1495–1545. doi:10.100710462-017-9599-6

Jain, A. K., & Gupta, B. B. (2019). A machine learning based approach for phishing detection using hyperlinks information. *Journal of Ambient Intelligence and Humanized Computing, 10*(5), 2015–2028. doi:10.100712652-018-0798-z

Jost, J. T., Barberá, P., Bonneau, R., Langer, M., Metzger, M., Nagler, J., Sterling, J., & Tucker, J. A. (2018). How social media facilitates political protest: Information, motivation, and social networks. *Political Psychology, 39*, 85–118. doi:10.1111/pops.12478

Karahoca, A., Karahoca, D., & Evirgen, E. (2019). Sentiment analysis of Turkish tweets by data mining methods. *International Journal of Mechanical Engineering and Technology*, *10*(1).

Karcioğlu, A. A., & Aydin, T. (2019, April). Sentiment analysis of Turkish and english twitter feeds using Word2Vec model. In *2019 27th Signal Processing and Communications Applications Conference (SIU)* (pp. 1-4). IEEE. 10.1109/SIU.2019.8806295

Karthikeyan, T., Sekaran, K., Ranjith, D., & Balajee, J. M. (2019). Personalized content extraction and text classification using effective web scraping techniques. *International Journal of Web Portals*, *11*(2), 41–52. doi:10.4018/IJWP.2019070103

Kaya, M., Fidan, G., & Toroslu, I. H. (2012, December). Sentiment analysis of turkish political news. In *2012 IEEE/WIC/ACM International Conferences on Web Intelligence and Intelligent Agent Technology* (Vol. 1, pp. 174-180). IEEE. 10.1109/WI-IAT.2012.115

Kirelli, Y., & Arslankaya, S. (2020). Sentiment Analysis of Shared Tweets on Global Warming on Twitter with Data Mining Methods: A Case Study on Turkish Language. *Computational Intelligence and Neuroscience*. PMID:32963511

Li, H. R., He, F. Z., & Yan, X. H. (2019). IBEA-SVM: An indicator-based evolutionary algorithm based on pre-selection with classification guided by SVM. *Applied Mathematics. A Journal of Chinese Universities*, *34*(1), 1–26. doi:10.100711766-019-3706-1

Mostafa, M. M. (2013). More than words: Social networks' text mining for consumer brand sentiments. *Expert Systems with Applications*, *40*(10), 4241–4251. doi:10.1016/j.eswa.2013.01.019

Ouaguid, A., Abghour, N., & Ouzzif, M. (2018). A novel security framework for managing android permissions using blockchain technology. *International Journal of Cloud Applications and Computing*, *8*(1), 55–79. doi:10.4018/IJCAC.2018010103

Prabowo, R., & Thelwall, M. (2009). Sentiment analysis: A combined approach. *Journal of Informetrics*, *3*(2), 143–157. doi:10.1016/j.joi.2009.01.003

Schonlau, M., Guenther, N., & Sucholutsky, I. (2017). Text mining with n-gram variables. *The Stata Journal*, *17*(4), 866–881. doi:10.1177/1536867X1801700406

Sharma, S., & Jain, A. (2019). Cyber social media analytics and issues: A pragmatic approach for twitter sentiment analysis. In *Advances in Computer Communication and Computational Sciences* (pp. 473–484). Springer. doi:10.1007/978-981-13-6861-5_41

Shastry, K. A., Sanjay, H. A., & Deexith, G. (2017). Quadratic-radial-basis-function-kernel for classifying multi-class agricultural datasets with continuous attributes. *Applied Soft Computing*, *58*, 65–74. doi:10.1016/j.asoc.2017.04.049

Surjandari, I., Naffisah, M. S., & Prawiradinata, M. I. (2015). Text mining of twitter data for public sentiment analysis of staple foods price changes. *Journal of Industrial and Intelligent Information*, *3*(3). Advance online publication. doi:10.12720/jiii.3.3.253-257

Vural, A. G., Cambazoglu, B. B., Senkul, P., & Tokgoz, Z. O. (2013). A framework for sentiment analysis in turkish: Application to polarity detection of movie reviews in Turkish. In *Computer and Information Sciences III* (pp. 437–445). Springer. doi:10.1007/978-1-4471-4594-3_45

Wikarsa, L., & Thahir, S. N. (2015, November). A text mining application of emotion classifications of Twitter's users using Naive Bayes method. In *2015 1st International Conference on Wireless and Telematics (ICWT)* (pp. 1-6). IEEE. 10.1109/ICWT.2015.7449218

APPENDIX

```
import tweepy as tw
import xlsxwriter # The library to be used to save the data
import datetime # Library required for the date range
import pandas as pd # Library used for files and assemblies

#Keys
consumer_key = " XXXXXXXXXXXXXXXXXX "
consumer_secret = " XXXXXXXXXXXXXXX "
access_key = " XXXXXXXXX-XXXXXXXXXXXXXXXXXXXXXXXXXXXX "
access_secret = " XXXXXXXXXXXXXXXXXXXXXXXXXXXXXXXXXXXXX "

# In [2]:
# Communication with Twitter section
try:
 auth = tw.OAuthHandler(consumer_key, consumer_secret)
 auth. set_access_token(access_key, access_secret)
 auth. get_authorization_url()
 api = tw.API(auth)
except tw. TweepError:
 print ('err')

# In [3]:
# Retrieving information of Twitter profile from excel file
mimet = pd. read_excel(open ("___", "rb"), sheet_name = "
Sheet1 ")
al = list (mimet [ "Unnamed: 3"] [1: -1])
mylist = []
for i in al:
    mylist. append (i.rpartition ("/") [-1])
mylist

# In [63]:
name = " mahfiegilmez " # The place where the person to search
is specified.
startDate = datetime. datetime (2019, 6, 24, 0, 0, 0)
endDate = datetime. datetime (2019, 12, 31, 23, 59, 59)
count = 0
```

```
tweets = []
# To get started, the first 200 tweets are received.
tmpTweets = api.user_timeline (name,count = 200)
# The initial 200 tweets are checked. It is added to the list
of tweets within the date range.
for tweet in tmpTweets:
        if tweet. created_at < endDate and tweet. created_at >
startDate:
                tweets. append (tweet)
# In each loop, new query is opened to go to the previous date
by comparing # the date of the previous last tweet
while (tmpTweets[-1]. created_at > startDate):
    print("Next Tweet @", tmpTweets [-1]. created_at, count)
    # The next 20 tweets are received. Each tweet set is
checked one by one.
    tmpTweets = api.user_timeline (name,max_id = tmpTweets[-1].
id, wait_on_rate_limit = True,tweet_mode = "extended",wait_on_
rate_limit_notify = True,timeout = 5,retry_count = 2,retry_
delay = 10)
    count += 1
    for tweet in tmpTweets:
    # The tweet is saved in the tweets list within the desired
date range.
        if tweet. created_at < endDate and tweet. created_at >
startDate:
                tweets. append(tweet)


# In [61]:
# The section that ensures that the tweets we receive are
passed through criteria and assigned to a new series
tweets2 = []
tweets.reverse()
count=0
for x in tweets:
    if(x. in_reply_to_status_id == None) or (x. in_reply_to_
screen_name == name):
        if (not x.retweeted) and ("RT @" not in x. full_text):
            tweets2. append (x)
            print(x. user.name, " >>", "DATE: ",x. created_
at,">> ",x.user.location, ">> ",x.full_text, "\n\n")
```

```
            count+=1
            print(count)


# In [51]:
# It serves to export periodic data from the criteria.
workbookfp = xlsxwriter. Workbook(name +"_Dönemlik" " .xlsx")
worksheetfp = workbookfp. add_worksheet()
row = 0
for tweet in tweets2:
    worksheetfp. write_string (row, 0, str(tweet.user.name))
    worksheetfp. write_string (row, 1, str(tweet.created_at))
    worksheetfp. write (row, 2, tweet.full_text)
    worksheetfp. write_string(row, 3, str(tweet.user.location))
    row += 1
workbookfp. close()
print("Excel file ready")


# In [6]:
name = "mahfiegilmez"
tweets = api. user_timeline (screen_name=name, tweet_
mode="extended", count = 200)
tmp = []
tweetler = [ tweet for tweet in tweets]
for j in tweetler:
    tmp. append (j)
tmp. reverse ()
count = 0
for i in tmp:
    if (i.in_reply_to_status_id == None) or (i.in_reply_to_
screen_name == name):
        if (not i.retweeted) and ("RT @" not in i. full_text):
            print(i.user.screen_name, " >>", "DATE: ",i.
created_at," >> ",i.user.location,">> ",i.full_text, "\n\n")
            count += 1
            print(count)
```

Chapter 9
The Stakes of Social Media:
Analyzing User Sentiments

Elodie Attié
iD https://orcid.org/0000-0003-3400-8927
Capgemini Engineering T.E.C., France

Anne Bouvet
iD https://orcid.org/0000-0003-4648-455X
Capgemini Engineering T.E.C., France

Jérôme Guibert
Capgemini Engineering T.E.C., France

ABSTRACT

The COVID-19 context affected the use of social media. Video and voice chat facilitate social interactions during the current social distancing requirements. However, social media creates unrealistic reference points of comparison. The time spent on social media can thus diminish well-being. Researchers and managers aspire to understand how sentiments can control social media. Another research interest regards which techniques create positive sentiments and enhance user experience. This chapter introduces the main stakes of social media, how sentiments change social media, and in turn, social media influences sentiments. The main focus presents a literature review regarding the techniques to analyze sentiments. Finally, solutions and recommendations contemplate the use of social media, for both users and social media platforms.

DOI: 10.4018/978-1-7998-8413-2.ch009

INTRODUCTION

Natural disasters motivate researchers to analyze users' behavior and sentiments on social media (Gao et al., 2020; Pathak et al., 2020). The Covid-19 pandemic has changed the way people used to live and behave on social media (Albahli et al., 2020). The situation heightened mental and physical issues due to diseases and stress (Campbell & Gavet, 2021). Social media gives various ways to communicate and create social bonds. It represents a timely concern to fight against isolation. People spend more time on social media, willing to enhance their well-being and social life (Boyd & Ellison, 2007; Nyagah et al., 2015). However, users' perceptions can be wrong. Research has shown that the use of social media enhances signs of depression, anxiety, and sleeping disorders (Milyavskaya et al., 2018; Utz et al., 2015; Verduyn et al., 2015). People tend to do upward comparisons, diminishing their self-esteem whereas most people on social media post filtered pictures (Hamasaki et al., 2009; Muqaddas et al., 2017). In addition, the development of video and voice chat facilitates social interactions, making them more realistic and human. More than text, the voice, and facial expressions enhance sentiments (Dai et al., 2015). Therefore, social media can analyze users' attitudes to improve user experience, and in turn sentiments and behaviors (Albahli et al., 2020). In marketing, researchers and managers can conduct tests to understand consumers' behavior and their level of trust in a brand's message (De Keyzer et al., 2017). Neuroscience and artificial intelligence techniques can analyze users' sentiments and behaviors during their social media experience (Zhang et al., 2020).

This chapter aims at explaining (1) the stakes of social media, (2) the way sentiments influence social media and in turn, social media influences sentiments, and (3) techniques to analyze user's sentiments. The first part presents the background of this chapter, with social media characteristics and the stakes of social media; the second part focuses on social media and sentiments, the type of data necessary to do sentiment analysis, and the techniques of sentiment analysis on social media; the third part suggests solutions and recommendations regarding unhealthy social comparisons and risky behaviors on social media, as well as solutions for social media platforms to develop a user-centric strategy; finally, the fourth part brings out future research directions regarding new ways of conducting sentiment analysis on social media, like media ethnography or neuromarketing, and discusses the role of social media moderators.

BACKGROUND

Social Media Characteristics

Social Media Content

Each social media displays some specific functionalities and has a different positioning and targets of users (i.e., age or socio-professional categories). Social media can respond to work purposes (i.e., LinkedIn, Twitter) or more personal and creative purposes (i.e., Instagram, Facebook, TikTok). Table 1 presents an overview of the main social media content. It shows that social media differentiate according to their functionalities. They can enable users to generate text, videos, photos, voice, messages, reactions, communities, and artificial intelligence control. Solely the social media Facebook, Linked In, and Twitter display all these functionalities.

Table 1. Social media content

Social media	Media content							
	Text	Video	Photo	Voice	Messages/chat	Community (follows, friends)	Reactions (likes, shares, comments)	Artificial intelligence control
Clubhouse				x		x	x	
Instagram		x	x	x	x	x	x	x
Facebook	x	x	x	x	x	x	x	x
LinkedIn	x	x	x	x	x	x	x	x
Pinterest		x	x			x	x	x
Snapchat		x	x	x	x	x		
TikTok		x		x	x	x	x	x
Twitter	x	x	x	x	x	x	x	x
YouTube		x		x		x	x	x
Twitch		x		x	x	x	x	x

Social Media Dimensions

Social media turn around four main dimensions, namely the human dimension, the entertaining dimension, the knowledge dimension, and the business dimension:

- **Human dimension:** Social media enables users to engage in a community, stay in touch with others, share knowledge and updates. For example, Facebook offers two mobile applications to differentiate users' needs: the Facebook application enables to follow and share updates, and the Facebook Messenger application enables users to communicate with others. Moreover, social media allows users to break the traditional barriers of distance and time through real-time messages, video chats, and reactions –this is the case for most social media.
- **Entertaining dimension:** Social media enables sharing content and following specific communities. For instance, Pinterest's users can create thematic boards and pin similar images from the Internet, whereas Instagram enables people to share pictures or videos they created. In addition, social media enables to relax, spend time watching shows, short movies, or video games, like YouTube, Instagram, Twitch, TikTok, Facebook, or Snapchat.
- **Knowledge dimension:** Social media can be used as learning tools, to look for updates from peers, brands, communities, news, or public sentiments and opinions about specific topics. For example, YouTube proposes tutorials about various subjects, allowing people to choose their interests. Moreover, all social media enables to share some information, content, and ideas –it can be private or public. The main objective of Snapchat is to build a safe place for people to express themselves and increase the sense of solidarity between them (Kelly, 2018).
- **Business dimension:** Social media can develop professional networks and communicate work updates. LinkedIn suggests job offers, enables people to share their resumes and to stay in touch with professional networks. Social media changes traditional marketing techniques to social media marketing techniques. Social media is a way to communicate in real-time with consumers and market a brand (De Vlack, 2020). It also facilitates interactions and co-creation with consumers to offer the best product at the right time, and to increase visibility and business profits (De Vlack, 2020).

Social Media Journey

Social media remain in non-stop competition with other social media, and they need to differentiate themselves to attract users and brands, increase the loyalty of use, and develop their activity and profits. For instance, Facebook bought Instagram and WhatsApp, and Twitter abandoned Periscope and Vine with the arrival of TikTok on the market. Thus, each social media implies a different strategy that can influence users differently during their day. Figure 1 illustrates users' sentiment journey on the main social media.

Figure 1. Users' sentiments journey on social media

The Stakes of Social Media

Understanding Consumer Behavior

Social media users can follow brands, business pages, communities, and share information with their peers (Baştuğ et al., 2020). Marketers use social media to interact with their consumers as well as analyze and predict their behavior (Baştuğ et al., 2020). For example, researchers and marketers believe that Twitter is a highly reliable tool for companies to connect with consumers (Barnes et al., 2012; Swani et al., 2014). Other researchers have shown the reliability of Facebook, YouTube, Linked In, and Pinterest as well (Jansen et al., 2009; Michaelidou et al., 2011). Social media feeds showed 50.5% neutral, 31.2% positive, and 18.3% negative sentiments during the Covid-19 context (Albahli et al., 2020). Understanding consumer behavior can guide marketers to choose which content to share and for which social media audience (Baştuğ et al., 2020). This can increase brand attachment and consumer engagement (Baştuğ et al., 2020). Indeed, social media enables companies to develop their strategies: interact with their target, develop their brand image, and do advertising (Baştuğ et al., 2020), or do pay referencing ads like YouTube and TikTok.

Responding to Users' Needs

According to the uses and gratifications theory, different needs explain the use of social media (Ruggiero, 2000; Whiting & Williams, 2013): the need for social interaction and communication (i.e., Facebook, Instagram, Snapchat); information and knowledge (i.e., YouTube, Twitter, LinkedIn, Facebook, Instagram, Clubhouse); entertainment and relaxation (i.e., TikTok, YouTube, Snapchat, Twitch); free expression of opinion and information (i.e., Facebook, Twitter, Clubhouse, Pinterest). Social media is a source of information, communication, entertainment, and/or support (Chang,

2019; De Vlack, 2020). People can use social media to share some good news and personal information, or spend time and evacuate stress (Munzel et al., 2018; Cho et al., 2020). For instance, students can use social media to get school information and work together (Aillerie & McNicol, 2016). Therefore, users expect the right information at the right time. Social media platforms acknowledge responsibility in distinguishing fake news from facts (De Vlack, 2020). For example, at the start of the Covid-19 pandemic, Instagram highlighted Covid-19 related posts and stories coming from health administrations (De Vlack, 2020). Furthermore, social media can enable people to express suicidal thoughts and dark feelings, such as depression and anxiety (Calear et al., 2010; Robinson et al., 2016). Social media can prevent deviant behaviors and provide anonymous non-judgmental advice (Robinson et al., 2016). This implies a system to capture users' sentiments and a safe and efficacy method to influence sentiments and risky behaviors (Robinson et al., 2016; Robinson et al., 2014).

Privacy Concerns

Social media are accessible through laptops, tablets, mobile applications, or some smartwatches. The way social media tracks and collects personal data can be perceived as too intrusive, and can arouse privacy concerns (Awad & Krishnan, 2006; Hong & Thong, 2013; Phelps et al., 2001). External databases usually collect the data, leading to ethical problems due to the unpredictable characteristics of social media (i.e., the data are automatically collected) (Van der Hoven, 2013). Information privacy and protection are key factors of acceptance and use of social media (Jia & Xu, 2016). When users perceive privacy risks about the use of the data, users tend to stress, which subsequently leads to the rejection of the technology (Lynch & Ariely, 2000). Social media platforms, therefore, focus on technological features, such as privacy settings or information withholding (Jiang et al., 2013, Acquisti et al., 2015). For example, Facebook and Snapchat users can control if they want to share their geographical position with their network; Instagram users can share stories and posts with a public or private setting. These privacy settings enable people to create social groups, share information accordingly, and reinforce and respond to the need to belong to a social group.

Making Profits Through Social Media

Brands can adapt their content and their presence on social media according to their positioning and targets. For example, YouTube can display advertisings before and during videos, enabling monetization of the videos for creators. In exchange, brands can control their content creation, such as the speech, presentation, video concept, logo, etc. Brands can integrate their ads in Instagram or Facebook feeds or collaborate directly with influencers, ensuring targeting, loyalty strategies, and pricing strategies with special offers and promotional codes. During the Covid-19 pandemic, the closure of many non-essential stores due to the risks of contamination pushed many people to increase their online purchases, and social media became another way of communicating. For example, Facebook has set up a marketplace for sales, rentals, and donations between people, whereas Instagram displays a special section highlighting the sales of designers and brands. Furthermore, brands can analyze customers' reactions to their product and competitors' strategies, and thus, highlight needs and tendencies to adapt their strategy to the market. For example, if a competitor announces that they are investing in a niche market, it could represent a relevant opportunity to make profits. Moreover, social media enables consumers to spread the news about their experience and either the product or customer experience is great or bad, it can spread quickly, and uncontrollably if companies do not react quickly and accordingly. Consumers now have the power to hold companies to account for their marketing promises.

MAIN FOCUS OF THE CHAPTER

Social Media and Sentiments

There is an endless circle of sentiments on social media. On the one hand, social media can create sentiments, and on the other hand, sentiments can influence the use of social media and behaviors as well. This part explores how creators and moderators can create sentiments to users (Diakopoulos & Shamma 2010; O'Connor et al., 2010; Tumasjan et al., 2010; Kim et al., 2009), and in turn, how sentiments influence social media content, behaviors, and reactions.

Social Media Creates Sentiments

Using social media can come from intrinsic motivations (i.e., enhancing social status through the perceived social image, looking for a sense of fame or social recognition), and/or extrinsic (i.e., TikTok or YouTube pay creators according to the number of views of their videos). The sentiments created due to the dissemination of positive and negative opinions from users, creators, moderators, and companies, enable researchers to predict real-time issues like box-office revenues for movies (Asur & Huberman, 2010) or political elections (Kim et al., 2009). Moreover, many people use social media to enhance their well-being and social lives by building or maintaining personal and professional relationships (Boyd & Ellison, 2007). For introverts, social media favors communication and social well-being (Amichai-Hamburger et al., 2010; Ellison et al., 2007). Furthermore, positive feedback from peers, including strangers, can increase self-esteem to a very high degree (Valkenburg et al., 2006). More specifically, social media can give users a sense of freedom and social identity, self-esteem and confidence, and positive vibes during hard times (Nyagah et al., 2015). However, social media hides some dark sides as well. An increase in the time spent on social media engenders a decrease in self-esteem (Chen & Lee, 2013; Muqaddas et al., 2017). Approximately 88% of users do social comparisons on social media, including 98% of upward social comparisons (i.e., comparing oneself with someone looking or doing better) (Muqaddas et al., 2017). In addition, filtered pictures displaying re-shaped bodies and faces seem realistic to users who compare to them, decreasing their self-image and confidence (Kleemans et al., 2018, O'Guinn & Shrum, 1997). Finally, moderators have a role to play in regulating users' behaviors, reactions, and thus sentiments on social media since they are in direct contact with brands and users.

Sentiments Create Social Media Interactions and Behaviors

Multitasking on social media can predict signs of depression (Becker et al., 2013). Social media can be associated with signs of depression and other issues, such as sleeping disorders, anxiety, envy, stress, and low self-esteem or well-being (Bjornsen & Archer, 2015; Milyavskaya et al., 2018; Utz et al., 2015). Moreover, the literature highlighted a fear of missing out where people stay connected on social media to not miss any news and show others they are always present. This fear of missing out implies more time spent on social media and more feelings of stress too (Alt, 2017; Blackwell et al., 2017). In addition, social comparisons moderate the relationship between the use of social media and sentiments of loneliness (Yang, 2016). Therefore, social anxiety seems to influence more the use of social media than the other way around (Dobrean & Pasarelu, 2016).

Figure 2 presents a visual resume of the lifecycle of sentiments on social media.

Figure 2 shows the different steps leading to reference points and sentiments on social media:

1. Event: The user, creator, or brand has a significant event or update, new idea, or a concept to share with peers (i.e., #BlackLivesMatter, #MeToo, #BodyPositive, etc.);
2. Writing: The influencer creates new content (i.e., a picture with a specific comment, a video, a post, etc.) in reaction to this event;
3. Broadcasting: The influencer shares new content to a close social circle, public or private, also depending on the social media. The social media algorithm

automatically scans the content to control, authorize, monetize, tag, or block following its own rules (i.e., automatic regulation);

4. Close subscribers' readings: The first reactions of the close circle lead the social media algorithm to upgrade or downgrade the post;

5. Re-use and additional postings: The reaction or concept can be re-posted and re-used by users, influencers, and companies;

6. Trend analysis and increased visibility: The algorithm understands the interest of the subject and upgrades every post/content about the event (i.e., public regulation);

7. Extended public broadcasting (subscribers and others): There is a multiplication of the content on different social media and informative media, such as the TV, press, radio, etc.;

8. Reading and appropriation of the viewers: Everyone, people, personalities and medias are able to express their opinion about the event;

9. Identification and creation of a movement: The movement is set in action, the people can identify themselves with the event and are able to unite to act in force. This induces a new reference point and norms like the #BlackLivesMatter, #MeToo, #BodyPositive, etc. movements.

Figure 2. Lifecycle of sentiments on social media

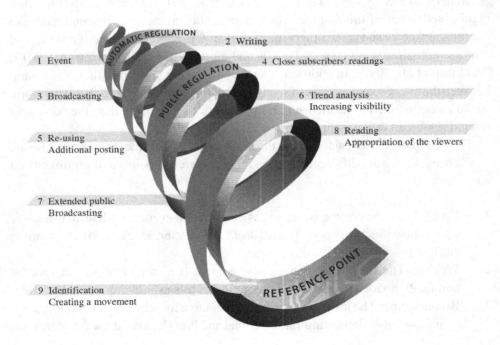

What data for Sentiment Analysis?

This part presents the type of data that enables conducting sentiment analysis on social media, such as text, image, voice and video.

Text

The analysis of a corpus of text data enables researchers to study sentiments on social media as well as the spread of misinformation, which can increase fear, notably during the Covid-19 pandemic (Alahmary et al., 2019). Moreover, research has shown that the use of emojis can substitute or enhance the sentiment orientation and meaning of the text (Almuraih et al., 2020). Researchers should take into account both text and emojis when studying users' sentiments on social media (Almuraih et al., 2020). Indeed, smiley emoji faces versus angry or crying emoji faces demonstrate the sentiment orientation or the intentions of the user (Almuraih et al., 2020). In addition, research has shown that images and texts can lead to sentiments that may influence users' engagement toward the post, like viewing, liking, commenting, sharing, and tagging a relative (Alibakhshi & Srivastava, 2019).

Image

The analysis of images on social media enables researchers to study users' sentiments (Poria et al., 2017; Bakhshi et al., 2014). Researchers want to know if a happy-looking person in a picture can lead to more positive sentiments and reactions than a sad-looking person (Alibakhshi & Srivastava, 2019). However, the relationship between the sentiment displayed through the image and its accompanying text remains unclear. Selfies influence self-esteem regarding the reactions and the use of beauty filters (Kleemans et al., 2018). Another example, posting a picture of a trip to Bali on Instagram can translate the pride and happiness of the creator, and engender social comparison or dreams to the viewers (Yang, 2016). Finally, regarding the symbolism of the colors, using a black and white picture (i.e., sadness, mystery, melancholia, vintage) versus a colorful picture (i.e., happiness or anger, realistic) can translate different sentiments as well.

Voice

The voice contains a multitude of information. Indeed, a verbal message can communicate non-verbal messages and express sentiments. Thanks to prosody, researchers can recognize a person's voice, age, sex, accent, intonations, and sentiments (Scherer, 2003). Several studies have already developed their algorithm to detect sentiments based on the acoustic parameters of the voice, reaching 80% accuracy. Researchers have developed algorithms that detect primary emotions in discrete forms, like anger, joy, sadness, surprise, disgust, fear, and neutral emotions. Others have classified the sentiments in continuous forms along axes: valence and pleasure (positive versus negative), and arousal and dominance (Dai et al., 2015). However, the voices on YouTube videos often result from several captures, which can induce a bias in the analysis of the sentiments. Voice analysis is the most effective with spontaneous speeches, like on Instagram, Snapchat, TikTok, or Facebook stories.

Video

Videos can evoke and engender many sentiments through voice, background, and images, leading to greater user emotional engagement through multiple stimuli (Schreiner et al., 2019). The analysis of videos, such as the degree of arousal, facial expressions, retention, and attention duration can provide further insight into what specific features can cause which corresponding emotional responses (Gupta et al., 2017; Schreiner et al., 2019). For example, a laughing man delivers a positive emotion, but this emotion becomes negative if this same laughing man carries a weapon, and the meaning of the same laughing changes (Gupta et al., 2017). Therefore, a video displays a simple and accurate indicator of the overall sentiment of the video (Gupta et al., 2017).

Techniques of Sentiments Analysis on Social Media

Research has shown that the valence of a message (positive versus negative) influences sentiments, whereas voice intonations (factual-emotional) do not have a significant influence (De Keyzer et al., 2017). Social media analytics enable brands to measure the performance of their marketing actions through specific reporting platforms. For example, researchers can extract fragments of text or speech to categorize, analyze and translate data into meaningful insights. More specifically, social media analytics enable companies to spot tendencies and analyze the marketplace, understand consumers' needs through their sentiments towards the brand, and measure the relevance of social media strategies. Research in marketing usually focuses on social media analytics but sentiment analysis should complement this research method (Baştuğ et al., 2020). Sentiment analysis started with text-based information (Hearst, 1992; Wiebe, 1994) and brought out different approaches: subjective lexicon, n-gram modeling, rule-based machine learning (Alrumaih et al., 2020; Pathak et al., 2020; Abdul-Mageed et al., 2020), data mining (Clement, 2020), natural language processing (Albahli et al., 2020; Singh et al., 2020) (see Table 2).

Table 2. Description of different techniques of sentiment analysis

Methodology	Description	Advantages & Limitations
Text-based information	Primary input and output based on text rather than graphics or sound, from vocabulary database	Advantages: AI can understand what the user says and sentiments linked to the post; Limitations: Twitter enables people to post 280 characters only, limiting self-expression.
Subjective lexicon	A list of words and grammatical rules to which is assigned a score that indicates its nature in terms of a positive, negative, or objective point of view	Advantages: A wider term coverage, companies can analyze and highlight positive and negative feedback from consumers; Limitations: AI cannot discern the use of sarcasm, there is a restricted number of words in the lexicons (which evolves very quickly on social media) and thus, the assignation of a fixed sentiment orientation and score to the lexicon.
N-gram modelling	Counting how often word sequences occur in corpus text to predict the next items	Advantages: simplicity and scalability; Limitations: predictability is greater with big samples.
Rule-based machine learning	The identification of information applied to a set of relational rules to predict future tendencies and behaviors	Advantages: the ability to adapt and create trained models for specific purposes and contexts, and predict consumer behavior; Limitations: low applicability to new data because it requires labeled data, and labeled data can be costly or even prohibitive in some contexts.
Data mining	The analysis of data from different perspectives to transform data into useful information by establishing relationships between data or identifying patterns	Advantages: data mining brings useful insights to marketers; Limitations: it collects personal information so privacy concerns can be high, and the data need to be updated for current relevant information.
Natural language processing (NLP)	The use of a built-in statistical model to perform a speech recognition routine that converts the natural language to a programming language	Advantages: process and analyze large amounts of natural language data; Limitations: NLP is mostly trained by languages, and usually it works better with English.

Table 2 shows that sentiment analysis can be conducted through different techniques such as:

- Text-based information: The text is classified according to specific criteria like the polarity of the sentiment expressed (i.e., positive, negative, neutral), of the outcome (i.e., happy versus sad or angry) (Niu et al., 2005), the agreement or disagreement with a topic (Balahur et al., 2009), good or bad news (Bansal et al., 2008), support or opposition (Terveen et al., 1997), and pros and cons about a subject (Kim & Hovy, 2006);

- Subjective lexicon analysis: Product reviews enable to highlight sentiments linked to the product, and thus predict intentions and behaviors (Jebaseeli & Kirubakaran, 2012);
- N-gram modeling: This technique implies the use of uni-gram, bi-grams, tri-grams, 4-grams, 5-grams, etc. A higher number of words predicts a more accurate model;
- Rule-based machine learning: This technique performs the semi and/or supervised learning through the extraction of the features from the data and suggests a predictive model;
- Data mining: This technique implies the association between the data, clustering, classification, and prediction to define sequential patterns;
- Natural language processing (NLP): This technique infers the polarity of common sense concepts and opinions from natural language text at a semantic level, rather than at the syntactic level (Cambria et al., 2010). NLP can continually monitor positive or negative expectations to refine brand strategies.

Based on the literature, there are five main steps to conduct sentiment analysis (Alahmary et al., 2019; Alrumaih et al., 2020; Aljasir et al., 2017; Rajan et al., 2014; He & Deyu, 2011):

1. Data collection: Collecting insightful data (i.e., Tweets, Instagram posts, Facebook comments, hashtags, etc.);
2. Data cleaning: Cleaning undesirable data and converting the data into understandable files for processing;
3. Pre-processing task: Transforming raw data into understandable formats;
4. Sentiment analysis: Identifying polarity within the text, voices, images, and videos;
5. Implementation and results: Analyzing the reliability and accuracy of the information.

SOLUTIONS AND RECOMMENDATIONS

How to Fade off Unhealthy Social Comparisons?

Social media creates reference points, like body shape, brand shopping, travels, etc. This social comparison can decrease users' well-being (Yang, 2016). Research has shown that the more people use Facebook, the more their self-esteem decreases with upward comparisons (Vogel et al., 2014). Upward comparisons bump up self-perception whereas downward comparisons add no bump of effect (Vogel et al., 2014). Furthermore, people usually show a bright side of their life that does not represent reality, whereas some can show a dark side of their life to increase empathy and attention (i.e., "Fuck my Life" posts on social media). Thus, social media can create sentiments that are not rooted in reality, which can engender negative sentiments (Yang, 2016). Thus, people should educate themselves about the risks of social comparisons on social media. For example, users could unfollow people and brands leading to upward comparisons. Since 2021, Instagram fade off these unhealthy social comparisons by hiding the number of likes on users' posts.

How to Prevent Risky Behaviors on Social Media?

Social media analytics lead to the concept of social listening, such as monitoring social media to solve problems and highlight opportunities. In addition, social media enables to express risky behaviors such as suicidal thoughts (Robinson et al., 2016). Social media algorithms should be able to detect and react to these risky behaviors and prevent people from harassment and being influenced (Robinson et al., 2016). For example, in France, we can cite the case of Mila, 17 years old, harassed for criticizing a religion (BBC, 2020). There are also worldwide challenges such as the "Blue whale challenge" created in 2018 in Russia, which consists of 50 dares for 50 days, or the "Momo Challenge", in 2019, targeting children on YouTube, which both led to suicide dares (Phippen, 2020). Social media could become a safer place with more privacy and ethical settings to increase well-being (Van der Hoven, 2013). Some social media like TalkLife aim to prevent these risky behaviors by connecting people from all over the world, and whose purpose is to support people going through anxiety, depression, and self-harm habits. In addition, Facebook analyzes users' messages to predict intentions to commit suicide and can transmit this information to authorities for help. There is also a way to fight against the spread of rumors with an algorithm inspired by nature that focuses on these criteria: public or private, tracing flows of information, and user account activity (Sahoo et al., 2020). The algorithm calculates the probability that a specific account is affected by rumor information and the Twitter profile can be censored (Sahoo et al., 2020). Nevertheless, some users can try to fraudulently spread fake information. To overcome the risk of user privacy violation on social media, data security by encryption, separation, or classification by machine learning can identify fake profile identification (Sahoo et al., 2019). Data security algorithms use various perspectives such as account viability, sequence of transactions, and spatial correlations between different accounts (Sahoo et al., 2019). Furthermore, machine learning algorithms can detect a human, legitimate bot, versus a malicious bot, thanks to the pattern of writing attached to the post. The content is classified using various classifiers to detect bot accounts (Sahoo et al., 2019).

How to Develop a User-Centric Strategy?

Brands should focus on user-centric strategies, instead of producer-centric strategies, to produce valuable content through helpful information and relevant advice (De Vlack, 2020). A user-centric strategy places users at the center of social media usage with specific platform design and functionalities. The goal is to provide a positive user experience and increase the activity and time spent on social media. More than ever, creators and moderators should take into consideration users' needs before posting public content (Muqaddas et al., 2017). For example, YouTube created YouTube Kids, and Facebook created Messenger Kids for children under 13 years old, displaying parental control to check the contacts and messages content. Therefore, educating people from a young age about the stakes and risks of social media could prevent them from risky behaviors.

FUTURE RESEARCH DIRECTIONS

Netnography: A Way to Observe Social Media Sentiments

Netnography could be a way to observe and understand social media practices and needs. This technique combines ethnographic methods –traditional participative observation and tools of netnography– and visual analysis. A netnography study about Donald Trump versus Hilary Clinton supporters on Twitter has shown that based on the way political supporters discuss car brands, researchers could predict either the person supports Trump or Clinton (Schaefer, 2017). Furthermore, social media networks could create a link between netnography and artificial intelligence (AI): netnography can teach AI and AI can learn from netnography to better capture and engender sentiments (e.g., Robinson et al., 2016).

Neuromarketing: A Way to Analyze Social Media Behaviors

The analysis of emotions is becoming an important issue for marketers to improve the impact and efficiency of marketing strategies. The act of buying is generated by 80% from the limbic system, the seat of emotions, which is the domain of cognitive neuroscience (Soyez, 2017). Neuromarketing tools imply functional magnetic resonance imaging and electroencephalography, as well as techniques based on biometric technologies or artificial intelligence and big data, facial recognition, and natural language processing. The aim is to synthesize and model emotions by studying the microexpressions that reveal sentiments (Soyez, 2017). In practice, the RealEyes software detects unconscious reactions caught on camera. Facebook, was busted in May 2017 for trying to determine users' emotions. The social media used smartphone or computer cameras to analyze emotions when people watched specific content (Soyez, 2017). Thus, neuromarketing techniques allow managers and researchers to analyze and predict users' behaviors from the brain processes that take place during content exposure (Zhang et al., 2020). Sentiments engender body indicators that neuromarketing can detect and interpret (Ciccarelli & Meyer, 2006; Solomon, 2017). Moderators on forums and brands could learn from neuromarketing to engender positive sentiments through videos, voice, images, text, and emojis. For example, Google used eye-tracking to measure users' attention and emotional arousal with pupil dilatation, while looking at new advertising formats (O'Reilly, 2013). Based on this experimentation, Google could recommend to its clients that overlay formats increase more attention and emotional involvement than banner formats.

The New Role of Social Media Moderators

Brands can moderate their communities' reactions and answers, influencing sentiments and behaviors. Moreover, social media also moderates the use of their platforms. For example, Instagram and Facebook censor pages, posts, or people who seem to violate their rules. For example, in France, the city Bitche has been banned for several days on Facebook. Another example, fourteen influencers promoting the feminist cause and sexual education have also assigned Facebook in the Paris Court of Justice for the censorship of their content. Thus, there is a cycle of responsibilities on social media, describing the roles of users, brands/moderators, and governments (see Figure 3):

- Users and creators should educate themselves on ways to favor their well-being, prevent themselves from social media risks, and be respectful to one another;
- Brands and moderators should create a safe place for expression and favor consumer well-being, following laws and regulations, and showing benevolence, respect, and human values;
- Governments and justice should play a role over laws and regulations to protect users and brands, users' education, and privacy design and settings. For example, governments could better understand how to help people going through the Covid-19 pandemic (Albahli et al., 2020).

Figure 3. Cycle of responsibilities on social media

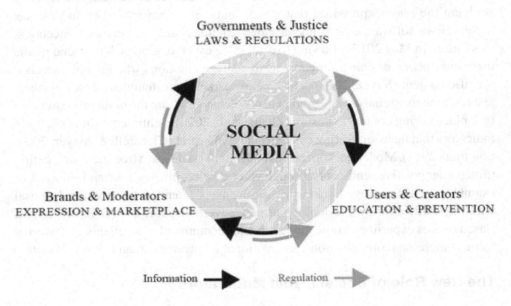

CONCLUSION

Researchers and managers can mine big data to understand sentiments, create new opportunities, and overcome rising challenges (Almuraih et al., 2020). Social media offers significant advantages to both brands and consumers, on a professional and personal level, as well as risks and stakes. People taking breaks from social media feel more well-being after only one week (Verduyn et al., 2015). Therefore, sentiment analysis could be a way for social media to prevent bad-being from the usage of their platforms and educate people to adopt better social media habits. In addition, social media analytics enable researchers to understand sentiments and predict behaviors. Thus, during the Covid-19 pandemic, social media represents an essential tool that could lead to drastic cultural and societal changes (Cook, 2020). Indeed, social media has the power to raise funds for various causes such as crowdfunding for artists and startups. For instance, Amira created a YouTube video which profits go to Black Lives Matter associations; Captain Tom Moore, a 99-year-old English citizen was able to raise over 5 million euros to help public hospitals during the first lockdown; and the Ice bucket challenge raises funds against the Charcot disease.

ACKNOWLEDGMENT

This research was supported by Capgemini Engineering.

REFERENCES

Abdul-Mageed, M., Zhang, C., Hashemi, A., & Nagoudi, E. M. (2020). *AraNet: New deep learning toolkit for arabic social media.* Medium. Accessed from: https://medium.com/syncedreview/aranet-new-deeplearning-toolkit-for-arabic-social-media-d4729887ca48

Acquisti, A., Brandimarte, L., & Loewenstein, G. (2015). Privacy and human behavior in the age of information. *Science, 347*(6221), 509–514. doi:10.1126cience. aaa1465 PMID:25635091

Aillerie, K., & McNicol, S. (2016). Information literacy and social networking sites: Challenges and stakes regarding teenagers' uses. *Journal for Communication Studies, 9*(2), 89–100.

Alahmary, R. M., Al-Dossari, H. Z., & Emam, A. Z. (2019). Sentiment analysis of saudi dialect using deep learning techniques. *International Conference on Electronics, Information, and Communication*, Auckland, New Zealand. 10.23919/ELINFOCOM.2019.8706408

Albahli, S., Algsham, A., Aeraj, S., Alsaeed, M., Alrashed, M., Rauf, H. T., Arif, M., & Mohammed, M. A. (2021). COVID-19 Public Sentiment Insights: A Text Mining Approach to the Gulf Countries. Computers. *Materials & Continua, 67*(2), 1613–1627. doi:10.32604/cmc.2021.014265

Alessia, D., Ferri, F., Grifoni, P., & Guzzo, T. (2015). Approaches, tools and applications for sentiment analysis implementation. *International Journal of Computers and Applications, 125*(3).

Alibakhshi, R., & Srivastava, S. C. (2019). *Should We Say What We Show? Examining the Influence of Image and Text Sentiments on Social Media Engagement. Fortieth International Conference on Information Systems*, Munich.

Aljasir, S., Bajnaid, A., Elyas, T., & Alnawasrah, M. (2017). University students usage of Facebook: The case of obtained gratifications and typology of its users. *Science, 229*, 61–66.

Alrumaih, A., Al-Sabbagh, A., Alsabah, R., Kharrufa, H., & Baldwin, J. (2020). Sentiment analysis of comments in social media. *Iranian Journal of Electrical and Computer Engineering*, *10*(6), 5917–5922.

Alt, D. (2017). Students' social media engagement and fear of missing out (FoMO) in a diverse classroom. *Journal of Computing in Higher Education*, *29*(2), 388–410. doi:10.100712528-017-9149-x

Amichai-Hamburger, Y., & Vinitzky, G. (2010). Social network use and personality. *Computers in Human Behavior*, *26*(6), 1289–1295. doi:10.1016/j.chb.2010.03.018

Asur, S., & Huberman, B. (2010). Predicting the future with social media. *Web Intelligence and Intelligent Agent Technology (WI-IAT). IEEE/WIC/ACM International Conference*, *1*, 492–499.

Awad, N. F., & Krishnan, M. S. (2006). The personalization privacy paradox: An empirical evaluation of information transparency and the willingness to be profiled online for personalization. *Management Information Systems Quarterly*, *30*(1), 13–28. doi:10.2307/25148715

Bakhshi, B., Shamma, D. A., & Gilbert, E. (2014). Faces Engage Us Photos with Faces Attract More Likes and Comments on Instagram. *Proceedings of the SIGCHI Conference on Human Factors in Computing Systems (CHI'14)*, 965-974. 10.1145/2556288.2557403

Balahur, A., Kozareva, Z., & Montoyo, A. (2009, March). Determining the polarity and source of opinions expressed in political debates. *International Conference on Intelligent Text Processing and Computational Linguistics*, 468-480. 10.1007/978-3-642-00382-0_38

Bansal, M., Cardie, C., & Lee, L. (2008). The power of negative thinking: Exploiting label disagreement in the min-cut classification framework. *Proceedings of the International Conference on Computational Linguistics (COLING)*, 15-18.

Barnes, N. G., Leschault, A. M., & Andonian, J. (2012). *Social media surge by the 2012 Fortune 500: Increase use of blogs, Facebook, Twitter and more.* Retrieved from https://www.umassd.edu/cmr/socialmedia/2012fortune500/

Baştuğ, S., Çalişir, V., Gülmez, S., & Ateş, A. (2020). Measuring port brand equity: A sentiment analysis on port social media messages. *Journal of Social Sciences*, *65*, 85–106.

BBC Article. (2020). Accessed from: https://www.bbc.com/news/world-europe-51369960

Becker, M. W., Alzahabi, R., & Hopwood, C. J. (2013). Media Multitasking is associated with symptoms of depression and social anxiety. *Cyberpsychology, Behavior, and Social Networking, 16*(2), 132–135.

Bjornsen, C. A., & Archer, K. J. (2015). Relations between college students cell phone use during class and grades. *Scholarship of Teaching and Learning in Psychology, 1*(4), 326–336.

Blackwell, D., Leaman, C., Tramposch, R., Osborne, C., & Liss, M. (2017). Extraversion, neuroticism, attachment style and fear of missing out as predictors of social media use and addiction. *Personality and Individual Differences, 116,* 69–72.

Boyd, D. M., & Ellison, N. B. (2007). Social network sites: Definition, history, and scholarship. *Journal of Computer-Mediated Communication, 13,* 210–230.

Calear, A. L., & Christensen, H. (2010). Review of internet-based prevention and treatment programs for anxiety and depression in children and adolescents. *Medical Journal, 192*(11).

Cambria, E., Speer, R., Havasi, C., & Hussain, A. (2010). SenticNet: A Publicly Available Semantic Resource for Opinion Mining. *AAAI Fall Symposium: Commonsense Knowledge, 10*(2), 5449.

Campbell, M., & Gavett, G. (2021). What Covid-19 Has Done to Our Well-Being, in 12 Charts. *Harvard Business Review*.

Chang, W.-L. (2019). The Impact of Emotion: A Blended Model to Estimate Influence on Social Media. *Information Systems Frontiers, 21,* 1137–1151.

Chen, W., & Lee, K. (2013). Sharing, liking, commenting, and distressed? The pathway between Facebook interaction and psychological distress. *Cyberpsychology, Behavior, and Social Networking, 16*(10), 728–734.

Cho, H., Li, P., & Goh, Z. H. (2020). Privacy Risks, Emotions, and Social Media: A Coping Model of Online Privacy. *ACM Transformation Computer-Human Interaction, 40*(6), 40–68.

Ciccarelli, S. K., & Meyer, G. E. (2006). *Psychology*. Prentice Hall.

Clement, J. (2020). *Twitter: Most users by country*. Statista. Available: https://www.statista.com/statistics/242606/number-of-active-twitter-users-in-selected-countries/

Cook, C. (2010). Mobile Marketing and Political Activities. *International Journal of Mobile Marketing, 5*(1), 154–163.

Dai, W., Han, D., Dai, Y., & Xu, D. (2015). Emotion recognition and affective computing on vocal social media. *Information & Management, 52*(7), 777–788.

De Keyzer, F., Dens, N., & De Pelsmacker, P. (2017). Don't be so emotional! How tone of voice and service type affect the relationship between message valence and consumer responses to WOM in social media. *Online Information Review, 41*(7), 905–920.

De Vlack, K. (2020). *What is the Role of Social Media during the COVID-19 Crisis?* Knowledge @HEC. Accessed from: https://www.hec.edu/en/knowledge/instants/what-role-social-media-during-covid-19-crisis-0

Diakopoulos, N. A., & Shamma, D. A. (2010). Characterizing debate performance via aggregated twitter sentiment. *Proceedings of the SIGCHI Conference on Human Factors in Computing Systems*, 1195-1198.

Dobrean, A., & Păsărelu, C.-R. (2016). Impact of Social Media on Social Anxiety. *Systematic Reviews*. Advance online publication. doi:10.5772/65188

Ellison, N., Steinfield, C., & Lampe, C. (2007). The benefits of Facebook "friends:" social capital and college students' use of online social network sites. *Journal of Computer-Mediated Communication, 12*, 1143–1168.

Gao, J., Zheng, P., Jia, Y., Chen, H., & Mao, Y. (2020). Mental health problems and social media exposure during COVID-19 outbreak. *PLoS One, 15*(4).

Gupta, P., Soundararajan, B., & Zachariah, T. (2017). *Image-based sentiment analysis of videos*. In *Thirtieth Annual Conference on Neural Information Processing Systems (NIPS)*, Barcelona, Spain.

Hamasaki, M., Takeda, H., Hope, T., & Nishimura, T. (2009, March). Network analysis of an emergent massively collaborative creation community: How can people create videos collaboratively without collaboration? *Proceedings of the International AAAI Conference on Web and Social Media, 3*(1).

He, Y., & Deyu, Z. (2011). Self-training from labeled features for sentiment analysis. *Information Processing & Management, 47*(4), 606–616.

Hearst, M. A. (1992). Direction-Based Text Interpretation as an Information Access Refinement. *Text Based Intelligent Systems: Current Research and Practice in Information Extraction and Retrieval*, 257-274.

Hong, W., & Thong, J. (2013). Internet privacy concerns: An integrated conceptualisation and four empirical studies. *MIS Quaterly, 37*(1), 275–298.

Jansen, B. J., Zhang, M., Sobel, K., & Chowdury, A. (2009). Twitter power: Tweets as electronic word of mouth. *Journal of the American Society for Information Science and Technology*, *60*(11), 2169–2188.

Jebaseeli, A. N., & Kirubakaran, E. (2012). A survey on sentiment analysis of (product) reviews. *International Journal of Computers and Applications*, *47*(11).

Jia, H., & Xu, H. (2016). Measuring individuals' concerns over collective privacy on social networking sites. *Cyberpsychology (Brno)*, *10*(1).

Jiang, Z., Heng, C. S., & Choi, B. C. F. (2013). Privacy concerns and privacy-protective behavior in synchronous online social interactions. *Information Systems Research*, *24*(3), 597–595.

Kelly, L. L. (2018). A snapchat story: How black girls develop strategies for critical resistance in school. *Learning, Media and Technology*, 1–16.

Kim, E., Gilbert, S., Edwards, M. J., & Graeff, E. (2009). Detecting sadness in 140 characters: Sentiment analysis and mourning Michael Jackson on Twitter. *Web Ecology*, *3*, 1–15.

Kim, S. M., & Hovy, E. (2006). Automatic identification of pro and con reasons in online reviews. *Proceedings of the COLING/ACL Main Conference Poster Sessions*, 483-490.

Kleemans, M., Daalmans, S., Carbaat, I., & Anschutz, D. (2018). Picture Perfect: The direct effect of manipulated Instagram photos on body image in adolescent girls. *Media Psychology*, *21*(1), 93–110.

Lynch, J. G. Jr, & Ariely, D. (2000). Competition on Price, Quality. *Marketing Science*, *19*(1).

Michaelidou, N., Siamagka, N. T., & Christodoulides, G. (2011). Usage, barriers and measurement of social media marketing: An exploratory investigation of small and medium B2B brands. *Industrial Marketing Management*, *40*, 1153–1159.

Milyavskaya, M., Saffran, M., Hope, N., & Koestner, R. (2018). Fear of missing out: Prevalence, dynamics, and consequences of experiencing FOMO. *Motivation and Emotion*, *42*, 725–737.

Munzel, A., Meyer-Waarden, L., & Galan, J. P. (2018). The social side of sustainability: Well-being as a driver and an outcome of social relationships and interactions on social networking sites. *Technological Forecasting and Social Change*.

Muqaddas, J., Soomro, A. S., & Ahmad, N. (2017). Impact of Social Media on Self-Esteem. *European Scientific Journal, 13*, 329–341. doi:10.19044/esj.2017. v13n23p329

Niu, Y., Zhu, X., Li, J., & Hirst, G. (2005). Analysis of polarity information in medical text. *Proceedings of the American Medical Informatics Association 2005 Annual Symposium.*

Nyagah, V. W., Stephen, A., & Mwania, J. M. (2015). Social networking sites and their influence on the self-esteem of adolescents in Embu county, Kenya. *Journal of Educational Policy and Entrepreneurial Research, 2*(1), 87–92.

O'Connor, B., Balasubramanyan, R., Routledge, B. R., & Smith, N. A. (2010). From Tweets to Polls: Linking Text Sentiment to Public Opinion Time Series. *ICWSM, 11*(122–129), 1-2.

O'Guinn, T., & Shrum, L. J. (1997). The Role of Television in the Construction of Consumer Reality. *The Journal of Consumer Research, 23*, 278–294.

O'Reilly, L. (2013). *Google patents 'pay-per-gaze' eye-tracking ad technology.* Accessed from: https://www.marketingweek.com/google-patents-pay-per-gaze-eye-tracking-ad-technology/

Pathak, A., Pandey, M., & Rautaray, S. (2020). Adaptive model for sentiment analysis of social media data using deep learning. *International Conference on Intelligent Computing and Communication Technologies.*

Phelps, J. E., D'Souza, G., & Nowak, G. J. (2001). Antecedents and consequences of consumer privacy concerns: An empirical investigation. *Journal of Interactive Marketing, 15*(4), 2–17.

Phippen, A., & Bond, E. (2020). Momo Week: A Perfect Social Media Storm and a Breakdown in Stakeholder Sanity? In Organisational Responses to Social Media Storms. Palgrave Macmillan.

Poria, S., Cambria, E., Hazarika, D., Majumder, N., Zadeh, A., & Morency, L.-P. (2017). Context-Dependent Sentiment Analysis in User-Generated Videos. *Proceedings of the 55th Annual Meeting of the Association for Computational Linguistics, 1*, 873-883.

Rajan, A., Pappu, S., & Victor, P. (2014). Web sentiment analysis for scoring positive or negative words using Tweeter data. *International Journal of Computers and Applications, 96*(6), 33–37.

Robinson, J., Cox, G., Bailey, E., Hetrick, S., Rodrigues, M., Fisher, S., & Herrman, H. (2016). Social media and suicide prevention: A systematic review. *Early Intervention in Psychiatry*, *10*(2), 103–121.

Robinson, J., Rodrigues, M., Fisher, S., & Herrman, H. (2014). *Suicide and Social Media Study: Report of the Internet Search*. Orygen Youth Health Research Centre, Community Works.

Ruggiero, T. (2000). Uses and Gratifications Theory in the 21st Century. *Mass Communication & Society*, *3*(1), 3–37.

Sahoo, S. R., & Gupta, B. B. (2019). Classification of various attacks and their defence mechanism in online social networks: A survey. *Enterprise Information Systems*, *13*(6), 832–864.

Sahoo, S. R., & Gupta, B. B. (2020). Classification of spammer and nonspammer content in online social network using genetic algorithm-based feature selection. *Enterprise Information Systems*, *14*(5), 710–736.

Schaefer, B. (2017). *Bumper Stickers & Social Data: How Trump and Clinton Supporters Measure Up*. Brandwatch. Accessed from: https://www.brandwatch.com/blog/bumper-stickers/

Scherer, K. (2003). Vocal communication of emotion: A review of research paradigms. *Speech Communication*, *40*(1-2), 227–256.

Schreiner, M., Fischer, T., & Riedl, R. (2019). Impact of content characteristics and emotion on behavioral engagement in social media: Literature review and research agenda. *Electronic Commerce Research*, 1–17.

Singh, P., Singh, S., Sohal, M., Dwivedi, Y. K., Kahlon, K. S., & Sawhney, R. S. (2020). Psychological fear and anxiety caused by COVID-19: Insights from Twitter analytics. *Asian Journal of Psychiatry*, *54*, 102280.

SolomonR. C. (2017). *Emotion*. Retrieved from http://www.britannica.com/topic/emotion

Soyez, F. (2017). *Advertising from the future: analyzing emotions, a risk of manipulating people*. Accessed from: https://www.cnetfrance.fr/news/pub-du-futur-l-analyse-des-emotions-un-risque-de-manipulation-39858642.html

Swani, K., Brown, B. P., & Milne, G. R. (2014). Should tweets differ for B2B and B2C? An analysis of Fortune 500 companies' Twitter communications. *Industrial Marketing Management*, *43*(5), 873–881.

Terveen, L., Hill, W., Amento, B., McDonald, D., & Creter, J. (1997). PHOAKS: A system for sharing recommendations. *Communications of the ACM, 40*(3), 59–62.

Tumasjan, A., Sprenger, T. O., Sandner, P. G., & Welpe, I. M. (2010). Predicting Elections with Twitter: What 140 Characters Reveal about Political Sentiment. *ICWSM, 10*, 178–185.

Utz, S., Muscanell, N., & Khalid, C. (2015). Snapchat elicits more jealousy than Facebook: A comparison of Snapchat and Facebook use. *Cyberpsychology, Behavior, and Social Networking, 18*(3), 141–146.

Valkenburg, P. M., Peter, J., & Schouten, M. A. (2006). Friend networking sites and their relationship to adolescents' well-being and social selfesteem. *Cyberpsychology & Behavior, 9*, 584–590.

Van der Hoven, E. (2013). *Fact sheet- Ethics Subgroup IoT-Version 4.01*. Delft University of Technology Chair Ethics Subgroup IoT Expert Group.

Verduyn, P., Lee, D. S., Park, J., Shablack, H., Orvell, A., Bayer, J., Ybarra, O., Jonides, J., & Kross, E. (2015). Passive Facebook Usage Undermines Affective Well-Being: Experimental and Longitudinal Evidence. *Journal of Experimental Psychology, 144*(2), 480–488.

Vogel, E. A., Rose, J. P., Roberts, L. R., & Eckles, K. (2014). Social comparison, social media, and self-esteem. *Psychology of Popular Media Culture, 3*(4), 206.

Whiting, A., & Williams, D. (2013). Why people use social media: A uses and gratifications approach. *Qualitative Market Research, 16*(4), 362–369.

Wiebe, J. M. (1994). Tracking Point of View in Narrative. *Computational Linguistics, 20*(2), 233–287.

Yang, C.-C. (2016). Instagram Use, Loneliness, and Social Comparison Orientation: Interact and Browse on Social Media, But Don't Compare. *Cyberpsychology, Behavior, and Social Networking, 19*.

Zhang, J., Yun, J. H., & Lee, E.-J. (2020). Brain buzz for Facebook? Neural indicators of SNS content engagement. *Journal of Business Research*.

ADDITIONAL READING

Anikin, A., & Lime, C. (2018). Perceptual and acoustic differences between authentic and acted nonverbal emotional vocalizations. *Quarterly Journal of Experimental Psychology*, *71*(3), 622–641. PMID:27937389

Gaind, B., Syal, V., Padgalwar, S. (2018). Emotion Detection and Analysis on Social Media. *Global Journal of Engineering Science and Researches*.

Rodriguez, A., Argueta, C., & Chen, Y. (2019). Automatic Detection of Hate Speech on Facebook Using Sentiment and Emotion Analysis. *1st International Conference on Artificial Intelligence in Information and Communication, ICAIIC 2019*, 169-174. 10.1109/ICAIIC.2019.8669073

Root, J. (2018). A model for sentiment and emotion analysis of unstructured social media text. *Electronic Commerce Research*, *18*(1), 181–199. doi:10.100710660-017-9257-8

KEY TERMS AND DEFINITIONS

Data Mining: Family of tools allowing the analysis of a large amount of data on social media.

Ethnography: A research method used by sociologists to study and comprehend groups, organizations, and communities.

Frequency: Number of oscillations per second expressed in Hertz (Hz). For the voice, the frequency corresponds to the number of opening and closing phases per second of the vocal folds.

Natural Language Processing: Opinion mining technique with extracting information about people's thoughts and feelings from a corpus of text data (Albahli et al., 2020).

Prosody: The melody of the voice represented by the acoustic and non-verbal parameters of voiced speech usually defined by the fundamental frequency, rhythm and intensity of the speech signal.

Sentiment: An emotional state occurring as the result of an emotion through external or internal causes (i.e., happy and joyful, or painful and sad).

Sentiment Analysis: The field of study that analyses people's opinions, sentiments, evaluations, appraisals, attitudes, and emotions towards products, services, organizations, individuals, issues, events, topics, and their attributes (Almuraih et al., 2020).

Social Media: Online networks through which users can create online communities to share information, ideas, personal messages, and other content like videos.

Subjective Lexicon: A word list nominated to a score that shows its nature in terms of positive, negative or objective opinion (Alessia et al., 2015).

Chapter 10
Predicting Catastrophic Events Using Machine Learning Models for Natural Language Processing

Muskaan Chopra
Chandigarh College of Engineering and Technology, India

Sunil K. Singh
(iD) https://orcid.org/0000-0003-4876-7190
Chandigarh College of Engineering

and Technology, India

Kriti Aggarwal
Chandigarh College of Engineering and Technology, India

Anshul Gupta
Chandigarh College of Engineering and Technology, India

ABSTRACT

In recent years, there has been widespread improvement in communication technologies. Social media applications like Twitter have made it much easier for people to send and receive information. A direct application of this can be seen in the cases of disaster prediction and crisis. With people being able to share their observations, they can help spread the message of caution. However, the identification of warnings and analyzing the seriousness of text is not an easy task. Natural language processing (NLP) is one way that can be used to analyze various tweets for the same. Over the years, various NLP models have been developed that are capable of providing high accuracy when it comes to data prediction. In the chapter, the authors will analyze various NLP models like logistic regression, naive bayes, XGBoost, LSTM, and word embedding technologies like GloVe and transformer encoder like BERT for the purpose of predicting disaster warnings from the scrapped tweets. The authors focus on finding the best disaster prediction model that can help in warning people and the government.

DOI: 10.4018/978-1-7998-8413-2.ch010

INTRODUCTION

Disasters and crises have always been dynamic and chaotic by nature (Guha-Sapir et al., 2016). Natural disasters disrupt people's lives in an instant, causing mental, physical, and societal damage. Communication is important in all aspects of disaster management in such a circumstance (Mukkamala et al., 2016). Earlier people used to use traditional media channels in order to communicate disaster warnings. The traditional media included devices such as television, newspaper, and radio channels. However, this method of communication was slow and difficult.

With the development of new technologies, the communication ability of people has also improved and developed tremendously. One of the major contributors to this change is the ever-evolving smartphone and internet technologies. The second reason is the plethora of software and applications available on these devices. Unlike before, now people are just "a few clicks" and one "app" away from being able to send or receive information.

One of the biggest influencers of all has been the social media applications and platforms like FaceBook, Instagram, and Twitter. All these platforms have played a vital role in the prediction, the announcement of disasters. Not only this, but these platforms have also served as a way for people to communicate and share their grief as well as send and receive help. Today, social media is recognized as one of the most popularly used media platforms for disaster management. (Gray et al., 2016, Ranjan Avasthi, 2017).

Social media gives people the freedom to become producers along with being consumers of information. The present paper focuses on Twitter which is one of the most widely used social media networks for disaster prediction and management research. Since the launch of Twitter in 2005, it has become one of the largest microblogging services. (Dhiraj Murthy, 2018).

With new hashtags and keywords trending on Twitter every day, the latest trend is spreading the news updates from around the world. This is something that has proved to be beneficial in the prediction of natural disasters and emergency situations (Ulvi, O et al, 2019) like floods (Vieweg S. et al., 2010, Vieweg S. et al., 2010, Starbird K et l., 2010), earthquakes (Earle, P et al., 2010, Kireyev, K, et al., 2009, Muralidharan S et al), wildfires, and hurricanes (Hughes AL, Palen L, 2009, Hughes AL et al., 2008), etc. The platform has shown great potential in increasing the survival rate during emergency situations caused due to disasters like tornadoes and wildfires. In one such paper (Lindsay B, 2011), authors emphasized the use of Twitter as a multidirectional communication network that can not only aid officials in compiling lists of the disaster-affected people but also help them in contacting the grieved family members. Tweeting has hence provided people a way to announce emergency situations in real-time. People use this channel to express and describe what they see and observe. Programmatically monitoring tweets can hence help in finding hints for upcoming calamities. Many disaster relief organizations and news agencies hence have been aiming to develop technologies and programs related to tweet analysis.

One point to take note of is that it cannot be guaranteed that a particular piece of information found on social media is "Truth" (Zhang, Z., & Gupta, B. B., 2018). Moreover, it is not easy to identify emergency tweets just by analyzing the words. In order to actually declare them as disaster announcements, much in-depth analysis is required. (Iruvanti, G, 2020). A study done in (Kate Starbird et al., 2010) exemplifies the dilemma of conversational microblogging. They focused on the use of Twitter for communicating the disasters where they found high discrepancies in the tweets and retweets.

The majority of the material retweeted during the 2009 Red River disaster in North Dakota was the one that previously existed on Twitter. However, the news that spread included less than 10% of the real tweets. The majority of news floating onto mainstream channels was found to be derivative. These synthetic and fake tweets spread like wildfire in the wake of original tweets.

The present paper hence focuses on developing a Natural Language Processing (NLP) based Disaster Prediction model. This model will help people as well as the government to detect whether a particular tweet is a premonition of disaster or a false warning. The result of this analysis will not only help people to be well aware of what is about to come but will also help in preventing the creation of fake commotion.

In section two of the present papers, the authors discuss the previous research works being done in the field of disaster prediction using Twitter. Section 3 briefs about the NLP techniques used in the paper. This section discusses different processes like data pre-processing and building prediction models. The last section of the paper compares these models based upon their test accuracy to find the most suitable model of disaster prediction.

LITERARY WORK & MOTIVATION

Twitter is one of the most popular microblogging sites. The platform receives millions of tweets on a daily basis. According to a survey done in (Srivastava, A et al., 2019), every second twitter disseminates around 6,000 tweets. This amounts to almost 500 million tweets per day and more than 200 billion tweets on an annual basis. The tweets range from informational to advertising and promotional content. However, in the current era of digitalization, where people are the content generators, determining the truth value of the information is very important (Mendoza et al., 2010). Many researchers have noted a surge in the spread of fake news especially during emergency situations like the Covid-19 pandemic (Gupta A et al., 2021, Sahoo, S. R., & Gupta, B. B., 2021).

The research problem in the present paper is motivated by various researchers that show the exponential increase in the frequency of tweets during any disaster period (Lamsal, R., & Kumar, T. V., 2021). Careful monitoring, processing, and analyses of these tweets can help in the identification of important information like a prediction of calamity, call for help, identification of missing people, etc. Discussions on Twitter vary between thousands of different topics. However, some studies suggest that the maximum number of daily users are only interested in viral tweets consisting of hot topics and top news (Murthy, J. S. et al., 2019). The number of Twitter users, as well as the number of tweets, increase daily, yet, the participation of official organizations during emergency situations and crises remains negligible (Latonero, M., & Shklovski, I., 2011).

Further studies and research work suggest that the automatic classification of tweets can play a crucial role in the identification of emergency situations. It can also help official organizations to take well-timed action, thus saving the lives of affected people. Over the years, a number of classification algorithms and solutions have been successfully used to detect and classify natural disaster tweets and messages. Some researches even extended beyond the simple disaster prediction and classification phase by enhancing the results using visualization techniques like mapping. One of the papers (Ian P. Benitez et al., 2018), used a feature vector matrix for the purpose of representing features extracted from Twitter messages. They applied an improved Genetic Algorithm for the extraction of features. Social media data supplied by catastrophe witnesses have been found to be extremely valuable for disaster management and response. To deal with the paucity of labeled data at the start of a target catastrophe, domain adaptation techniques have been utilized. The approaches for designing the models range from conventional machine learning algorithms (Li et al.2017) to newer deep learning-based ones (Li, X., & Caragea, C. 2019). One such paper (Li et al.2017) proposed a self-training type approach. The approach used Naïve Bayes as the base classifier. (David Graf et al., 2018) also designed a cross-domain classifier for different disaster types. Xukun Li and Doina Caragea (Li, Xukun & Caragea, Doina., 2020) surveyed various DRCN approaches for disaster tweet classification. Figure 1 Previously done work in Disaster predictions using Twitter (Seddighi H et al., 2020) shows the collective research topics and work that has been done on various disaster prediction phases using Twitter.

Figure 1. Previously done work in Disaster predictions using Twitter
Source: Seddighi H et al., 2020

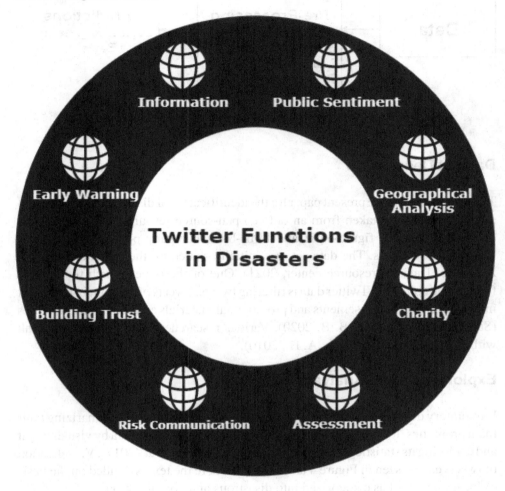

METHODOLOGIES

For the prediction and analysis of disasters in Tweets, several procedures were achieved. This process is illustrated in Figure 2 and the steps are further explained in detail in the following sections.

Figure 2. Methodology and workflow

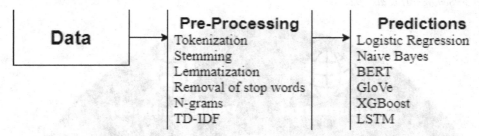

Dataset Description

The data set used in the present paper for the identification of disaster and emergency-related tweets were taken from an online open-source resource. The dataset was originally created by figure-eight, an AI ML-based company, popular for providing high trained datasets. The data set was initially shared on the website 'Data For Everyone'(Datasets resource center, 2021). One of the issues which the authors faced while collecting Twitter data is filtering tweets. Tweets often contain irrelevant information like advertisements and promotional materials and spamming activities (Sahoo, S. R., & Gupta, B. B. 2020). Various researchers have studied and dealt with this problem like (Wang, A. H., 2010).

Exploratory Data Analysis

Exploratory data analysis is a process for taking data insights and summarizing their main properties. It enables us to make some inferences from the data by visualizing it and exploring its statistical properties (Oleksandr Zaytsev et al., 2017). Visualization of tweets can be seen in Figure 4 and Figure 5 where the text is divided on the basis of location as well as categorized into disastrous and non-disastrous.

EDA can be particularly helpful to get information about the inside structure of a large dataset, detecting missing values, determining the relations among the dataset through visualizations, and selecting particular models for further predictions and analysis. This is shown in Figure 3.

Figure 3. Identification of Missing Values through EDA in the dataset

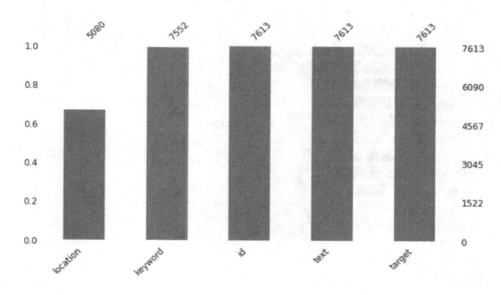

Figure 4. Classification of Tweets by location as Non- Disaster

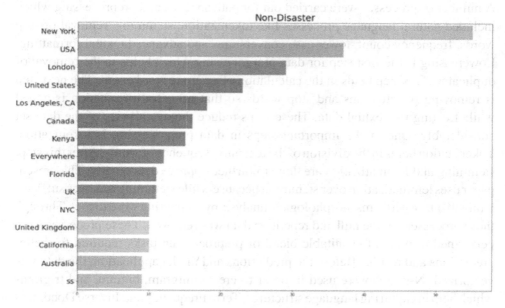

Figure 5. Classification of Tweets by location as Disaster

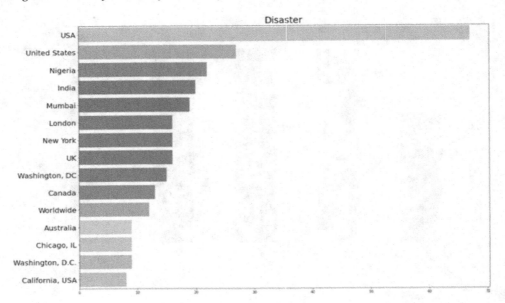

Data Pre-Processing

A number of processes were carried out for data analysis and preprocessing which included natural language processes like tokenization, stemming, removal of stop words, frequency count, lower case conversions, and advanced textual formatting. Lowercasing is the first step for data preprocessing which helps in the removal of duplicates. This step helps in the calculation of accurate word count. The next step is removing punctuations and stop words so that no extra information is added while treating the textual data. These steps reduce the overall size of the data set considerably. One of the important steps in data preprocessing is tokenization. Tokenization helps in the division of the text into a sequence of words. After this step, stemming and lemmatization are done to further improve data quality. The present paper uses lemmatization over stemming because while stemming removes suffices, lemmatization performs morphological analysis by converting word to root. Through these processes, all the null and repetitive data was removed. These processes were performed to obtain the suitable blend of preprocessing tasks required for better predictions and results. Before the predictions and model application, the data was vectorized. N-grams were used in order to create unigram, bigram, and trigrams which help in capturing language structures. Term Frequency and Inverse Document Frequency were used to generate TF-IDF. TD is the ratio of the word count present in a sentence to the length of the sentence. IDF value indicates the uniqueness of a word, the more the IDF value, the more unique the word is (Analytics Vidhya, 2020).

Figure 6. Most occurring after cleaning and preprocessing the data set

Figure 6 shows the keywords or the most occurring words in the datasets through a word cloud visualization. Furthermore, preprocessed and cleaned data has been used for training the models. The models have been discussed in detail in the next section.

MODELS

Logistic Regression

One of the popular statistical approaches to Machine Learning and NLP is Logistic regression. This technique uses relationships of outputs or independent variables or dependent variables. The result is used to analyze whether the dependent variable is dichotomous, unordered polytomous, or ordered polytomous:

(a) dichotomous:- A dependent variable is dichotomous when it has only two categories. Some examples of this are categorizing data into negative and positive.

(b) unordered polytomous:- An unordered polytomous is a nominal scale variable having three or more classifications. One of the popular examples of this can be seen in the case of the political party identification problem.

(c) ordered polytomous: Unlike unordered polytomous, an ordered polytomous is an ordinal scale variable having three or more classifications. An example of this can be seen in (Salkind, N. J. 2010), where the researchers have used it to complete the level of education.

In the present paper, the dataset is categorized into only two categories. The first category is the real disaster represented by 1 and the second one is the fake disaster represented by 0, it falls under dichotomous. The model is used over the preprocessed data set to predict the results as shown in Figure 7.

Figure 7. Confusion Matrix for Logistic Regression

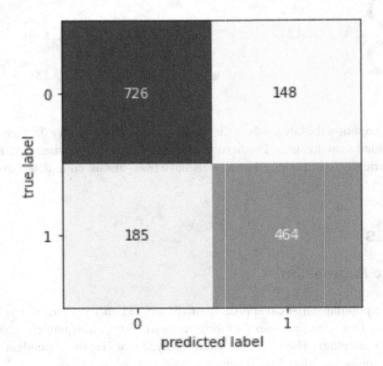

The confusion matrix in figure 7 gives the description of the classifier. The model gives an accuracy of 0.781 on the data set.

XGBoost

The second model is the XGBoost which is another version of the gradient boosted decision tree classifier. In this model, the trees are built sequentially. The goal of each succeeding tree is to decrease the mistakes of the preceding tree. These succeeding trees are known as basic or weak learners. Each of these weak learners offers some crucial information for prediction, allowing the boosting approach to successfully combine these weak learners to generate a strong learner. The strength of XGBoost resides in its scalability, which enables rapid learning via parallel and distributed computation and economical memory consumption. The confusion matrix in figure 8 gives the description of the classifier. The model gives an accuracy of 0.745 on the data set.

Figure 8. Confusion Matrix for XGBoost

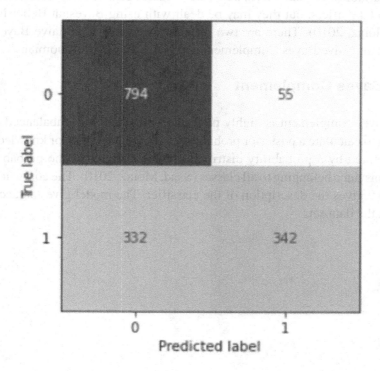

Naive Bayes

Naive Bayes uses prior information to compute a posterior probability which is represented as a probability distribution. Probability distribution indicates the likelihood of a particular instance belonging to a specific class. This algorithm is said to be "naive" as it makes two important assumptions about the environment which are defined as follows:

1. Each variable is statistically independent of the others
2. Each characteristic is equally important.

Although these two criteria are extremely unusual in reality, these simplifying assumptions help in deducing the likelihood of a certain occurrence. This is done using the basic idea of Bayesian conditional probabilities and decision making.

The naive Bayes classifier has the benefit of using a little quantity of training data to estimate the parameters. The drawback of NB is the class conditional independence assumption, which means that NB loses accuracy when there are relationships among variables. Dependencies between variables cannot be represented by naive Bayesian Classifiers, but they may be dealt with using Bayesian Belief Networks (Saad, Motaz, 2010). There are two different ways in which naive Bayes can be represented: Naive Bayes Complement and Naive Bayes Multinomial.

Naive Bayes Complement

Naive Bayes complement is highly preferred with small but imbalanced datasets. It is used to calculate a posterior probability with the help of prior knowledge. This is represented by a probability distribution which calculates the probability of a specific instance belonging to all classes (Saad, Motaz, 2010). The confusion matrix in figure 9 gives the description of the classifier. The model gives an accuracy of 0.795 on the data set.

Figure 9. Confusion Matrix for Naive Bayes Complement

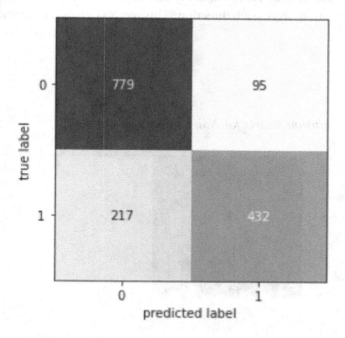

Naive Bayes Multinomial

This method employs basic, heuristic solutions to some of the issues associated with naive Bayes classifiers. The technique tackles both fundamental difficulties as well as those that occur as a result of the text not being created using a multinomial model (Saad, Motaz, 2010). The confusion matrix in figure 10 gives the description of the classifier. The model gives an accuracy of 0.789 on the data set.

LSTM

Long Short-Term Memory Networks (LSTMs) are Recurrent Neural Network (RNN) versions that tackle RNN gradient vanishing/exploding issues. LSTMs are intended to capture long-distance relationships within texts. Each LSTM unit has three gates that govern which information to remember, forget, and pass to the next phase. LSTMs maintain lengthy dependencies between words and hold the contextual meaning of each word based on the surrounding information. However, they only pay attention to one direction of information, which is the past. Bi-LSTMs, on the other hand, concentrate on the input's past and future orientations (O'Keefe, Simon & Alrashdi, Mohammed, 2018). This technique allows the network to collect more information than before. This is done by concatenating hidden representations, at each token location, from each direction. This method gives an accuracy of 0.719.

GloVe

Figure 10. Confusion Matrix for Naive Bayes Multinomial

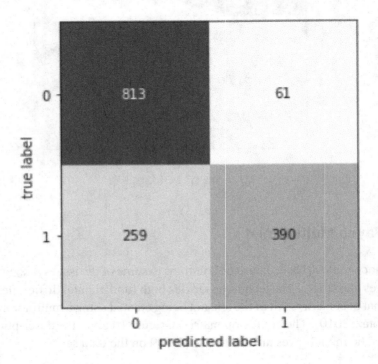

The application of word embedding has piqued the curiosity of many NLP researchers in recent years. Word embedding is a class of feature learning approaches or language models in which texts (words or phrases) are mapped to real-world vectors of numbers. The primary objective of word embedding is to develop expressive and efficient text representations in which related words or phrases have representations capable of conveying their semantic meaning. (Naili et al., 2017).GloVe embedding is a well-known universal pre-trained word embedding that the authors in (Pennington et al., 2014) produced. This embedding has been shown to have an important impact in the improvement of several NLP tasks (Pennington et al., 2014). GloVe embedding is a freely accessible 100-dimensional embedding that has been trained on 6 billion words from online text and Wikipedia and is comparable to tweets (O'Keefe, Simon & Alrashdi, Mohammed, 2018). This method gives an accuracy of 0.81.

BERT

Because of its capacity to capture contextual word embeddings, BERT and its variations have been widely utilised as building blocks for a wide range of applications (Song, G.; Huang, D, 2021). Transformers are altering the entire path of NLP in order to get SOTA (State of the Art) outcomes.

BERT is an acronym that stands for Bidirectional Encoder Representations from Transformers. BERT is a model that is "deeply bidirectional." The use of the term

Figure 11. High-level description of the Transformer encoder

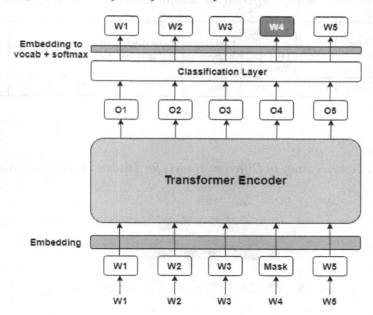

bidirectional, here, indicates the ability of BERT to learn information from both the left and right sides of a token's context, during the training phase. A model's bidirectionality is critical for properly comprehending the meaning of a language. This approach gives the highest accuracy of 0.846 on the data set.

CONCLUSION

The field of Tweet analysis and predictions has witnessed some impressive advancements in recent years. Initially, the extracted and scraped tweets were analyzed and visualized. Things have come a long way, and advanced natural language processing models are being used instead. The results have also improved steadily and are tending more and more towards realism.

In this review, the authors have studied various models proposed for performing the task of natural language processing which include Word Embeddings, Logistic Regression, Naive Bayes, BERT. Table I compares the accuracy of the above-mentioned Natural Language Processing Models trained on the Disaster Tweet Dataset.

Table 1. Test Accuracy of Different Models for Disaster Prediction using Tweets

Model Used for Prediction	LSTM	XGBoost & Decision Trees	Logistic Regression	Naive Bayes Multinomial	Naive Bayes Complement	GloVe	Transformer / BERT
Test Accuracy	0.719	0.745	0.781	0.789	0.795	0.813	0.846

Figure 12. Test Accuracy of Different Models for Disaster Prediction using Tweets

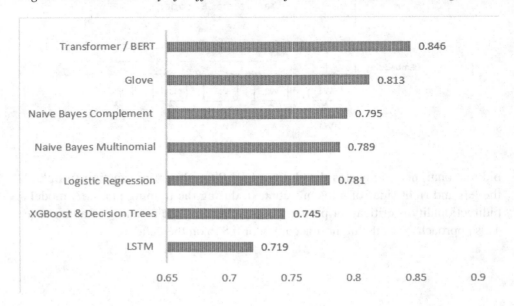

Figure. 12 gives a pictorial representation of the data which is provided in tables I. From Figure. 12, the Transformer/BERT has generated the most impressive results as compared to the other models. On the basis of the values, the authors also conclude that the results of the Naive Bayes are only slightly better than the Logistic Regression. Similarly, XG Boost and LSTM have also shown similar results, but XG Boost does perform better on the dataset due to its effectiveness in dealing with large datasets.

Notable developments in the future will involve improving the training stability of these models and increasing the accuracy of predictions in real-time also.

REFERENCES

Al-Qurishi, M., Rahman, S. M. M., Alamri, A., & Mostafa, M. A., & Al-Rubaian. (2018). SybilTrap: A graph-based semi-supervised Sybil defense scheme for online social networks. *Concurrency and Computation, 30*(5), e4276.

Avasthi, R. (2017). Social Media and Disasters: A Literature Review. *Journal of the American Academy of Child & Adolescent Psychiatry, 56*(10). doi:10.1016/j.jaac.2017.07.317

Benitez, Sison, & Medina. (2018). Implementation of GA-Based Feature Selection in the Classification and Mapping of Disaster-Related Tweets. In *Proceedings of the 2nd International Conference on Natural Language Processing and Information Retrieval (NLPIR 2018)*. Association for Computing Machinery. doi:10.1145/3278293.3278297

Bouarara, H. A. (2021). Recurrent Neural Network (RNN) to Analyse Mental Behaviour in Social Media. *International Journal of Software Science and Computational Intelligence, 13*(3), 1–11.

Candon, P. (2019). Twitter: Social communication in the Twitter era. *New Media & Society, 21*. doi:10.1177/1461444819831987

Chaudhary, P., Gupta, B. B., & Yamaguchi, S. (2016, October). XSS detection with automatic view isolation on online social network. In *2016 IEEE 5th Global Conference on Consumer Electronics* (pp. 1-5). IEEE.

Chen, T. Y., Chen, Y. M., & Tsai, M. C. (2020). A Status Property Classifier of Social Media User's Personality for Customer-Oriented Intelligent Marketing Systems: Intelligent-Based Marketing Activities. *International Journal on Semantic Web and Information Systems, 16*(1), 25–46.

Datasets Resource Center. (2021, March 11). *Appen*. https://appen.com/open-source-datasets/

Disasters on social media - dataset by crowdflower. (2016, November 21). https://data.world/crowdflower/disasters-on-social-media/access.

Earle, P., Guy, M., Buckmaster, R., Ostrum, C., Horvath, S., & Vaughan, A. (2010, March). OMG Earthquake! Can Twitter improve earthquake response? *Seismological Research Letters*, *81*(2), 246–251.

Graf, D., Retschitzegger, W., Schwinger, W., Pröll, B., & Elisa-beth, K. (2018). Cross-domain informativeness classification for disaster situations. *Proceedings of the 10th international conference on management of digital ecosystems*, 183–190.

Gray, B., Weal, M., & Martin, D. (2016). *Social media and disasters: A new conceptual framework*. Academic Press.

Guha-Sapir, D., Vos, F., Below, R., & Ponserre, S. (2016). Annual Disaster Statistical Review 2016: The Numbers and Trends. Brussels: Centre for Research on the Epidemiology of Disasters (CRED).

Gupta, A. (in press). An Exploratory Analysis on the Unfold of Fake News During COVID-19 Pandemic. *Smart Systems: Innovations in Computing*.

Gupta, S., Gupta, B. B., & Chaudhary, P. (2018). Hunting for DOM-Based XSS vulnerabilities in mobile cloud-based online social network. *Future Generation Computer Systems*, *79*, 319–336.

Hughes, A. L., & Palen, L. (2009). Twitter adoption and use in mass convergence and emergency events. *ISCRAM Conference*.

Hughes, A. L., Palen, L., Sutton, J., Liu, S., & Vieweg, S. (2008). *"Site-seeing" in disaster: an examination of on-line social convergence'*. Paper presented at the ISCRAM (Information Systems for Crisis Response and Management) Conference, Washington, DC.

Iruvanti, G. (2020, August 1). *Real or NOT? NLP with DISASTER Tweets (classification using google bert)*. Medium. https://levelup.gitconnected.com/real-or-not-nlp-with-disaster-tweets-classification-using-google-bert-76d2702807b4

Kireyev, K., Palen, L., & Anderson, K. (2009). Applications of topics models to the analysis of disaster-related Twitter data. In *NIPS Workshop on Applications for Topic Models: Text and Beyond (Vol. 1)*. Academic Press.

Lamsal, R., & Kumar, T. V. (2021). Twitter-Based Disaster Response Using Recurrent Nets. *International Journal of Sociotechnology and Knowledge Development (IJSKD), 13*(3), 133-150. doi:10.4018/IJSKD.2021070108

Latonero, M., & Shklovski, I. (2011). Emergency Management, Twitter, and Social Media Evangelism. *International Journal of Information Systems for Crisis Response and Management, 3*(4), 1–16. https://doi.org/10.4018/jiscrm.2011100101

Li, X., & Caragea, C. (2019). *Identifying Disaster Damage Images Using a Domain Adaptation Approach*. ISCRAM.

Li & Caragea. (2020). *Domain Adaptation with Reconstruction for Disaster Tweet Classification.* . doi:10.1145/3397271.3401242

Li, Caragea, Caragea, & Herndon. (2017). Disaster response aided by tweet classification with a domain adaptation approach. *Journal of Contingencies and Crisis Management, 26*. doi:10.1111/1468-5973.12194

Lindsay B. (2011). *Social media and disasters: Current uses, future options and policy considerations*. Washington, DC: Congressional Research Service CRS Report for Congress, Analyst in American National Government.

Mendoza, M., Poblete, B., & Castillo, C. (2010). *Twitter under Crisis: Can we trust what we RT?* Paper presented at First Workshop on Social Media Analytics, Washington, DC.

Mukkamala, A., & Beck, R. (2016). *Enhancing Disaster Management Through Social Media Analytics To Develop Situation Awareness: What Can Be Learned From Twitter Messages About Hurricane Sandy?* Academic Press.

Muralidharan, S., Rasmussen, L., Patterson, D., & Shin, J. (2011). Hope for Haiti: An analysis of Facebook and Twitter usage during the earthquake relief efforts. *Public Relations Review, 37*(2), 175–177.

Murthy, J. S., G.M., S., & K.G., S. (2019). A Real-Time Twitter Trend Analysis and Visualization Framework. *International Journal on Semantic Web and Information Systems (IJSWIS), 15*(2), 1-21. doi:10.4018/IJSWIS.2019040101

Naili, Habacha, & Ben Ghezala. (2017). Comparative study of word embedding methods in topic segmentation. *Procedia Computer Science, 112*, 340-349. . doi:10.1016/j.procs.2017.08.009

Noor, S., Guo, Y., Shah, S. H. H., Nawaz, M. S., & Butt, A. S. (2020). Research synthesis and thematic analysis of twitter through bibliometric analysis. *International Journal on Semantic Web and Information Systems, 16*(3), 88–109.

O'Keefe. (2018). Deep Learning and Word Embeddings for Tweet Classification for Crisis Response. Academic Press.

Pennington, Socher, & Manning. (2014). Glove: Global Vectors for Word Representation. *EMNLP, 14*, 1532-1543. . doi:10.3115/v1/D14-1162

Saad, M. (2010). *The Impact of Text Preprocessing and Term Weighting on Arabic Text Classification.* doi:10.13140/2.1.4677.2164

Sahoo, S. R., & Gupta, B. B. (2020). Classification of spammer and nonspammer content in online social network using genetic algorithm-based feature selection. *Enterprise Information Systems, 14*(5), 710–736.

Sahoo, S. R., & Gupta, B. B. (2021). Multiple features based approach for automatic fake news detection on social networks using deep learning. *Applied Soft Computing, 100*, 106983.

Salkind, N. J. (2010). *Encyclopedia of research design* (Vol. 1-0). SAGE Publications, Inc., doi:10.4135/9781412961288

Seddighi, H., Salmani, I., & Seddighi, S. (2020). Saving Lives and Changing Minds with Twitter in Disasters and Pandemics: A Literature Review. *Journalism and Media., 1*(1), 59–77. https://doi.org/10.3390/journalmedia1010005

Sharma, Y., Bhargava, R., & Tadikonda, B. V. (2021). Named Entity Recognition for Code Mixed Social Media Sentences. *International Journal of Software Science and Computational Intelligence, 13*(2), 23–36.

Song, G., & Huang, D. (2021). A Sentiment-Aware Contextual Model for Real-Time Disaster Prediction Using Twitter Data. *Future Internet, 13*, 163. doi:10.3390/fi13070163

Srivastava, A., Singh, V., & Drall, G. S. (2019). Sentiment Analysis of Twitter Data: A Hybrid Approach. *International Journal of Healthcare Information Systems and Informatics, 14*(2), 1–16. doi:10.4018/IJHISI.2019040101

Starbird, K., Palen, L., Hughes, A. L., & Vieweg, S. (2010). Chatter on the red: what hazards threat reveals about the social life of microblogged information. In *Proceedings of the 2010 ACM conference on Computer supported cooperative work (CSCW '10).* Association for Computing Machinery. doi:10.1145/1718918.1718965

Starbird, K., Palen, L., Hughes, A. L., & Vieweg, S. (2010). Chatter on the red: what hazards threat reveals about the social life of microblogged information. In *CSCW '10: Proceedings of the 2010 ACM conference on Computer supported cooperative work.* ACM.

Ultimate guide to deal with text data. (2020, December 23). *Analytics Vidhya.* https://www.analyticsvidhya.com/blog/2018/02/the-different-methods-deal-text-data-predictive-python/

Ulvi, O., Lippincott, N., Khan, M. H., Mehal, P., Bass, M., Lambert, K., Lentz, E., & Haque, U. (2019, December 10). The role of social and mainstream media during storms. *Journal of Public Health and Emergency.* https://jphe.amegroups.com/article/view/5543/html

Vieweg, S. (2010). Microblogged contributions to the emergency arena: Discovery, interpretation, and implications. Computer Supported Collaborative Work.

Vieweg, S., Hughes, A. L., Starbird, K., & Palen, L. (2010). Microblogging during two natural hazards events: What Twitter may contribute to situational awareness. In *Proceedings of SIGCHI Conference on Human Factors in Computing Systems.* ACM.

Wang, A. (2010). *Don't Follow Me - Spam Detection in Twitter.* doi:10.7312/wang15140-003

Wang, H., Li, Z., Li, Y., Gupta, B. B., & Choi, C. (2020). Visual saliency guided complex image retrieval. *Pattern Recognition Letters, 130,* 64–72.

Yen, S., Moh, M., & Moh, T. S. (2021). Detecting Compromised Social Network Accounts Using Deep Learning for Behavior and Text Analyses. *International Journal of Cloud Applications and Computing, 11*(2), 97–109.

Zaytsev, O., Papoulias, N., & Stinckwich, S. (2017). Towards Exploratory Data Analysis for Pharo. In *Proceedings of the 12th edition of the International Workshop on Smalltalk Technologies (IWST '17).* Association for Computing Machinery. doi:10.1145/3139903.3139918

Zhang, L., Zhang, Z., & Zhao, T. (2021). A Novel Spatio-Temporal Access Control Model for Online Social Networks and Visual Verification. *International Journal of Cloud Applications and Computing, 11*(2), 17–31.

Zhang, Z., & Gupta, B. B. (2018). Social media security and trustworthiness: Overview and new direction. *Future Generation Computer Systems, 86,* 914–925.

Zhang, Z., Jing, J., & Wang, X. (2020). A crowdsourcing method for online social networks security assessment based on human-centric computing. *Human-centric Computing and Information Sciences, 10,* 1–19.

Zhang, Z., Sun, R., Zhao, C., Wang, J., & Chang, C. K. (2017). CyVOD: A novel trinity multimedia social network scheme. *Multimedia Tools and Applications, 76*(18), 18513–18529.

Chapter 11
Clubhouse Experience:
Sentiment Analysis of an Alternative Platform From the Eyes of Classic Social Media Users

Ipek Deveci Kocakoç
Dokuz Eylul University, Turkey

Pınar Özkan
iD https://orcid.org/0000-0003-2765-7224
Dokuz Eylul University, Turkey

ABSTRACT

Clubhouse is an invitation-only social networking application that differs from the usual social media platforms in that it is "audio only." In this chapter, the sentiments in the social media messages about Clubhouse in the classic SMPs are examined by supervised learning (by using Hugging Face Transformer Library), and the user feelings are analyzed. Because Turkey is in the first ranks among European countries in terms of both the number of social media users and the number of messages, the analysis is conducted using the Turkish users. Mentions of Clubhouse have begun on Twitter and Sourtimes platforms in Turkey in early 2021. In this study, the aim is to demonstrate how Clubhouse, a new and different SMP, is evaluated by Twitter and Sourtimes users and to reveal user thoughts about this SMP along the timeline by using sentiment analysis.

DOI: 10.4018/978-1-7998-8413-2.ch011

INTRODUCTION

Clubhouse, which was launched on the App Store on 17.03.2020, differs from the usual social media platforms in that it is based on "audio". Although the application was only available for the iOS operating system until May 2021 and participation is on the basis of invitation, which caused a limited number of participants for a long time, the Lion King event, which was held on 27.12.2020 and where the casting was done on the Clubhouse platform, spread by the word of mouth and increased the number of users. At the beginning of 2021, in Turkey, users started to talk about Clubhouse on Twitter and Sourtimes platforms, especially the Turkish users living in the USA. Since the second half of January 2021, people started to see the Clubhouse invitations, which aroused great curiosity and attracted users, especially with the viral effect of Twitter. Clubhouse invitations were also offered for sale on e-commerce sites such as "Ebay". The platform, which increased the number of participants in Turkey as well as in the world in a very short time with the participation of celebrities, has active participants from many different professions and age groups.

In the loneliness imposed by the pandemic period and in the clamp of written communication imposed by other social media platforms, the superior aspects of the application are that it provides the two-way audio chat environment that people long for, on many different topics, with many different people, without prior planning, being lively, interactive and open to surprises. With these superiorities, the effect created by Clubhouse raises questions in the minds of researchers such as: "Is this platform and similar ones the future of social media?", "Is Clubhouse a fashion?", "What are the attitudes of other social media users towards the platform?", "For which platforms could it be a threat?".

In this study which was designed as a preliminary research to answer these questions, it is aimed to reveal how Clubhouse (CH), a new and different social media platform (SMP), is evaluated by Twitter and Sourtimes users, which are powerful and effective SMPs, by conducting sentiment analysis with preliminary data. Thus, it is aimed to reveal the user attitudes towards this SMP using sentiment analysis on big data while Clubhouse is still at the beginning of the ladder. This is one of the leading and largest studies on sentiments towards Clubhouse.

In this chapter, firstly, brief information will be given about the concept of social media, Twitter, and Sourtimes, which are chosen as the research platforms, and Clubhouse, which is determined as the research topic. Then, the concept of sentiment analysis is briefly explained, and the results of the sentiment analysis on all Turkish tweets containing the word "Clubhouse" and all entries in the Clubhouse heading in the Sourtimes between July 1, 2020, and July 1, 2021, were presented and examined.

BACKGROUND

Social Media Platforms

Social media platforms, which have increased and diversified since the second half of the 1990s, have become indispensable in many areas, from connecting with friends to communicating with potential and existing customers. The information obtained from social media, which has become one of the most important data sources for people and companies, directs many sectors. Ideas spread on social media reflect how successful the product or service is and therefore affect sales and the economy. The resulting economic impact has led to the need for companies to explore the perception in social media over time and has pioneered perception analysis studies in social media. Millions of people every day share their positive and negative opinions on social media about the issues like the products they buy, the services and brands they use, institutions, economy, politics, sports, etc. (Meral and Diri, 2014: 690).

In recent years, many scientists from different fields of expertise have argued that content analysis is necessary for social media platforms (John et al., 2018; Strain et al., 2015; Drakett et al., 2018; Dubrofsky & Wood, 2014). Social media analysis, which people use to tell others about their daily activities and experiences and to share their ideas, is used in decision-making processes in many business activities, especially in marketing. Especially during the 2016 US presidential elections, the manipulation and use of social media as a political marketing communication tool and its impact on voter preferences have been examined in a wide range of platforms ranging from news in the press to academic studies and documentaries (Isaac&Hanna, 2018; Berghel, 2018; Cadwalladr&Graham- Harrison,2018; et al.) Social media is both an application for many marketing areas such as Wom (Jansen et al. 2009), CRM (Harringan et al., 2015), consumer behavior (Ruths & Pfeffer, 2014), retailing (Samogia et al. 2019), etc. and the results of applications. Researchers make inferences by analyzing consumer comments, likes, and shares about brands and products with different algorithms, and help companies develop strategies. Social media, which has become an integral part of daily life, is a real-time customer satisfaction measurement platform. It has become an important resource for businesses.

According to Statista's 2021 "Social media usage worldwide" report, the number of people actively using social media in the world is 4.2 billion. Turkey[1] is among the countries with the highest number of social media users in the world, with the number of social media users reaching 54.34 million. When the number of users of social media platforms is examined, Facebook (2.74 billion users), Youtube (2.29 billion users), and Whatsapp (2 billion users) are among the top three SMPs. In the last two years, Tiktok, Instagram, Snapchat, etc. also became big global players

(Statista, 2021). Although the number of users is much less than those companies, the characteristics of the user base, the difference in the way of use, and the effect it creates distinguish Twitter positively from other social media platforms for both businesses and researchers. Twitter is frequently used by researchers in social media analysis, especially because of its API, allowing companies and private individuals to access data easily, and tweets limited to 280 characters.

In addition to these global players that come to mind first in the social media ecosystem, sometimes the legal conditions of the countries and sometimes the cultural differences cause some local social media platforms to come to the fore. Tik Tok, Weixin, Douyin, Sina Weibo have very high user numbers as PRC originated social media companies (Yu et al. 2011). Line in Japan, Telegram, VK, and OK in Russia are local social media platforms (Usmed,2020). In Turkey, there are local initiatives such as friendplans, curbaa, Hocam, follow-up, although they are not used by large masses (Onedio, 2014). Sourtimes, Turkey's oldest and most influential local social media platform, can be described as a participatory dictionary. It has led to many academic studies on the user profile of the Sourtimes and being an important reference source for Turkish internet users (Açıköz & Buber, 2012; Sine & Özsoy, 2017; Uzunoğlu, 2015; Üngüren,2019).

Twitter

Founded by Jack Dorsey in 2006, Twitter is a social networking and microblogging site that allows users to post messages of up to 280 characters called "tweets". According to the "2021-We are Social (January) Report", it is the 4th most visited website today and the 6th most time spent on a social media platform. Among 353.1 million monthly active users, 79% of the users of the platform are from countries other than the USA.

For its users, Twitter provides the opportunity to share and communicate by expressing their opinions, ideas, judgments, concerns, and attitudes about events in the economy, politics, environment, culture, education, and many other fields. Twitter is perceived as a news platform as well as being a social network. The fact that it was used by participants and members of the press to communicate with large masses in social events such as the Arab spring, the Gezi resistance, and Blacklivesmatters also supported this perception. According to research by Pew Research, 71% of Twitter users use Twitter to read the news (Wojcik & Hughes, 2019).

Twitter's 280-character limitation directs its users to use phrases that are commonly used with the hashtag (#) symbol to classify shared content, which is written without spaces and allows the content to reach more people. Hashtags serve to appropriately tag content so that users can easily find posts related to a topic of interest or a specific person. Hashtags used to categorize items on chat sites in the 1990s are the names of the designer Messina, who used the username @chrismessina on 23.08.2007, and wrote "how do you feel about using # (pound) for groups. As in #barcamp [msg]? It came to the fore again with its tweet, and later it was widely used to disseminate information in the 2007 San Diego wildfire. Although the fuse for the spread of the hashtag was ignited here, its popularity came when Twitter turned English hashtags into clickable links in 2009, allowing users to see relevant tweets (Azder, 2019).

Sourtimes – Ekşisözlük

The most frequently visited websites in Turkey are google.com, youtube.com, and facebook.com. The twelfth place on the list is ekisozluk.com (IAB Turkey Internet Measurement Research Gemius, 2019). Sourtimes (ST) has been operating at www. eksisozluk.com -sozluk.sourtimes.org- since February 1999. It can be defined as an interactive platform and database containing information, experiences, observations, jokes, comments, surveys, links, and resources about words, terms, concepts, and people. With this structure, Sourtimes is the first participatory dictionary in Turkey and the world. The site, which has many similar clones in Turkey, has similar ones in the world. Urbandictionary is the most well-known dictionary in this category worldwide.

Participatory dictionaries are dynamic dictionaries on the web-based on mutual interaction between authors (Duman & Özdoyran, 2018). Participatory dictionary sites are considered to be one of the first examples of the web 2.0 era and social media (Susar & Narin, 2011). In the participatory dictionary format, writers can open a topic, concept, event, or person themselves, as well as define, interpret, or share encyclopedic information with the entries they enter under the opened headings. Most of these interpretations and definitions are based on the author's personal experience. As an interactive database, authors produce content about the title in participatory dictionaries.

Sourtimes, a successful and pioneering internet formation that plays an essential role in the establishment of Turkish cyberculture, attracts attention as a successful and pioneering internet formation (Çelik, 2018). It can be qualified as a solid reference source for local, ethnic, religious, and national culture. Authors' alternative definitions of concepts, phenomena, and processes; their comments and evaluations on the agenda, their handling of the agenda items as a member of the public, and taking the pulse of the public ensure that ST is perceived as a phenomenon and left its mark on cyber life. Sourtimes is nowadays used by readers and writers for different purposes such as a search engine, discussion platform, subculture medium, socialization tool, and advertising medium (Gurel & Yakin, 2007).

Clubhouse

Clubhouse is an audio-based social media application. The company describes itself as "a new type of audio-based social product that allows people from all over the world to talk, tell stories, develop ideas, deepen friendships, and meet interesting new people around the world" (Clubhouse Privacy Policy, 2021). It is possible to engage in activities such as telling stories, asking questions, discussing, learning, singing, acting, or simply listening, by entering independent and different rooms where conversations similar to a free-flowing podcast take place.

Figure 1. Number of Clubhouse active users
Source: Statista, Clubhouse Report, 2021b

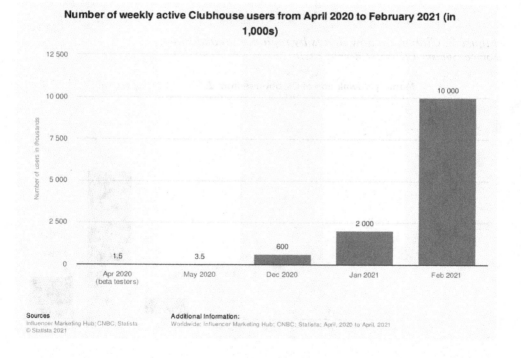

Developed by Paul Davison and Rohan Seth and released in beta version on the IOS operating system in March 2020, the application reached only 1,500 users until May 2020 but managed to reach the market value of approximately 100 million dollars. Particularly, the participation of some of the world's richest and most important figures - such as Elon Musk and Mark Zuckerberg - as well as technology influencers and celebrities in the Silicon Valley, has increased the attractiveness of the application for users from different groups. In this process, the presence of reviews about the platform in many influential media outlets such as The New Tork Times and Vogue caused the platform to be recognized by the wider masses (Dean, 2021; Subair, 2021; Marcin, 2021). In March-April 2021, the first statistics on the number of users of Clubhouse began to appear on independent data platforms. According to the Clubhouse Report of Statista (2021), the total number of users of the application reached 10 million as of April 2021, as seen in Figure 1.

By February 2021, North and Latin America accounted for the largest share of global downloads, with users from Europe, Middle East, and Africa regions increasing since then. When the download data of Clubhouse in Figure 2 is examined, it is seen that there was a large increase in the number of downloads in February, and this increase was due to Europe, the Middle East and Asia, and Asia-Pacific countries (Statista, 2021b).

Figure 2. Clubhouse downloads by regional breakdown
Source: Statista, Clubhouse Report, 2021b

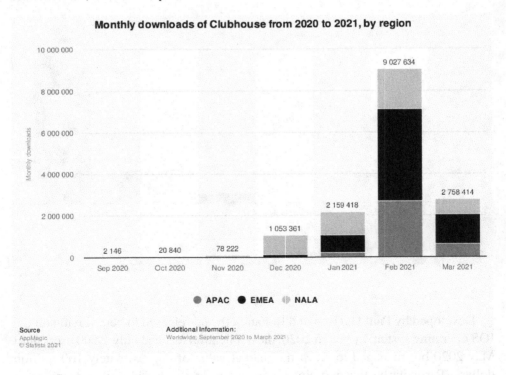

Although audio media has existed for a very long time, new audio media shaped by user-generated content and audio platforms created live by many users have given the first signs of being the new focus of the social media world with their impact. The effect of Clubhouse has caused 2021 to be described as "the year of the ear" (Kelly, 2021) in some media outlets.

Although Clubhouse seems to be a simple mobile app, it also has some privacy and security issues like most new social networking apps do. The data breach on April 2020, a fake Android app, and the back-end infrastructure being in China are some security problems. There are also some privacy issues to be solved such as using the contact list in the phone, conversations being recorded temporarily by Clubhouse, privacy policy being available only in English. These issues are to be solved by the next updates. Nevertheless, as noted by Kaspersky (2021), compared to other popular social media apps, Clubhouse gathers less information about its users. As an audio-only app, it doesn't request access to your camera or photos.

Sentiment Analysis

There is no semantic tag information (subject, positivity, negativity, etc.) in social media messages shared with content in different formats such as text, pictures, videos. Therefore, the knowledge of what the perception is about a subject is hidden in the bulk of raw data on social media (Meral and Diri; 2014: 690). In order to make this scattered data set, which makes it difficult for researchers to produce information, meaningful and therefore to measure the effectiveness of social media, modern data analysis methods are used as well as traditional analytical methods.

Social media analytics is the practice of collecting data from blogs and social media websites and analyzing that data to make a decision about a particular business/topic. Social media mining has emerged with the application of data mining principles on social media. In social media mining studies, data is collected, organized, and analyzed through social media, and meaningful results are tried to be drawn. The most well-known social media platforms with big data can be given as Facebook, Google+, and Twitter. About 500 million messages (tweets) are shared daily on Twitter. While the information of the tweets sent is stored, much more information such as hashtags, user information, the tweet time, and tweet location are also recorded as well as the content. In this case, a raw data size of 1 KB is created per tweet. In other words, the raw data size of tweets sent in only one day in the world is around 500 GB. The dimensions of the data show that social media mining is a big data application.

Sentiment analysis (SA) is an advanced form of web and text mining. It applies a combination of statistics, natural language processing (NLP), and machine learning to classify and extract subjective knowledge from text files, for instance, a reviewer's emotions, opinions, decisions, or observations about a specific matter, case, or an organization and its activities. This style of research is often referred to as opinion mining (with an extraction focus) or effective rating. The terms emotion classification and extraction are used by some experts as well.

Sentiment analysis allows for an accurate assessment of people's attitudes towards a company in the age of information. People's ability to connect with companies and the general perception of brands depends heavily on social opinion. Customers may not give the company a chance if they've read a few negative reviews. In this sense, companies that continuously track their reputations will resolve problems promptly and enhance feedback-based operations. The data gathered from consumers' reactions like tweets, remarks, reviews, and any writing that's relevant to products or services are analyzed in sentiment analysis. Thanks to sentiment analysis on large volumes of texts available in many online channels such as news sites, social media platforms, shopping sites, and forums, lots of valuable information, which is of great importance for companies or institutions, such as customers' views on brands and products, the happiness level of the society, and the opinions and attitudes of the public about politicians, can be accessed.

Many tasks can be achieved by sentiment analysis. In this chapter, we introduce an actual case study on the assessment of a new social media experience. Since the book is all about sentiment analysis, a detailed introduction to sentiment analysis will not be given in this chapter. Instead, the practical use of sentiment analysis on social media data will be focused on.

Sentiment analysis attempts to categorize the text according to its contextual substance. In general, texts, as a binary classification, are polarized as positive or negative. This is called coarse-grained analysis. Although sentiment analysis seems to classify only a text as positive or negative when viewed from the outside, it may differ according to its usage areas. Subjectivity/objectivity analysis, fine-grained analysis, detection of emotions, aspect-based emotion analysis are other areas we can go further by sentiment analysis. Despite the many useful aspects, there are also many disadvantages or challenges in the sensitivity analysis. People express ideas in complex ways, which makes their views incomprehensible. The tools of sarcasm, irony, and allusion can mislead sentiment analysis. Therefore, concise and focused insights such as product, book, movie, and music reviews are easier to analyze. Since sensitivity analysis heavily depends on computing, programming, natural language processing, and text mining technologies, the extend, quality, and reliability of its applications are expanding every day in parallel with the developments in those technologies. Document-level, sentence-level, aspect-based, and comparative sentiment analysis, and sentiment lexicon acquisition are some other problematic areas (Feldman, 2013).

In the current literature, there are many different classifications for sentiment analysis approaches. The detailed overview is not in the scope of this chapter. Here we follow the most basic classification. Lexicon-based approaches, machine learning-based methods, or a hybrid of the two may be utilized for SA. Unsupervised emotion lexicon and word polarity are used in lexicon-based approaches, whereas supervised architecture and word features are used in machine learning approaches.

For lexicon-based approaches, each language should be handled separately because of the grammar and architecture of the language. Lexicon-based, dictionary-based, and corpus-based approaches are available. As stated by Dehkharghani et al. (2016), English has the richest set of sentiment analysis resources such as SentiWordNet (Esuli and Sebastiani 2006), and SenticNet (Cambria, Olsher and Rajagopal 2014). SentiWordNet adopts a polar classification method, labeling words as positive, negative, and neutral, while SenticNet classifies words according to five different criteria: happiness, attention, sensitivity, ability, and general polarity.

Turkish's unique traits, as a member of the Turkic family of Altaic languages, make NLP and sentiment analysis tasks challenging. SentiTurkNet (Dehkharghani et al. 2016), and a sentiment analysis system for Turkish by Dehkharghani et al.(2016) are some studies on the Turkish language. Zemberek (Akın and Akın 2007) is another lexicon-based system. KeNet is one of the most comprehensive Turkish WordNet, which has 80,000 synsets covering 110,000 word-sense pairs (Bakay et al., 2020).

Machine learning-based approaches, on the other hand, mostly use supervised learning to train a model that can predict the sentiment of a sentence. Neural networks, deep learning, naive Bayes, maximum entropy, and support vector machines are the most popular methods for supervised learning-based sentiment analysis. A model is trained to include a representative sample of the language and a new sentence is evaluated for sentiment prediction. One of the most comprehensive libraries is the HuggingFace Transformers, a python-based library, that exposes an API to use many well-known transformer architectures, such as BERT, RoBERTa, GPT-2 or DistilBERT, that obtain state-of-the-art results on a variety of NLP tasks like text classification, information extraction, question answering, and text generation (Hugging Face team, 2019). The library includes many models trained for different languages.

SENTIMENT ANALYSIS OF CLUBHOUSE DATA

One years' data from Twitter are taken by Python codes from Twitter API for Academic Research Track, beginning from 01.07.2020. This track of Twitter Developer Environment allows academic users to draw up to 10 million historical twits per month. Sentiment analysis is performed on data beginning from January 2021, which is the time Clubhouse was a trending topic for the first time in Turkey. All entries of Sourtimes are also taken for the same time period.

The analysis process is given in Figure 3 and the data summary is given in Table 1.

Figure 3. Sentiment analysis process

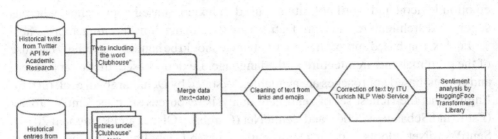

Table 1. The data summary

Data source	Data labels	#All tweets/entries	#Turkish tweets/ entries
Twitter	'id', 'date', 'tweet', 'url','username'	10,184,042	135,092
Sourtimes	'entry', 'date'	3,010	3,010

The raw data is first investigated to have a few basic statistics. The daily tweet/ entry counts for one year for all tweets/entries are given in Figure4. It can be seen that the popularity of "Clubhouse" has a peak in mid-February, 2021 for both Twitter and Sourtimes. Since there are no entries in Sourtimes before January 2021, the figures have different timelines. The peak at the mid-May is the date when Clubhouse App for Android is announced. It seems that the Android App did not bring much enthusiasm as the IOS App. The reason for this (although there is no data to prove) can be seen that traditional social media platforms are quick to release audio-based plug-ins such as Twitter Spaces, Facebook Hotline, Instagram, etc. Android users had the opportunity to chat with more users without the need for an invitation.

When the language of the tweets is examined, it can be seen that English is the first one and Turkish is the ninth one (Table 2).

Figure 4. Tweet/Entry counts

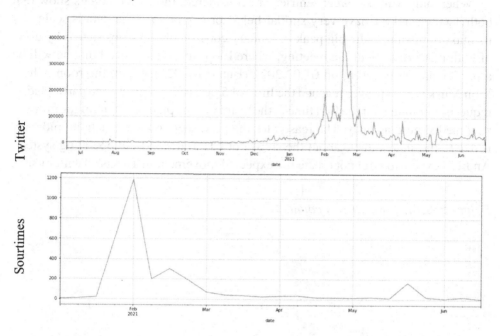

Table 2. Language of tweets

Language code	Language	#tweets
en	English	3,969,837
th	Thai	2,795,819
ja	Japan	1,874,326
in	Indonesian	217,532
und	Undefined	173,056
ar	Arabic	169,531
pt	Portuguese	162,124
de	German	146,459
tr	**Turkish**	**135,143**
es	Spanish	106,671
fr	French	71,171
it	Italian	64,934
tl	Tagalog	44,823
hi	Hindi	43,003
ru	Russian	41,775

When only Turkish tweets/entries are considered, the scaled counts show that both Twitter and ST have very similar behavior (Figure 5). The data is scaled by its maximum value. The big peak in January consists of messages shared by users of both platforms about the meeting, where Elon Musk announced that he will be a participant by tweeting on 01.02.2021 (Butcher, 2021). When the room where Elon Musk was a speaker reached the limit of 5,000 users, because the participation requests continued, for the first time in the history of the platform, tens of rooms were streamed simultaneously. The reason for the peak seen in the ST data in mid-May is due to the shares made about the arrival of CH to the android operating system. Android expansion did not create the expected movement in Turkish Twitter users.

Figure 5. Scaled tweet/entry counts

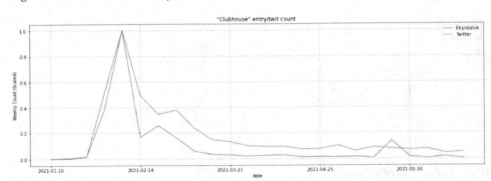

After preprocessing (cleaning stop words, punctuations, hashtags, links, etc.), the data is subjected to coarse-grained sentiment analysis by a pipeline composed of ITU Turkish NLP Web Service to correct the words in Turkish, and Hugging Face Transformers Library for sentiment analysis. In this chapter, the Bert-base Turkish Sentiment Model by Yıldırım (2020) (https://huggingface.co/savasy/bert-base-turkish-sentiment-cased) is utilized. The model based on BERTurk for Turkish Language (https://huggingface.co/dbmdz/bert-base-turkish-cased) and pretrained by tagged data of movie and product reviews and tweets in Turkish.

```
from transformers import AutoModelForSequenceClassification,
AutoTokenizer, pipeline
model = AutoModelForSequenceClassification.from_
pretrained("savasy/bert-base-turkish-sentiment-cased")
tokenizer = AutoTokenizer.from_pretrained("savasy/bert-base-
turkish-sentiment-cased")
```

```
sa= pipeline("sentiment-analysis", tokenizer=tokenizer,
model=model)
```

The amount and polarity of entries and tweets are then compared and interpreted for Twitter and ST along the timeline. Table 3 shows the results of sentiment analysis. It is seen that while most of the tweets are positive, most of the entries are negative. While the majority of twitter (a global social media platform) users view CH positively, Sourtimes (a local SMP) writers view it negatively. It can be thought that the culture of criticism that is generally dominant in ST is effective in this result. The innovative audience of all ages that Twitter reached, welcomed this new platform very positively. In fact, Twitter, which realized this positive point of view, was the first among the traditional platforms which started the conversation rooms as Twitter Spaces.

Table 3. Sentiment Results

Data source	#Turkish tweets/entries	Positive (%)	Negative (%)
Twitter	135,092	77546 (57%)	57546 (43%)
Sourtimes	3,010	1118 (37%)	1892 (63%)

When positive and negative tweet/entry counts are examined through the timeline in Figure 6, no change of sentiment in time is detected for both Twitter and ST.

Figure 6. Positive and negative tweet/entry counts through the timeline

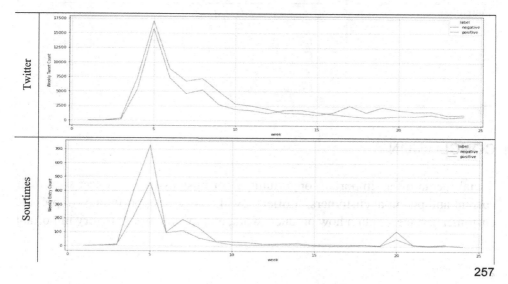

Wordclouds for most frequent keywords for positive and negative tweets/entries are given in Figure 7. Since the data is on Turkish tweets/entries, all word lists are translated into English in order to report here. The word Boğaziçi (Bosphorus), which appears in tweets about CH, is used in tweets within the scope of the student resistance that took place at Boğaziçi University during the time when CH was first popular in Turkey (January-February 2021). Twitter users, who listened to the rooms which are opened to announce the interventions made by the security teams to the students who set up tents on the school campus, and reached thousands of listeners, tagged the words CH and Bosphorus to reach wider audiences. Therefore, the word is included in both positive and negative word clouds. In general, it is seen that the prominent words for both emotions are the same. Similar to Twitter, the words used in positive and negative entries in the ST are almost the same. This is because users describe the features of this social media (voice, chat, invitation, follow, live, etc.). While these features were found positive by some of the users, they were described as negative by some others. On the negative side, the word "android" comes from tweets in response to the app being only in IOS. On the positive side, words such as "beautiful", "pleasant", "happy" stand out.

Figure 7. Wordclouds for sentiments

	Positive	Negative
Twitter		
Sourtimes		

CONCLUSION

Social media offers important opportunities for businesses to connect with their current and potential customers. It offers a wide range of opportunities to provide customer service, explain how products work, and much more. It is very important to test and monitor product/service results to determine the most effective strategies with social media. Traditionally, social media has a model of written and/or visual sharing.

The social media industry witnessed the birth of a new and limited user phenomenon, Clubhouse, in 2020. Developed by a very small company, this sound-based social media platform reached a limited market segment with the preference of application developers for a while, both determining the trends of its target market and becoming a curiosity for those who could not reach it. Using Clubhouse for social media users in the rest of the world, especially in the USA, with the effects it has created in Silicon Valley, in the Twitter messages of technology influencers and famous users in the USA, has become, in a sense, "conspicuous consumption".

Although the application is only on the IOS operating system and there is a condition to be invited by someone who is already using the application to use the application, -perhaps thanks to- the platform has started to be talked about by a very large audience, especially on Twitter and other social media platforms, and news about it in the press is published.

In this study, the attitudes of the users of Twitter and ST, two social media platforms that Turkish social media users actively use and that affect large masses, towards this new and different social media platform were determined by sentiment analysis method. For this purpose, a data set consisting of tweets between July 2020-July 2021 and entries written under the Clubhouse heading between January 2021-July 2021 was collected and machine learning-based sentiment analysis was carried out with the help of Python language codes and libraries.

The first thing that drew attention in the data set was the number of tweets about CH and its periodic distribution. The fact that so many tweets about it show that CH is a platform that attracts the attention of Twitter users. Users of ST also showed interest in this new platform and shared informative entries about the platform in accordance with the nature of the dictionary.

The results of the sentiment analysis show that there are differences between the two platforms in terms of viewpoints on CH. While Twitter users evaluated this new platform with positive expressions (57%), the words they used the most were application, social, nice, and invitation. Only 37% of the entries on ST were positive. Speech, invitation, social, live, and new are the words that stand out in entries. The prominence of similar words in negative and positive expressions stems from the subjective evaluations made by the users after descriptive/introductory posts about the platform are made. For example, while some users think that access to the platform by invitation is positive, some users evaluate this situation negatively. This is also an example of one of the problematic issues of sentiment analysis. Since the sentiment approaches for the Turkish language do not include subjective/objective sentiment evaluations yet, the sentiment analysis gives less practical information.

The new breath that Clubhouse has brought to the market and the growth potential it has demonstrated has provided the opportunity to develop a differentiated market offering with voice-based applications for traditional social media platforms that have already reached the maturity stage.

There is a lot of news in the press that all players, including the Facebook group of companies, which still continues to grow in the market, have started to work on integrating voice-based applications into their systems. Twitter, one of the most effective social media platforms, has been the fastest-acting platform at this stage. In time, it will be seen what steps Clubhouse will take to maintain its leadership in this market, in which it is a pioneer.

Voice-based social media will also make a significant difference for social data analysts and miners. The fact that it is currently not possible to record on these platforms has made it impossible at this stage to collect data on topics such as the activity times, the number of users, and the topics discussed for CH and other audio-based plug-ins without APIs. If a model cannot be developed that will enable businesses to use this platform healthily in decision processes, especially in marketing activities, it is very difficult for Clubhouse to be sustainable, especially since these models are only voice-based.

REFERENCES

Açıköz, T., & Büber, H. (2012). *Eksisozluk as a learning platform.* Spring 2012 Independent Study Final Report School of Information Sciences University of Pittsburgh. https://www.pitt.edu/~peterb/indepstudies/2970-AcikozBuber-122.pdf

Akın, A. A., & Akın, M. D. (2007). Zemberek, an open source nlp framework for turkic languages. *Structure (London, England), 10,* 1–5.

Azder, B. (2019). Hashtag Nedir? En Etkili Nasıl Kullanılır? [What is a hashtag? How to Use It Most Effectively]. Netvent Blog.

Berghel, H. (2018). Malice Domestic: The Cambridge Analytica Dystopia. *Computer, 51*(5), 84–89. doi:10.1109/MC.2018.2381135

Butcher, M. (2021). *Elon Musk busts Clubhouse limit, fans stream to YouTube, he switches to interviewing Robinhood CEO.* TechCrunch.

Cadwalladr, C., & Graham-Harrison, E. (2018). *50 million Facebook profiles harvested for Cambridge Analytica in major data breach.* freestudio21.com

Çelik, N. (2018). The influence of media on moral values: Examination of the series named ufak tefek cinayetler through comments of eksi sozluk. *Journal of International Social Research*, *11*(55), 474–479. doi:10.17719/jisr.20185537220

Clubhouse Privacy Policy. (2021). *Privacy Policy*. https://www.notion.so/Privacy-Policy-cd4b415950204a46819478b31f6ce14f

Dean, B. (2021). *How Many Users Does Clubhouse Have? 40+ Clubhouse Stats.* Backlinko.

Dehkharghani, R., Saygin, Y., Yanikoglu, B., & Oflazer, K. (2016). SentiTurkNet: A Turkish Polari-ty Lexicon for Sentiment Analysis. *Language Resources and Evaluation*, *50*(3), 667–685. doi:10.100710579-015-9307-6

Dehkharghani, R., Saygin, Y., Yanikoglu, B., & Oflazer, K. (2016). SentiTurkNet: A Turkish polarity lexicon for sentiment analysis. *Language Resources and Evaluation*, *50*(3), 667–685. doi:10.100710579-015-9307-6

Drakett, J., Rickett, B., Day, K., & Milnes, K. (2018). Old jokes, new media – online sexism and constructions of gender in internet memes. *Feminism & Psychology*, *28*(1), 109–127. doi:10.1177/0959353517727560

Dubrofsky, R. E., & Wood, M. M. (2014). Posting racism and sexism: Authenticity, agency and self-reflexivity in social media. *Communication and Critical/Cultural Studies*, *11*(3), 282–287. doi:10.1080/14791420.2014.926247

Duman, K., & Özdoyran, G. (2018). Dijital emek ve kullanıcı içeriğinin metalaşması: Katılımcı sözlük yazarları üzerine inceleme. *Erciyes İletişim Dergisi*, *5*(4), 75–99. doi:10.17680/erciyesiletisim.419811

Esuli, A., & Sebastiani, F. (2006). SentiWordNet: a publicly available lexical resource for opinion mining. *Proceedings of LREC*, (6), 417–22.

Feldman, R. (2013). Techniques and applications for sentiment analysis. *Communications of the ACM*, *56*(4), 82–89. doi:10.1145/2436256.2436274

Gu, C., & Kurov, A. (2020). Informational role of social media: Evidence from Twitter sentiment. *Journal of Banking & Finance*, *121*(C).

Gürel, E., & Yakın, M. (2013). Ekşi Sözlük: Postmodern elektronik kültür. *Selçuk İletişim*, *4*(4), 203-219. Retrieved from https://dergipark.org.tr/en/pub/josc/issue/19014/200751

Gürel, E., & Yakın, M. (2005). Bir Reklam Mecrası Olarak Ekşi Sözlük. *Pi - Pazarlama ve İletişim Kültürü Dergisi*, *4*(14), 26 - 42.

Harrigan, P., Soutar, G., Choudhury, M. M., & Lowe, M. (2015). Modelling CRM in a social media age. *Australasian Marketing Journal, 23*(1), 27–37. doi:10.1016/j. ausmj.2014.11.001

Hugging Face Team. (2019). *Hugging Face: State-of-the-Art Natural Language Processing in ten lines of TensorFlow 2.*. https://blog.tensorflow.org/2019/11/hugging-face-state-of-art-natural.html

Türkiye İnternet Ölçümleme Araştırması Gemius, I. A. B. (2019). *Aralık overnight 2019 top 20 listeleri.* https://www.iabturkiye.org/UploadFiles/TopTwentyFiles/Internet_audiencetoplist_12_2019_Overnight.pdf

Isaak, J., & Hanna, M. J. (2018). User Data Privacy: Facebook, Cambridge Analytica, and Privacy Protection. *Computer, 51*(8), 8, 56–59. doi:10.1109/MC.2018.3191268

John, L. K., Kim, T., & Barasz, K. (2018). Ads that don't overstep. *Harvard Business Review, 96*(1), 62–69.

Kaspersky. (2021). *Clubhouse security and privacy - Is Clubhouse safe to use?* https://www.kaspersky.com/resource-center/preemptive-safety/is-clubhouse-safe-to-use

Kelly, H. (2021). From podcasts to Clubhouse, audio is filling more of our time. For some families, that's a problem. *The Washington Post.* https://www.washingtonpost.com/ technology/ 2021/03/15/ audio-time-Clubhouse-podcasts/

Marcin, T. (2021). *Here's what you need to know about Clubhouse, the invite-only social app.* Mashable. https://mashable.com/article/what-is-Clubhouse-app/

Meral, M., & Diri, B. (2014). Sentiment analysis on Twitter. *2014 22nd Signal Processing and Communications Applications Conference (SIU)*, 690-693. 10.1109/SIU.2014.6830323

Bakay, O., Ergelen, O., Sarmis, E., Yildirim, S., Kocabalcioglu, A., Arican, B. N., Ozcelik, M., Saniyar, E., Kuyrukcu, O., Avar, B., & Yıldız, O. T. (2020). Turkish WordNet KeNet. *Proceedings of GWC 2020.*

Popüler Uzakdoğu Sosyal Medya Platformları. (2020). *Uluslararası sosyal medya derneği Blog sayfası.* www.usmed.org.tr/populer-uzakdogu-sosyal-medya-platformlari/

Ruths, D., & Pfeffer, J. (2014). Social media for large studies of behavior. *Science, 346*(6213), 1063–1064. doi:10.1126cience.346.6213.1063 PMID:25430759

Samoggia, A., Bertazzoli, A., & Ruggeri, A. (2019). Food retailing marketing management: Social media communication for healthy food. *International Journal of Retail & Distribution Management, 47*(9), 928–956. doi:10.1108/IJRDM-08-2018-0178

Sine, R., & Özsoy, S. (2017). Ekşi Sözlük kullanıcılarının yeni medya kullanım pratikleri. *Route Educational and Social Science Journal, 4*(8), 53–65. doi:10.17121/ressjournal.885

Statista. (2021). *Social media - Statistics & Facts, Social media usage worldwide.* Statista. https://www.statista.com/topics/1164/social-networks/

Statista. (2021b). *Clubhouse - statistics & facts.* Author.

Strain, M., Saucier, D., & Martens, A. (2015). Sexist humor in Facebook profiles: Perceptions of humor targeting women and men. *Humor: International Journal of Humor Research, 28*(1), 119–141. doi:10.1515/humor-2014-0137

Subair, E. (2021). Drake, Oprah Winfrey and Virgil Abloh Are Fans: Here's Everything You Need to Know About Clubhouse. *Vogue.* https://www.vogue.com/article/everything-you-need-to-know-about-Clubhouse

Susar, F., & Narin, B. (2011). Sosyal paylaşımın tecimselleştirilmesi bağlamında internet reklamcılığı: Ekşi Sözlük örneği [In the context of commercialization of social sharing internet advertising: The example of sour dictionary]. *İstanbul Arel Üniversitesi İletişim Fakültesi İletişim Çalışmaları Dergisi, 3,* 1-14.

TÜİK. (2021). *Adrese Dayalı Nüfus Kayıt Sistemi Sonuçları, 2020.* tuik.gov.tr

Türk İşi Sosyal Ağlar. (2014). Onedio.

Üngören, E. (2019). Yeni medya iletişim kanalı olarak katılımcı sözlük sitelerine yönelik bir değerlendirme. *OPUS–Uluslararası Toplum Araştırmaları Dergisi, 11*(18), 2878–2907. doi:10.26466/opus.567125

Uzunoğlu, S. (2015). Bir postmodern intiharın ardından Ekşi Sözlük'te kanaatlerin oluşumu ve grupların biçimlenme süreçleri. *Intermedia International Peer-Reviewed E-Journal Of Communication Sciences, 2*(2), 424–439.

We Are Social. (2021). *Digital 2021 Global overview report.* We Are Social.

Wojcik, S., & Hughes, A. (2019). *Sizing Up Twitter Users, How Twitter Users Compare to the General Public.* Pew Research Center.

Yıldırım, S. (2020). Comparing Deep Neural Networks to Traditional Models for Sentiment Analysis in Turkish Language. In B. Agarwal, R. Nayak, N. Mittal, & S. Patnaik (Eds.), *Deep Learning-Based Approaches for Sentiment Analysis.* Algorithms for Intelligent Systems. doi:10.1007/978-981-15-1216-2_12

Yu, L., Asur, S., & Huberman, B. A. (2011). *What Trends in Chinese Social Media?* arXiv preprint arXiv:1107.3522.

KEY TERMS AND DEFINITIONS

Clubhouse: Clubhouse is a new audio-based social media form with invitation-based participation, where people can chat instantly on any topic.

Hugging Face: Hugging Face is the #1 NLP startup, with over a thousand firms, including Bing, Apple, and Monzo, using the library in their production.

Sentiment Analysis: Sentiment Analysis is a sub-research area of Natural Language Processing (NLP) studies. With sentiment analysis, also known as Opinion Mining, subjective language elements in oral or written texts about a particular subject can be interpreted.

Social Media: Users construct online communities to exchange information, ideas, career, interests, personal messages, and other content via social media (such as websites for social networking and microblogging) (such as videos).

Sourtimes: Sourtimes is a participatory dictionary containing comments from registered authors.

Supervised Learning: A supervised learning technique uses a known set of input data and known responses to train a model to make credible predictions for new data.

Text Mining: Text mining, which is a special area of data mining, is the application of data mining methods on texts written or shared by people with the help of natural language processing techniques. Many methods have already been developed on the analysis of texts, identifying important terms, summarizing, classifying, or grouping texts.

Unsupervised Learning: Unsupervised learning is the approach used when little or no idea of what the desired output from the data looks like. Various models and structures can be created by clustering the data based on the relationships between the variables.

ENDNOTE

[1]   The population of Turkey in 2020 is 83,614,312 according to the data of the Turkish Statistical Institute-TUIK (TUIK Institutional (tuik.gov.tr)).

Compilation of References

ways to use social media for Education. (2021, March 31). *Sprout Social.* https://sproutsocial. com/insights/social-media-for-education/

Abbe, A., Grouin, C., Zweigenbaum, P., & Falissard, B. (2016). Text mining applications in psychiatry: A systematic literature review. *International Journal of Methods in Psychiatric Research, 25*(2), 86–100. doi:10.1002/mpr.1481 PMID:26184780

Abdulla, N. A., Ahmed, N. A., Shehab, M. A., & Al-Ayyoub, M. (2013). *Arabic sentiment analysis: Lexicon-based and corpus-based. In 2013 IEEE Jordan conference on applied electrical engineering and computing technologies.* AEECT.

Abdul-Mageed, M., Zhang, C., Hashemi, A., & Nagoudi, E. M. (2020). *AraNet: New deep learning toolkit for arabic social media.* Medium. Accessed from: https://medium.com/syncedreview/ aranet-new-deeplearning-toolkit-for-arabic-social-media-d4729887ca48

Abu-Salih, B., Wongthongtham, P., Zhu, D., Chan, K. Y., Rudra, A., Abu-Salih, B., ... Rudra, A. (2021). Sentiment Analysis on Big News Media Data. *Social Big Data Analytics: Practices, Techniques, and Applications,* 177-218.

Achirul Nanda, M., Boro Seminar, K., Nandika, D., & Maddu, A. (2018). A comparison study of kernel functions in the support vector machine and its application for termite detection. *Information (Basel), 9*(1), 5. doi:10.3390/info9010005

Açıköz, T., & Büber, H. (2012). *Eksisozluk as a learning platform.* Spring 2012 Independent Study Final Report School of Information Sciences University of Pittsburgh. https://www.pitt. edu/~peterb/indepstudies/2970-AcikozBuber-122.pdf

Acquisti, A., Brandimarte, L., & Loewenstein, G. (2015). Privacy and human behavior in the age of information. *Science, 347*(6221), 509–514. doi:10.1126cience.aaa1465 PMID:25635091

Addo-Tenkorang, R., & Helo, P. T. (2016). Big data applications in operations/supply-chain management: A literature review. *Computers & Industrial Engineering, 101,* 528–543. doi:10.1016/j.cie.2016.09.023

Adegun, A., & Viriri, S. (2021). Deep learning techniques for skin lesion analysis and melanoma cancer detection: A survey of state-of-the-art. *Artificial Intelligence Review*, *54*(2), 811–841. doi:10.100710462-020-09865-y

Agarwal, A., Xie, B., Vovsha, I., Rambow, O., & Passonneau, R. J. (2011, June). Sentiment analysis of twitter data. In *Proceedings of the workshop on language in social media (LSM 2011)* (pp. 30-38). Academic Press.

Aggarwal, C. C. (2016). Neighborhood-based collaborative filtering. In *Recommender systems* (pp. 29–70). Springer. doi:10.1007/978-3-319-29659-3_2

Agreste, S., De Meo, P., Ferrara, E., Piccolo, S., & Provetti, A. (2015). Trust networks: Topology, dynamics, and measurements. *IEEE Internet Computing*, *19*(6), 26–35.

Ahmadian, S., Joorabloo, N., Jalili, M., Ren, Y., Meghdadi, M., & Afsharchi, M. (2020). A social recommender system based on reliable implicit relationships. *Knowledge-Based Systems*, *192*, 105371. doi:10.1016/j.knosys.2019.105371

Ahmad, M., Aftab, S., Muhammad, S. S., & Ahmad, S. (2017). Machine learning techniques for sentiment analysis: A review. *Int. J. Multidiscip. Sci. Eng*, *8*(3), 27.

Ahmed Abbasi, A. H., & Dhar, M. (2014). Benchmarking twitter sentiment analysis tools. *Proceedings of the Ninth International Conference on Language Resources and Evaluation (LREC'14)*.

Aichner, T., Grünfelder, M., Maurer, O., & Jegeni, D. (2021). Twenty-Five Years of Social Media: A Review of Social Media Applications and Definitions from 1994 to 2019. *Cyberpsychology, Behavior, and Social Networking*, *24*(4), 215–222. doi:10.1089/cyber.2020.0134

Aillerie, K., & McNicol, S. (2016). Information literacy and social networking sites: Challenges and stakes regarding teenagers' uses. *Journal for Communication Studies*, *9*(2), 89–100.

Akaichi, J. (2013, September). Social networks' Facebook'statutes updates mining for sentiment classification. In *2013 International Conference on Social Computing* (pp. 886-891). IEEE.

Akama, S., Kudo, Y., & Murai, T. (2020). Neighbor Selection for User-Based Collaborative Filtering Using Covering-Based Rough Sets. In *Topics in Rough Set Theory* (pp. 141–159). Springer. doi:10.1007/978-3-030-29566-0_9

Akhtar, M. S., Gupta, D., Ekbal, A., & Bhattacharyya, P. (2017). Feature selection and ensemble construction: A two-step method for aspect based sentiment analysis. *Knowledge-Based Systems*, *125*, 116–135. doi:10.1016/j.knosys.2017.03.020

Akın, A. A., & Akın, M. D. (2007). Zemberek, an open source nlp framework for turkic languages. *Structure (London, England)*, *10*, 1–5.

Al Fararni, K., Aghoutane, B., Riffi, J., Sabri, A., & Yahyaouy, A. (2020). Comparative Study on Approaches of Recommendation Systems. In *Embedded Systems and Artificial Intelligence* (pp. 753–764). Springer. doi:10.1007/978-981-15-0947-6_72

Alahmary, R. M., Al-Dossari, H. Z., & Emam, A. Z. (2019). Sentiment analysis of saudi dialect using deep learning techniques. *International Conference on Electronics, Information, and Communication*, Auckland, New Zealand. 10.23919/ELINFOCOM.2019.8706408

Albahli, S., Algsham, A., Aeraj, S., Alsaeed, M., Alrashed, M., Rauf, H. T., Arif, M., & Mohammed, M. A. (2021). COVID-19 Public Sentiment Insights: A Text Mining Approach to the Gulf Countries. Computers. *Materials & Continua, 67*(2), 1613–1627. doi:10.32604/cmc.2021.014265

Alena, N., Helmut, P., & Mitsuru, I. (2010). Recognition of Affect, Judgment, and Appreciation in Text. *Proceedings of the 23rd international conference on computational linguistics (Coling 2010)*, 806–814.

Alessia, D., Ferri, F., Grifoni, P., & Guzzo, T. (2015). Approaches, tools and applications for sentiment analysis implementation. *International Journal of Computers and Applications, 125*(3).

Alfaro, C., Cano-Montero, J., Gómez, J., Moguerza, J. M., & Ortega, F. (2016). A multi-stage method for content classification and opinion mining on weblog comments. *Annals of Operations Research, 236*(1), 197–213.

Ali Taha, V., Pencarelli, T., Škerháková, V., Fedorko, R., & Košíková, M. (2021). The use of social media and its impact on shopping behavior of Slovak and Italian consumers during COVID-19 pandemic. *Sustainability, 13*(4), 1710. https://doi.org/10.3390/su13041710

Alibakhshi, R., & Srivastava, S. C. (2019). *Should We Say What We Show? Examining the Influence of Image and Text Sentiments on Social Media Engagement. Fortieth International Conference on Information Systems*, Munich.

Aljasir, S., Bajnaid, A., Elyas, T., & Alnawasrah, M. (2017). University students usage of Facebook: The case of obtained gratifications and typology of its users. *Science, 229*, 61–66.

Al-Qurishi, M., Rahman, S. M. M., Alamri, A., & Mostafa, M. A., Al-Rubaian, et al. (2018). SybilTrap: A graph-based semi-supervised Sybil defense scheme for online social networks. *Concurrency and Computation, 30*(5), e4276.

Alrumaih, A., Al-Sabbagh, A., Alsabah, R., Kharrufa, H., & Baldwin, J. (2020). Sentiment analysis of comments in social media. *Iranian Journal of Electrical and Computer Engineering, 10*(6), 5917–5922.

Al-Smadi, M., Qawasmeh, O., Al-Ayyoub, M., Jararweh, Y., & Gupta, B. (2018). Deep Recurrent neural network vs. support vector machine for aspect-based sentiment analysis of Arabic hotels' reviews. *Journal of Computational Science, 27*, 386–393. doi:10.1016/j.jocs.2017.11.006

Alt, D. (2017). Students' social media engagement and fear of missing out (FoMO) in a diverse classroom. *Journal of Computing in Higher Education, 29*(2), 388–410. doi:10.100712528-017-9149-x

Amichai-Hamburger, Y., & Vinitzky, G. (2010). Social network use and personality. *Computers in Human Behavior, 26*(6), 1289–1295. doi:10.1016/j.chb.2010.03.018

Amini, M., Nasiri, M., & Afzali, M. (2014). *Proposing a new hybrid approach in movie recommender system.* Academic Press.

An Integrated Marketing Communications Perspective on Social Media Metrics. (n.d.). Available online: https://papers.ssrn.com/sol3/papers.cfm?abstract_id=2280132

Anandhan, A., Shuib, L., Ismail, M. A., & Mujtaba, G. (2018). *Social media recommender systems: review and open research issues.* Academic Press.

Ansari, J. A. N., & Khan, N. A. (2020). Exploring the role of social media in collaborative learning the new domain of learning. *Smart Learn. Environ, 7,* 9. doi:10.1186/s40561-020-00118-7

Asur, S., & Huberman, B. (2010). Predicting the future with social media. *Web Intelligence and Intelligent Agent Technology (WI-IAT). IEEE/WIC/ACM International Conference, 1,* 492–499.

Avasthi, R. (2017). Social Media and Disasters: A Literature Review. *Journal of the American Academy of Child & Adolescent Psychiatry, 56*(10). doi:10.1016/j.jaac.2017.07.317

Awad, N. F., & Krishnan, M. S. (2006). The personalization privacy paradox: An empirical evaluation of information transparency and the willingness to be profiled online for personalization. *Management Information Systems Quarterly, 30*(1), 13–28. doi:10.2307/25148715

Awwalu, J., Bakar, A. A., & Yaakub, M. R. (2019). Hybrid N-gram model using Naïve Bayes for classification of political sentiments on Twitter. *Neural Computing & Applications, 31*(12), 9207–9220. doi:10.100700521-019-04248-z

Azder, B. (2019). Hashtag Nedir? En Etkili Nasıl Kullanılır? [What is a hashtag? How to Use It Most Effectively]. Netvent Blog.

Azizan, S. A., & Aziz, I. A. (2017). Terrorism detection based on sentiment analysis using machine learning. *Journal of Engineering and Applied Sciences (Asian Research Publishing Network), 12*(3), 691–698.

Bakay, O., Ergelen, O., Sarmis, E., Yildirim, S., Kocabalcioglu, A., Arican, B. N., Ozcelik, M., Saniyar, E., Kuyrukcu, O., Avar, B., & Yıldız, O. T. (2020). Turkish WordNet KeNet. *Proceedings of GWC 2020.*

Bakhshi, B., Shamma, D. A., & Gilbert, E. (2014). Faces Engage Us Photos with Faces Attract More Likes and Comments on Instagram. *Proceedings of the SIGCHI Conference on Human Factors in Computing Systems (CHI'14),* 965-974. 10.1145/2556288.2557403

Balahur, A., Kozareva, Z., & Montoyo, A. (2009, March). Determining the polarity and source of opinions expressed in political debates. *International Conference on Intelligent Text Processing and Computational Linguistics,* 468-480. 10.1007/978-3-642-00382-0_38

Ballesteros C. (2019). *El índice de engagement en redes sociales, una medición emergente en la comunicación académica y organizacional.* Academic Press.

Bankov, B. (2019). *The Impact of Social Media on Video Game Communities and the Gaming Industry.* Academic Press.

Bansal, M., Cardie, C., & Lee, L. (2008). The power of negative thinking: Exploiting label disagreement in the min-cut classification framework. *Proceedings of the International Conference on Computational Linguistics (COLING),* 15-18.

Barbier, G., & Liu, H. (2011). Data mining in social media. In *Social network data analytics* (pp. 327–352). Springer.

Barbosa, L., & Feng, J. (2010). Robust sentiment detection on twitter from biased and noisy data. Coling 2010, 36-44.

Barbosa, R. R. L., Sánchez-Alonso, S., & Sicilia-Urban, M. A. (2015). Evaluating hotels rating prediction based on sentiment analysis services. *Aslib Journal of Information Management.*

Barnes, N. G., Leschault, A. M., & Andonian, J. (2012). *Social media surge by the 2012 Fortune 500: Increase use of blogs, Facebook, Twitter and more.* Retrieved from https://www.umassd.edu/cmr/socialmedia/2012fortune500/

Barros, M., Moitinho, A., & Couto, F. M. (2020). Hybrid semantic recommender system for chemical compounds. *European Conference on Information Retrieval,* 94–101.

Baştuğ, S., Çalişir, V., Gülmez, S., & Ateş, A. (2020). Measuring port brand equity: A sentiment analysis on port social media messages. *Journal of Social Sciences, 65,* 85–106.

Batty, M., Axhausen, K. W., Giannotti, F., Pozdnoukhov, A., Bazzani, A., Wachowicz, M., Ouzounis, G., & Portugali, Y. (2012). Smart cities of the future. *The European Physical Journal. Special Topics, 214*(1), 481–518. doi:10.1140/epjst/e2012-01703-3

Bautin, M., Vijayarenu, L., & Skiena, S. (2008). International Sentiment analysis for news and blogs. *Proceedings of the International Conference on Weblogs and Social Media (ICWSM).*

BBC Article. (2020). Accessed from: https://www.bbc.com/news/world-europe-51369960

Beaudoin & Hong. (2021). Emotions in the time of coronavirus: Antecedents of digital and social media use among Millennials. *Computers in Human Behavior, 123.* doi:10.1016/j.chb.2021.106876

Becker, M. W., Alzahabi, R., & Hopwood, C. J. (2013). Media Multitasking is associated with symptoms of depression and social anxiety. *Cyberpsychology, Behavior, and Social Networking, 16*(2), 132–135.

Bektaş, J., & Ibrikci, T. (2017, February). Hybrid classification procedure using SVM with LR on two distinctive datasets. In *Proceedings of the 6th International Conference on Software and Computer Applications* (pp. 68-71). 10.1145/3056662.3056717

Ben Schafer, J., Frankowski, D., Herlocker, J., & Sen, S. (2007). Collaborative filtering recommender systems. In *The adaptive web* (pp. 291–324). Springer. doi:10.1007/978-3-540-72079-9_9

Benitez, Sison, & Medina. (2018). Implementation of GA-Based Feature Selection in the Classification and Mapping of Disaster-Related Tweets. In *Proceedings of the 2nd International Conference on Natural Language Processing and Information Retrieval (NLPIR 2018)*. Association for Computing Machinery. doi:10.1145/3278293.3278297

Berghel, H. (2018). Malice Domestic: The Cambridge Analytica Dystopia. *Computer, 51*(5), 84–89. doi:10.1109/MC.2018.2381135

Bergström, A., & Jervelycke Belfrage, M. (2018). News in Social Media. *Digital Journalism, 6*(5), 583–598. doi:10.1080/21670811.2018.1423625

Bhatia, N. (2010). Survey of nearest neighbor techniques. *ArXiv Preprint ArXiv:1007.0085*.

Bhuta, S., Doshi, A., Doshi, U., & Narvekar, M. (2014, February). A review of techniques for sentiment analysis Of Twitter data. In *2014 International conference on issues and challenges in intelligent computing techniques (ICICT)* (pp. 583-591). IEEE.

Bifet, A., & Frank, E. (2010). Sentiment knowledge discovery in twitter streaming data. *International conference on discovery science*.

Bjornsen, C. A., & Archer, K. J. (2015). Relations between college students cell phone use during class and grades. *Scholarship of Teaching and Learning in Psychology, 1*(4), 326–336.

Blackwell, D., Leaman, C., Tramposch, R., Osborne, C., & Liss, M. (2017). Extraversion, neuroticism, attachment style and fear of missing out as predictors of social media use and addiction. *Personality and Individual Differences, 116*, 69–72.

Bokde, D., Girase, S., & Mukhopadhyay, D. (2015). Matrix factorization model in collaborative filtering algorithms: A survey. *Procedia Computer Science, 49*, 136–146. doi:10.1016/j.procs.2015.04.237

Bolshakov & Gelbukh. (2004). *Comput Linguis: Models, Resources, Applications*. Academic Press.

Bonzanini, M. (2016). *Mastering social media mining with Python*. Packt Publishing Ltd.

Bouarara, H. A. (2021). Recurrent Neural Network (RNN) to Analyse Mental Behaviour in Social Media. *International Journal of Software Science and Computational Intelligence, 13*(3), 1–11.

Boulesteix, A. L., Janitza, S., Kruppa, J., & König, I. R. (2012). Overview of random forest methodology and practical guidance with emphasis on computational biology and bioinformatics. *Wiley Interdisciplinary Reviews. Data Mining and Knowledge Discovery, 2*(6), 493–507.

Boyd, D. M., & Ellison, N. B. (2007). Social network sites: Definition, history, and scholarship. *Journal of Computer-Mediated Communication, 13*, 210–230.

Boynukalin, Z., & Karagoz, P. (2013). Emotion analysis on Turkish texts. In *Information Sciences and Systems, 264* (pp. 159–168). Springer.

Briciu, V.-A., & Briciu, A. (2021). Social Media and Organizational Communication. In Encyclopedia of Organizational Knowledge, Administration, and Technology (pp. 2609–2624). IGI Global.

Brynielsson, J., Horndahl, A., & Johansson, F. (2012). *Analysis of Weak Signals for Detecting Lone Wolf Terrorists. In European Intelligence & Security Informatics Conference.* EISIC.

Bureau, O. (2021, May 27). *Covid-19 pandemic fuelled digital payments modes: RBI annual report.* @businessline. https://www.thehindubusinessline.com/money-and-banking/covid-19-pandemic-fuelled-digital-payments-modes-rbi-annual-report/article34657571.ece

Burke, R. (2000). *Knowledge-based recommender systems.* Academic Press.

Butcher, M. (2021). *Elon Musk busts Clubhouse limit, fans stream to YouTube, he switches to interviewing Robinhood CEO.* TechCrunch.

Cadwalladr, C., & Graham-Harrison, E. (2018). *50 million Facebook profiles harvested for Cambridge Analytica in major data breach.* freestudio21.com

Calear, A. L., & Christensen, H. (2010). Review of internet-based prevention and treatment programs for anxiety and depression in children and adolescents. *Medical Journal, 192*(11).

Cambria, E., Speer, R., Havasi, C., & Hussain, A. (2010). SenticNet: A Publicly Available Semantic Resource for Opinion Mining. *AAAI Fall Symposium: Commonsense Knowledge, 10*(2), 5449.

Cambria, E., Schuller, B., Xia, Y., & Havasi, C. (2013). New avenues in opinion mining and sentiment analysis. *IEEE Intelligent Systems, 28*(2), 15–21.

Cambria, E., & White, B. (2014). Jumping NLP curves: A review of natural language processing research. *IEEE Computational Intelligence Magazine, 9*(2), 48–57. doi:10.1109/MCI.2014.2307227

Campbell, M., & Gavett, G. (2021). What Covid-19 Has Done to Our Well-Being, in 12 Charts. *Harvard Business Review*.

Can, E. F., Ezen-Can, A., & Can, F. (2018). *Multilingual sentiment analysis: An RNN-based framework for limited data.* Retrieved from arXiv preprint arXiv:1806.04511

Candon, P. (2019). Twitter: Social communication in the Twitter era. *New Media & Society, 21.* doi:10.1177/1461444819831987

Cavus, N., & Ibrahim, D. (2008). *A mobile tool for learning English words.* Retrieved from http://libezproxy.open.ac.uk/login?url=http://search.ebscohost.com/login.aspx?direct=true&db=eric&AN=ED504283&site=ehost-live&scope=site

Cavus, N., & Ibrahim, D. (2009). M-learning: An experiment in using SMS to support learning new English language words. *British Journal of Educational Technology, 40*(1), 78–91.

Çelik, N. (2018). The influence of media on moral values: Examination of the series named ufak tefek cinayetler through comments of eksi sozluk. *Journal of International Social Research, 11*(55), 474–479. doi:10.17719/jisr.20185537220

Ceron, A., Curini, L., Iacus, S. M., & Porro, G. (2014). Every tweet counts? How sentiment analysis of social media can improve our knowledge of citizens' political preferences with an application to Italy and France. *New Media & Society*, *16*(2), 340–358.

Chae, D.-K., Lee, S.-C., Lee, S.-Y., & Kim, S.-W. (2018). On identifying k-nearest neighbors in neighborhood models for efficient and effective collaborative filtering. *Neurocomputing*, *278*, 134–143. doi:10.1016/j.neucom.2017.06.081

Chang, H. H., & Meyerhoefer, C. D. (2021). COVID-19 and the demand for online food shopping services: Empirical Evidence from Taiwan. *American Journal of Agricultural Economics*, *103*(2), 448–465. doi:10.1111/ajae.12170

Chang, W.-L. (2019). The Impact of Emotion: A Blended Model to Estimate Influence on Social Media. *Information Systems Frontiers*, *21*, 1137–1151.

Chaudhary, P., Gupta, B. B., & Yamaguchi, S. (2016, October). XSS detection with automatic view isolation on online social network. In *2016 IEEE 5th Global Conference on Consumer Electronics* (pp. 1-5). IEEE.

Chaudhary, P., Gupta, B. B., & Yamaguchi, S. (2016, October). XSS detection with automatic view isolation on online social network. In *2016 IEEE 5th Global Conference on Consumer Electronics* (pp. 1-5). IEEE. 10.1109/GCCE.2016.7800354

Chaudhary, P., Gupta, B. B., Chang, X., Nedjah, N., & Chui, K. T. (2021). Enhancing big data security through integrating XSS scanner into fog nodes for SMEs gain. *Technological Forecasting and Social Change*, *168*, 120754. doi:10.1016/j.techfore.2021.120754

Chaudhary, P., Gupta, B. B., Choi, C., & Chui, K. T. (2020, December). XSSPro: XSS Attack Detection Proxy to Defend Social Networking Platforms. In *International Conference on Computational Data and Social Networks* (pp. 411-422). Springer.

Chehal, D., Gupta, P., & Gulati, P. (2020). Implementation and comparison of topic modeling techniques based on user reviews in e-commerce recommendations. *Journal of Ambient Intelligence and Humanized Computing*, 1–16.

Chen, W., Cai, Y., Lai, K., & Xie, H. (2016, January). A topic-based sentiment analysis model to predict stock market price movement using Weibo mood. In Web Intelligence (Vol. 14, No. 4, pp. 287-300). IOS Press.

Chen, C.-M., Tsai, M.-F., Lin, Y.-C., & Yang, Y.-H. (2016). Query-based music recommendations via preference embedding. *Proceedings of the 10th ACM Conference on Recommender Systems*, 79–82. 10.1145/2959100.2959169

Chen, S., Wang, G., & Jia, W. (2015). κ-FuzzyTrust: Efficient trust computation for large-scale mobile social networks using a fuzzy implicit social graph. *Information Sciences*, *318*, 123–143.

Chen, T. Y., Chen, Y. M., & Tsai, M. C. (2020). A Status Property Classifier of Social Media User's Personality for Customer-Oriented Intelligent Marketing Systems: Intelligent-Based Marketing Activities. *International Journal on Semantic Web and Information Systems*, *16*(1), 25–46.

Chen, W., & Lee, K. (2013). Sharing, liking, commenting, and distressed? The pathway between Facebook interaction and psychological distress. *Cyberpsychology, Behavior, and Social Networking, 16*(10), 728–734.

Chen, X., & Zhang, X. (2003). A popularity-based prediction model for web prefetching. *Computer, 36*(3), 63–70. doi:10.1109/MC.2003.1185219

Cho, H., Li, P., & Goh, Z. H. (2020). Privacy Risks, Emotions, and Social Media: A Coping Model of Online Privacy. *ACM Transformation Computer-Human Interaction, 40*(6), 40–68.

Chowdhary. (2012). *Natural Language Processing*. Academic Press.

Chu, F. (2021, February 10). *Social Commerce is leading the future of ecommerce.* Digital Commerce 360. https://www.digitalcommerce360.com/2021/02/10/social-commerce-is-leading-the-future-of-ecommerce/

Chui, K. T., Liu, R. W., Zhao, M., & De Pablos, P. O. (2020). Predicting students' performance with school and family tutoring using generative adversarial network-based deep support vector machine. *IEEE Access: Practical Innovations, Open Solutions, 8*, 86745–86752. doi:10.1109/ACCESS.2020.2992869

Chui, K. T., Lytras, M. D., & Liu, R. W. (2020). A generic design of driver drowsiness and stress recognition using MOGA optimized deep MKL-SVM. *Sensors (Basel), 20*(5), 1474. doi:10.339020051474 PMID:32156100

Chui, K. T., Lytras, M. D., & Vasant, P. (2020). Combined generative adversarial network and fuzzy C-means clustering for multi-class voice disorder detection with an imbalanced dataset. *Applied Sciences (Basel, Switzerland), 10*(13), 4571. doi:10.3390/app10134571

Chui, K. T., & Shen, C. W. (2019). Tolerance analysis in scale-free social networks with varying degree exponents. *Library Hi Tech, 37*(1), 57–71. doi:10.1108/LHT-07-2017-0146

Chung, W., & Zeng, D. (2016). Social-media-based public policy informatics: Sentiment and network analyses of US Immigration and border security. *Journal of the Association for Information Science and Technology, 67*(7), 1588–1606.

Ciccarelli, S. K., & Meyer, G. E. (2006). *Psychology*. Prentice Hall.

Cinelli & Quattrociocchi. (2020). The COVID-19 social media infodemic. *Sci Rep, 10*, 16598. doi:10.1038/s41598-020-73510-5

Clarizia, F., Colace, F., Pascale, F., Lombardi, M., & Santaniello, D. (2019). Sentiment Analysis in Social Networks: A Methodology Based on the Latent Dirichlet Allocation Approach. In *11th Conference of the European Society for Fuzzy Logic and Technology (EUSFLAT 2019)*, (pp. 241-248). Academic Press.

Clement, J. (2020). *Twitter: Most users by country.* Statista. Available: https://www.statista.com/statistics/242606/number-of-active-twitter-users-in-selected-countries/

Clubhouse Privacy Policy. (2021). *Privacy Policy*. https://www.notion.so/Privacy-Policy-cd4b415950204a46819478b31f6ce14f

Çoban, Ö., Özyer, B., & Özyer, G. T. (2015, May). Sentiment analysis for Turkish Twitter feeds. In *2015 23nd Signal Processing and Communications Applications Conference (SIU)* (pp. 2388-2391). IEEE. 10.1109/SIU.2015.7130362

Colace, F., De Santo, M., & Greco, L. (2013, September). A probabilistic approach to tweets' sentiment classification. In *2013 Humaine Association Conference on Affective Computing and Intelligent Interaction* (pp. 37-42). IEEE.

Cook, C. (2010). Mobile Marketing and Political Activities. *International Journal of Mobile Marketing*, *5*(1), 154–163.

Cui, Z., Xu, X., Fei, X. U. E., Cai, X., Cao, Y., Zhang, W., & Chen, J. (2020). Personalized recommendation system based on collaborative filtering for IoT scenarios. *IEEE Transactions on Services Computing*, *13*(4), 685–695. doi:10.1109/TSC.2020.2964552

D'Andrea, A., Ferri, F., Grifoni, P., & Guzzo, T. (2015). Approaches, Tools and Applications for Sentiment Analysis Implementation. *International Journal of Computers and Applications*, *125*(3), 26–33. doi:10.5120/ijca2015905866

Da Silva, N. F., Hruschka, E. R., & Hruschka, E. R. Jr. (2014). Tweet sentiment analysis with classifier ensembles. *Decision Support Systems*, *66*, 170–179. doi:10.1016/j.dss.2014.07.003

Dai, W., Han, D., Dai, Y., & Xu, D. (2015). Emotion recognition and affective computing on vocal social media. *Information & Management*, *52*(7), 777–788.

Datasets Resource Center. (2021, March 11). *Appen*. https://appen.com/open-source-datasets/

Davenport, T. H., & Dyché, J. (2013). Big data in big companies. *International Institute for Analytics*, *3*, 1–31.

David, C. (2011). *How Traditional Entertainment Can Use Social Media*. GigaOm. Retrieved 2011-06-19. https://gigaom.com/2011/05/10/how-traditional-entertainment-can-use-social-media/

Davidov, D., Tsur, O., & Rappoport, A. (2010). Enhanced sentiment learning using twitter hashtags and smileys. Coling 2010.

De Keyzer, F., Dens, N., & De Pelsmacker, P. (2017). Don't be so emotional! How tone of voice and service type affect the relationship between message valence and consumer responses to WOM in social media. *Online Information Review*, *41*(7), 905–920.

De Meo, P., Ferrara, E., Rosaci, D., & Sarné, G. M. (2014). Trust and compactness in social network groups. *IEEE Transactions on Cybernetics*, *45*(2), 205–216.

De Vlack, K. (2020). *What is the Role of Social Media during the COVID-19 Crisis?* Knowledge @HEC. Accessed from: https://www.hec.edu/en/knowledge/instants/what-role-social-media-during-covid-19-crisis-0

De', R., Pandey, N., & Pal, A. (2020). Impact of digital surge during Covid-19 pandemic: A viewpoint on research and practice. *International Journal of Information Management*. doi:10.1016/j.ijinfomgt.2020.102171

Dean, B. (2021). *How Many Users Does Clubhouse Have? 40+ Clubhouse Stats*. Backlinko.

DeBell, M., & Chapman, C. (2006). *Computer and internet use by students in 2003*. Statistical analysis report. NCES 2006-065. National Center for education statistics.

Dehkharghani, R., Saygin, Y., Yanikoglu, B., & Oflazer, K. (2016). SentiTurkNet: A Turkish Polari-ty Lexicon for Sentiment Analysis. *Language Resources and Evaluation*, *50*(3), 667–685. doi:10.100710579-015-9307-6

Diakopoulos, N. A., & Shamma, D. A. (2010). Characterizing debate performance via aggregated twitter sentiment. *Proceedings of the SIGCHI Conference on Human Factors in Computing Systems*, 1195-1198.

Disasters on social media - dataset by crowdflower. (2016, November 21). https://data.world/crowdflower/disasters-on-social-media/access.

Dobrean, A., & Păsărelu, C.-R. (2016). Impact of Social Media on Social Anxiety. *Systematic Reviews*. Advance online publication. doi:10.5772/65188

Dodds, K. (2006). Popular geopolitics and audience dispositions: James Bond and the internet movie database (IMDb). *Transactions of the Institute of British Geographers*, *31*(2), 116–130. doi:10.1111/j.1475-5661.2006.00199.x

Do, H. H., Prasad, P. W. C., Maag, A., & Alsadoon, A. (2019). Deep learning for aspect-based sentiment analysis: A comparative review. *Expert Systems with Applications*, *118*, 272–299. doi:10.1016/j.eswa.2018.10.003

Dong, X., Yu, Z., Cao, W., Shi, Y., & Ma, Q. (2020). A survey on ensemble learning. *Frontiers of Computer Science*, *14*(2), 241–258. doi:10.100711704-019-8208-z

Drakett, J., Rickett, B., Day, K., & Milnes, K. (2018). Old jokes, new media – online sexism and constructions of gender in internet memes. *Feminism & Psychology*, *28*(1), 109–127. doi:10.1177/0959353517727560

Dubey, A., Gupta, A., Raturi, N., & Saxena, P. (2018). Item-Based Collaborative Filtering Using Sentiment Analysis of User Reviews. *International Conference on Application of Computing and Communication Technologies*, 77–87. 10.1007/978-981-13-2035-4_8

Dubrofsky, R. E., & Wood, M. M. (2014). Posting racism and sexism: Authenticity, agency and self-reflexivity in social media. *Communication and Critical/Cultural Studies*, *11*(3), 282–287. doi:10.1080/14791420.2014.926247

Du, J., & Jing, H. (2017). Collaborative Filtering-Based Matching and Recommendation of Suppliers in Prefabricated Component Supply Chain. *International Conference on Applications and Techniques in Cyber Security and Intelligence*, 128–139.

Duman, K., & Özdoyran, G. (2018). Dijital emek ve kullanıcı içeriğinin metalaşması: Katılımcı sözlük yazarları üzerine inceleme. *Erciyes İletişim Dergisi*, *5*(4), 75–99. doi:10.17680/erciyesiletisim.419811

Earle, P., Guy, M., Buckmaster, R., Ostrum, C., Horvath, S., & Vaughan, A. (2010, March). OMG Earthquake! Can Twitter improve earthquake response? *Seismological Research Letters*, *81*(2), 246–251.

Ellison, N., Steinfield, C., & Lampe, C. (2007). The benefits of Facebook "friends:" social capital and college students' use of online social network sites. *Journal of Computer-Mediated Communication*, *12*, 1143–1168.

Elshakankery, K., & Ahmed, M. F. (2019). HILATSA: A hybrid Incremental learning approach for Arabic tweets sentiment analysis. *Egyptian Informatics Journal*, *20*(3), 163–171. doi:10.1016/j.eij.2019.03.002

Esuli, A., & Sebastiani, F. (2006). SentiWordNet: a publicly available lexical resource for opinion mining. *Proceedings of LREC*, (6), 417–22.

Fang, X., & Zhan, J. (2015). Sentiment analysis using product review data. *Journal of Big Data*, *2*(5), 1–14.

Fatemi, M., & Rezaei-Moghaddam, K. (2020). Sociological factors influencing the performance of organic activities in Iran. *Life Sciences, Society and Policy*, *16*(1), 1–16. doi:10.118640504-020-00098-z PMID:32390089

Feizollah, A., Ainin, S., Anuar, N. B., Abdullah, N. A., & Hazim, M. (2019). Halal Products on Twitter: Data Extraction and Sentiment Analysis Using Stack of Deep Learning Algorithms. *IEEE Access: Practical Innovations, Open Solutions*, *7*, 83354–83362. doi:10.1109/ACCESS.2019.2923275

Feldman, R. (2013). Techniques and applications for sentiment analysis. *Communications of the ACM*, *56*(4), 82–89. doi:10.1145/2436256.2436274

Felfernig, A., Jeran, M., Ninaus, G., Reinfrank, F., Reiterer, S., & Stettinger, M. (2014). Basic approaches in recommendation systems. In *Recommendation Systems in Software Engineering* (pp. 15–37). Springer. doi:10.1007/978-3-642-45135-5_2

Fernando, K. R. M., & Tsokos, C. P. (2021). Dynamically weighted balanced loss: Class imbalanced learning and confidence calibration of deep neural networks. *IEEE Transactions on Neural Networks and Learning Systems*, 1–12. doi:10.1109/TNNLS.2020.3047335 PMID:33444149

Fogues, R., Such, J. M., Espinosa, A., & Garcia-Fornes, A. (2015). Open challenges in relationship-based privacy mechanisms for social network services. *International Journal of Human-Computer Interaction*, *31*(5), 350–370.

Fouad, M. M., Gharib, T. F., & Mashat, A. S. (2018). Efficient Twitter Sentiment Analysis System with Feature Selection and Classifier Ensemble. *International Conference on Advanced Machine Learning Technologies and Applications (AMLTA2018)*, *723*, 516–527.

Friedman, L., & Friedman, H. (2013). Using Social Media Technologies to Enhance Online Learning. *Journal of Educators Online., 10*. Advance online publication. doi:10.9743/JEO.2013.1.5

Fullerton, N. (2020). *Instagram vs. Reality: The Pandemic's Impact on Social Media and Mental Health.* https://www.pennmedicine.org/news/news-blog/2021/april/instagram-vs-reality-the-pandemics-impact-on-social-media-and-mental-health

Gallagher, C., Furey, E., & Curran, K. (2019). The application of sentiment analysis and text analytics to customer experience reviews to understand what customers are really saying. *International Journal of Data Warehousing and Mining, 15*(4), 21–47. doi:10.4018/IJDWM.2019100102

Gamallo, P., & Garcia, M. (2014). Citius: A NaiveBayes Strategy for Sentiment Analysis on English Tweets. *Proceedings of the 8th International Workshop on Semantic Evaluation.* 10.3115/v1/S14-2026

Gao, J., Zheng, P., Jia, Y., Chen, H., & Mao, Y. (2020). Mental health problems and social media exposure during COVID-19 outbreak. *PLoS One, 15*(4).

Giachanou, A., & Crestani, F. (2016). Like it or not: A survey of twitter sentiment analysis methods. *ACM Computing Surveys, 49*(2), 1–41. doi:10.1145/2938640

Gikas, J., & Grant, M. M. (2013). Mobile computing devices in higher education: Student perspectives on learning with cellphones, smartphones & social media. *Internet and Higher Education Mobile, 19*, 18–26. doi:10.1016/j.iheduc.2013.06.002

Global internet penetration rate as of April 2021, by region. (2021). *Statista.* Retrieved 3 August 2021 Online https://www.statista.com/statistics/269329/penetration-rate-of-the-internet-by-region/

Go, A., Bhayani, R., & Huang, L. (2009). Twitter sentiment classification using distant supervision. CS224N project report, Stanford.

Go, A., Huang, L., & Bhayani, R. (2009). Twitter sentiment analysis. *Entropy (Basel, Switzerland), 17.*

Gökçe, O. Z., Hatipoğlu, E., Göktürk, G., Luetgert, B., & Saygin, Y. (2014). Twitter and politics: Identifying Turkish opinion leaders in new social media. *Turkish Studies, 15*(4), 671–688. doi:10.1080/14683849.2014.985425

Gou, Z., Yamaguchi, S., & Gupta, B. B. (2017). Analysis of various security issues and challenges in cloud computing environment: a survey. In Identity Theft: Breakthroughs in Research and Practice (pp. 221-247). IGI Global. doi:10.4018/978-1-5225-0808-3.ch011

Graf, D., Retschitzegger, W., Schwinger, W., Pröll, B., & Elisa-beth, K. (2018). Cross-domain informativeness classification for disaster situations. *Proceedings of the 10th international conference on management of digital ecosystems*, 183–190.

Gray, B., Weal, M., & Martin, D. (2016). *Social media and disasters: A new conceptual framework.* Academic Press.

Greenhow, C. (2011a). Online social networks and learning. *On the Horizon, 19*(1), 4–12.

Greenhow, C. (2011b). Youth, learning, and social media. *Journal of Educational Computing Research, 45*(2), 139–146. https://doi.org/10.2190/EC.45.2.a

Grossi, E., & Buscema, M. (2007). Introduction to artificial neural networks. *European Journal of Gastroenterology & Hepatology, 19*(12), 1046–1054.

Gu, C., & Kurov, A. (2020). Informational role of social media: Evidence from Twitter sentiment. *Journal of Banking & Finance, 121*(C).

Guellil, I., & Boukhalfa, K. (2015, April). Social big data mining: A survey focused on opinion mining and sentiments analysis. In *2015 12th international symposium on programming and systems (ISPS)* (pp. 1-10). IEEE.

Guha-Sapir, D., Vos, F., Below, R., & Ponserre, S. (2016). Annual Disaster Statistical Review 2016: The Numbers and Trends. Brussels: Centre for Research on the Epidemiology of Disasters (CRED).

Gundecha, P., & Liu, H. (2012). Mining social media: a brief introduction. *New directions in informatics, optimization, logistics, and production*, 1-17.

Gupta, A. (in press). An Exploratory Analysis on the Unfold of Fake News During COVID-19 Pandemic. *Smart Systems: Innovations in Computing*.

Gupta, B. B., Sangaiah, A. K., Nedjah, N., Yamaguchi, S., Zhang, Z., & Sheng, M. (2018). *Recent research in computational intelligence paradigms into security and privacy for online social networks (OSNs)*. Academic Press.

Gupta, A. (2022). An Exploratory Analysis on the Unfold of Fake News During COVID-19 Pandemic. In *Smart Systems: Innovations in Computing* (pp. 259–272). Springer Singapore.

Gupta, B. B., Agrawal, D. P., Yamaguchi, S., & Sheng, M. (2020). Soft computing techniques for big data and cloud computing. *Soft Computing, 24*(8), 5483–5484. doi:10.100700500-020-04766-2

Gupta, P., Soundararajan, B., & Zachariah, T. (2017). *Image-based sentiment analysis of videos.* In *Thirtieth Annual Conference on Neural Information Processing Systems (NIPS)*, Barcelona, Spain.

Gupta, S., & Dave, M. (2020). An Overview of Recommendation System: Methods and Techniques. In *Advances in Computing and Intelligent Systems* (pp. 231–237). Springer. doi:10.1007/978-981-15-0222-4_20

Gupta, S., & Gupta, B. B. (2016). JS-SAN: Defense mechanism for HTML5-based web applications against javascript code injection vulnerabilities. *Security and Communication Networks, 9*(11), 1477–1495.

Gupta, S., & Gupta, B. B. (2017). Detection, avoidance, and attack pattern mechanisms in modern web application vulnerabilities: Present and future challenges. *International Journal of Cloud Applications and Computing, 7*(3), 1–43.

Gupta, S., Gupta, B. B., & Chaudhary, P. (2018). Hunting for DOM-Based XSS vulnerabilities in mobile cloud-based online social network. *Future Generation Computer Systems, 79,* 319–336. doi:10.1016/j.future.2017.05.038

Gürel, E., & Yakın, M. (2005). Bir Reklam Mecrası Olarak Ekşi Sözlük. *Pi - Pazarlama ve İletişim Kültürü Dergisi, 4*(14), 26 - 42.

Gürel, E., & Yakın, M. (2013). Ekşi Sözlük: Postmodern elektronik kültür. *Selçuk İletişim, 4*(4), 203-219. Retrieved from https://dergipark.org.tr/en/pub/josc/issue/19014/200751

Gu, Y., Chanussot, J., Jia, X., & Benediktsson, J. A. (2017). Multiple kernel learning for hyperspectral image classification: A review. *IEEE Transactions on Geoscience and Remote Sensing, 55*(11), 6547–6565. doi:10.1109/TGRS.2017.2729882

Hadj Ameur, M. S., & Aliane, H. (2021). Aracovid19-MFH: Arabic covid-19 multi-label fake news & hate speech detection dataset. *Procedia Computer Science, 189,* 232–241. https://doi.org/10.1016/j.procs.2021.05.086

Hailong, Z., Wenyan, G., & Bo, J. (2014, September). Machine learning and lexicon based methods for sentiment classification: A survey. In *2014 11th web information system and application conference* (pp. 262-265). IEEE.

Hajiali, M. (2020). Big data and sentiment analysis: A comprehensive and systematic literature review. *Concurrency and Computation, 32*(14), e5671. doi:10.1002/cpe.5671

Hamasaki, M., Takeda, H., Hope, T., & Nishimura, T. (2009, March). Network analysis of an emergent massively collaborative creation community: How can people create videos collaboratively without collaboration? *Proceedings of the International AAAI Conference on Web and Social Media, 3*(1).

Hancu-Budui, A., Zorio-Grima, A., & Blanco-Vega, J. (2020). Audit Institutions in the European Union: Public Service Promotion, Environmental Engagement and COVID Crisis Communication through Social Media. *Sustainability, 2020*(12), 9816.

Han, E. J., & Sohn, S. Y. (2015). Patent valuation based on text mining and survival analysis. *The Journal of Technology Transfer, 40*(5), 821–839. doi:10.100710961-014-9367-6

Harper, F. M., & Konstan, J. A. (2015). The movielens datasets: History and context. *Acm Transactions on Interactive Intelligent Systems (Tiis), 5*(4), 1–19.

Harrigan, P., Soutar, G., Choudhury, M. M., & Lowe, M. (2015). Modelling CRM in a social media age. *Australasian Marketing Journal, 23*(1), 27–37. doi:10.1016/j.ausmj.2014.11.001

Hassonah, M. A., Al-Sayyed, R., Rodan, A., Ala'M, A. Z., Aljarah, I., & Faris, H. (2020). An efficient hybrid filter and evolutionary wrapper approach for sentiment analysis of various topics on Twitter. *Knowledge-Based Systems, 192,* 105353. doi:10.1016/j.knosys.2019.105353

Hatzivassiloglou, V., & McKeown, K. (1997). Predicting the semantic orientation of adjectives. In *35th annual meeting of the association for computational linguistics and 8th conference of the European chapter of the association for computational linguistics*, (pp. 174-181). Academic Press.

Hayran, A., & Sert, M. (2017, May). Sentiment analysis on microblog data based on word embedding and fusion techniques. In *2017 25th Signal Processing and Communications Applications Conference (SIU)* (pp. 1-4). IEEE. 10.1109/SIU.2017.7960519

Hearst, M. A. (1992). Direction-Based Text Interpretation as an Information Access Refinement. *Text Based Intelligent Systems: Current Research and Practice in Information Extraction and Retrieval*, 257-274.

Hemmatian, F., & Sohrabi, M. K. (2019). A survey on classification techniques for opinion mining and sentiment analysis. *Artificial Intelligence Review*, *52*(3), 1495–1545. doi:10.100710462-017-9599-6

Hernández-Nieves, E., Hernández, G., Gil-González, A.-B., Rodríguez-González, S., & Corchado, J. M. (2020). Fog computing architecture for personalized recommendation of banking products. *Expert Systems with Applications*, *140*, 112900. doi:10.1016/j.eswa.2019.112900

He, Y., & Deyu, Z. (2011). Self-training from labeled features for sentiment analysis. *Information Processing & Management*, *47*(4), 606–616.

Hong, W., & Thong, J. (2013). Internet privacy concerns: An integrated conceptualisation and four empirical studies. *MIS Quaterly*, *37*(1), 275–298.

Hovorka, D., & Rees, M. J. (2009). Active collaboration learning environments: The class of Web 2.0. *20th Australasian Conference on Information Systems: ACIS 2009*.

Huang, J., Nie, F., Huang, H., Tu, Y. C., & Lei, Y. (2013). Social trust prediction using heterogeneous networks. *ACM Transactions on Knowledge Discovery from Data*, *7*(4), 1–21.

Hugging Face Team. (2019). *Hugging Face: State-of-the-Art Natural Language Processing in ten lines of TensorFlow 2.*. https://blog.tensorflow.org/2019/11/hugging-face-state-of-art-natural.html

Hughes, A. L., Palen, L., Sutton, J., Liu, S., & Vieweg, S. (2008). *"Site-seeing" in disaster: an examination of on-line social convergence'*. Paper presented at the ISCRAM (Information Systems for Crisis Response and Management) Conference, Washington, DC.

Hughes, A. L., & Palen, L. (2009). Twitter adoption and use in mass convergence and emergency events. *ISCRAM Conference*.

Hu, H., Ahn, G. J., & Jorgensen, J. (2012). Multiparty access control for online social networks: Model and mechanisms. *IEEE Transactions on Knowledge and Data Engineering*, *25*(7), 1614–1627.

Iruvanti, G. (2020, August 1). *Real or NOT? NLP with DISASTER Tweets (classification using google bert)*. Medium. https://levelup.gitconnected.com/real-or-not-nlp-with-disaster-tweets-classification-using-google-bert-76d2702807b4

Isaak, J., & Hanna, M. J. (2018). User Data Privacy: Facebook, Cambridge Analytica, and Privacy Protection. *Computer, 51*(8), 8, 56–59. doi:10.1109/MC.2018.3191268

It's Curtains for Blockbuster Stores. (2013, Nov. 13). *ABC News.*

Jain, A. K., Sahoo, S. R., & Kaubiyal, J. (2021). Online social networks security and privacy: comprehensive review and analysis. *Complex & Intelligent Systems*, 1-21.

Jain, A. K., & Gupta, B. B. (2019). A machine learning based approach for phishing detection using hyperlinks information. *Journal of Ambient Intelligence and Humanized Computing, 10*(5), 2015–2028. doi:10.100712652-018-0798-z

Jain, A. K., & Gupta, B. B. (2019). Feature Based Approach for Detection of Smishing Messages in the Mobile Environment. *Journal of Information Technology Research, 12*(2), 17–35. doi:10.4018/JITR.2019040102

Jalilifard, A., Caridá, V., Mansano, A., & Cristo, R. (2020). Semantic sensitive TF-IDF to determine word relevance in documents. *ArXiv Preprint ArXiv:2001.09896.*

Jannach, D., Manzoor, A., Cai, W., & Chen, L. (2020). A survey on conversational recommender systems. *ArXiv Preprint ArXiv:2004.00646.*

Jansen, B. J., Zhang, M., Sobel, K., & Chowdury, A. (2009). Twitter power: Tweets as electronic word of mouth. *Journal of the American Society for Information Science and Technology, 60*(11), 2169–2188.

Järvinen, A. (2009). Game Design for Social Networks. *Proceedings of the 2009 ACM SIGGRAPH Symposium on Video Games - Sandbox '09.* doi:10.1145/1581073.1581088

Jebaseeli, A. N., & Kirubakaran, E. (2012). A survey on sentiment analysis of (product) reviews. *International Journal of Computers and Applications, 47*(11).

Jia, H., & Xu, H. (2016). Measuring individuals' concerns over collective privacy on social networking sites. *Cyberpsychology (Brno), 10*(1).

Jiang, Z., Heng, C. S., & Choi, B. C. F. (2013). Privacy concerns and privacy-protective behavior in synchronous online social interactions. *Information Systems Research, 24*(3), 597–595.

John, L. K., Kim, T., & Barasz, K. (2018). Ads that don't overstep. *Harvard Business Review, 96*(1), 62–69.

Johnson, J. M., & Khoshgoftaar, T. M. (2019). Survey on deep learning with class imbalance. *Journal of Big Data, 6*(1), 1–54. doi:10.118640537-019-0192-5

Joshi, A., Balamurali, A. R., Bhattacharyya, P., & Mohanty, R. (2011). C-feel-it: a sentiment analyzer for microblogs. *Proceedings of ACL: Systems Demonstrations, HLT '11*, 127–132.

Joshi, M., Prajapati, P., Shaikh, A., & Vala, V. (2017). A Survey on Sentiment Analysis. *International Journal of Computers and Applications, 163*(6), 34–38. doi:10.5120/ijca2017913552

Jost, J. T., Barberá, P., Bonneau, R., Langer, M., Metzger, M., Nagler, J., Sterling, J., & Tucker, J. A. (2018). How social media facilitates political protest: Information, motivation, and social networks. *Political Psychology*, *39*, 85–118. doi:10.1111/pops.12478

Kanayama, H., & Nasukawa, T. (2006). Fully automatic lexicon expansion for domain-oriented sentiment analysis. In *Proceedings of the 2006 conference on empirical methods in natural language processing*, (pp. 355-363). 10.3115/1610075.1610125

Kaplan & Haenlein. (2010). Users of the world, unite! The challenges and opportunities of social media. *Business Horizons*, *53*(1), 61. doi:10.1016/j.bushor.2009.09.003

Kaplan, A. M., & Haenlein, M. (2010). Users of the world, unite! The challenges and opportunities of social media. *Business Horizons*, *53*(1), 59–68.

Karahoca, A., Karahoca, D., & Evirgen, E. (2019). Sentiment analysis of Turkish tweets by data mining methods. *International Journal of Mechanical Engineering and Technology*, *10*(1).

Karamibekr, M., & Ghorbani, A. A. (2012, December). Sentiment analysis of social issues. In *2012 International Conference on Social Informatics* (pp. 215-221). IEEE.

Karcioğlu, A. A., & Aydin, T. (2019, April). Sentiment analysis of Turkish and english twitter feeds using Word2Vec model. In *2019 27th Signal Processing and Communications Applications Conference (SIU)* (pp. 1-4). IEEE. 10.1109/SIU.2019.8806295

Karthikeyan, T., Sekaran, K., Ranjith, D., & Balajee, J. M. (2019). Personalized content extraction and text classification using effective web scraping techniques. *International Journal of Web Portals*, *11*(2), 41–52. doi:10.4018/IJWP.2019070103

Kaspersky. (2021). *Clubhouse security and privacy - Is Clubhouse safe to use?* https://www.kaspersky.com/resource-center/preemptive-safety/is-clubhouse-safe-to-use

Kaubiyal, J., & Jain, A. K. (2019). A feature based approach to detect fake profiles in Twitter. In *Proceedings of the 3rd International Conference on Big Data and Internet of Things* (pp. 135-139). ACM. 10.1145/3361758.3361784

Kaya, M., Fidan, G., & Toroslu, I. H. (2012, December). Sentiment analysis of turkish political news. In *2012 IEEE/WIC/ACM International Conferences on Web Intelligence and Intelligent Agent Technology* (Vol. 1, pp. 174-180). IEEE. 10.1109/WI-IAT.2012.115

Ke, J., Zheng, H., Yang, H., & Chen, X. M. (2017). Short-term forecasting of passenger demand under on-demand ride services: A spatio-temporal deep learning approach. *Transportation Research Part C, Emerging Technologies*, *85*, 591–608. doi:10.1016/j.trc.2017.10.016

Kelly, H. (2021). From podcasts to Clubhouse, audio is filling more of our time. For some families, that's a problem. *The Washington Post*. https://www.washingtonpost.com/ technology/ 2021/03/15/ audio-time-Clubhouse-podcasts/

Kelly, L. L. (2018). A snapchat story: How black girls develop strategies for critical resistance in school. *Learning, Media and Technology*, 1–16.

Kemp, S. (2020, January 30). *Digital 2020: 3.8 billion people use social media.* We Are Social. https://wearesocial.com/blog/2020/01/digital-2020-3-8-billion-people-use-social-media

Khan, M. T., Durrani, M., Ali, A., Inayat, I., Khalid, S., & Khan, K. H. (2016). Sentiment analysis and the complex natural language. *Complex Adaptive Systems Modeling, 4*(1), 1–19. doi:10.118640294-016-0016-9

Kietzmann, J. H., & Kristopher, H. (2021, May-June). Social media? Get serious! Understanding the functional building blocks of social media. *Business Horizons, 54*(3), 241–251. doi:10.1016/j.bushor.2011.01.005

Kim, D., Kim, D., Hwang, E., & Choi, H. G. (2013). A user opinion and metadata mining scheme for predicting box office performance of movies in the social network environment. *New Review of Hypermedia and Multimedia, 19*(3-4), 259–272.

Kim, E. H. J., Jeong, Y. K., Kim, Y., Kang, K. Y., & Song, M. (2016). Topic-based content and sentiment analysis of Ebola virus on Twitter and in the news. *Journal of Information Science, 42*(6), 763–781.

Kim, E., Gilbert, S., Edwards, M. J., & Graeff, E. (2009). Detecting sadness in 140 characters: Sentiment analysis and mourning Michael Jackson on Twitter. *Web Ecology, 3,* 1–15.

Kim, S. M., & Hovy, E. (2006). Automatic identification of pro and con reasons in online reviews. *Proceedings of the COLING/ACL Main Conference Poster Sessions,* 483-490.

Kirelli, Y., & Arslankaya, S. (2020). Sentiment Analysis of Shared Tweets on Global Warming on Twitter with Data Mining Methods: A Case Study on Turkish Language. *Computational Intelligence and Neuroscience.* PMID:32963511

Kireyev, K., Palen, L., & Anderson, K. (2009). Applications of topics models to the analysis of disaster-related Twitter data. In *NIPS Workshop on Applications for Topic Models: Text and Beyond* (Vol. *1*). Academic Press.

Kirkpatrick, D. (2011). *The Facebook effect: The real inside story of Mark Zuckerberg and the world's fastest-growing company.* Academic Press.

Kleemans, M., Daalmans, S., Carbaat, I., & Anschutz, D. (2018). Picture Perfect: The direct effect of manipulated Instagram photos on body image in adolescent girls. *Media Psychology, 21*(1), 93–110.

Korenkova, M., Maros, M., Levicky, M., & Fila, M. (2020). Consumer Perception of Modern and Traditional Forms of Advertising. *Sustainability, 2020*(12), 9996.

Korkontzelos, I., Nikfarjam, A., Shardlow, M., Sarker, A., Ananiadou, S., & Gonzalez, G. H. (2016). Analysis of the effect of sentiment analysis on extracting adverse drug reactions from tweets and forum posts. *Journal of Biomedical Informatics, 62,* 148–158.

Kwon, H. J., Ban, H. J., Jun, J. K., & Kim, H. S. (2021). Topic modeling and sentiment analysis of online review for airlines. *Information (Basel), 12*(2), 78. doi:10.3390/info12020078

Lai, C.-H., Lee, S.-J., & Huang, H.-L. (2019). A social recommendation method based on the integration of social relationship and product popularity. *International Journal of Human-Computer Studies, 121*, 42–57. doi:10.1016/j.ijhcs.2018.04.002

Lalji, T., & Deshmukh, S. (2016). Twitter sentiment analysis using hybrid approach. *International Research Journal of Engineering and Technology, 3*(6), 2887–2890.

Lamsal, R., & Kumar, T. V. (2021). Twitter-Based Disaster Response Using Recurrent Nets. *International Journal of Sociotechnology and Knowledge Development (IJSKD), 13*(3), 133-150. doi:10.4018/IJSKD.2021070108

Latonero, M., & Shklovski, I. (2011). Emergency Management, Twitter, and Social Media Evangelism. *International Journal of Information Systems for Crisis Response and Management, 3*(4), 1–16. https://doi.org/10.4018/jiscrm.2011100101

Le, D. N., Parvathy, V. S., Gupta, D., Khanna, A., Rodrigues, J. J., & Shankar, K. (2021). IoT enabled depthwise separable convolution neural network with deep support vector machine for COVID-19 diagnosis and classification. *International Journal of Machine Learning and Cybernetics*, 1–14. PMID:33727984

Leevy, J. L., Khoshgoftaar, T. M., Bauder, R. A., & Seliya, N. (2018). A survey on addressing high-class imbalance in big data. *Journal of Big Data, 5*(1), 1–30. doi:10.118640537-018-0151-6

Lenhart, A., Madden, M., & Hitlin, P. (2005). *Teens and technology*. Washington, DC: Pew Charitable Trusts.

Lenhart, A., Arafeh, S., & Smith, A. (2008). *Writing, technology and teens*. Pew Internet & American Life Project.

Li & Caragea. (2020). *Domain Adaptation with Reconstruction for Disaster Tweet Classification.* . doi:10.1145/3397271.3401242

Li & Wu. (2010). Using text mining and sentiment analysis for online forums hotspot detection and forecast. *Decision Support Systems Archive, 48*(2), 354-368.

Li, Caragea, Caragea, & Herndon. (2017). Disaster response aided by tweet classification with a domain adaptation approach. *Journal of Contingencies and Crisis Management, 26.* doi:10.1111/1468-5973.12194

Liang, T. P., Li, X., Yang, C. T., & Wang, M. (2015). What in consumer reviews affects the sales of mobile apps: A multifacet sentiment analysis approach. *International Journal of Electronic Commerce, 20*(2), 236–260.

Li, F., Tang, H., Shang, S., Mathiak, K., & Cong, F. (2020). Classification of heart sounds using convolutional neural network. *Applied Sciences (Basel, Switzerland), 10*(11), 3956. doi:10.3390/app10113956

Ligthart, A., Catal, C., & Tekinerdogan, B. (2021). Systematic reviews in sentiment analysis: A tertiary study. *Artificial Intelligence Review*, *54*(7), 4997–5053. Advance online publication. doi:10.100710462-021-09973-3

Li, H. R., He, F. Z., & Yan, X. H. (2019). IBEA-SVM: An indicator-based evolutionary algorithm based on pre-selection with classification guided by SVM. *Applied Mathematics. A Journal of Chinese Universities*, *34*(1), 1–26. doi:10.100711766-019-3706-1

Li, J., & Meesad, P. (2016). Combining sentiment analysis with socialization bias in social networks for stock market trend prediction. *International Journal of Computational Intelligence and Applications*, *15*(01), 1650003.

Li, K., Zhang, R., Li, F., Su, L., Wang, H., & Chen, P. (2019). A new rotation machinery fault diagnosis method based on deep structure and sparse least squares support vector machine. *IEEE Access: Practical Innovations, Open Solutions*, *7*, 26571–26580. doi:10.1109/ACCESS.2019.2901363

Lindsay B. (2011). *Social media and disasters: Current uses, future options and policy considerations*. Washington, DC: Congressional Research Service CRS Report for Congress, Analyst in American National Government.

Lin, K.-S. (2020). A case-based reasoning system for interior design using a new cosine similarity retrieval algorithm. *Journal of Information and Telecommunication*, *4*(1), 91–104. doi:10.1080/24751839.2019.1700338

Lippman, R. P., Weller-Fahy, D. J., Mensch, A. C., Campbell, W. M., Campbell, J. P., Streilein, W. W., & Carter, K. M. (2017, March). Toward finding malicious cyber discussions in social media. *Workshops at the Thirty-First AAAI Conference on Artificial Intelligence*.

Li, S., & Tsai, F. (2011). Noise control in document classification based on fuzzy formal concept analysis. *IEEE International Conference on Fuzzy Systems (FUZZ)*, 2583-2588. 10.1109/FUZZY.2011.6007449

Li, T., Zhao, Z., Sun, C., Yan, R., & Chen, X. (2020). Adaptive channel weighted CNN with multisensor fusion for condition monitoring of helicopter transmission system. *IEEE Sensors Journal*, *20*(15), 8364–8373. doi:10.1109/JSEN.2020.2980596

Liu, B. (2012). Sentiment analysis and opinion mining. *Synthesis Lectures on Human Language Technologies*, *5*(1), 1-167.

Liu, B., Hu, M., & Cheng, J. (2005). Opinion observer: analyzing and comparing opinions on the web. In *Proceedings of the 14th international conference on World Wide Web*, (pp. 342-351). 10.1145/1060745.1060797

Liu, B., & Zhang, L. (2012). A survey of opinion mining and sentiment analysis. In *Mining text data* (pp. 415–463). Springer. doi:10.1007/978-1-4614-3223-4_13

Liu, M., Kalk, D., Kinney, L., & Orr, G. (2009). Web 2.0 and its use in higher education: A review of literature. *World Conference on E-learning in Corporate, Government, Healthcare, and Higher Education (ELEARN).*

Li, W., Zhu, L., Shi, Y., Guo, K., & Cambria, E. (2020). User reviews: Sentiment analysis using lexicon integrated two-channel CNN–LSTM family models. *Applied Soft Computing, 94,* 106435. doi:10.1016/j.asoc.2020.106435

Li, X., & Caragea, C. (2019). *Identifying Disaster Damage Images Using a Domain Adaptation Approach.* ISCRAM.

Li, Y. M., & Li, T. Y. (2013). Deriving market intelligence from microblogs. *Decision Support Systems, 55*(1), 206–217. doi:10.1016/j.dss.2013.01.023

Lops, P., Jannach, D., Musto, C., Bogers, T., & Koolen, M. (2019). Trends in content-based recommendation. *User Modeling and User-Adapted Interaction, 29*(2), 239–249. doi:10.100711257-019-09231-w

Lund, A. M. (2001). Measuring usability with the use questionnaire 12. *Usability Interface, 8*(2), 3-6.

Lynch, J. G. Jr, & Ariely, D. (2000). Competition on Price, Quality. *Marketing Science, 19*(1).

Mahadik, K., Wu, Q., Li, S., & Sabne, A. (2020). Fast distributed bandits for online recommendation systems. *Proceedings of the 34th ACM International Conference on Supercomputing,* 1–13. 10.1145/3392717.3392748

Majid, A., Chen, L., Chen, G., Mirza, H. T., Hussain, I., & Woodward, J. (2013). A context-aware personalized travel recommendation system based on geotagged social media data mining. *International Journal of Geographical Information Science, 27*(4), 662–684. doi:10.1080/136 58816.2012.696649

Malviya, A. (2020). *Machine Learning: An Overview of Classification Techniques.* Academic Press.

Mangan, T. (2020, September 6). *5 Social Media Marketing Strategies For Video Games* [web log]. http://blog.hellosocial.com.au/blog/5-social-media-marketing-strategies-for-video-games

Marcin, T. (2021). *Here's what you need to know about Clubhouse, the invite-only social app.* Mashable. https://mashable.com/article/what-is-Clubhouse-app/

Market Research Reports - Welcome. (n.d.). https://www.researchandmarkets.com/reports/5013565/impact-of-covid-19-on-the-video-conferencing?utm_source=dynamic&utm_medium=BW&utm_code=bpftq7&utm_campaign=1379168%2B-%2BImpact%2Bof%2BCOVID-19%2Bon%2Bthe%2BVideo%2BConferencing%2BMarket%2C%2B2020&utm_exec=joca220bwd

Matsumoto, S., Takamura, H., & Okumura, M. (2005). Sentiment classification using word sub-sequences and dependency sub-trees. In Pacific-Asia conference on knowledge discovery and data mining, (pp. 301-311). Academic Press.

McCulloch, W. S., & Pitts, W. (1943). A logical calculus of the ideas immanent in nervous activity. *The Bulletin of Mathematical Biophysics, 5*(4), 115–133.

Medhat, W., Hassan, A., & Korashy, H. (2014). Sentiment analysis algorithms and applications : A survey. *Ain Shams Engineering Journal, 5*(4), 1093–1113. doi:10.1016/j.asej.2014.04.011

Melville & Gryc. (2009). Sentiment Analysis of Blogs by Combining Lexical Knowledge with Text Classification. *KDD '09: Proceedings of the 15th ACM SIGKDD international conference on Knowledge discovery and data mining,* 1275-1284.

Melville, P., & Sindhwani, V. (2010). Recommender systems. Encyclopedia of Machine Learning, 1, 829–838.

Melville, P., Gryc, W., & Lawrence, R. D. (2009). Sentiment analysis of blogs by combining lexical knowledge with text classification. In *Proceedings of the 15th ACM SIGKDD international conference on Knowledge discovery and data mining* (pp. 1275-1284). ACM. 10.1145/1557019.1557156

Mendoza, M., Poblete, B., & Castillo, C. (2010). *Twitter under Crisis: Can we trust what we RT?* Paper presented at First Workshop on Social Media Analytics, Washington, DC.

Mendoza, M., Poblete, B., & Castillo, C. (2010). Twitter under crisis: Can we trust what we RT? *Proceedings of the first workshop on social media analytics* 71–79.

Meral, M., & Diri, B. (2014). Sentiment analysis on Twitter. *2014 22nd Signal Processing and Communications Applications Conference (SIU),* 690-693. 10.1109/SIU.2014.6830323

Michaelidou, N., Siamagka, N. T., & Christodoulides, G. (2011). Usage, barriers and measurement of social media marketing: An exploratory investigation of small and medium B2B brands. *Industrial Marketing Management, 40,* 1153–1159.

Milyavskaya, M., Saffran, M., Hope, N., & Koestner, R. (2018). Fear of missing out: Prevalence, dynamics, and consequences of experiencing FOMO. *Motivation and Emotion, 42,* 725–737.

Mir, J., & Usman, M. (2015). An effective model for aspect based opinion mining for social reviews. *2015 Tenth International Conference on Digital Information Management (ICDIM),* 49-56. 10.1109/ICDIM.2015.7381851

Misra, A., Sharma, A., Gulia, P., & Bana, A. (2014). Big data: Challenges and opportunities. *International Journal of Innovative Technology and Exploring Engineering, 4*(2), 41–42.

Mittal, N., Agarwal, B., Agarwal, S., Agarwal, S., & Gupta, P. (2013). A hybrid approach for twitter sentiment analysis. In *10th international conference on natural language processing (ICON-2013),* (pp. 116-120). Academic Press.

Moreo, A., Romero, M., Castro, J. L., & Zurita, J. M. (2012). Lexicon-based comments-oriented news sentiment analyzer system. *Expert Systems with Applications, 39*(10), 9166–9180. doi:10.1016/j.eswa.2012.02.057

Morinaga, S., Yamanishi, K., Tateishi, K., & Fukushima, T. (2002). Mining product reputations on the web. In *Proceedings of the eighth ACM SIGKDD international conference on Knowledge discovery and data mining*, (pp. 341-349). 10.1145/775047.775098

Mostafa, M. M. (2013). More than words: Social networks' text mining for consumer brand sentiments. *Expert Systems with Applications*, *40*(10), 4241–4251. doi:10.1016/j.eswa.2013.01.019

Mouthami, Devi, & Bhask. (2013). Sentiment Analysis and Classification Based On Textual Reviews. *Information Communication and Embedded Systems (ICICES)*, 271-276.

Mudinas, Zhang, & Levene. (2012). Combining Lexicon and Learning based Approaches for Concept-Level Sentiment Analysis. *Journal of American Society*, 1-8.

Mukkamala, A., & Beck, R. (2016). *Enhancing Disaster Management Through Social Media Analytics To Develop Situation Awareness: What Can Be Learned From Twitter Messages About Hurricane Sandy?* Academic Press.

Mukkamala, R. R., Hussain, A., & Vatrapu, R. (2014, September). Fuzzy-set based sentiment analysis of big social data. In *2014 IEEE 18th International Enterprise Distributed Object Computing Conference* (pp. 71-80). IEEE.

Munzel, A., Meyer-Waarden, L., & Galan, J. P. (2018). The social side of sustainability: Well-being as a driver and an outcome of social relationships and interactions on social networking sites. *Technological Forecasting and Social Change*.

Muqaddas, J., Soomro, A. S., & Ahmad, N. (2017). Impact of Social Media on Self-Esteem. *European Scientific Journal*, *13*, 329–341. doi:10.19044/esj.2017.v13n23p329

Muralidharan, S., Rasmussen, L., Patterson, D., & Shin, J. (2011). Hope for Haiti: An analysis of Facebook and Twitter usage during the earthquake relief efforts. *Public Relations Review*, *37*(2), 175–177.

Murthy, J. S., G.M., S., & K.G., S. (2019). A Real-Time Twitter Trend Analysis and Visualization Framework. *International Journal on Semantic Web and Information Systems (IJSWIS)*, *15*(2), 1-21. doi:10.4018/IJSWIS.2019040101

Musto, C., Semeraro, G., & Polignano, M. (2014). A Comparison of Lexicon-based Approaches for Sentiment Analysis of Microblog Posts. DART@ AI* IA, 59-68.

Naili, Habacha, & Ben Ghezala. (2017). Comparative study of word embedding methods in topic segmentation. *Procedia Computer Science, 112*, 340-349. . doi:10.1016/j.procs.2017.08.009

Nallaperuma, D., Nawaratne, R., Bandaragoda, T., Adikari, A., Nguyen, S., Kempitiya, T., De Silva, D., Alahakoon, D., & Pothuhera, D. (2019). Online incremental machine learning platform for big data-driven smart traffic management. *IEEE Transactions on Intelligent Transportation Systems*, *20*(12), 4679–4690. doi:10.1109/TITS.2019.2924883

Nash, W., Drummond, T., & Birbilis, N. (2018). A review of deep learning in the study of materials degradation. *NPJ Materials Degradation, 2*(1), 1-12.

Nehe, M. P. B., & Nawathe, A. N. (2020). *Aspect based sentiment classification using machine learning for online Reviews*. EasyChair.

Neviarouskaya, A., Prendinger, H., & Ishizuka, M. (2011). SentiFul: A lexicon for sentiment analysis. *IEEE Transactions on Affective Computing, 2*(1), 22–36. doi:10.1109/T-AFFC.2011.1

Ngak, C. (2011, July 6). *Then and now: A history of social networking sites*. CBS News. https://www.cbsnews.com/pictures/then-and-now-a-history-of-social-networking-sites/

Ngoc, P. T., & Yoo, M. (2014, February). The lexicon-based sentiment analysis for fan page ranking in Facebook. In *The International Conference on Information Networking 2014 (ICOIN2014)* (pp. 444-448). IEEE.

Nguyen, T. H., Shirai, K., & Velcin, J. (2015). Sentiment analysis on social media for stock movement prediction. *Expert Systems with Applications, 42*(24), 9603–9611.

Nikil Prakash, T., & Aloysius, A. (2020). Applications, Approaches, and Challenges in Sentiment Analysis. *International Research Journal of Modernization in Engineering Technology and Science, 02*(07), 910–915.

Nisa, Z. U. (2021, January 9). *The role of Social Media in Education: 2021*. ITSABUZAR. https://itsabuzar.net/role-of-social-media-in-education/

Niu, Y., Zhu, X., Li, J., & Hirst, G. (2005). Analysis of polarity information in medical text. *Proceedings of the American Medical Informatics Association 2005 Annual Symposium*.

Noor, S., Guo, Y., Shah, S. H. H., Nawaz, M. S., & Butt, A. S. (2020). Research synthesis and thematic analysis of twitter through bibliometric analysis. *International Journal on Semantic Web and Information Systems, 16*(3), 88–109.

Nyagah, V. W., Stephen, A., & Mwania, J. M. (2015). Social networking sites and their influence on the self-esteem of adolescents in Embu county, Kenya. *Journal of Educational Policy and Entrepreneurial Research, 2*(1), 87–92.

O'Guinn, T., & Shrum, L. J. (1997). The Role of Television in the Construction of Consumer Reality. *The Journal of Consumer Research, 23*, 278–294.

O'Keefe. (2018). Deep Learning and Word Embeddings for Tweet Classification for Crisis Response. Academic Press.

O'Reilly, L. (2013). *Google patents 'pay-per-gaze' eye-tracking ad technology*. Accessed from: https://www.marketingweek.com/google-patents-pay-per-gaze-eye-tracking-ad-technology/

ObarJ. A.WildmanS. (n.d.). Social media definition and the governance challenge: An introduction to the special issue. *Telecommunications Policy*, 745–750. doi:10.1016/j.telpol.2015.07.014

O'Connor, B., Balasubramanyan, R., Routledge, B. R., & Smith, N. A. (2010). From Tweets to Polls: Linking Text Sentiment to Public Opinion Time Series. *ICWSM, 11*(122–129), 1-2.

Okwuashi, O., & Ndehedehe, C. E. (2020). Deep support vector machine for hyperspectral image classification. *Pattern Recognition, 103*, 107298. doi:10.1016/j.patcog.2020.107298

Ordorica, S. (2021, August 30). *Council post: Why your business needs a multilingual social media presence.* Forbes. https://www.forbes.com/sites/forbesbusinesscouncil/2021/08/30/why-your-business-needs-a-multilingual-social-media-presence/?sh=53aceeac27f6

Organization, W. H. (2020). *Director-general's remarks at the media briefing on 2019 novel Coronavirus on 8 February 2020.* https://www.who.int/dg/speeches/detail/director-general-s-remarks-at-the-media-briefing-on-2019-novel-coronavirus---8-february-2020

Ouaguid, A., Abghour, N., & Ouzzif, M. (2018). A novel security framework for managing android permissions using blockchain technology. *International Journal of Cloud Applications and Computing, 8*(1), 55–79. doi:10.4018/IJCAC.2018010103

Padmaja, S. (2013). Opinion Mining and Sentiment Analysis –An Assessment of Peoples' Belief: A Survey. *International Journal of Ad hoc Sensor & Ubiquitous Computing, 4*(1), 21–33. doi:10.5121/ijasuc.2013.4102

Pak, A., & Paroubek, P. (2010). Twitter as a corpus for sentiment analysis and opinion mining. LREc, 10, 1320-1326.

Pandya, S., Shah, J., Joshi, N., Ghayvat, H., Mukhopadhyay, S. C., & Yap, M. H. (2016). A novel hybrid based recommendation system based on clustering and association mining. *2016 10th International Conference on Sensing Technology (ICST)*, 1–6.

Pang, B., & Lee, L. (2004). *A sentimental education: Sentiment analysis using subjectivity summarization based on minimum cuts.* Retrieved from arXiv preprint cs/0409058

Pang, B., Lee, L., & Vaithyanathan, S. (2002). *Thumbs up? Sentiment classification using machine learning techniques.* Retrieved from arXiv preprint cs/0205070

Pang, B., & Lee, L. (2008). Opinion mining and sentiment analysis. *Foundations and Trends in Information Retrieval, 2*(1-2), 1–135. doi:10.1561/1500000011

Parikh, R., & Movassate, M. (2009). *Sentiment analysis of user-generated twitter updates using various classification techniques.* CS224N Final Report.

Pasupa, K., Vatathanavaro, S., & Tungjitnob, S. (2020). Convolutional neural networks based focal loss for class imbalance problem: A case study of canine red blood cells morphology classification. *Journal of Ambient Intelligence and Humanized Computing*, 1–17. doi:10.100712652-020-01773-x

Pathak, A., Pandey, M., & Rautaray, S. (2020). Adaptive model for sentiment analysis of social media data using deep learning. *International Conference on Intelligent Computing and Communication Technologies.*

Pavlopoulos, I. (2014). *Aspect Based Sentiment Analysis* (Ph.D. thesis). Department of Informatics, Athens University of Economics and Business.

Pazzani, M. J., & Billsus, D. (2007). Content-based recommendation systems. In *The adaptive web* (pp. 325–341). Springer. doi:10.1007/978-3-540-72079-9_10

Peddinti, V. M., & Chintalapoodi, P. (2011). Domain adaptation in sentiment analysis of twitter. *Workshops at the Twenty-Fifth AAAI Conference on Artificial Intelligence.*

Pennington, Socher, & Manning. (2014). Glove: Global Vectors for Word Representation. *EMNLP*, *14*, 1532-1543. . doi:10.3115/v1/D14-1162

Perez, S. (2020). Video conferencing apps saw a record 62m downloads during one week in March. *Tech Crunch*. https://techcrunch.com/2020/03/30/videoconferencing-apps-saw-a-record-62m-downloads-during-one-week-in-march/

Pérez-Escoda, A., Jiménez-Narros, C., Perlado-Lamo-de-Espinosa, M., & Pedrero-Esteban, L. M. (2020). Social Networks' Engagement During the COVID-19 Pandemic in Spain: Health Media vs. Healthcare Professionals. *International Journal of Environmental Research and Public Health*, *17*(14), 5261. https://doi.org/10.3390/ijerph17145261

Pérez-Soler, S. (2017). *Periodismo y Redes Sociales*. Claves Para la Gestión de Contenidos Digitales. Editorial UOC.

Phelps, J. E., D'Souza, G., & Nowak, G. J. (2001). Antecedents and consequences of consumer privacy concerns: An empirical investigation. *Journal of Interactive Marketing*, *15*(4), 2–17.

Philander, K., & Zhong, Y. (2016). Twitter sentiment analysis: Capturing sentiment from integrated resort tweets. *International Journal of Hospitality Management*, *55*, 16–24.

Phippen, A., & Bond, E. (2020). Momo Week: A Perfect Social Media Storm and a Breakdown in Stakeholder Sanity? In Organisational Responses to Social Media Storms. Palgrave Macmillan.

Piplani, S. (2020, April 13). *Is Online Gaming The New Social Media?* [web log]. https://blog.synclarity.in/marketing/is-online-gaming-the-new-social-media

Popüler Uzakdoğu Sosyal Medya Platformları. (2020). *Uluslararası sosyal medya derneği Blog sayfası*. www.usmed.org.tr/populer-uzakdogu-sosyal-medya-platformlari/

Poria, S., Cambria, E., Hazarika, D., Majumder, N., Zadeh, A., & Morency, L.-P. (2017). Context-Dependent Sentiment Analysis in User-Generated Videos. *Proceedings of the 55th Annual Meeting of the Association for Computational Linguistics*, *1*, 873-883.

Prabowo, R., & Thelwall, M. (2009). Sentiment analysis: A combined approach. *Journal of Informetrics*, *3*(2), 143–157. doi:10.1016/j.joi.2009.01.003

PricewaterhouseCoopers. (n.d.). *Impact of the COVID-19 outbreak on digital payments*. PwC. https://www.pwc.in/consulting/financial-services/fintech/dp/impact-of-the-covid-19-outbreak-on-digital-payments.html

Priss, U. (2006). *Formal concept analysis in information science*. Presented at the annual review of information science and technology. 10.1002/aris.1440400120

Qazi, A., Tamjidyamcholo, A., Raj, R. G., Hardaker, G., & Standing, C. (2017). Assessing consumers' satisfaction and expectations through online opinions: Expectation and disconfirmation approach. *Computers in Human Behavior*, *75*, 450–460. doi:10.1016/j.chb.2017.05.025

Quigley, M. (Ed.). (2007). *Encyclopedia of information ethics and security*. IGI global. doi:10.4018/978-1-59140-987-8

Rafea, A., & Mostafa, N. A. (2013, May). Topic extraction in social media. In *2013 International Conference on Collaboration Technologies and Systems (CTS)* (pp. 94-98). IEEE.

Rajan, A., Pappu, S., & Victor, P. (2014). Web sentiment analysis for scoring positive or negative words using Tweeter data. *International Journal of Computers and Applications*, *96*(6), 33–37.

Raji, F., Jazi, M. D., & Miri, A. (2014). PESCA: A peer-to-peer social network architecture with privacy-enabled social communication and data availability. *IET Information Security*, *9*(1), 73–80.

Ramzan, B., Bajwa, I. S., Jamil, N., Amin, R. U., Ramzan, S., Mirza, F., & Sarwar, N. (2019). An intelligent data analysis for recommendation systems using machine learning. *Scientific Programming*, *2019*, 2019. doi:10.1155/2019/5941096

Rashid, M., Hamid, A., & Parah, S. A. (2019). Analysis of Streaming Data Using Big Data and Hybrid Machine Learning Approach. In Handbook of Multimedia Information Security: Techniques and Applications (pp. 629-643). Springer. doi:10.1007/978-3-030-15887-3_30

Riaz, S., Fatima, M., Kamran, M., & Nisar, M. W. (2019). Opinion mining on large scale data using sentiment analysis and k-means clustering. *Cluster Computing*, *22*(3), 7149–7164. doi:10.100710586-017-1077-z

Richardson, J., & Lenarcic, J. (2008). Text Messaging as a Catalyst for Mobile Student Administration: The "Trigger" Experience. *International Journal of Emerging Technologies & Society*, *6*(2), 140–155.

Robertson, S. (2004). Understanding inverse document frequency: On theoretical arguments for IDF. *The Journal of Documentation*, *60*(5), 503–520. doi:10.1108/00220410410560582

Robinson, J., Cox, G., Bailey, E., Hetrick, S., Rodrigues, M., Fisher, S., & Herrman, H. (2016). Social media and suicide prevention: A systematic review. *Early Intervention in Psychiatry*, *10*(2), 103–121.

Robinson, J., Rodrigues, M., Fisher, S., & Herrman, H. (2014). *Suicide and Social Media Study: Report of the Internet Search*. Orygen Youth Health Research Centre, Community Works.

Rodrigues, R. G., das Dores, R. M., Camilo-Junior, C. G., & Rosa, T. C. (2016). SentiHealth-Cancer: A sentiment analysis tool to help detecting mood of patients in online social networks. *International Journal of Medical Informatics*, *85*(1), 80–95.

Romadon, A. W., Lhaksmana, K. M., Kurniawan, I., & Richasdy, D. (2020). Analyzing TF-IDF and Word Embedding for Implementing Automation in Job Interview Grading. *2020 8th International Conference on Information and Communication Technology (ICoICT)*, 1–4.

Rout, J. K., Choo, K. K. R., Dash, A. K., Bakshi, S., Jena, S. K., & Williams, K. L. (2018). A model for sentiment and emotion analysis of unstructured social media text. *Electronic Commerce Research*, *18*(1), 181–199. doi:10.100710660-017-9257-8

Ruggiero, T. (2000). Uses and Gratifications Theory in the 21st Century. *Mass Communication & Society*, *3*(1), 3–37.

Runge, K. K., & Yeo, S. K. (2013). Tweeting nano: How public discourses about nanotechnology develop in social media environments. *Journal of Nanoparticle Research*, *15*(1), 1381.

Ruths, D., & Pfeffer, J. (2014). Social media for large studies of behavior. *Science*, *346*(6213), 1063–1064. doi:10.1126cience.346.6213.1063 PMID:25430759

Saad, M. (2010). *The Impact of Text Preprocessing and Term Weighting on Arabic Text Classification.* doi:10.13140/2.1.4677.2164

Sahoo, S. R., & Gupta, B. B. (2019). Classification of various attacks and their defence mechanism in online social networks: A survey. *Enterprise Information Systems*, *13*(6), 832–864.

Sahoo, S. R., & Gupta, B. B. (2019). Hybrid approach for detection of malicious profiles in twitter. *Computers & Electrical Engineering*, *76*, 65–81. doi:10.1016/j.compeleceng.2019.03.003

Sahoo, S. R., & Gupta, B. B. (2020). Classification of spammer and nonspammer content in online social network using genetic algorithm-based feature selection. *Enterprise Information Systems*, *14*(5), 710–736. doi:10.1080/17517575.2020.1712742

Sahoo, S. R., & Gupta, B. B. (2021). Multiple features based approach for automatic fake news detection on social networks using deep learning. *Applied Soft Computing*, *100*, 106983.

Sahoo, S. R., & Gupta, B. B. (2021). Real-time detection of fake account in twitter using machine-learning approach. In *Advances in computational intelligence and communication technology* (pp. 149–159). Springer. doi:10.1007/978-981-15-1275-9_13

Saif, H., He, Y., & Alani, H. (2012). Semantic sentiment analysis of twitter. In *International semantic web conference* (pp. 508-524). Springer.

Salkind, N. J. (2010). *Encyclopedia of research design* (Vol. 1-0). SAGE Publications, Inc., doi:10.4135/9781412961288

Samoggia, A., Bertazzoli, A., & Ruggeri, A. (2019). Food retailing marketing management: Social media communication for healthy food. *International Journal of Retail & Distribution Management*, *47*(9), 928–956. doi:10.1108/IJRDM-08-2018-0178

Sarlan, A., Nadam, C., & Basri, S. (2014). Twitter sentiment analysis. In *Proceedings of the 6th International conference on Information Technology and Multimedia* (pp. 212-216). IEEE. 10.1109/ICIMU.2014.7066632

Schaefer, B. (2017). *Bumper Stickers & Social Data: How Trump and Clinton Supporters Measure Up.* Brandwatch. Accessed from: https://www.brandwatch.com/blog/bumper-stickers/

Scheibenzuber, C., Hofer, S., & Nistor, N. (2021). Designing for fake news literacy training: A problem-based undergraduate online-course. *Computers in Human Behavior, 121*, 106796. https://doi.org/10.1016/j.chb.2021.106796

Scherer, K. (2003). Vocal communication of emotion: A review of research paradigms. *Speech Communication, 40*(1-2), 227–256.

Schonlau, M., Guenther, N., & Sucholutsky, I. (2017). Text mining with n-gram variables. *The Stata Journal, 17*(4), 866–881. doi:10.1177/1536867X1801700406

Schreiner, M., Fischer, T., & Riedl, R. (2019). Impact of content characteristics and emotion on behavioral engagement in social media: Literature review and research agenda. *Electronic Commerce Research*, 1–17.

Seddighi, H., Salmani, I., & Seddighi, S. (2020). Saving Lives and Changing Minds with Twitter in Disasters and Pandemics: A Literature Review. *Journalism and Media., 1*(1), 59–77. https://doi.org/10.3390/journalmedia1010005

Selwyn, N. (2012). Making sense of young people, education and digital technology: The role of sociological theory. *Oxford Review of Education, 38*(1), 81–96.

Shahheidari, S., Dong, H., & Daud, M. N. R. B. (2013, July). Twitter sentiment mining: A multi domain analysis. In *2013 Seventh International Conference on Complex, Intelligent, and Software Intensive Systems* (pp. 144-149). IEEE.

Shahi, G. K., Dirkson, A., & Majchrzak, T. A. (2021). An exploratory study of covid-19 misinformation on Twitter. *Online Social Networks and Media, 22*, 100104. doi:10.1016/j.osnem.2020.100104

Shamma, D. A., Kennedy, L., & Churchill, E. F. (2009). Tweet the debates: understanding community annotation of uncollected sources. *Proceedings of the first SIGMM workshop on Social Media*, 3-10. 10.1145/1631144.1631148

Shani, G., & Gunawardana, A. (2011). Evaluating recommendation systems. In *Recommender systems handbook* (pp. 257–297). Springer. doi:10.1007/978-0-387-85820-3_8

Sharma, R., Gopalani, D., & Meena, Y. (2017). Collaborative filtering-based recommender system: Approaches and research challenges. *2017 3rd International Conference on Computational Intelligence & Communication Technology (Cict)*, 1–6.

Sharma, S., & Jain, A. (2019). Cyber social media analytics and issues: A pragmatic approach for twitter sentiment analysis. In *Advances in Computer Communication and Computational Sciences* (pp. 473–484). Springer. doi:10.1007/978-981-13-6861-5_41

Sharma, Y., Bhargava, R., & Tadikonda, B. V. (2021). Named Entity Recognition for Code Mixed Social Media Sentences. *International Journal of Software Science and Computational Intelligence, 13*(2), 23–36.

Shastry, K. A., Sanjay, H. A., & Deexith, G. (2017). Quadratic-radial-basis-function-kernel for classifying multi-class agricultural datasets with continuous attributes. *Applied Soft Computing*, *58*, 65–74. doi:10.1016/j.asoc.2017.04.049

Shayaa, S., Jaafar, N. I., Bahri, S., Sulaiman, A., Wai, P. S., Chung, Y. W., ... Al-Garadi, M. A. (2018). Sentiment analysis of big data: Methods, applications, and open challenges. *IEEE Access: Practical Innovations, Open Solutions*, *6*, 37807–37827.

Shi, X., Ye, H., & Gong, S. (2008). A personalized recommender integrating item-based and user-based collaborative filtering. *2008 International Seminar on Business and Information Management*, *1*, 264–267.

Shu, J., Shen, X., Liu, H., Yi, B., & Zhang, Z. (2018). *A content-based recommendation algorithm for learning resources*. Academic Press.

Sine, R., & Özsoy, S. (2017). Ekşi Sözlük kullanıcılarının yeni medya kullanım pratikleri. *Route Educational and Social Science Journal*, *4*(8), 53–65. doi:10.17121/ressjournal.885

Singh, D. (2019, July 3). *Sarcasm Detection: Step towards Sentiment Analysis*. Retrieved January 22, 2021, from https://towardsdatascience.com/sarcasm-detection-step-towards-sentiment-analysis-84cb013bb6db/

Singh, V. K., Piryani, R., Uddin, A., & Waila, P. (2013, March). Sentiment analysis of movie reviews: A new feature-based heuristic for aspect-level sentiment classification. In *2013 International Mutli-Conference on Automation, Computing, Communication, Control and Compressed Sensing (iMac4s)* (pp. 712-717). IEEE.

Singh, P., Singh, S., Sohal, M., Dwivedi, Y. K., Kahlon, K. S., & Sawhney, R. S. (2020). Psychological fear and anxiety caused by COVID-19: Insights from Twitter analytics. *Asian Journal of Psychiatry*, *54*, 102280.

Singh, S. K., & Sachan, M. K. (2021). Classification of Code-Mixed Bilingual Phonetic Text Using Sentiment Analysis. *International Journal on Semantic Web and Information Systems*, *17*(2), 59–78. doi:10.4018/IJSWIS.2021040104

Singh, T., & Kumari, M. (2016). Role of text pre-processing in twitter sentiment analysis. *Procedia Computer Science*, *89*, 549–554. doi:10.1016/j.procs.2016.06.095

Sivanandam, S. N., & Deepa, S. N. (2008). Genetic algorithms. In *Introduction to genetic algorithms* (pp. 15–37). Springer.

Social Media: What Countries Use It Most & What Are They Using? (2019, January 31). *Digital Marketing Institute*. https://digitalmarketinginstitute.com/blog/social-media-what-countries-use-it-most-and-what-are-they-using

Sohrabi, B., Mahmoudian, P., & Raeesi, I. (2012). A framework for improving e-commerce websites usability using a hybrid genetic algorithm and neural network system. *Neural Computing & Applications*, *21*(5), 1017–1029. doi:10.100700521-011-0674-7

SolomonR. C. (2017). *Emotion*. Retrieved from http://www.britannica.com/topic/emotion

Song, G., & Huang, D. (2021). A Sentiment-Aware Contextual Model for Real-Time Disaster Prediction Using Twitter Data. *Future Internet, 13*, 163. doi:10.3390/fi13070163

Soofi, A. A., & Awan, A. (2017). *Classification techniques in machine learning: applications and issues*. Academic Press.

Soyez, F. (2017). *Advertising from the future: analyzing emotions, a risk of manipulating people*. Accessed from: https://www.cnetfrance.fr/news/pub-du-futur-l-analyse-des-emotions-un-risque-de-manipulation-39858642.html

Spertus, E. (1997). Smokey: Automatic recognition of hostile messages. *Proceedings of the 14th National Conference on Artificial Intelligence and 9th Innovative Applications of Artificial Intelligence Conference*, 1058-1065.

Sridevi, M., Rao, R. R., & Rao, M. V. (2016). *A survey on recommender system*. Academic Press.

Srivastava, A., Singh, V., & Drall, G. S. (2019). Sentiment Analysis of Twitter Data: A Hybrid Approach. *International Journal of Healthcare Information Systems and Informatics, 14*(2), 1–16. doi:10.4018/IJHISI.2019040101

Starbird, K., Maddock, J., Orand, M., Achterman, P. & Mason, R. M. (2014). Rumors, false flags, and digital vigilantes: Misinformation on twitter after the 2013 Boston marathon bombing. *IConference 2014 Proceedings*.

Starbird, K., Palen, L., Hughes, A. L., & Vieweg, S. (2010). Chatter on the red: what hazards threat reveals about the social life of microblogged information. In *Proceedings of the 2010 ACM conference on Computer supported cooperative work (CSCW '10)*. Association for Computing Machinery. doi:10.1145/1718918.1718965

Starbird, K., Palen, L., Hughes, A. L., & Vieweg, S. (2010). Chatter on the red: what hazards threat reveals about the social life of microblogged information. In *CSCW '10: Proceedings of the 2010 ACM conference on Computer supported cooperative work*. ACM.

Statista. (2021). *Global social networks ranked by number of users 2021*. Retrieved July 29, 2021, from https://www.statista.com/statistics/272014/global-social-networks-ranked-by-number-of-users/

Statista. (2021). *Social media - Statistics & Facts, Social media usage worldwide*. Statista. https://www.statista.com/topics/1164/social-networks/

Statista. (2021b). *Clubhouse - statistics & facts*. Author.

Stock Comparison: Compare DISH Network Corporation (DISH) to Other Stocks. (2017, Mar. 13). NASDAQ.com.

Stone, P. J., Dunphy, D. C., & Smith, M. S. (1966). *The general inquirer: A computer approach to content analysis*. M.I.T. Press.

Strain, M., Saucier, D., & Martens, A. (2015). Sexist humor in Facebook profiles: Perceptions of humor targeting women and men. *Humor: International Journal of Humor Research, 28*(1), 119–141. doi:10.1515/humor-2014-0137

Su, X., & Khoshgoftaar, T. M. (2009). *A survey of collaborative filtering techniques.* Academic Press.

Subair, E. (2021). Drake, Oprah Winfrey and Virgil Abloh Are Fans: Here's Everything You Need to Know About Clubhouse. *Vogue.* https://www.vogue.com/article/everything-you-need-to-know-about-Clubhouse

Suman, J. S. (2017). Sentiment Analysis of Tweets using Support Vector Machine. *International Journal of Computer Science and Mobile Applications, 5*(10), 83–91.

Sumida, N., Walker, M., & Mitchell, A. (2019, December 31). *The role of social media in news.* Pew Research Center's Journalism Project. https://www.pewresearch.org/journalism/2019/04/23/the-role-of-social-media-in-news/

Suri, P. R., & Taneja, H. (2010). Object Oriented Information Computing over WWW. *International Journal of Computer Science Issues, 7*(3), 38–41.

Surjandari, I., Naffisah, M. S., & Prawiradinata, M. I. (2015). Text mining of twitter data for public sentiment analysis of staple foods price changes. *Journal of Industrial and Intelligent Information, 3*(3). Advance online publication. doi:10.12720/jiii.3.3.253-257

Susar, F., & Narin, B. (2011). Sosyal paylaşımın tecimselleştirilmesi bağlamında internet reklamcılığı: Ekşi Sözlük örneği [In the context of commercialization of social sharing internet advertising: The example of sour dictionary]. *İstanbul Arel Üniversitesi İletişim Fakültesi İletişim Çalışmaları Dergisi, 3*, 1-14.

Swani, K., Brown, B. P., & Milne, G. R. (2014). Should tweets differ for B2B and B2C? An analysis of Fortune 500 companies' Twitter communications. *Industrial Marketing Management, 43*(5), 873–881.

Taboada, M., Brooke, J., Tofiloski, M., Voll, K., & Stede, M. (2011). Lexicon-based methods for sentiment analysis. *Computational Linguistics, 37*(2), 267–307. doi:10.1162/COLI_a_00049

Tang, J., Chang, Y., & Liu, H. (2014). Mining social media with social theories: A survey. *SIGKDD Explorations, 15*(2), 20–29.

Tang, J., Hu, X., & Liu, H. (2013). Social recommendation: A review. *Social Network Analysis and Mining, 3*(4), 1113–1133.

Tang, J., & Liu, H. (2012, April). Feature selection with linked data in social media. In *Proceedings of the 2012 SIAM International Conference on Data Mining* (pp. 118-128). Society for Industrial and Applied Mathematics.

Tan, S., Wang, Y., & Cheng, X. (2008). Combining learn-based and lexicon-based techniques for sentiment detection without using labeled examples. *Proceedings of the 31st annual international ACM SIGIR conference on Research and development in information retrieval*, 743-744. 10.1145/1390334.1390481

Tayal, D. K., & Yadav, S. K. (2017). entiment analysis on social campaign "Swachh Bharat Abhiyan" using unigram method. *AI & Society*, *32*(4), 633–645. doi:10.100700146-016-0672-5

Técnica, S. (2020, February 29). *Coronavirus. Por Qué La comunicación tradicional no sirve.* Inicio - Asociación Nacional de Informadores de la Salud. http://www.anisalud.com/index. php?option=com_content&view=article&id=5741

Terveen, L., Hill, W., Amento, B., McDonald, D., & Creter, J. (1997). PHOAKS: A system for sharing recommendations. *Communications of the ACM*, *40*(3), 59–62.

Tewari, A., & Gupta, B. B. (2017). A lightweight mutual authentication protocol based on elliptic curve cryptography for IoT devices. *International Journal of Advanced Intelligence Paradigms*, *9*(2-3), 111–121.

The Law Commission. (2018). Abusive and Offensive Online Communications: A Scoping Report. *WHO Situation Report 13* https://www.who.int/docs/default-source/coronaviruse/ situation-reports/20200202-sitrep-13-ncov-v3.pdf?sfvrsn=195f4010_6

Times of India Blog. (2021, February 5). https://timesofindia.indiatimes.com/blogs/voices/outlook-for-2021-the-evolution-of-social-media-and-the-role-it-can-play-in-the-future-of-education/

Tong, Evangelista, M., Parsons, A. B., Xu, H., Bader, G. D., Pagé, N., Robinson, M., Raghibizadeh, S., Hogue, C. W. V., Bussey, H., Andrews, B., Tyers, M., & Boone, C. (2001). Systematic genetic analysis with ordered arrays of yeast deletion mutants. *Science*, *294*(5550), 2364–2368. doi:10.1126cience.1065810 PMID:11743205

Tran, Y. H., & Tran, Q. N. (2017, December). Estimating public opinion in social media content using aspect-based opinion mining. In *International Conference on Mobile Networks and Management* (pp. 101-115). Springer.

Tubishat, M., Idris, N., & Abushariah, M. A. (2018). Implicit aspect extraction in sentiment analysis: Review, taxonomy, oppportunities, and open challenges. *Information Processing & Management*, *54*(4), 545–563. doi:10.1016/j.ipm.2018.03.008

TÜİK. (2021). *Adrese Dayalı Nüfus Kayıt Sistemi Sonuçları, 2020.* tuik.gov.tr

Tumasjan, A., Sprenger, T. O., Sandner, P. G., & Welpe, I. M. (2010). Predicting Elections with Twitter: What 140 Characters Reveal about Political Sentiment. *ICWSM*, *10*, 178–185.

Türk İşi Sosyal Ağlar. (2014). Onedio.

Türkiye İnternet Ölçümleme Araştırması Gemius, I. A. B. (2019). *Aralık overnight 2019 top 20 listeleri.* https://www.iabturkiye.org/UploadFiles/TopTwentyFiles/Internet_ audiencetoplist_12_2019_Overnight.pdf

Turney, P. D. (2002). *Thumbs up or thumbs down? Semantic orientation applied to unsupervised classification of reviews*. Retrieved from arXiv preprint cs/0212032

Turney, P. (2002). Thumbs Up or Thumbs Down? Semantic Orientation Applied to Unsupervised Classification of Reviews. *Proceedings of the 40th Annual Meeting of the Association for Computational Linguistics (ACL)*, 417-424.

Turney, P. D., & Littman, M. L. (2003). Measuring praise and criticism: Inference of semantic orientation from association. *ACM Transactions on Information Systems, 21*(4), 315–346. doi:10.1145/944012.944013

Tuten, T. L., & Solomon, M. R. (2018). *Social media marketing*. Sage.

Ultimate guide to deal with text data. (2020, December 23). *Analytics Vidhya*. https://www.analyticsvidhya.com/blog/2018/02/the-different-methods-deal-text-data-predictive-python/

Ulvi, O., Lippincott, N., Khan, M. H., Mehal, P., Bass, M., Lambert, K., Lentz, E., & Haque, U. (2019, December 10). The role of social and mainstream media during storms. *Journal of Public Health and Emergency*. https://jphe.amegroups.com/article/view/5543/html

Umar, S., & Maryam, F. A. (2018). Sentiment Analysis Approaches and Applications: A Survey. *International Journal of Computers and Applications, 181*(1), 1–9. doi:10.5120/ijca2018916630

Üngören, E. (2019). Yeni medya iletişim kanalı olarak katılımcı sözlük sitelerine yönelik bir değerlendirme. *OPUS–Uluslararası Toplum Araştırmaları Dergisi, 11*(18), 2878–2907. doi:10.26466/opus.567125

United Nations. (n.d.). https://www.un.org/en/un-coronavirus-communications-team/un-tackling-%E2%80%98infodemic%E2%80%99-misinformation-and-cybercrime-covid-19

United Nations. (n.d.). *Un tackles 'infodemic' of misinformation and cybercrime in covid-19 crisis*. Author.

Utz, S., Muscanell, N., & Khalid, C. (2015). Snapchat elicits more jealousy than Facebook: A comparison of Snapchat and Facebook use. *Cyberpsychology, Behavior, and Social Networking, 18*(3), 141–146.

Uzunoğlu, S. (2015). Bir postmodern intiharın ardından Ekşi Sözlük'te kanaatlerin oluşumu ve grupların biçimlenme süreçleri. *Intermedia International Peer-Reviewed E-Journal Of Communication Sciences, 2*(2), 424–439.

Valakunde, N. D., & Patwardhan, M. S. (2013, November). Multi-aspect and multi-class based document sentiment analysis of educational data catering accreditation process. In *2013 International Conference on Cloud & Ubiquitous Computing & Emerging Technologies* (pp. 188-192). IEEE.

Valkenburg, P. M., Peter, J., & Schouten, M. A. (2006). Friend networking sites and their relationship to adolescents' well-being and social selfesteem. *Cyberpsychology & Behavior, 9*, 584–590.

Van der Hoven, E. (2013). *Fact sheet- Ethics Subgroup IoT-Version 4.01*. Delft University of Technology Chair Ethics Subgroup IoT Expert Group.

Vapnik, V. (1995). *The Nature of Statistical Learning Theory*. Springer-Verlag. doi:10.1007/978-1-4757-2440-0

Varsha, S., Shete, V., & Pathan, A. (2015). Sentiment analysis on twitter data. *International Journal of Innovative Research in Advanced Engineering*, *2*(1), 178–183.

Verduyn, P., Lee, D. S., Park, J., Shablack, H., Orvell, A., Bayer, J., Ybarra, O., Jonides, J., & Kross, E. (2015). Passive Facebook Usage Undermines Affective Well-Being: Experimental and Longitudinal Evidence. *Journal of Experimental Psychology*, *144*(2), 480–488.

Viejo, A., & Sánchez, D. (2016). Enforcing transparent access to private content in social networks by means of automatic sanitization. *Expert Systems with Applications*, *62*, 148–160.

Vieweg, S. (2010). Microblogged contributions to the emergency arena: Discovery, interpretation, and implications. Computer Supported Collaborative Work.

Vieweg, S., Hughes, A. L., Starbird, K., & Palen, L. (2010). Microblogging during two natural hazards events: What Twitter may contribute to situational awareness. In *Proceedings of SIGCHI Conference on Human Factors in Computing Systems*. ACM.

Vishal, A. (2016). Sentiment Analysis of Twitter Data: A Survey of Techniques. *International Journal of Computers and Applications*, *139*(11), 5–15. doi:10.5120/ijca2016908625

Vogel, E. A., Rose, J. P., Roberts, L. R., & Eckles, K. (2014). Social comparison, social media, and self-esteem. *Psychology of Popular Media Culture*, *3*(4), 206.

Vural, A. G., Cambazoglu, B. B., Senkul, P., & Tokgoz, Z. O. (2013). A framework for sentiment analysis in turkish: Application to polarity detection of movie reviews in Turkish. In *Computer and Information Sciences III* (pp. 437–445). Springer. doi:10.1007/978-1-4471-4594-3_45

Wahl-Jorgensen, K., & Hanitzsch, T. (2009). *The Handbook of Journalism Studies*. Routledge. doi:10.4324/9780203877685

Wang, A. (2010). *Don't Follow Me - Spam Detection in Twitter*. doi:10.7312/wang15140-003

Wang, H., & Fu, W. (2021). Personalized learning resource recommendation method based on dynamic collaborative filtering. *Mobile Networks and Applications*, *26*(1), 473–487. doi:10.100711036-020-01673-6

Wang, H., Li, Z., Li, Y., Gupta, B. B., & Choi, C. (2020). Visual saliency guided complex image retrieval. *Pattern Recognition Letters*, *130*, 64–72.

Wang, J., Zhong, D., Adeli, H., Wang, D., & Liu, M. (2018). Smart bacteria-foraging algorithm-based customized kernel support vector regression and enhanced probabilistic neural network for compaction quality assessment and control of earth-rock dam. *Expert Systems: International Journal of Knowledge Engineering and Neural Networks*, *35*(6), e12357. doi:10.1111/exsy.12357

Wang, W., Zhao, M., & Wang, J. (2019). Effective android malware detection with a hybrid model based on deep autoencoder and convolutional neural network. *Journal of Ambient Intelligence and Humanized Computing*, *10*(8), 3035–3043. doi:10.100712652-018-0803-6

Wang, Z., Victor, J. C. T., & Chin, H. C. (2014). *Enhancing Machine Learning Methods for Sentiment Classification of Web Data*. Springer International Publishing. doi:10.1007/978-3-319-12844-3_34

We Are Social. (2021). *Digital 2021 Global overview report*. We Are Social.

Whiting, A., & Williams, D. (2013). Why people use social media: A uses and gratifications approach. *Qualitative Market Research*, *16*(4), 362–369.

Wiebe, J. M. (1994). Tracking Point of View in Narrative. *Computational Linguistics*, *20*(2), 233–287.

Wikarsa, L., & Thahir, S. N. (2015, November). A text mining application of emotion classifications of Twitter's users using Naive Bayes method. In *2015 1st International Conference on Wireless and Telematics (ICWT)* (pp. 1-6). IEEE. 10.1109/ICWT.2015.7449218

Wille, R. (1982). Restructuring lattice theory: an approach based on hierarchies of concepts. In *I. Rival* (pp. 445–470). Reidel. doi:10.1007/978-94-009-7798-3_15

Wojcik, S., & Hughes, A. (2019). *Sizing Up Twitter Users, How Twitter Users Compare to the General Public*. Pew Research Center.

Wolter L.-C., Chan-Olmsted S., Altobelli C.F. (2017). *Understanding video engagement on global service networks—The case of Twitter users on mobile platforms*. Dienstleistungen 4.0.

Wu, C.-S. M., Garg, D., & Bhandary, U. (2018). Movie recommendation system using collaborative filtering. *2018 IEEE 9th International Conference on Software Engineering and Service Science (ICSESS)*, 11–15.

Xia, R., Xu, F., Yu, J., Qi, Y., & Cambria, E. (2016). Polarity shift detection, elimination and ensemble: A three-stage model for document-level sentiment analysis. *Information Processing & Management*, *52*(1), 36–45. doi:10.1016/j.ipm.2015.04.003

Xia, R., Zong, C., & Li, S. (2011). Ensemble of feature sets and classification algorithms for sentiment classification. *Information Sciences*, *181*(6), 1138–1152. doi:10.1016/j.ins.2010.11.023

Xu, F., Pan, Z., & Xia, R. (2020). E-commerce product review sentiment classification based on a naïve Bayes continuous learning framework. *Information Processing & Management*, *57*(5), 102221. doi:10.1016/j.ipm.2020.102221

Yadav, A., & Vishwakarma, D. K. (2020). Sentiment analysis using deep learning architectures: A review. *Artificial Intelligence Review*, *53*(6), 4335–4385. doi:10.100710462-019-09794-5

Yadollahi, A., Shahraki, A. G., & Zaiane, O. R. (2017). Current state of text sentiment analysis from opinion to emotion mining. *ACM Computing Surveys*, *50*(2), 1–33. doi:10.1145/3057270

Yamashita, R., Nishio, M., Do, R. K. G., & Togashi, K. (2018). Convolutional neural networks: An overview and application in radiology. *Insights Into Imaging, 9*(4), 611–629. doi:10.100713244-018-0639-9 PMID:29934920

Yang, C.-C. (2016). Instagram Use, Loneliness, and Social Comparison Orientation: Interact and Browse on Social Media, But Don't Compare. *Cyberpsychology, Behavior, and Social Networking, 19.*

Yang, L., & Jin, R. (2006). Distance metric learning: A comprehensive survey. *Michigan State Universiy, 2*(2), 4.

Yang, M., & Chen, H. (2012). Partially supervised learning for radical opinion identification in hate group web forums. *IEEE International Conference on Intelligence and Security Informatics,* 96-101. 10.1109/ISI.2012.6284099

Yasin, A., Ben-Asher, Y., & Mendelson, A. (2014, October). Deep-dive analysis of the data analytics workload in cloudsuite. In *2014 IEEE International Symposium on Workload Characterization (IISWC)* (pp. 202-211). IEEE. 10.1109/IISWC.2014.6983059

Yen, S., Moh, M., & Moh, T. S. (2021). Detecting Compromised Social Network Accounts Using Deep Learning for Behavior and Text Analyses. *International Journal of Cloud Applications and Computing, 11*(2), 97–109.

Yıldırım, S. (2020). Comparing Deep Neural Networks to Traditional Models for Sentiment Analysis in Turkish Language. In B. Agarwal, R. Nayak, N. Mittal, & S. Patnaik (Eds.), *Deep Learning-Based Approaches for Sentiment Analysis.* Algorithms for Intelligent Systems. doi:10.1007/978-981-15-1216-2_12

YouTube TV Gets Ready to Take on Cable. (2017, Mar. 8). *KTLA.*

Yu, L., Asur, S., & Huberman, B. A. (2011). *What Trends in Chinese Social Media?* arXiv preprint arXiv:1107.3522.

Yue, L., Chen, W., Li, X., Zuo, W., & Yin, M. (2019). A survey of sentiment analysis in social media. *Knowledge and Information Systems, 60*(2), 617–663. doi:10.100710115-018-1236-4

Zarocostas, J. (2020). How to fight an infodemic. *Lancet, 395,* 676.

Zaslavsky, A., Perera, C., & Georgakopoulos, D. (2013). *Sensing as a service and big data.* arXiv preprint arXiv:1301.0159.

Zaytsev, O., Papoulias, N., & Stinckwich, S. (2017). Towards Exploratory Data Analysis for Pharo. In *Proceedings of the 12th edition of the International Workshop on Smalltalk Technologies (IWST '17).* Association for Computing Machinery. doi:10.1145/3139903.3139918

Zhai, Z., Bing, L., Hua, X., & Hua, X. (2011). Clustering Product Features for Opinion Mining. *Proceedings of WSDM'11,* 347-354.

Zhang, Ghosh, Dekhil, & Liu. (2011). *Combining Lexicon-based and Learning-based Methods for Twitter Sentiment Analysis.* HP Laboratories.

Zhang, L., Ghosh, R., Dekhil, M., Hsu, M., & Liu, B. (2011). *Combining lexicon-based and learning-based methods for Twitter sentiment analysis.* HP Laboratories, Technical Report.

Zhang, J., Yun, J. H., & Lee, E.-J. (2020). Brain buzz for Facebook? Neural indicators of SNS content engagement. *Journal of Business Research.*

Zhang, L., & Liu, B. (2014). Aspect and entity extraction for opinion mining. In *Data mining and knowledge discovery for big data* (pp. 1–40). Springer.

Zhang, L., Zhang, Z., & Zhao, T. (2021). A Novel Spatio-Temporal Access Control Model for Online Social Networks and Visual Verification. *International Journal of Cloud Applications and Computing, 11*(2), 17–31.

Zhang, Q., Yang, L. T., Chen, Z., & Li, P. (2018). A tensor-train deep computation model for industry informatics big data feature learning. *IEEE Transactions on Industrial Informatics, 14*(7), 3197–3204. doi:10.1109/TII.2018.2791423

Zhang, Q., Yang, L. T., Chen, Z., Li, P., & Bu, F. (2018). An adaptive dropout deep computation model for industrial IoT big data learning with crowdsourcing to cloud computing. *IEEE Transactions on Industrial Informatics, 15*(4), 2330–2337. doi:10.1109/TII.2018.2791424

Zhang, S., Wang, W., Ford, J., Makedon, F., & Pearlman, J. (2005). Using singular value decomposition approximation for collaborative filtering. *Seventh IEEE International Conference on E-Commerce Technology (CEC'05)*, 257–264. 10.1109/ICECT.2005.102

Zhang, W., Xu, H., & Wan, W. (2012). Weakness Finder: Find product weakness from Chinese reviews by using aspects based sentiment analysis. *Expert Systems with Applications, 39*(11), 10283–10291. doi:10.1016/j.eswa.2012.02.166

Zhang, X. L., He, X. Y., Yu, F. M., Liu, L. X., Zhang, H. X., & Li, Z. L. (2019). Distributed and personalised social network privacy protection. *International Journal of High Performance Computing and Networking, 13*(2), 153–163.

Zhang, Y., Miao, D., Wang, J., & Zhang, Z. (2019). A cost-sensitive three-way combination technique for ensemble learning in sentiment classification. *International Journal of Approximate Reasoning, 105*, 85–97. doi:10.1016/j.ijar.2018.10.019

Zhang, Z., & Gupta, B. B. (2018). Social media security and trustworthiness: Overview and new direction. *Future Generation Computer Systems, 86*, 914–925.

Zhang, Z., Jing, J., & Wang, X. (2020). A crowdsourcing method for online social networks security assessment based on human-centric computing. *Human-centric Computing and Information Sciences, 10*, 1–19.

Zhang, Z., Jing, J., & Wang, X. (2020). A crowdsourcing method for online social networks security assessment based on human-centric computing. *Human-Centric Computing and Information Sciences*, *10*, 1–19.

Zhang, Z., Sun, R., Zhao, C., Wang, J., Chang, C. K., & Gupta, B. B. (2017). CyVOD: A novel trinity multimedia social network scheme. *Multimedia Tools and Applications*, *76*(18), 18513–18529. doi:10.100711042-016-4162-z

Zhang, Z., & Wang, K. (2013). A trust model for multimedia social networks. *Social Network Analysis and Mining*, *3*(4), 969–979.

Zhao, R., Zhou, A., & Mao, K. (2016). Automatic detection of cyberbullying on social networks based on bullying features. *Proceedings of the 17th international conference on distributed computing and networking*. 10.1145/2833312.2849567

Zhao, W., Guan, Z., Chen, L., He, X., Cai, D., Wang, B., & Wang, Q. (2017). Weakly-supervised deep embedding for product review sentiment analysis. *IEEE Transactions on Knowledge and Data Engineering*, *30*(1), 185–197. doi:10.1109/TKDE.2017.2756658

Zheng, H., He, J., Zhang, Y., Wu, J., & Ji, Z. (2019). A mathematical model for intimacy-based security protection in social network without violation of privacy. *International Journal of High Performance Computing and Networking*, *15*(3-4), 121–132.

Zhou, Q., Xia, R., & Zhang, C. (2016). Online shopping behavior study based on multi-granularity opinion mining: China versus America. *Cognitive Computation*, *8*(4), 587–602.

Zhuang, F., Qi, Z., Duan, K., Xi, D., Zhu, Y., Zhu, H., Xiong, H., & He, Q. (2020). A comprehensive survey on transfer learning. *Proceedings of the IEEE*, *109*(1), 43–76. doi:10.1109/JPROC.2020.3004555

Ziegelmayer, D., & Schrader, R. (2012). Sentiment polarity classification using statistical data compression models. In *2012 IEEE 12th international conference on data mining workshops* (pp. 731-738). IEEE.

Zúñiga, H. G., Jung, N., & Valenzuela, S. (2012). Social Media Use for News and Individuals' Social Capital, Civic Engagement and Political Participation. *Journal of Computer-Mediated Communication*, *17*(3), 319–336. doi:10.1111/j.1083-6101.2012.01574.x

About the Contributors

Brij B. Gupta received PhD degree from Indian Institute of Technology Roorkee, India in the area of information security. He has published more than 250 research papers in international journals and conferences of high repute. He has visited several countries to present his research work. His biography has published in the Marquis Who's Who in the World, 2012. At present, he is working as an Assistant Professor in the Department of Computer Engineering, National Institute of Technology Kurukshetra, India. His research interest includes information security, cyber security, cloud computing, web security, intrusion detection, computer networks and phishing.

Dragan Peraković received a B.Sc. degree in 1995, an M.Sc. degree in 2003, and a PhD in 2005, all at the University of Zagreb, Croatia, EU. Dragan is Head of the Department for Information and Communication Traffic and Head of Chair of Information Communication Systems and Services Management, all at the Faculty of Transport and Traffic Sciences, University of Zagreb, where he is currently a full professor. Dragan is visiting professor at the University of Mostar, Faculty of Science and Education Sciences, Mostar / Bosnia and Herzegovina. Area of scientific interests and activities is modelling of innovative communication ecosystems in the environment of the transport system (ITS) and Industry 4.0; AI & ML in cybersecurity, DDoS, Internet of Things; AI in e-forensic of communication ecosystems (terminal devices/services); design and development of new innovative services and modules.

Ahmed A. Abd El-Latif received the B.Sc. degree with honor rank in Mathematics and Computer Science in 2005 and M.Sc. degree in Computer Science in 2010, all from Menoufia University, Egypt. He received his Ph. D. degree in Computer Science & Technology at Harbin Institute of Technology (H.I.T), Harbin, P. R. China in 2013. He is an associate professor of Computer Science at Menoufia University, Egypt. He is author and co-author of more than 130 papers in reputal journal and conferences. He received many awards, State Encouragement Award in Engineering Sciences 2016, Arab Republic of Egypt; the best Ph.D student award from Harbin Institute of Technology, China 2013; Young scientific award, Menoufia University,

Egypt 2014. He is a fellow at Academy of Scientific Research and Technology, Egypt. His areas of interests are multimedia content encryption, secure wireless communication, IoT, applied cryptanalysis, perceptual cryptography, secret media sharing, information hiding, biometrics, forensic analysis in digital images, and quantum information processing. Dr. Abd El-Latif is an associate editor of Journal of Cyber Security and Mobility, and Mathematical Problems in Engineering.

* * *

Kriti Aggarwal is an Undergraduate Scholar at Chandigarh College of Engineering and Technology, Panjab University, Chandigarh. Her research interests include parallel architectures, artificial intelligence, machine learning, and data science. She has accepted research articles and works across renowned journals, and conferences like AAP & CRC Press: Taylor & Francis Group.

Elodie Attié is currently a scientific project manager at Capgemini Engineering. She obtained a PhD in management science about the acceptance of the Internet of Things and its influence on consumer well-being in 2019. Her research interests relate to innovations, marketing, consumer behavior and well-being.

Jale Bektaş received her PhD degree in Electrical and Electronics Engineering, Computer Sciences from Cukurova University, Adana, Turkey in 2017. She received her MS degree from Computer Engineering Department, Cukurova University, Adana, Turkey in 2010. She is currently working as an instructor at School of Applied Technology and Management, Department of Computer Technology and Information Systems, Mersin University, Mersin, Turkey. Her main research interests are deep learning, image processing and data mining.

Muskaan Chopra is an Undergraduate Scholar at Chandigarh College of Engineering and Technology, Panjab University, Chandigarh. Her research interests include artificial intelligence, machine learning, and data science. She has accepted research articles and works across renowned journals, and conferences like International Journal of Software Science and Computational Intelligence, International Conference on Advances in Data Computing, Communication and Security,2021, and AAP & CRC Press: Taylor & Francis Group.

Kwok Tai Chui received the B.Eng. degree in Electronic and Communication Engineering – Business Intelligence Minor, with first-class honor, and Ph.D. degree in Electronic Engineering from City University of Hong Kong. He was the recipient of international awards in several IEEE events. For instance, he received the 2nd Prize Award (Postgraduate Category) of 2014 IEEE Region 10 Student Paper Contest, and Best Paper Award in IEEE The International Conference on Consumer Electronics-China, in both 2014 and 2015. He had industry experience as Senior Data Scientist in Internet of Things (IoT) company. He joined the School of Science and Technology at the Hong Kong Metropolitan University as a Research Assistant Professor.

Ipek Deveci Kocakoç received her PhD in Econometrics with a major in Industrial Engineering from Dokuz Eylul University, Turkey. Her recent research interests include Artificial Intelligence, Scientific Programming and Quantitative methods. She is currently a full time professor at Econometrics Department of Dokuz Eylul University. ORCID: 0000-0001-9155-8269

M. Govindarajan is currently an Associate Professor in the Department of Computer Science and Engineering, Annamalai University, Tamil Nadu, India. He received the B.E, M.E and Ph.D Degree in Computer Science and Engineering from Annamalai University, Tamil Nadu, India in 2001, 2005 and 2010 respectively. He did his post-doctoral research in the Department of Computing, Faculty of Engineering and Physical Sciences, University of Surrey, Guildford, Surrey, United Kingdom in 2011 and at CSIR Centre for Mathematical Modelling and Computer Simulation, Bangalore in 2013. He has visited countries like Czech Republic, Austria, Thailand, United Kingdom (twice), Malaysia, U.S.A (twice), and Singapore. He has presented and published more than 120 papers at Conferences and Journals and also received best paper awards. He has delivered invited talks at various national and international conferences. His current research interests include Data Mining and its applications, Web Mining, Text Mining, and Sentiment Mining. He has completed two major projects as principal investigator and has produced four Ph.Ds. He was the recipient of the Achievement Award for the field in the Conference in Bio-Engineering, Computer Science, Knowledge Mining (2006), Prague, Czech Republic. He received Career Award for Young Teachers (2006), All India Council for Technical Education, New Delhi, India and Young Scientist International Travel Award (2012), Department of Science and Technology, Government of India, New Delhi. He is a Young Scientists awardee under Fast Track Scheme (2013), Department of Science and Technology, Government of India, New Delhi and also granted Young Scientist Fellowship (2013), Tamil Nadu State Council for Science and Technology, Government of Tamil Nadu, Chennai. He also received the Senior Scientist International Travel Award (2016), Department of Science and Technology, Government of India. He has published eight book chapters and also applied patent in the area of data mining. He is an active Member of various professional bodies and Editorial Board Member of various conferences and journals.

Jérôme Guibert is a graphic designer, illustrator, Ux designer, experimented technician. He had multiple experiences in communication agency as an art director, and developed additional skills such as user experience, typography, photography and object design. Curious about new technologies, he worked with IBM on the development of a graphical interface for touch screens, an electronic ID card for the French government and the design of a videoconferencing tool for a pioneer in this field. In 2020, he joined Capgemini engineering and then the research project First Unit of Neuromarketing (FUN).

Anshul Gupta is an Undergraduate Scholar at the Department of Computer Science and Engineering, Chandigarh College of Engineering and Technology. His main area of interest is research involving extensive Data Science related technologies like Artificial Intelligence, Machine Learning, Deep Learning, Data Analytics, and Visualization. He has published an article 'An exploratory analysis on the unfold of Fake News during COVID-19 Pandemic' and has accepted, and submitted works across international journals, conferences, and book chapters on research topics comprising Digital Media, Fuzzy Logic, and Time Series Forecasting. He also worked on a research-based project submitted to Oxford Press entitled 'Molecular Dynamics, Server Design, and Data Mining' in which he designed a Peptide Utility Server for bioresearchers and also helped in finding characteristic features amongst the interface residues for helix-helix interactions of the proteins with the Department of Biophysics, Panjab University. Recently, he completed his internshipas a Research and AI Intern at Design Innovation Centre, Panjab University, and MHRD working on a project entitled 'AI for Predictive Maintenance'

Ankit Kumar Jain is presently working as Assistant Professor in National Institute of Technology, Kurukshetra, India. He received Master of technology from Indian Institute of Information Technology Allahabad (IIIT) India and PhD degree from National Institute of Technology, Kurukshetra. His general research interest is in the area of Information and Cyber security, Phishing Website Detection, Web security, Mobile Security, Online Social Network and Machine Learning. He has published many papers in reputed journals and conferences.

Lap-Kei Lee is an Assistant Professor of the School of Science and Technology at the Hong Kong Metropolitan University. He received his Bachelor of Engineering in Computer Engineering and Doctor of Philosophy in Computer Science from the University of Hong Kong. His research interests include the design and analysis of algorithms (especially in online job scheduling and data stream algorithms), natural language processing, algorithm engineering, and educational technology.

Mutwalibi Nambobi is a research assistant at Motion Analysis Research Lab, Islamic University in Uganda. He is also working as the Head of Science and Technology, Labour College of East Africa. He was a research assistant in Technical and Vocational Education (TVE) department at Islamic University of Technology, Dhaka, Bangladesh (IUT, 2018). He holds an MBA (Virtual University of Uganda, Muyenga, Kampala), BSc. Technical Education (Islamic University of Technology, Dhaka, Bangladesh) specializing in computer science and engineering. His research interest on Disruptive Innovations, Wargaming Strategy, Game theory, Coopetition, Blue Ocean Strategy, Blended learning, Green Skills, TVET and ICTs in a developing country.

Pinar Özkan is an assistant professor of marketing at Business Department of Dokuz Eylul University. She holds a Ph.D. from the same university. Her areas of research are relationship marketing, key account management, and service marketing.

Sunil K. Singh is working as Professor and HOD, Department of Computer Science and Engineering (CSE), Chandigarh College of Engineering and Technology (Degree Wing), Affiliated to Panjab University, Chandigarh, Sector-26, Chandigarh, India. He did his graduation (Bachelor of Engineering), postgraduation (Master of Engineering), and Doctor of Philosophy (Ph.D.) in computer science and engineering, and he has a great passion for both teaching and research. His areas of expertise are high- performance computing, Linux/Unix, Data Mining, Internet of Things (IOT), Machine Learning, Computer Architecture, Embedded System and Computer Network. He has published more than 50 research papers in reputed international/national journals and conferences. He is a reviewer of several renowned national and international research journals, and a member of professional bodies such as ACM, IE, LMISTE, ACEEE, IACSIT, and IAENG. He has also received 01 patent granted and 02 patents published, and he is also on many other research and book projects. He is very active as an ACM professional member. He also has contributed to the Eminent Speaker Program (ESP) of ACM India.

Rajab Ssemwogerere is pursuing a Master's of Science in Computer Science from Makerere University (MUK) Kampala, Uganda, also pursuing a postgraduate diploma in management at higher education at Islamic University in Uganda. He received his honors B.Sc. in Computer Science (2018) and a diploma in Computer science and Information Technology (2014) at the Islamic University in Uganda. Rajab gained certificates in Introduction to cybersecurity (2018) and an introduction to the internet of things and digital transformation (2018) from CISCO networking Academy. Currently, he works as a research assistant in the Motion Analysis Research Lab as well as a computer lab officer based at the Islamic University in Uganda. He

Led a team of six that developed an autonomous smart office system that later won the Rector award at Islamic University In Uganda (2018). He has research interests in computer vision, Artificial intelligence (IoT) and Machine learning.

Surabhi Verma has completed Master of Technology from National Institute of Technology, Kurukshetra in 2021.

Jingjing Wang is a Ph.D. student from the Hong Kong Metropolitan University.

Index

A

applications 1-3, 7, 11, 14, 19-22, 25-26,
  53-56, 60, 70, 81, 83, 88, 92-94, 98,
  101-102, 104, 106-108, 110, 117, 120-
  121, 130, 134-135, 137-141, 144-146,
  153, 157, 166-167, 170, 175, 188-191,
  199, 201, 213, 217-218, 223-224, 237,
  240, 243, 246, 252, 260-262
Artificial Intelligence 7, 20-21, 23, 52, 77,
  88, 125, 153, 155-156, 165, 169, 190,
  197-198, 210, 221
aspect-based level 22

B

BERT 223, 237-240, 253
big data 20, 33, 87-88, 116-118, 120-121,
  123, 127-128, 135, 137-138, 140-141,
  153, 163, 166-170, 210, 212, 245, 251
blogs 1, 11, 15, 19-20, 58, 70, 88, 104, 114,
  186, 214, 251

C

classification 2, 4, 7-9, 11, 13, 16-17, 19-22,
  24, 29-32, 38, 54-55, 58, 60, 63-64,
  68, 70, 74, 77-80, 82, 84, 87-90, 113,
  126, 130-131, 133, 135, 137, 139-140,
  157, 162-163, 165, 167-174, 179-181,
  183-184, 186-191, 208-209, 214, 219,
  226, 229-230, 239-242, 252-253
Clubhouse 200, 244-245, 249-251, 253-
  254, 259-264
collaborative filtering 24, 33, 39, 41, 44-45,

47, 49-53, 55-56
content-based filtering 24, 45, 50-51
convolutional neural network 155-156,
  164, 168-169
COVID-19 91-97, 100, 102-103, 107-110,
  112-114, 156, 166, 168, 196-197,
  200-202, 205, 211-213, 215-216,
  219, 226, 240

D

data mining 20, 24, 28, 32, 54, 57, 60, 88,
  90, 116, 123-124, 135-137, 140-141,
  172, 183, 187, 191, 206, 208, 221,
  251, 264
deep learning 86, 113, 133, 139, 155, 157,
  163-169, 213, 218, 242-243, 253
digital learning 102-104
digitalization 91, 94, 97, 108, 225
DISASTER Tweets 223, 226, 240
document level 2, 4, 22-23, 69-70, 82, 144
Domain Specific 23

E

Ethnography 197, 221

F

fake news 106-108, 110, 113, 139, 201,
  223, 225, 240, 242
forums 1, 14, 19-20, 22, 58, 70, 119, 134,
  211, 252
frequency 6, 8, 27, 38, 55, 155-157, 159-
  160, 182-183, 221, 226, 230

G

Gaming 98, 101-102, 109, 113

H

Health 15, 95, 99, 110, 112, 157, 201, 216, 219, 243
Hugging Face 244, 253, 256, 262, 264

I

infodemic 91, 93, 106-109, 114-115

L

latent semantic indexing 155, 159
lexicon-based approach 6-7, 23, 74, 80, 128
LSTM 156-157, 168, 223, 235, 239

M

Machine Leaning Approach 7, 23
machine learning 1-2, 7-9, 13, 19-20, 22-24, 26, 29-30, 32, 39, 54-55, 60, 67, 71-74, 77, 79-80, 82-85, 88, 119, 126-130, 132-133, 144, 153, 161, 168, 171-172, 188-190, 206, 208-209, 223, 226, 231, 251, 253
micro-blogs 19

N

Naive Bayes 8, 63-64, 70, 85, 130, 156, 171, 173, 179, 183, 186, 188, 192, 223, 234-236, 238-239, 253
natural language processing 1, 6, 20, 23, 58, 62, 69, 77, 83, 87-88, 118, 125, 142, 144, 153, 155-156, 173, 206, 208, 211, 221, 223, 225, 238-239, 251-252, 262, 264
N-gram 126, 178-179, 183, 186, 188-189, 191, 206, 208
NLP 6, 60, 62, 69, 77, 81, 119, 144-146, 153, 156, 171, 173-174, 186-187, 208, 223, 225, 231, 236-237, 240, 251, 253, 256, 260, 264

O

online social network 89, 109, 113, 116, 120, 137, 139, 157-158, 166-167, 216, 219, 239-240, 242
opinion mining 2, 4, 10, 12, 17, 21-22, 85, 87-88, 116, 119, 123, 125, 131, 135-138, 141-142, 149, 153, 169, 172, 188, 190, 215, 221, 251, 261, 264
Opinionated data 1, 116
opinions 1, 4-6, 10-11, 13-15, 17-19, 23, 38, 41, 57-59, 62-63, 69-71, 77-78, 83-84, 87, 94, 118, 135, 139, 143-144, 158, 199, 202, 208, 214, 221, 246-247, 251-252

P

Pandas 23, 175, 188, 193
prediction 7, 39, 49, 53, 77, 121, 124, 126, 129, 131, 136, 138-139, 157, 180, 208, 223-227, 233, 238, 242, 253
Prosody 205, 221

R

Rapid miner 23
recommendation systems 10, 23-25, 32, 46, 49-50, 52-55
reviews 9-17, 19-22, 39, 41, 50, 53-54, 62, 64, 70-71, 86, 90, 121, 126, 128, 136, 138, 140, 153, 155-157, 162, 165, 168, 186, 190, 192, 208, 216-217, 250, 252, 256

S

sentence level 2, 4, 22-23, 69, 71, 81, 125, 144
sentiment 1-6, 10-11, 13-23, 53-54, 57-66, 68-74, 76-90, 116, 118-120, 123, 125-129, 131-140, 142, 144-146, 148-149, 153, 155-159, 162-170, 172-174, 186, 188-192, 197, 199, 205-208, 212-214, 216-218, 220-221, 242, 244-245, 251-254, 256-257, 259, 261-264
sentiment analysis 1-6, 10-11, 13-23, 53,

57-66, 68-74, 77, 80-90, 116, 118-120, 123, 125-127, 129, 131, 133-136, 138-140, 142, 144-146, 148-149, 153, 155-159, 162-170, 172-174, 186, 188-192, 197, 205-208, 212-214, 216-218, 221, 242, 244-245, 251-254, 256-257, 259, 261-264

social comparison 205, 208, 220

social media 9, 11, 13, 19, 21-22, 25, 51-52, 54, 57-59, 67, 81, 83, 89, 91-94, 98-115, 117, 120-124, 126, 134-137, 139-144, 148, 152-154, 157, 165, 169, 171-173, 175, 186-190, 192, 196-206, 208-226, 239-249, 251-252, 254, 257-264

social networks 1, 58, 86-87, 91, 94-96, 100, 102, 106, 110-113, 115-116, 120-123, 126, 135-141, 153, 166, 172, 190-191, 219, 239, 242-243

Sourtimes 244-245, 247-248, 253-254, 257, 264

Subjective Lexicon 206, 208, 222

supervised learning 7-8, 22, 68, 77, 128, 131, 179, 208, 244, 253, 264

T

term frequency-inverse document frequency 155

text analysis 57, 120, 172, 196

text mining 12, 20, 28, 38, 57, 118-120, 125, 171-172, 177, 187-192, 213, 244, 251-252, 264

TF-IDF 27-28, 38, 54-55, 155, 159-161, 163, 165, 171, 178, 182, 188, 230

Turkish tweets 171, 174, 186, 191, 245, 256, 258

tweet classification 171, 184, 186, 226, 241-242

tweets 1, 11, 21, 58, 60-65, 67-69, 77, 82-86, 105, 107, 132-134, 137-139, 166, 171, 173-177, 183, 185-186, 188, 191, 194-195, 208, 217-219, 223, 225-230, 237-240, 245, 247-248, 251-252, 254-259

Twitter 20, 22, 25, 57-64, 67-68, 77, 81-90, 99, 102, 105-107, 112-114, 117, 121-122, 131-133, 135-136, 138-139, 143, 171-178, 183, 186-193, 198-200, 209-210, 214-217, 219-220, 223-228, 239-245, 247-248, 251, 253-254, 256-263

Twitter Data 22, 63, 67, 84, 136, 173, 176-177, 189, 192, 228, 240, 242

U

Unsupervised learning 9, 82, 128, 264

user behavior 26, 33, 196

V

Voice analysis 196, 206

W

WordCloud 175, 183-185, 188

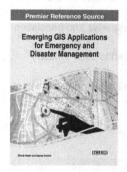
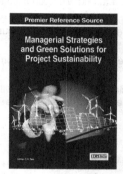

Printed in the United States
by Baker & Taylor Publisher Services